I0729501

Watercolors in the Garden

Beginner-Friendly Projects
Inspired by Chinese Aesthetics

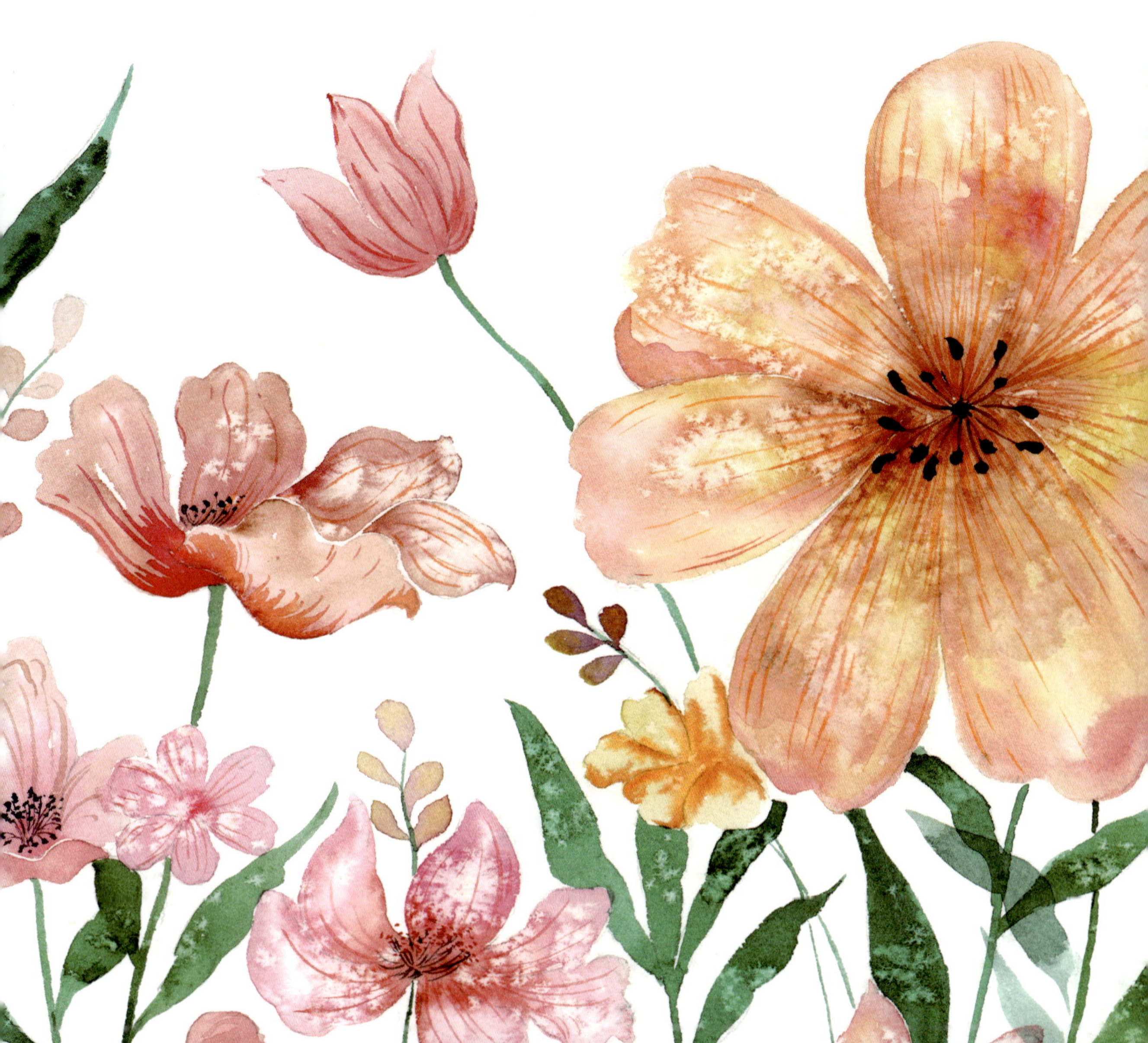

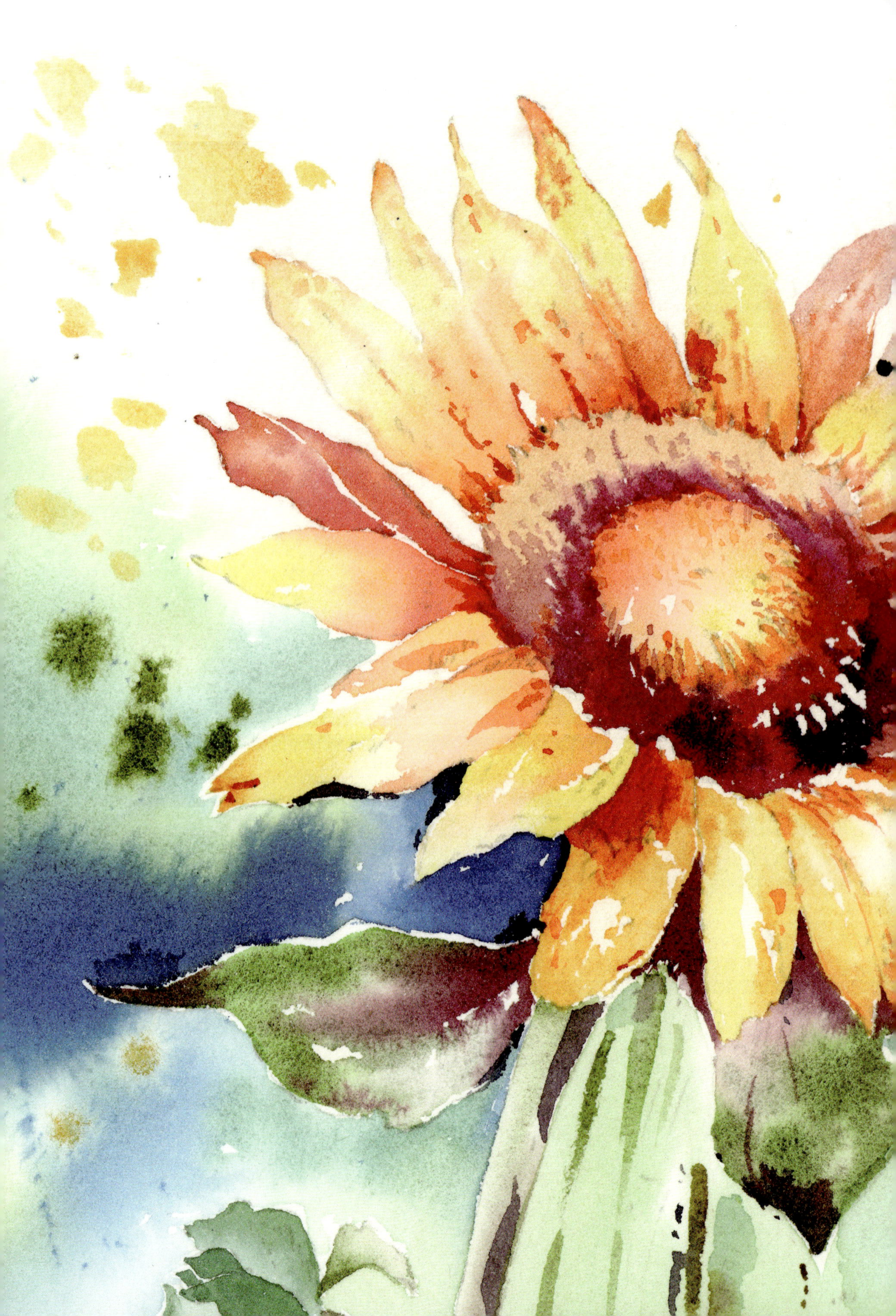

Blooms, Bugs, and Pets

Watercolors in the Garden

Beginner-Friendly Projects Inspired by Chinese Aesthetics

By Zhou Feiyu

SCPG

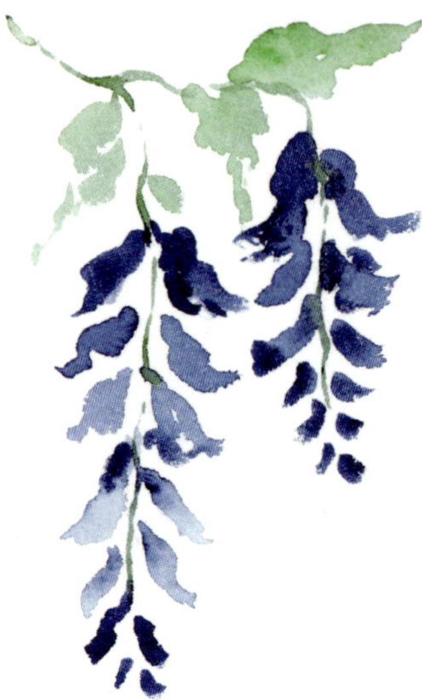

Copyright © 2025 Shanghai Press and Publishing Development Co., Ltd.

All rights reserved. Unauthorized reproduction, in any manner, is prohibited.

Text and Photographs: Zhou Feiyu
Translation: Shelly Bryant
Cover Design: Chen Ruiduo
Interior Design: Li Jing, Hu Bin (Yuan Yinchang Design Studio)

Editors: Cao Yue, Yang Wenjing

ISBN: 978-1-63288-053-6

Address any comments about *Watercolors in the Garden* to:

SCPG
401 Broadway, Ste. 1000
New York, NY 10013
USA

or

Shanghai Press and Publishing Development Co., Ltd.
Floor 5, No. 390 Fuzhou Road, Shanghai, China (200001)
Email: sppd@sppdbook.com

Printed in China by RR Donnelley Asia Printing Solutions Limited

1   3   5   7   9   10   8   6   4   2

On page 1
Fig. 1 **Warm-Colored Blossoms**
A large composition of warm-toned blossoms features broad, unfolding petals arranged in a graceful and expansive display.

On pages 2–3
Fig. 2 **A Sunflower in Full Bloom**
A symbol of vitality and warmth, the sunflower turns toward the light, embodying the spirit of summer.

Top
Fig. 3 **Wisteria**
Dangling like whispers in the wind, wisteria drapes the garden in quiet elegance.

Bottom
Fig. 4 **Cherry Blossoms**
A few delicate cherry blossoms bloom quietly on a bare branch, heralding the first sign of spring.

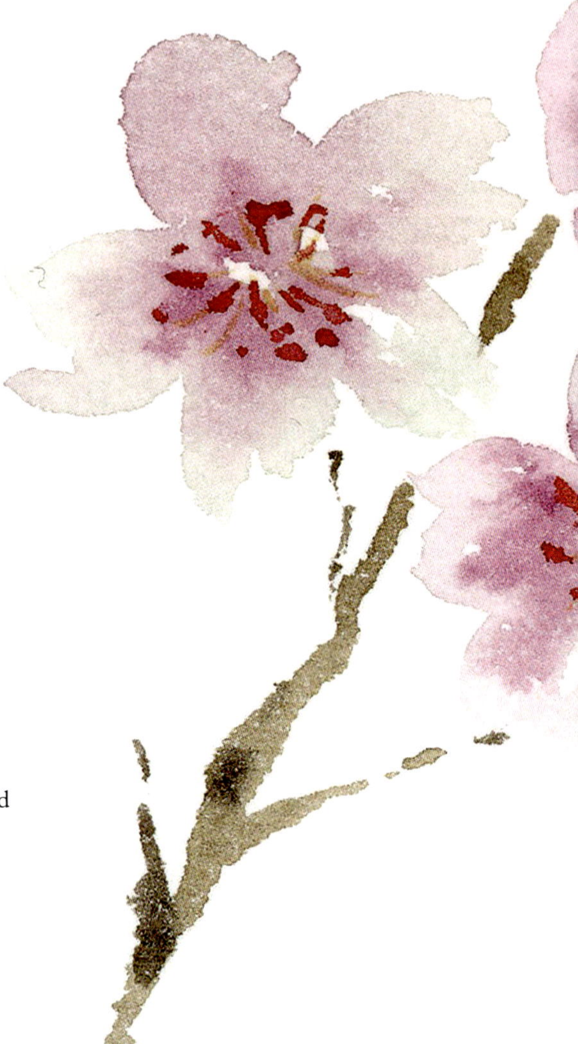

CONTENTS

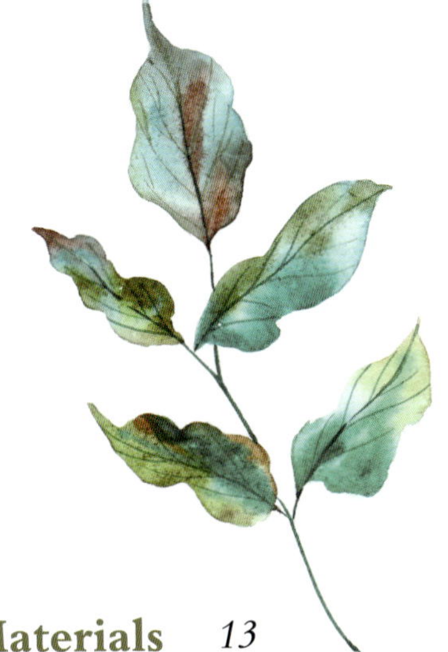

Preface *9*

Chapter One   Tools and Materials *13*

Brushes *13*

Paints *16*

Paper *20*

Other Tools and Materials *22*

Chapter Two   Basic Techniques *27*

Wet-on-Dry Technique *27*

Wet-on-Wet Technique *28*

Control of Brush Tip and Paper Moisture *30*

Other Common Techniques *32*

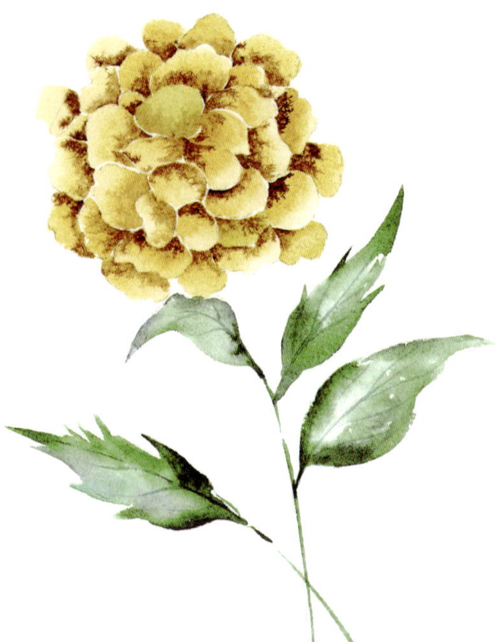

Top
Fig. 5 **A Leaf**
A single outstretched leaf, tinged with soft hues of yellow and green, reflects the quiet transition of the seasons.

Bottom
Fig. 6 **A Golden Hydrangea**
A golden hydrangea blooms with a gentle warmth, each petal softly blending shades of yellow and light brown, capturing the subtle dance of sunlight.

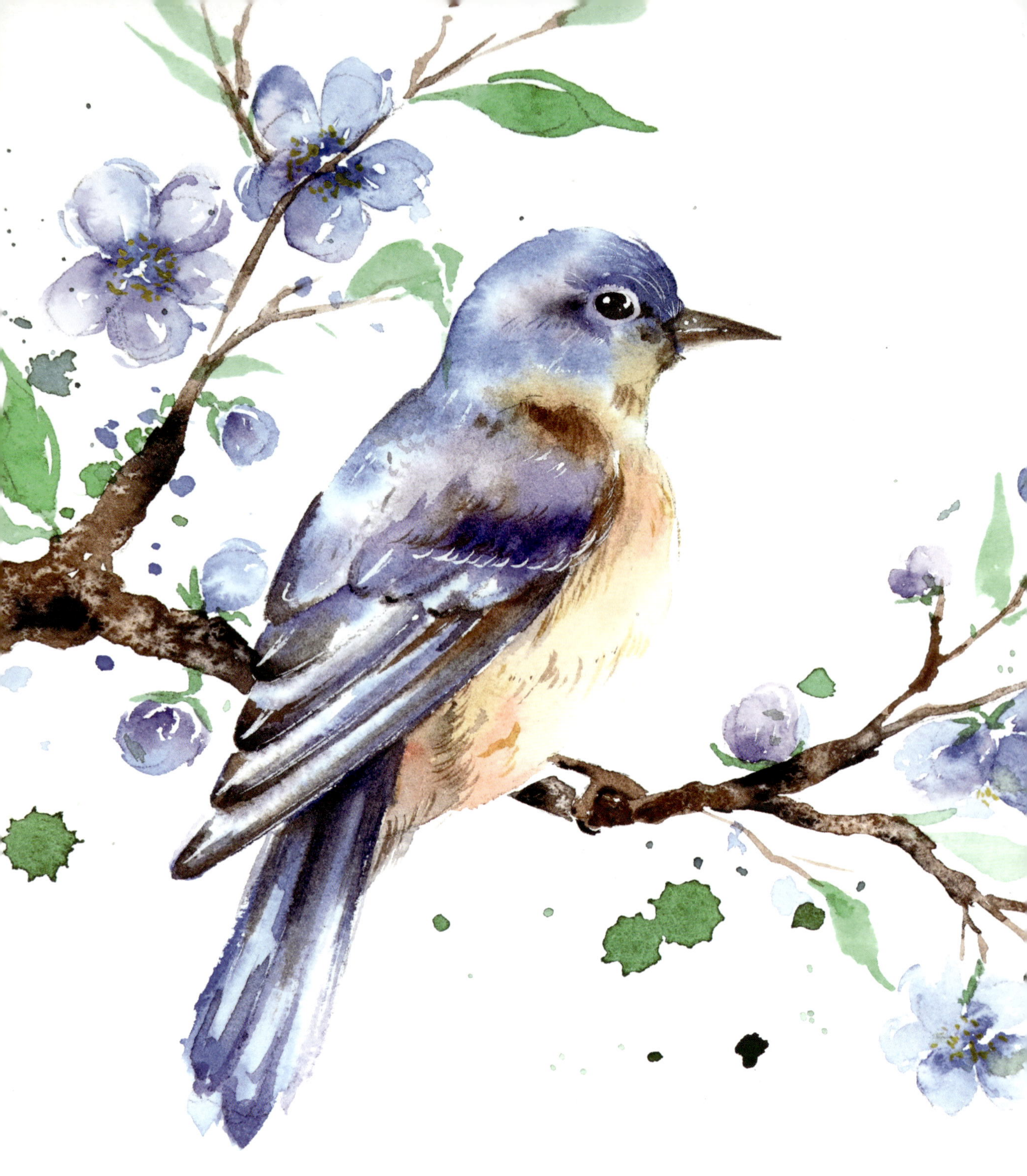

Fig. 7 **A Bird Perched Among Blue Blossoms**
A small bird perches among vibrant blue blossoms, in a
scene alive with color and quiet energy.

CONTENTS

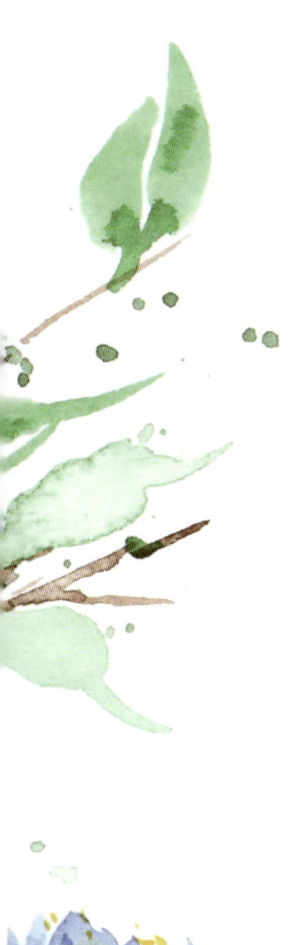

Chapter Three   Tutorials and Projects   *35*

Grape Hyacinth   *36*

Torch Lily   *40*

Butterfly   *47*

Cherry Blossom   *56*

King Protea   *62*

Praying Mantis   *68*

Poppy   *74*

Daisy   *81*

Owl   *89*

Lily   *95*

Bee   *103*

Peony   *111*

Cat   *118*

Sunflower   *125*

Iris   *133*

Bulldog   *140*

Line Art   *148*

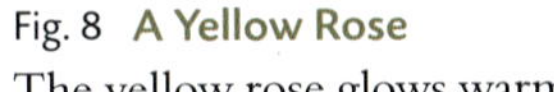

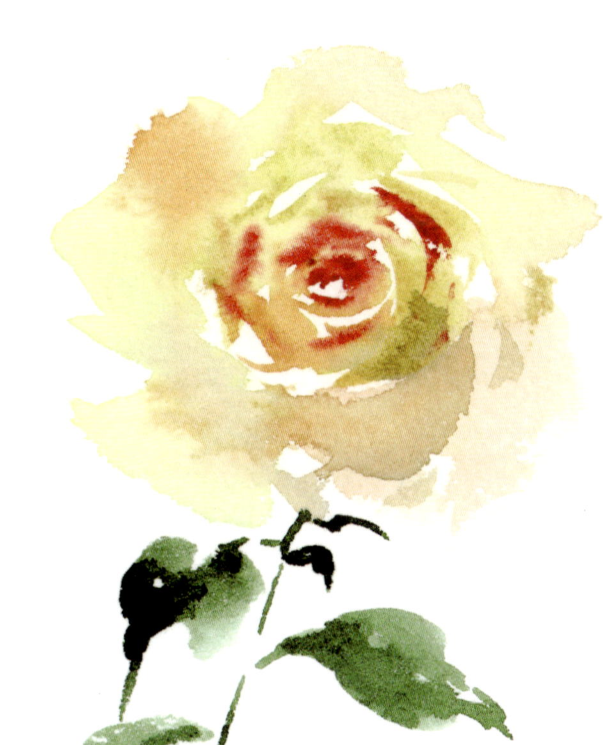

Fig. 8   **A Yellow Rose**
The yellow rose glows warmly as its soft petals unfold,
evoking feelings of joy and gentle sunshine.

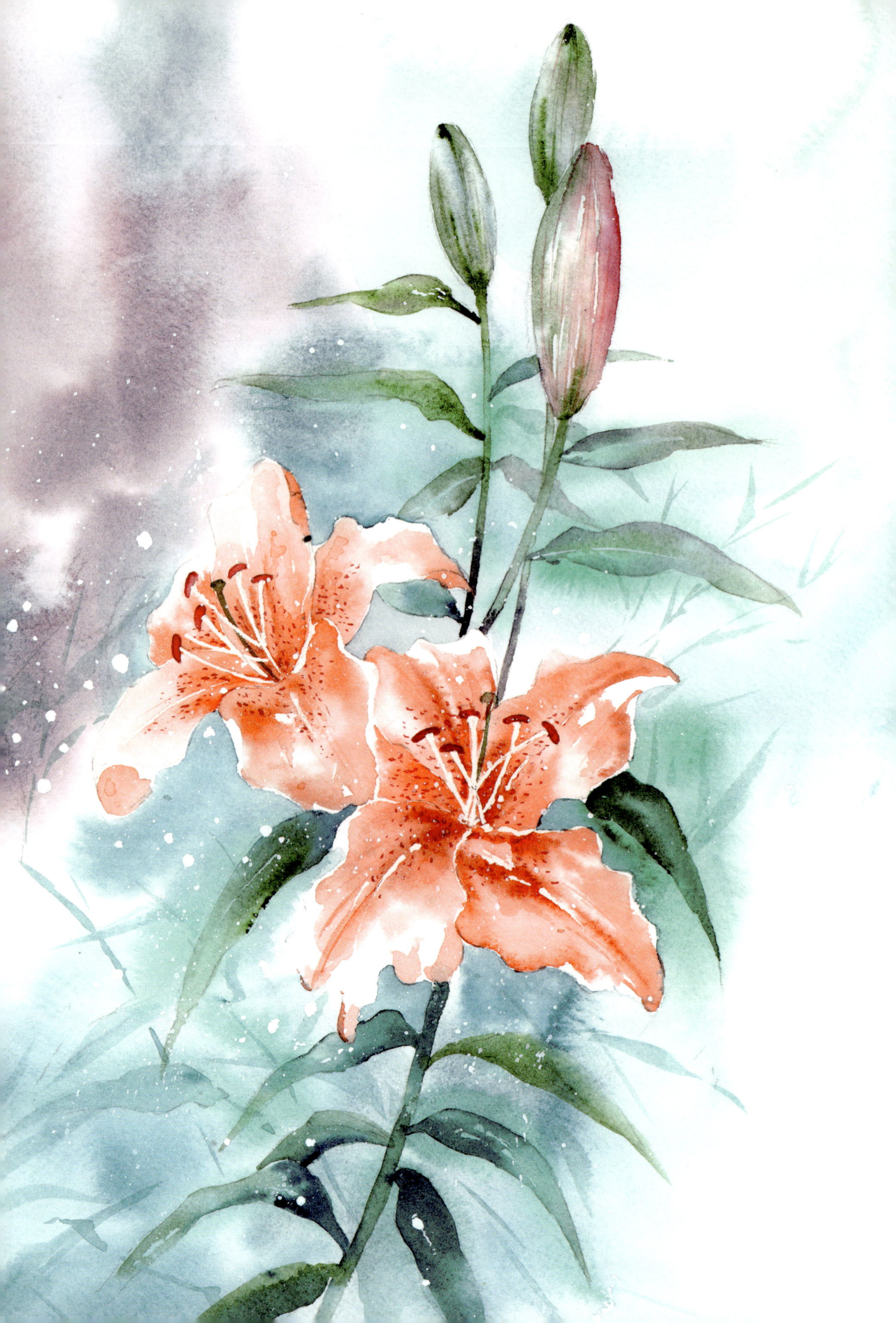

Preface

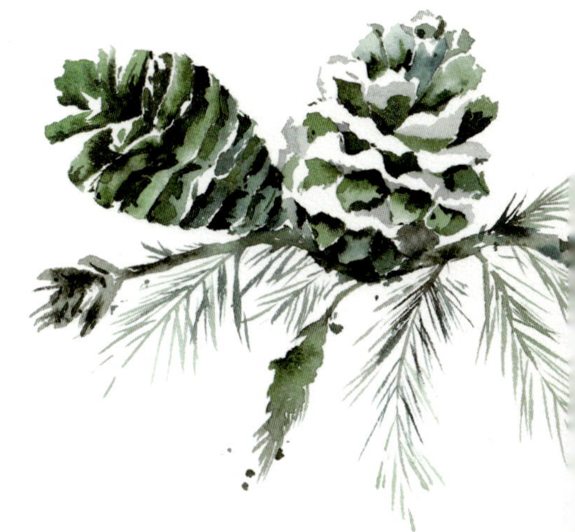

In this busy, fast paced world, a garden feels like a tranquil sanctuary, embodying my love for life and my keen observations. My garden is the source of my inspiration. I am always captivated by the beauty of flowers and the vitality of animals. Whenever I see them, I instinctively reach for my camera or pick up my paintbrush. This is how I converse with nature.

When I was invited to publish a watercolor tutorial on gardens scenes, I was incredibly happy. I began envisioning the framework of the book and preparing its content. As winter faded and spring arrived, I witnessed my garden's vibrant display of a variety of flowers blooming in every season. My pets frolicked joyfully there, and birds chirped merrily on the branches. With my paintbrush, I captured the main characters of the garden throughout the four seasons of the year. Each piece of work reflects my admiration for life and my heartfelt reflections on it.

In this garden, the spring irises bloom quietly, filling the air with an enchanting fragrance. In summer, the sunflowers lift their heads high, chasing the sunlight, as if demonstrating the

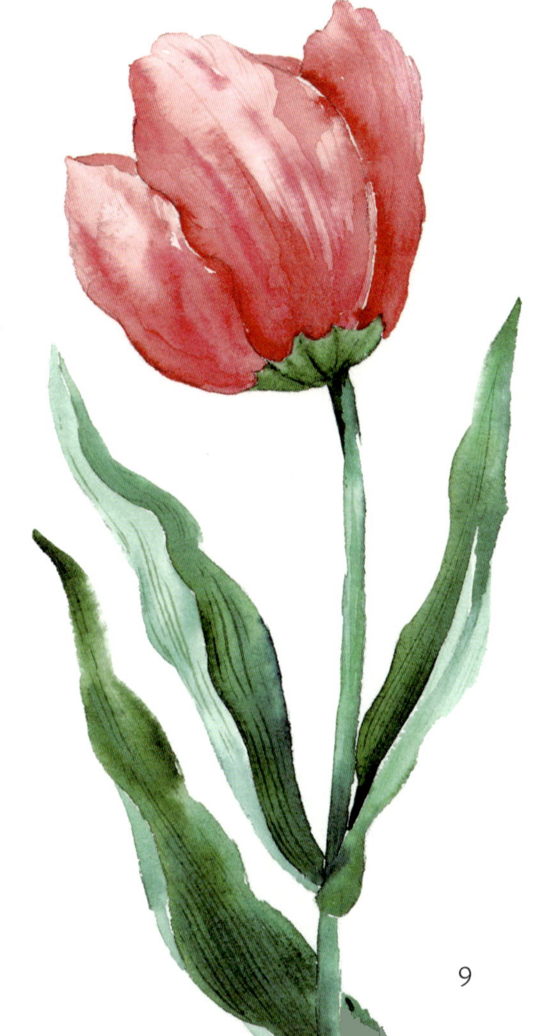

On the facing page
Fig. 9 Lilies in Various Stages
Lilies, whether in tight buds or full blossom, illustrate life's elegant transition and the promise of renewal.

Top
Fig. 10 Pine Cones
Two pine cones display their distinct natural texture and form, rendered in understated, earthy tones.

On the right
Fig. 11 A Tulip
A bright tulip stands tall, its smooth petals gently curving to unveil fresh, vibrant hues.

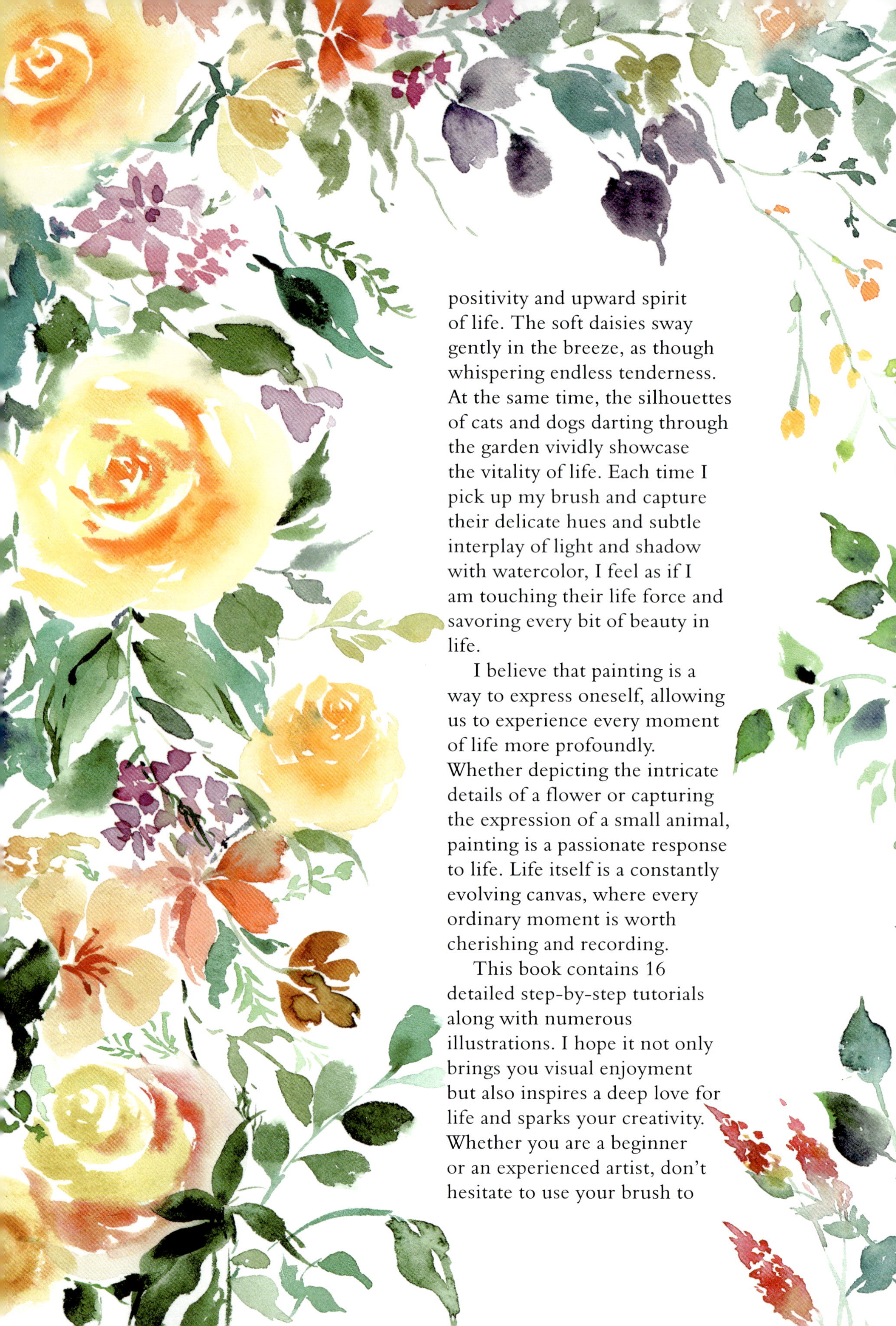

positivity and upward spirit
of life. The soft daisies sway
gently in the breeze, as though
whispering endless tenderness.
At the same time, the silhouettes
of cats and dogs darting through
the garden vividly showcase
the vitality of life. Each time I
pick up my brush and capture
their delicate hues and subtle
interplay of light and shadow
with watercolor, I feel as if I
am touching their life force and
savoring every bit of beauty in
life.

I believe that painting is a
way to express oneself, allowing
us to experience every moment
of life more profoundly.
Whether depicting the intricate
details of a flower or capturing
the expression of a small animal,
painting is a passionate response
to life. Life itself is a constantly
evolving canvas, where every
ordinary moment is worth
cherishing and recording.

This book contains 16
detailed step-by-step tutorials
along with numerous
illustrations. I hope it not only
brings you visual enjoyment
but also inspires a deep love for
life and sparks your creativity.
Whether you are a beginner
or an experienced artist, don't
hesitate to use your brush to

express the stories in your heart. Do not fear failure or imperfection. What truly matters is that your voice and emotions can be conveyed through your artwork. The beauty of art lies in its uniqueness and individuality, just like each person's life experiences, which are precious, irreplaceable memories. Remember, there is no standard answer in art. Paint what you want to paint and express what you wish to convey. Let colors intertwine with life, giving your creations genuine meaning.

May this book serve as an inspiration on your creative journey, guiding you to use your brush to capture the wonderful world that belongs uniquely to you.

On pages 10–11
Figs. 12–13 **Blossoms in Full Flourish**
A lively cluster of blossoms bursts into full bloom, radiating vivid hues and abundant vitality.

On page 12
Fig. 14 **Blue-Purple Hydrangea**
Clusters of hydrangea blooms reveal a cool harmony of blue and purple, evoking a serene and refreshing mood.

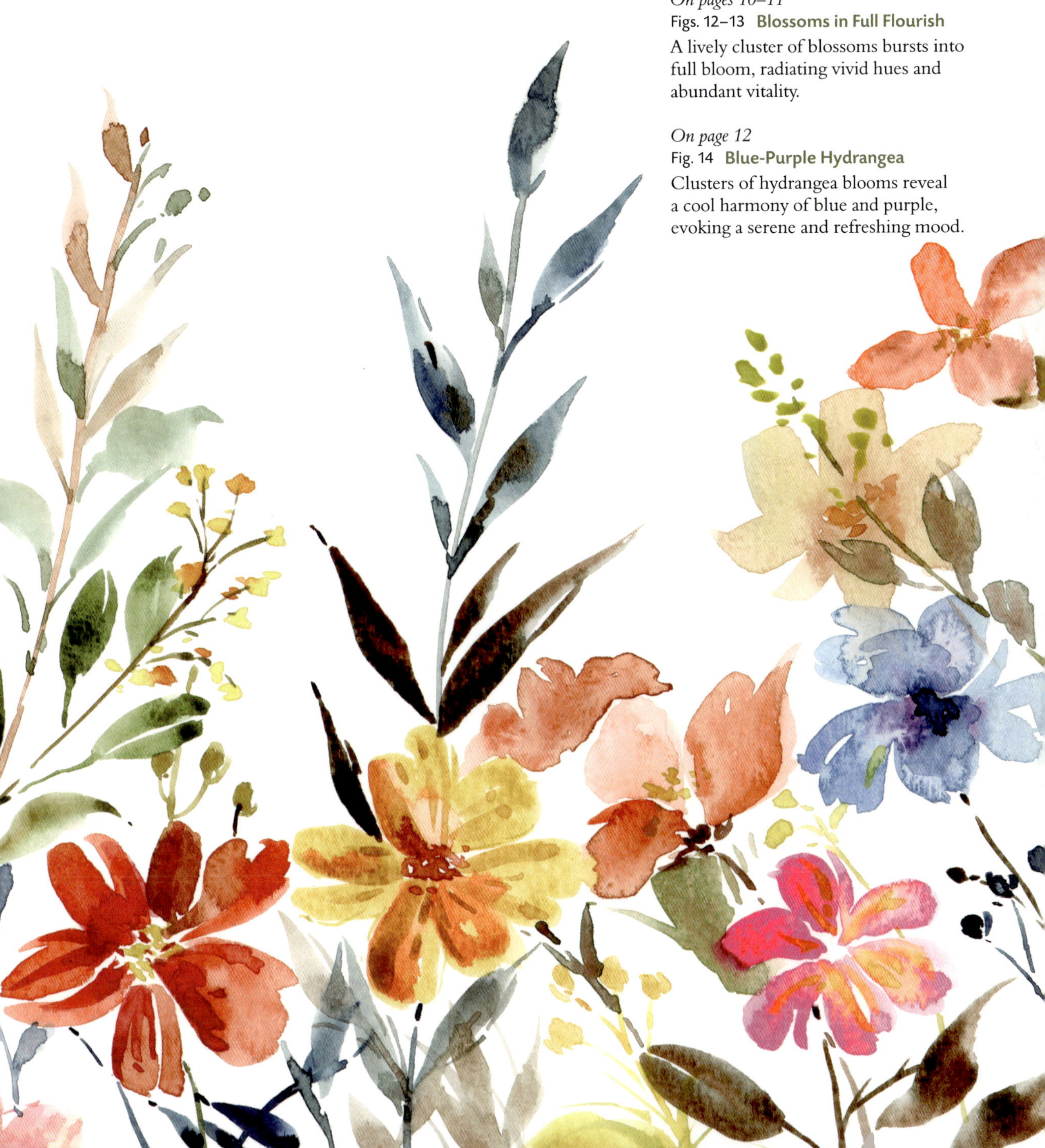

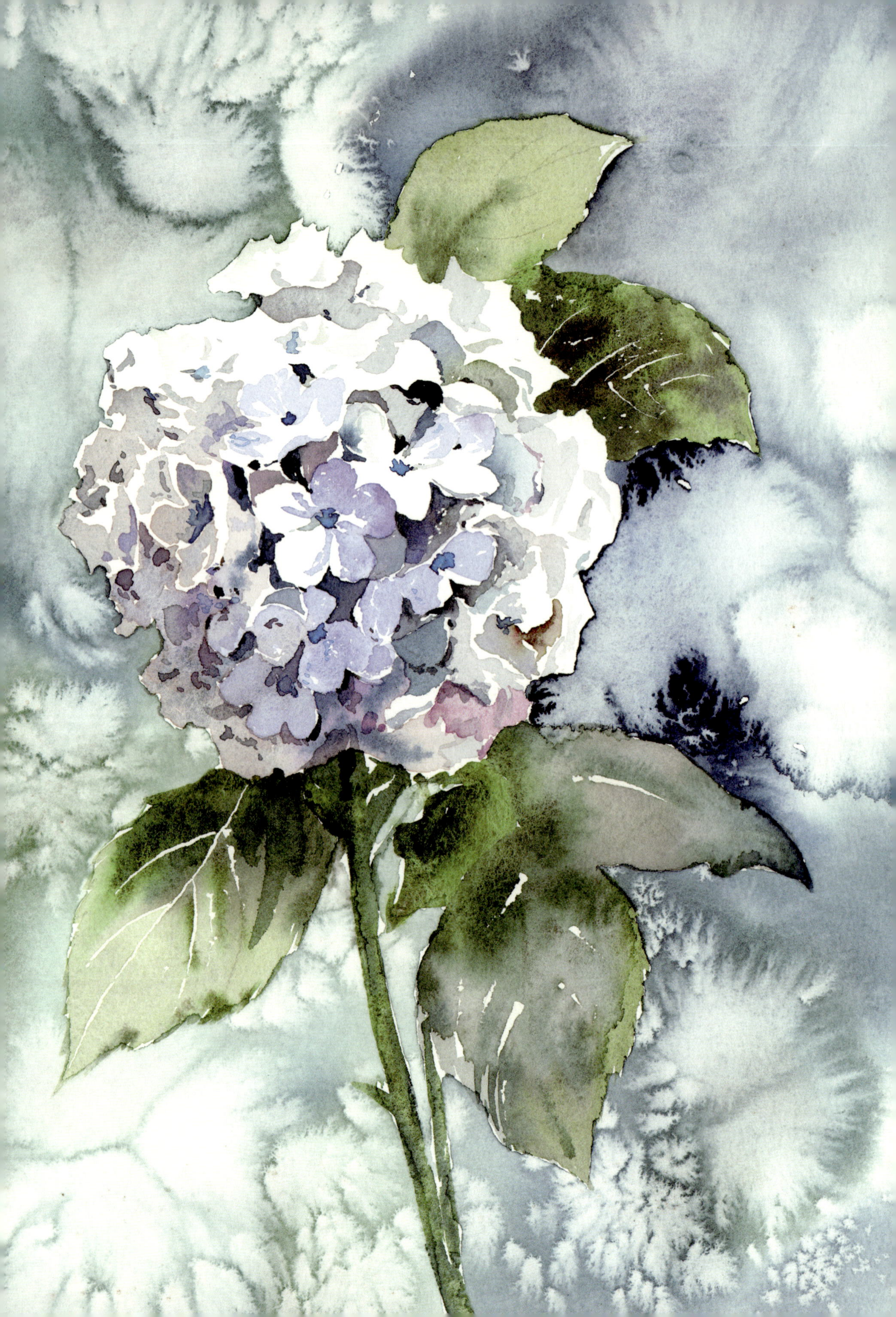

Chapter One

Tools and Materials

I n the world of watercolor, the right tools can help a painter more effortlessly capture the changes in light and color. From the material of the brushes to the texture of the paper, every choice of instrument influences the final result. In this chapter, we give a detailed introduction to the characteristics and suitable applications of different brushes, paints, and papers and share tips on using various supporting tools to help you better control moisture and color, making your creative process more confident and expressive.

Brushes

Brushes are essential tools in watercolor painting. A high quality brush should have good elasticity and excellent water holding capacity to better control moisture and the flow of color during the painting process.

Common materials for watercolor brushes include sable and squirrel hair. These natural hair brushes are soft and highly absorbent, capable of holding a large amount of paint, allowing for longer painting with a single dip and providing a smooth painting experience. However, they tend to be relatively expensive. There are also high quality synthetic fiber brushes available on the market, which generally have better elasticity and moderate water absorption. They perform especially well when rendering fine details or textural effects, offering excellent value for money.

The choice of watercolor brushes involves not only the material, but also the size and shape of the brush. In terms of size, brushes are typically categorized as large, medium, or small. The brush tip can come in various shapes, such as flat, round, or pointed. Different sizes suit different painting needs, while variations in brush tip shape affect the type of brushstroke and the overall painting effect.

Wide brush: Ideal for covering large areas with water or laying down base colors, these brushes can evenly coat the surface of the paper.

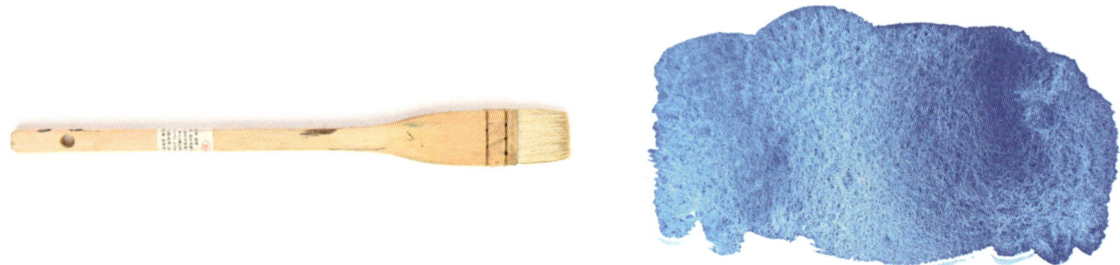

Square brush: Suitable for painting color blocks and outlining objects with clear edges, such as buildings, tree trunks, or sharp edged rocks.

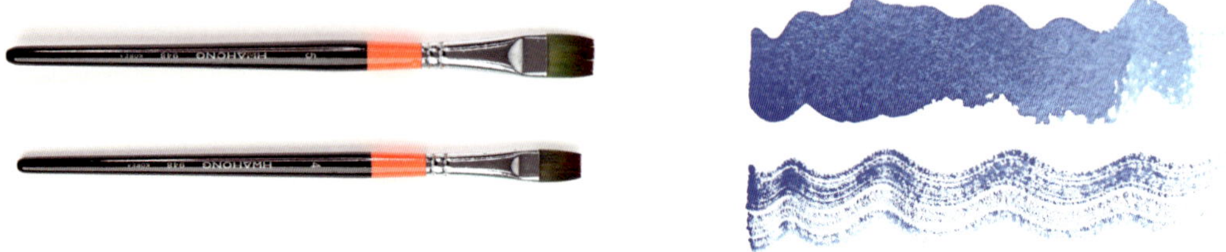

Round brush: This is the brush I use most often in my daily painting. Whether for laying down color or refining details, it handles both with ease. You could call it an all purpose brush.

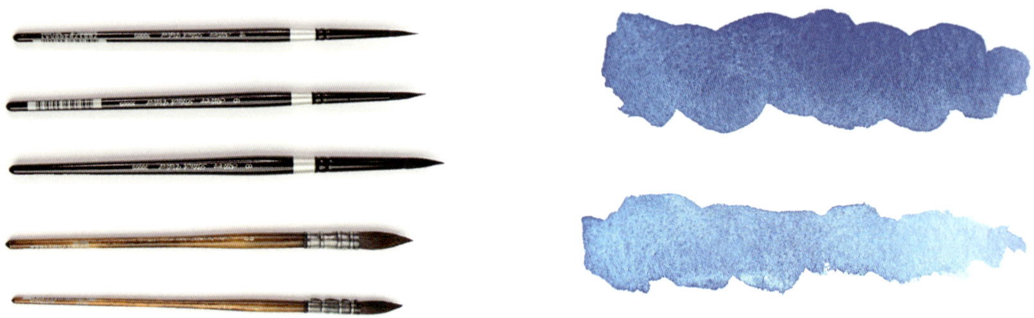

Filbert brush: Commonly used for shaping petals or creating circular and oval forms.

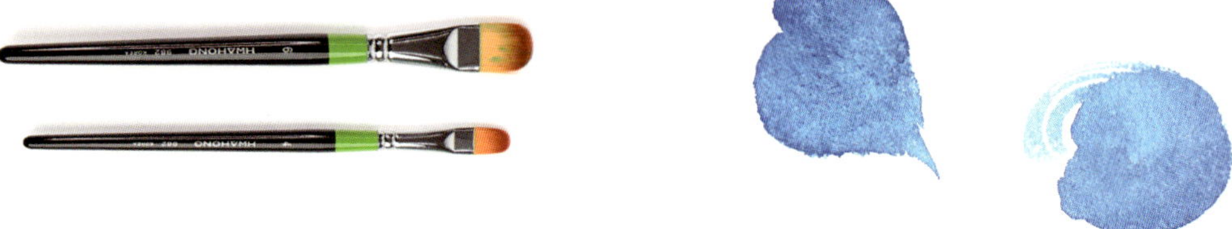

Cat tongue brush: It forms a point well and is often used for painting large leaves and petals.

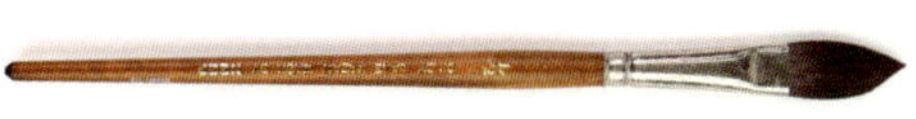

Liner brush: With a longer tip and less hair, this brush has limited water holding capacity and is mainly used for outlining lines or adding highlight accents.

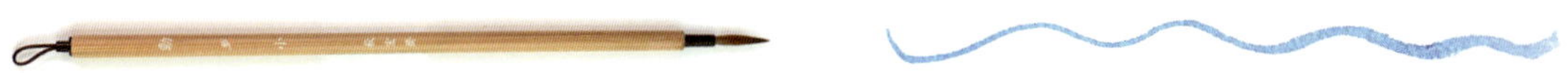

Bristle brush: Primarily used for creating textures.

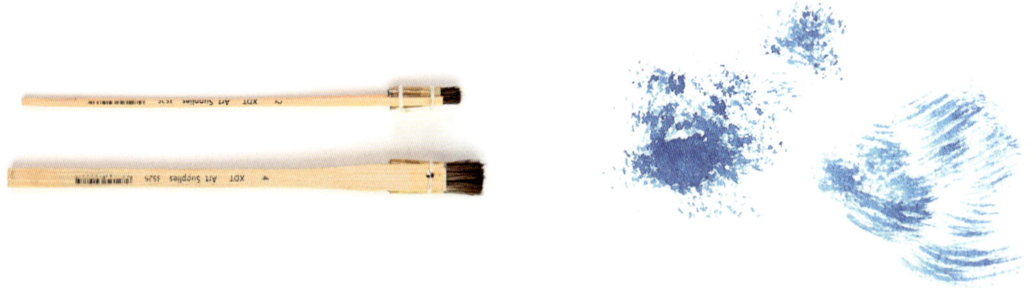

In most of the projects featured in this book, I used only the American brand Black Velvet round squirrel hair watercolor brushes, sizes 6 and 8, which are listed as Black Velvet 3000S brush for watercolor, size 6, and Black Velvet 3000S brush for watercolor, size 8 in the tutorial tools. Occasionally, I pair these with a brush that holds water better for laying down background washes, and a pointed brush for detailing. In practice, we often complete a painting using just one brush in a single, uninterrupted flow, without switching back and forth, which could disrupt our creative rhythm. That said, not using other brushes doesn't mean we shouldn't learn about them. Understanding the uses of different brushes can enrich your painting journey and add that extra touch of finesse.

After using a watercolor brush, it should be cleaned promptly. Gently blot excess water with a paper towel or sponge, and reshape the tip to help it return to its original form. It's best to hang the brush with the tip facing down to dry, to prevent moisture from remaining at the base of the brush, which helps extend the brush's lifespan.

Choosing the right watercolor brushes and maintaining good usage habits can not only enhance the expressiveness of your paintings but also make the creative process more effortless and enjoyable.

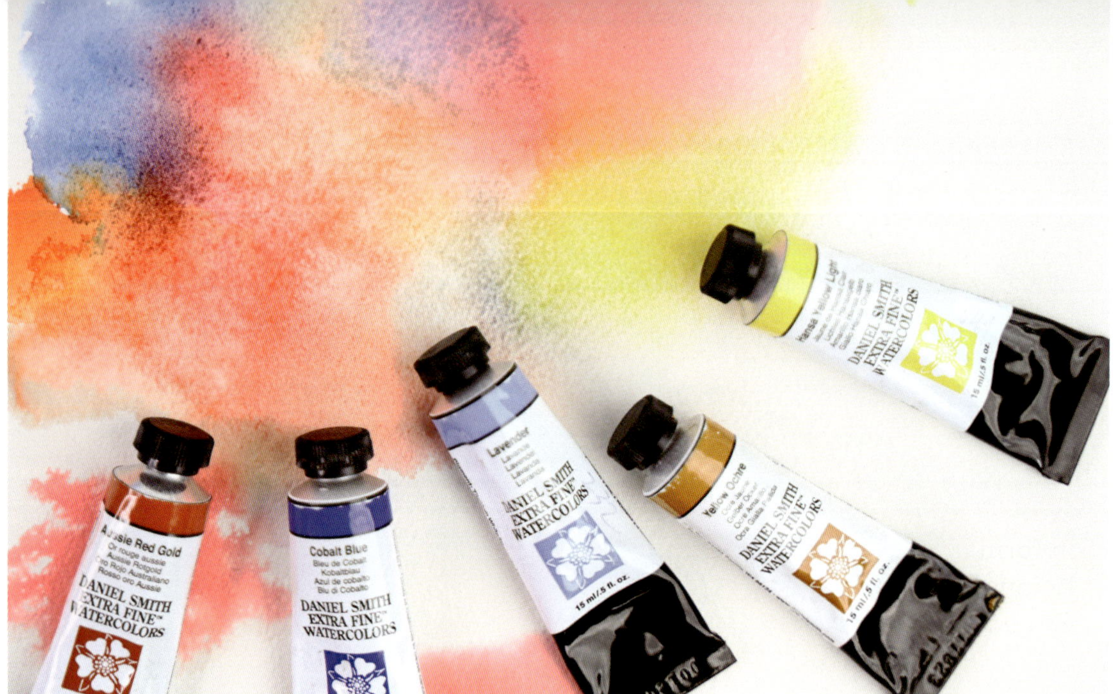

Paints

Watercolor paints are the core material in watercolor painting, and they are essentially divided into transparent and opaque types.

Transparent watercolor paints: High transparency allows the underlying layers of paint to show through when layered. The colors are light and luminous, making them ideal for delicate gradient effects and creating a fresh, airy feel in the painting.

Opaque watercolor paints: The rich, dense colors and strong coverage easily mask underlying layers. They help prevent uneven colors or water marks. Opaque watercolors are often used for detail refinement, image adjustments, and additions. All the projects in this book are completed using opaque watercolors.

Paint Brands

Apart from the fundamental differences, different types and brands of paint can also affect the final outcome of the artwork. There are numerous watercolor paint brands available on the market, ranging from beginner-level to professional grade, with varying prices and characteristics.

Brands with good value for money: Rembrandt and Van Gogh, which are ideal for beginners.

High end watercolor brands: M. Graham (MG), Daniel Smith (DS), Schmincke, and Holbein, among others. These are suited for painting enthusiasts who have higher demands for color quality.

For beginners, it is recommended to start with a 18 or 24 color set. After becoming familiar with these colors for a while, you can then add additional shades based on your personal needs. Of course, for beginners with a certain budget, it's worth considering high end watercolors right from the start.

High quality watercolor paints can greatly enhance the results of your work, boosting your confidence and motivation to continue painting. All the projects in this book were completed using Daniel Smith watercolor paints.

Paint Forms

Watercolor paints can also be categorized by their form into tube watercolor, solid watercolor, and liquid watercolor. Each form is suited to different painting techniques.

Tube watercolor is the most commonly used form by most artists. The paint is rich in color and comes out in a paste-like consistency. It is typically squeezed into a sealed mixing box (see image below) for storage, where it can be used by dipping, or directly squeezed onto a palette, where water is added to mix or dilute the colors. Tube watercolors have good fluidity, making it easy to mix and blend colors. It's important to spray a small amount of water into the tube when not in use to keep the paint moist and prevent it from drying out and becoming hard.

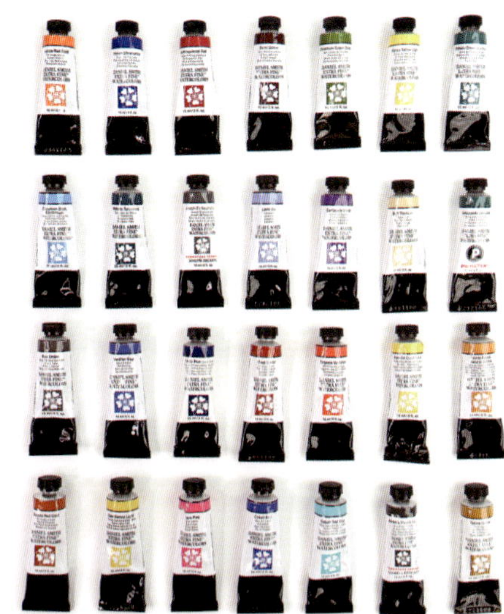

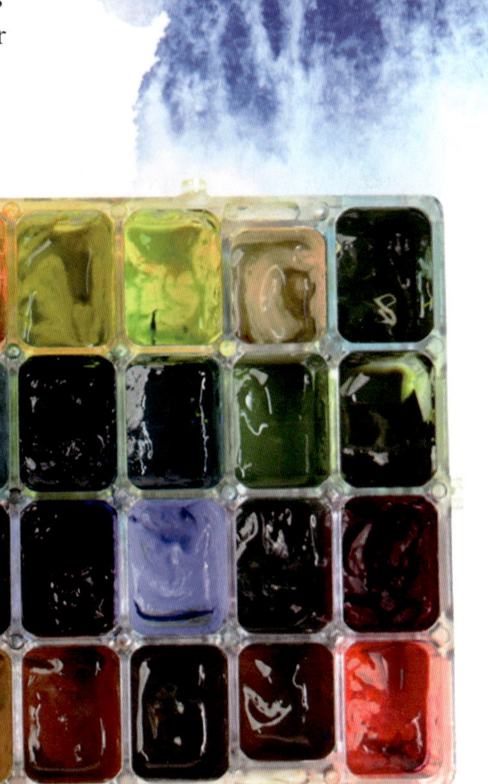

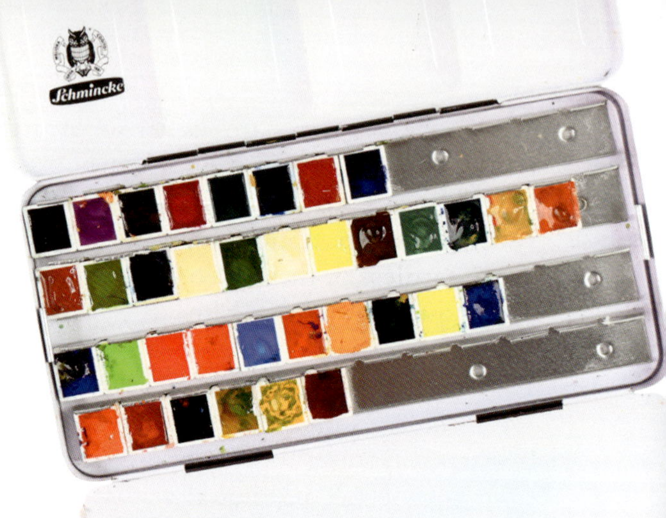

Solid watercolors are highly portable, making them ideal for outdoor sketching or carrying with you. Before use, they need to be activated with a spray of water or lightly brushed with a damp brush to moisten the surface, then mixed on the palette. However, be cautious when dipping your brush, as it is easy to mix colors. Make sure to clean the brush promptly to avoid unintended color blending.

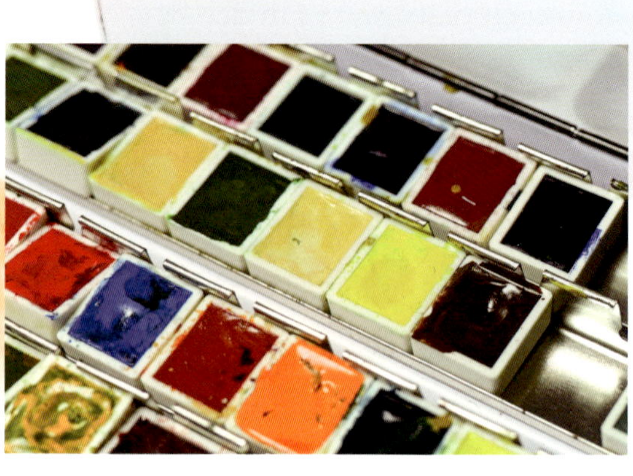

Liquid watercolors have delicate colors and higher concentration, typically requiring dilution with water, although some lighter colors can be used directly. They have excellent fluidity.

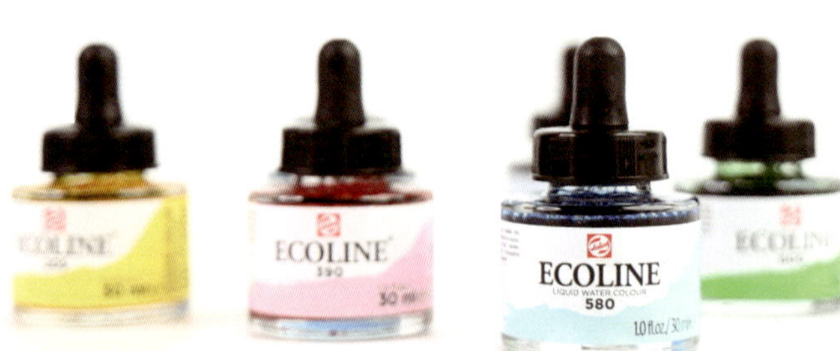

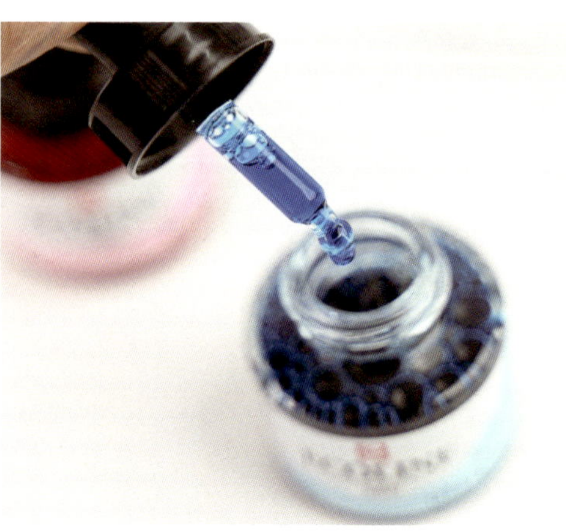

Watercolor paints are darker when wet, and the colors will slightly lighten once the painting is completely dry. Therefore, it's important to adjust the color concentration during the painting process to ensure the final result meets your expectations.

Regardless of the type or brand of watercolor paints used, the basic techniques of painting remain the same. The key is to understand the characteristics of watercolor, control the moisture and paint concentration effectively, and, through continuous practice, find the painting style that works best for you.

For the projects in this book, I used the Daniel Smith (DS) color chart. This color chart displays all the colors used in the book and clearly shows how each color varies in depth when adjusted for different levels of water concentration. You can use this color chart as a reference for applying colors in the later stages.

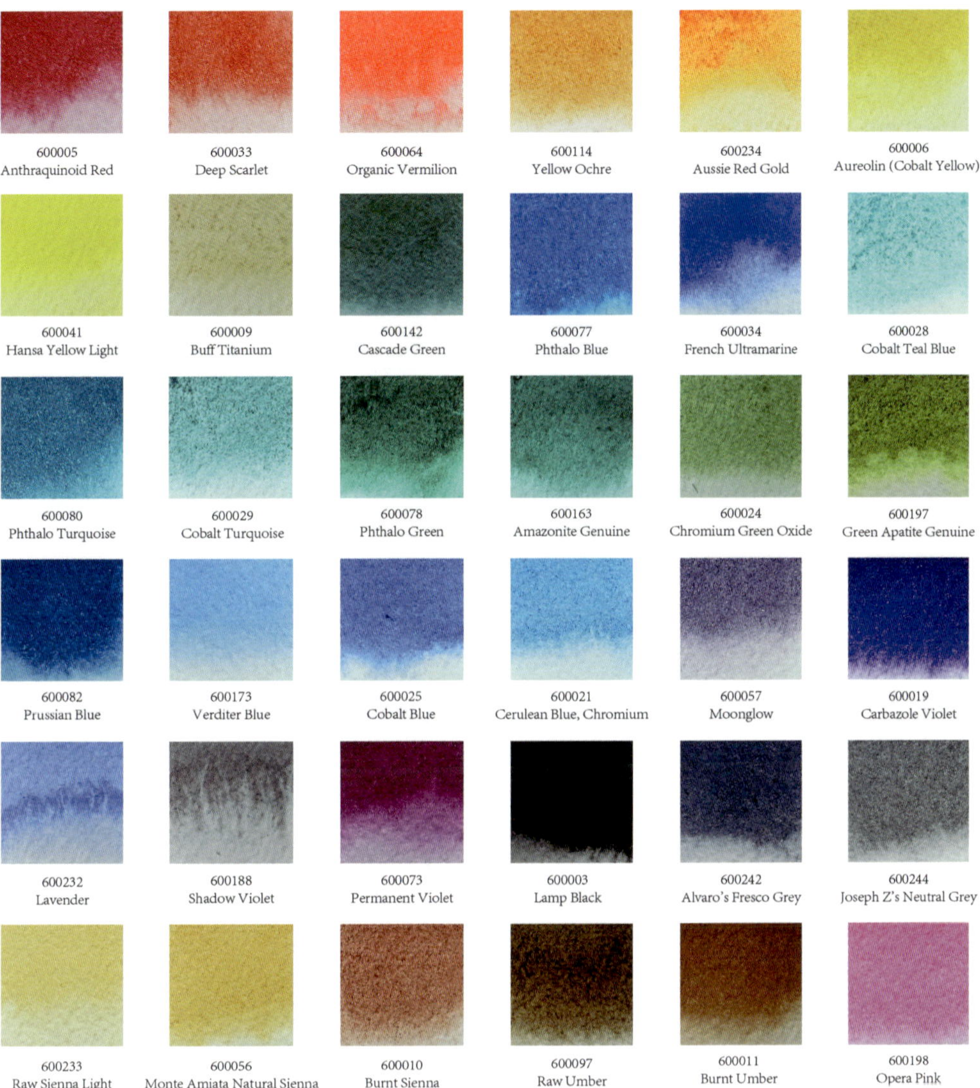

Paper

Watercolor paper is a crucial component in watercolor painting, and its material, texture, and thickness, all influence the final result of the artwork. Choosing the right watercolor paper not only enhances the ease of painting but also helps to better showcase the unique qualities of watercolor.

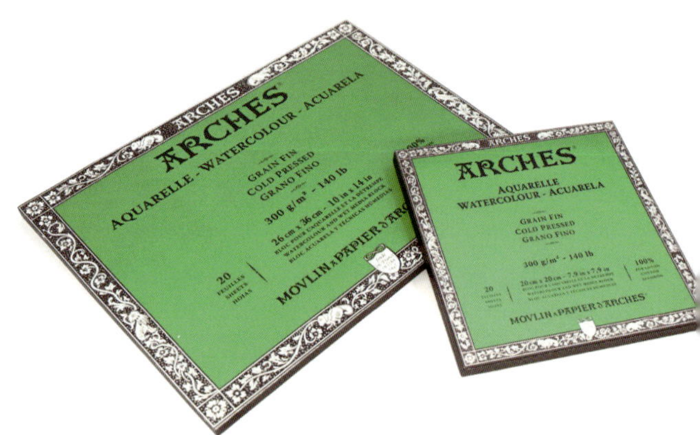

Material

Watercolor paper can be divided into two main types based on its composition: wood pulp paper and cotton pulp paper.

Wood pulp paper has a smoother surface with average absorbency, which causes the paint to stay more on the surface, resulting in vibrant colors. It's ideal for creating smooth watercolor effects. However, it is prone to water marks and is not suitable for complex layering or corrections. Wood pulp paper is relatively inexpensive and is great for practice or short-term projects, such as painting plants or simple sketches.

Cotton pulp paper is highly absorbent, making it easier to control the colors. It is ideal for detailed work and layering, and it resists fraying even with multiple modifications. Cotton pulp paper is especially suitable for large washes and long painting sessions, as it creates soft, natural color transitions. However, it is more expensive and, in terms of cost effectiveness, does not offer as much value as wood pulp paper.

Texture

Watercolor paper can be divided into three categories based on the texture of the surface: coarse, medium coarse, and fine texture. The texture of the paper affects the brushstroke effects and drying speed in watercolor paintings.

The images on the facing page show, from top to bottom, the same color displayed on coarse, medium coarse, and fine textured watercolor paper, highlighting the different textures and how each surface affects the appearance of the paint.

Coarse texture: The surface has noticeable texture, strong absorbency, and a slow drying speed, making it ideal for creating rich textural effects, such as landscapes or free flowing watercolor works. It is prone to producing "flying white" (*feibai*)—white spaces or broken brushstrokes left on the paper when the brush quickly sweeps across the surface due to the texture of the paper or insufficient moisture. This effect creates a light, dynamic feel and enhances the sense of light and breath in the painting.

Medium coarse texture: This texture is between rough and fine, allowing for both detailed work and moderate blending. It has a medium drying speed and is versatile enough for various types of watercolor paintings. It is the most commonly used and popular type of watercolor paper.

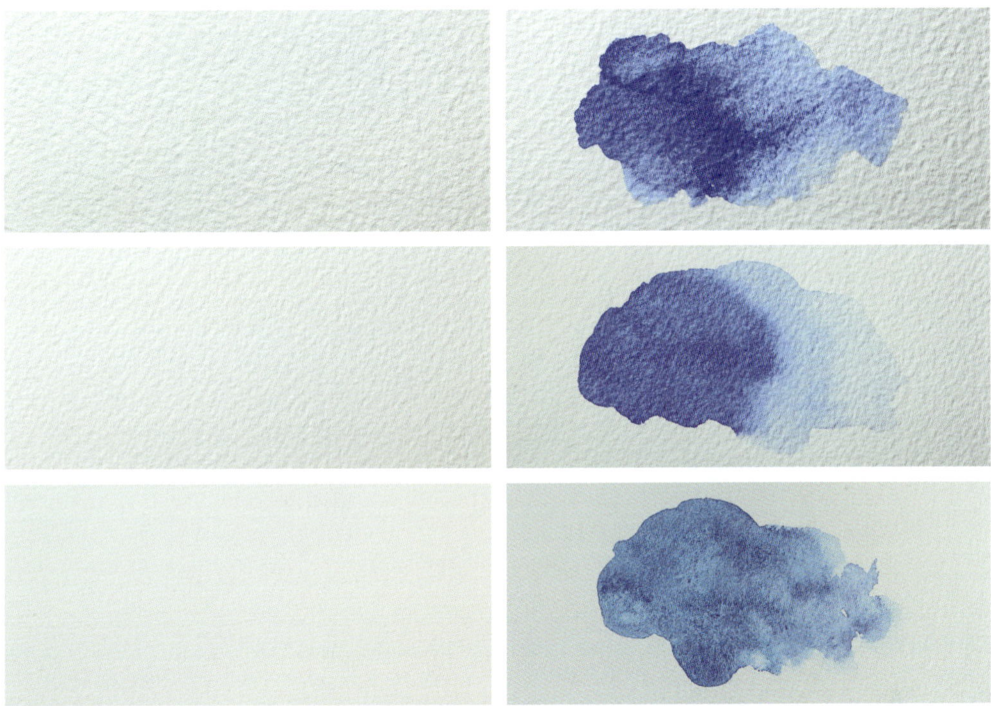

Fine texture: The surface is smooth with fine texture, offering fast absorbency, making it ideal for detailed illustrations. However, because it dries quickly, it requires more precise control of water and moisture.

Thickness

The thickness of watercolor paper is measured in grams per square meter (g/m²). The higher the gram weight, the thicker the paper, which generally means better absorbency and less likelihood of wrinkling during painting. Common gram weights are as follows:

Below 200 g: Relatively thin and prone to wrinkling, suitable for practice or projects that will be mounted.

240 g to 300 g: Ideal for most watercolor paintings, as it can handle multiple layers of color without warping easily. 300 g is the most recommended thickness, as it remains flat without needing to be mounted.

Above 300 g: Suitable for professional work, with extremely high absorbency and minimal wrinkling. However, it absorbs more paint, and colors may appear slightly darker once dried.

There are many brands of watercolor paper, and I generally prefer ARCHES. Although its price is slightly higher than other brands, it is the best watercolor paper I have used so far. It has excellent color rendering, strong absorbency, and a slow drying time, allowing ample time to work on the piece. In addition to ARCHES, Barbizon, Fabriano, and Saunders Waterford are also great choices.

All the projects in this book are created using ARCHES cotton pulp paper with a medium coarse texture and 300 g weight.

Other Tools and Materials

In watercolor painting, aside from the basic tools and materials such as brushes, paints, and paper, various auxiliary tools each have their own unique functions and value. Proper use of these tools not only enhances the smoothness of the creative process, but also expands the range of techniques that can be expressed, making the details of the artwork more refined and enriched.

Opaque white gouache: Due to its opacity, it is often used to outline or highlight fine details, such as the center of a flower (see image on the right).

Acrylic medium: Used to create transparent textures. When applying, you can dip a toothbrush into an appropriate amount of acrylic medium and flick the bristles in one direction using your hand. This takes advantage of the brush's rebound force, causing the medium to scatter onto the painting like raindrops, resulting in a natural textured effect.

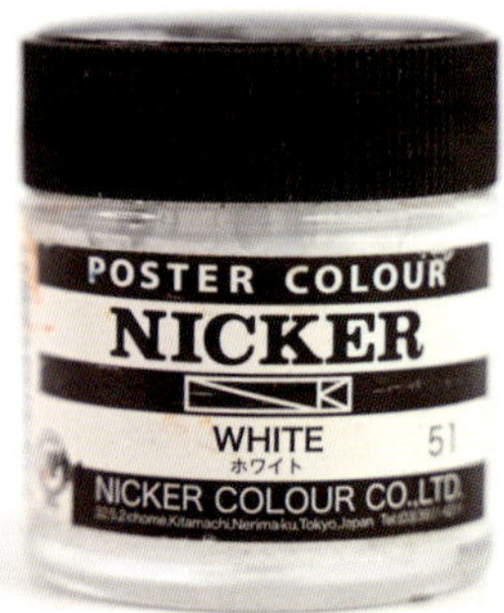

Opaque white gouache

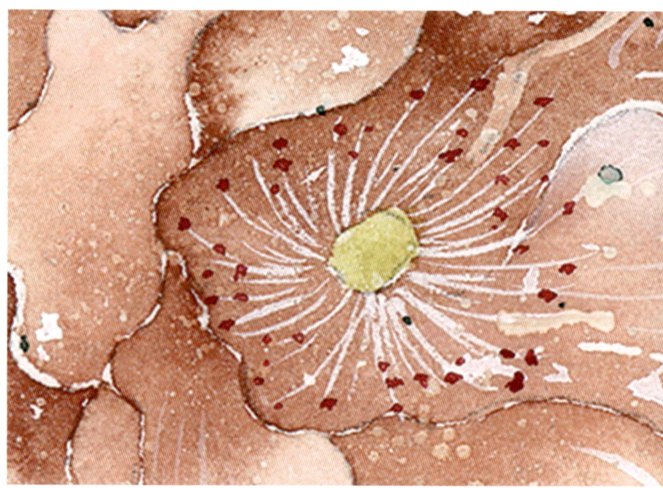

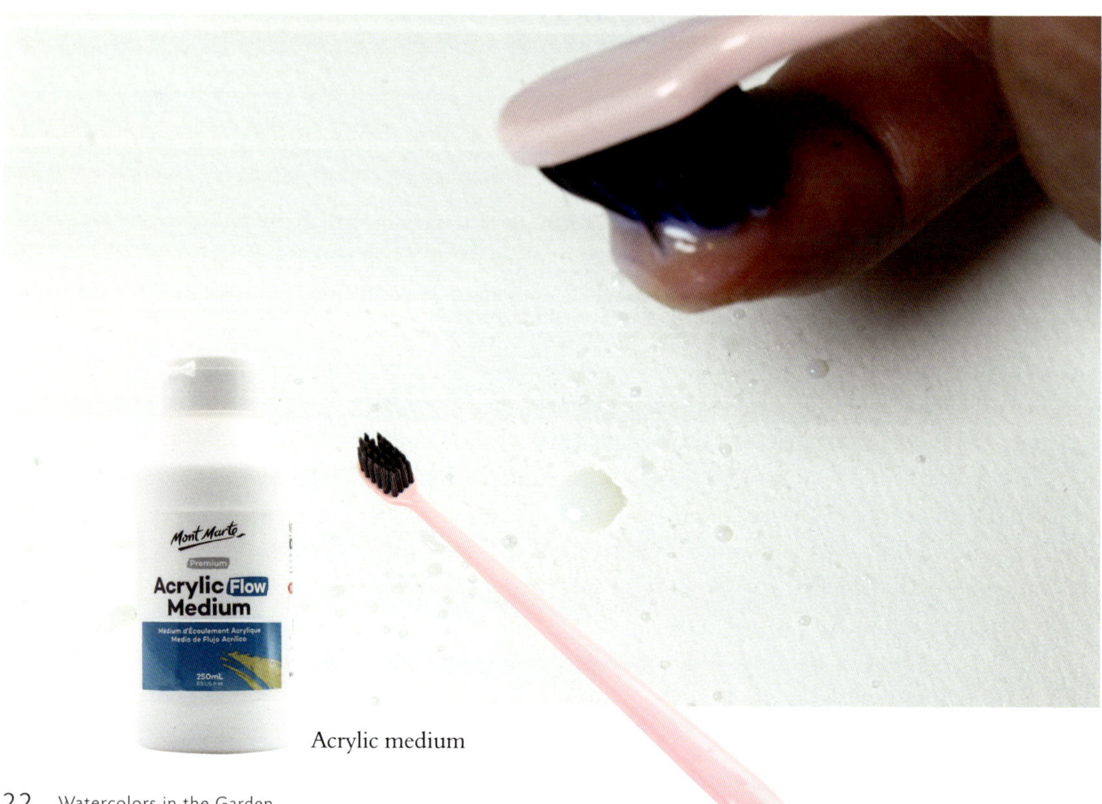

Acrylic medium

Bottled masking fluid: Used with a toothpick. Dip the toothpick into the masking fluid and draw the areas you want to keep unpainted.

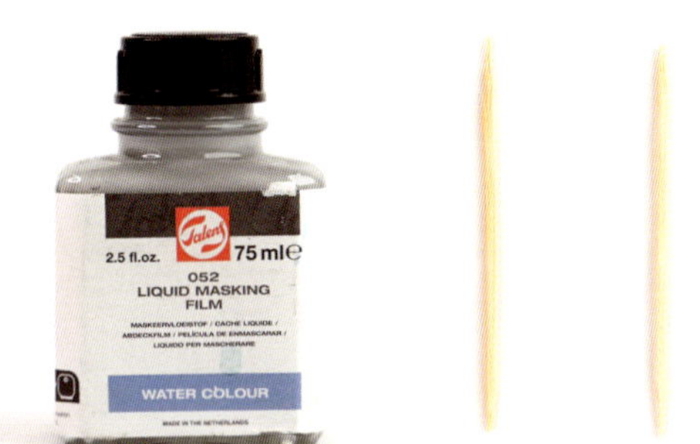

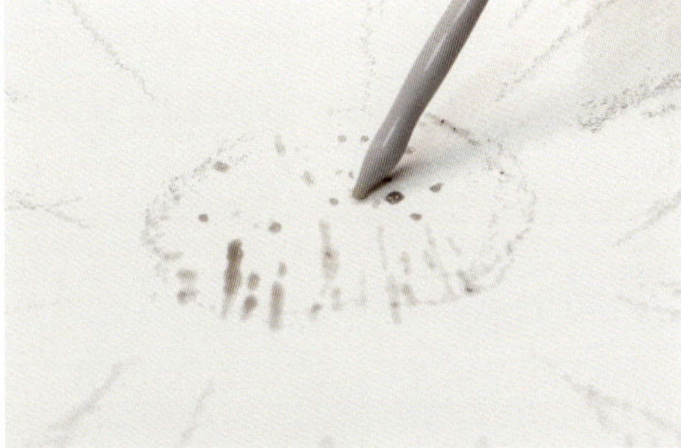

Large mixing palette: Allows for smoother and more convenient color mixing.

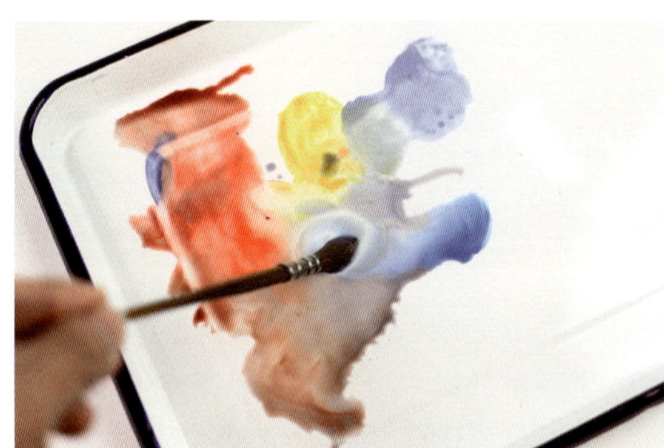

Dish: Used for diluting and mixing colors that need to be applied in large areas.

Spray bottle: Used to mist the paint to keep it constantly moist. It can also be sprayed onto the artwork just before it dries to help maintain a wet surface.

Water container: Used for cleaning watercolor brushes.

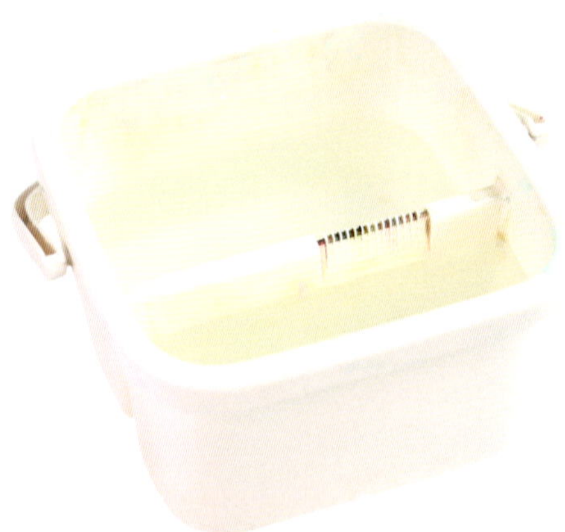

Water container

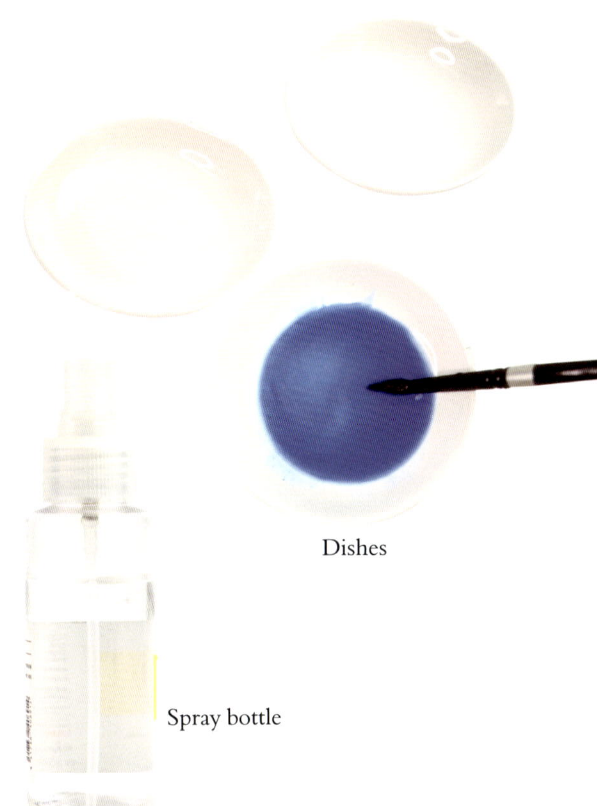

Dishes

Spray bottle

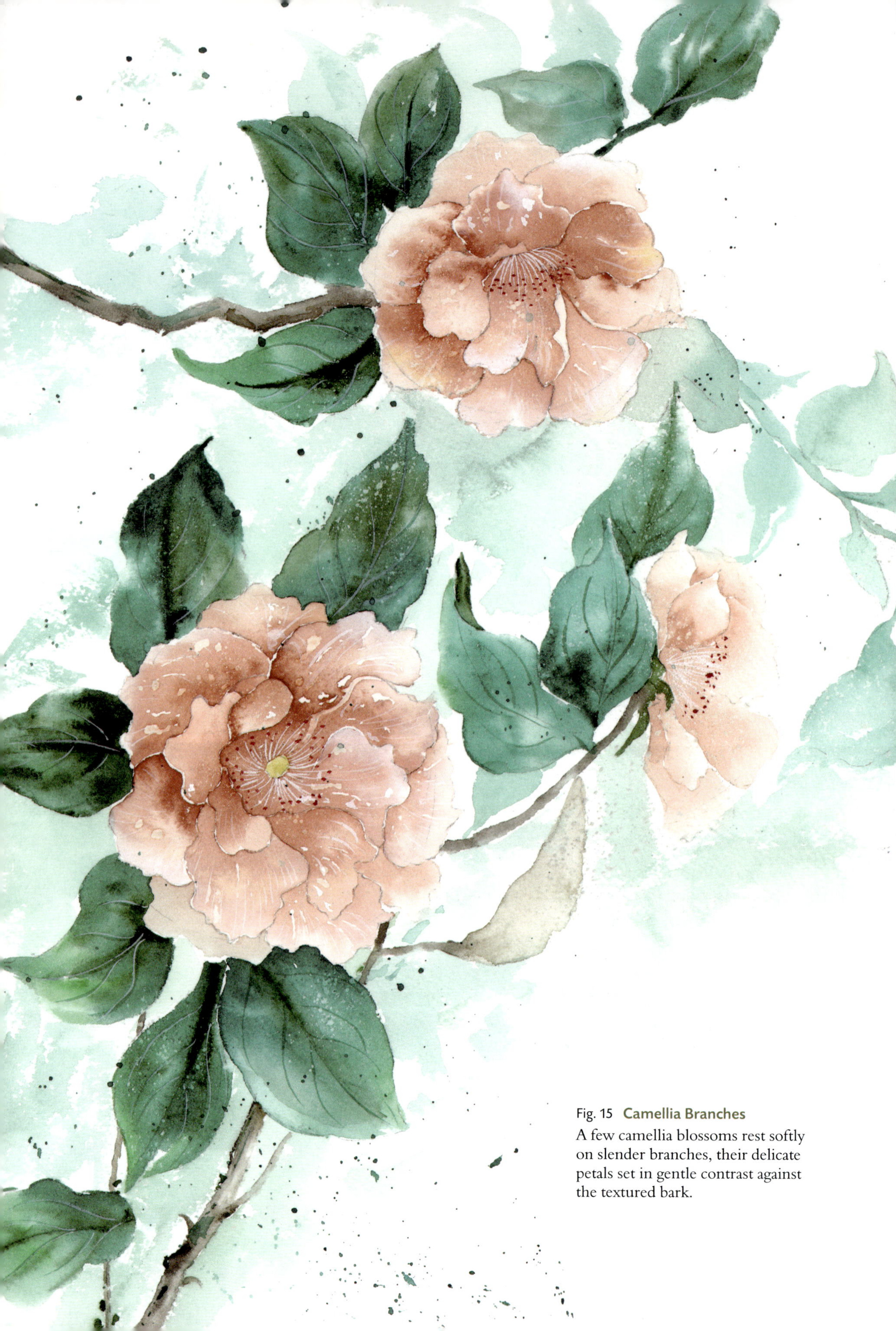

Fig. 15 Camellia Branches
A few camellia blossoms rest softly on slender branches, their delicate petals set in gentle contrast against the textured bark.

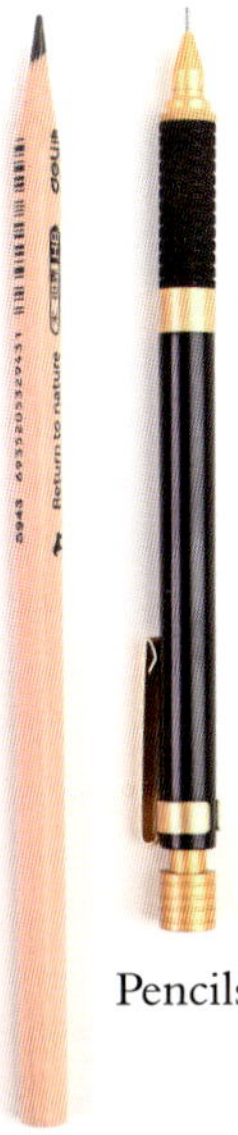

Eraser

Pencils

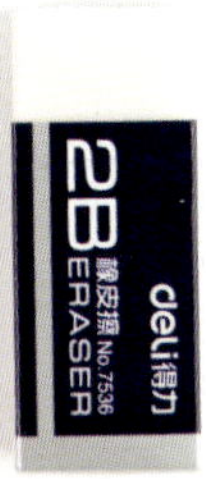

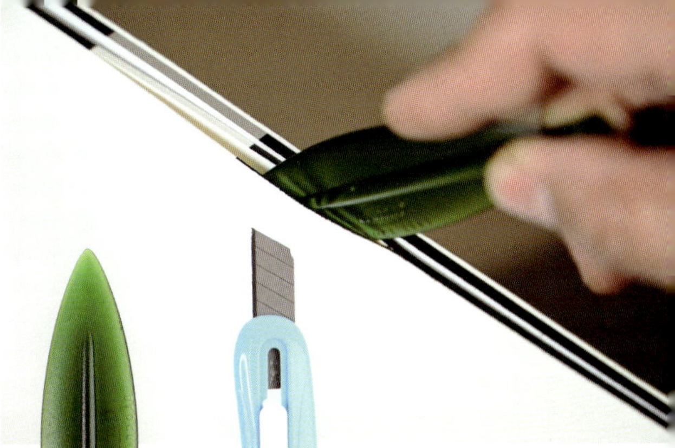

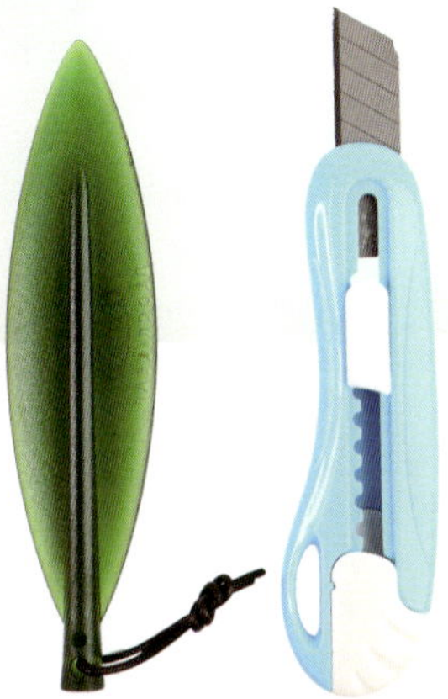

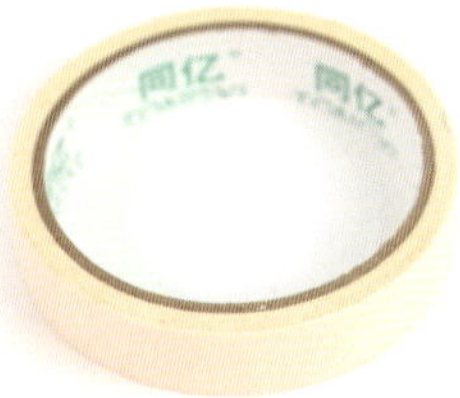

Masking tape

Craft knife   Utility knife

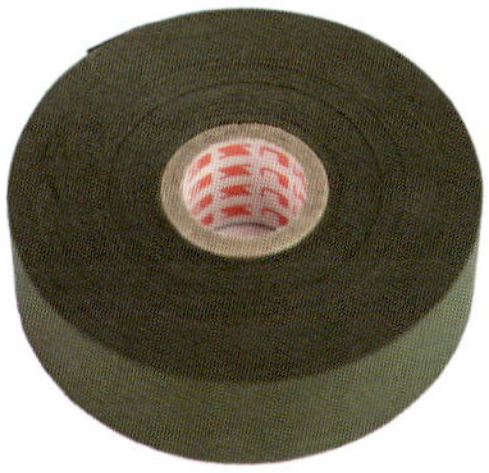

Water-activated tape

Pencil: Used during the sketching stage to help establish the composition and basic shapes. A model with moderate hardness is usually preferred, as it allows for clear line work while avoiding heavy indentations on the paper that could interfere with later painting.

Drawing board

Eraser: Used to correct sketch mistakes or remove masking fluid.

Water-activated tape: It becomes adhesive when wet and is an important tool for mounting paper.

Masking tape: Used to secure a single sheet of watercolor paper onto a drawing board, sealing the edges to prevent the paper from shifting or wrinkling when wet. It also helps create clean and neat edges on the artwork, and is easy to remove without damaging the paper surface.

Drawing board: Provides a solid and smooth surface for painting, making it easier to secure watercolor paper and reduce deformation or wrinkles while painting. When not working in a watercolor sketchbook, we typically use water-activated tape or masking tape to secure a single sheet of watercolor paper onto the drawing board for painting.

Craft knife or utility knife: If painting directly in a watercolor sketchbook with all four sides sealed, this tool is used to carefully cut the artwork from the sketchbook once the piece is finished, making it easier for future framing or storage.

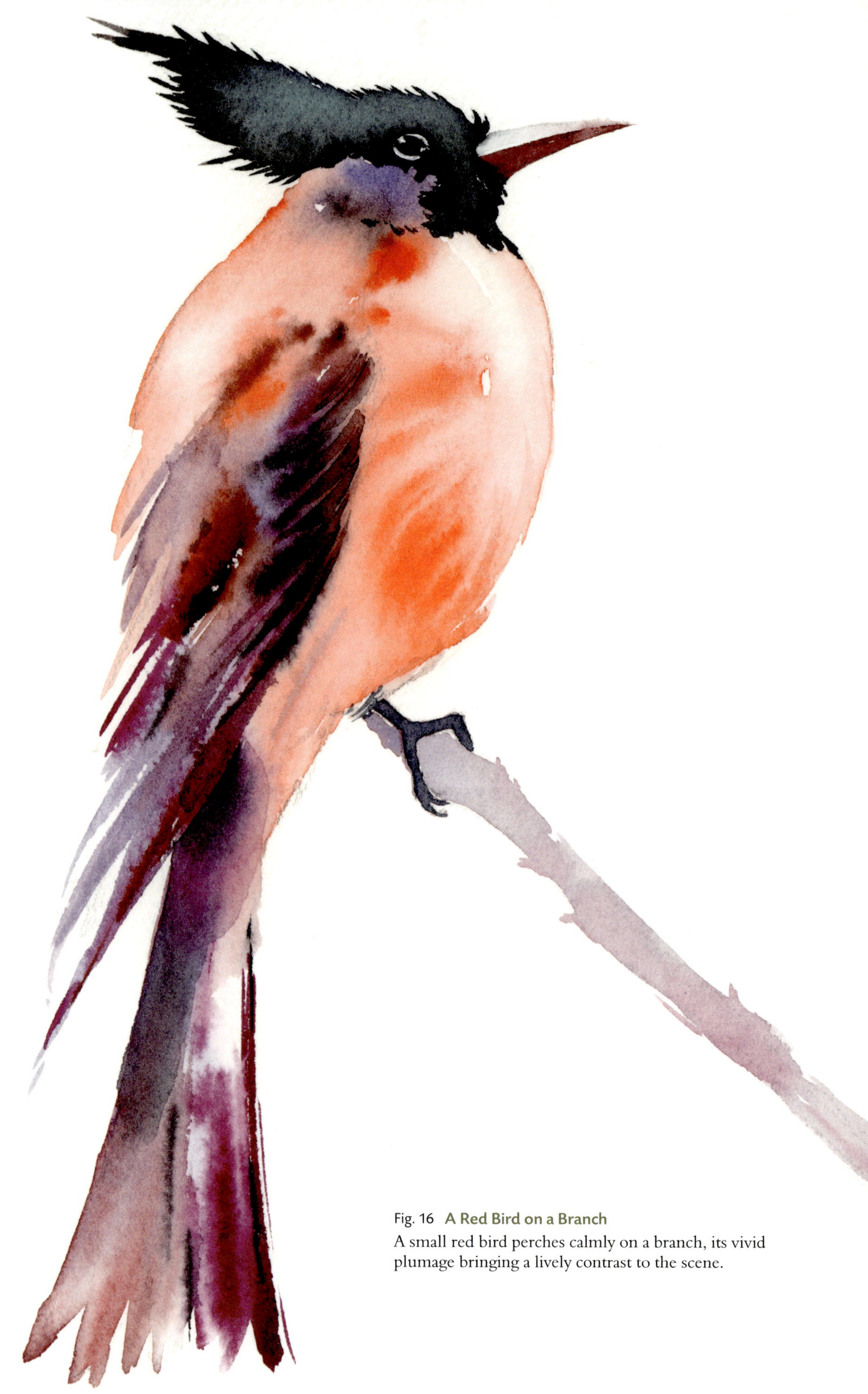

Fig. 16 **A Red Bird on a Branch**
A small red bird perches calmly on a branch, its vivid
plumage bringing a lively contrast to the scene.

Chapter Two
Basic Techniques

All watercolor paintings are based on two fundamental, essential techniques, wet-on-dry and wet-on-wet painting techniques. The key distinction lies in whether the painting is done on a dry surface or a wet one, not in whether the brush itself is dry or wet.

Wet-on-Dry Technique

Painting on a dry paper surface allows the paint to form clear brushstrokes and rich textures on the paper, making it ideal for depicting details, textures, and dry, granular effects such as tree bark, rocks, fur, and more.

For example, in the projects in this book, the peony's center, the fur of the cat and bee, and the petals of the lily are all depicted using the wet-on-dry technique.

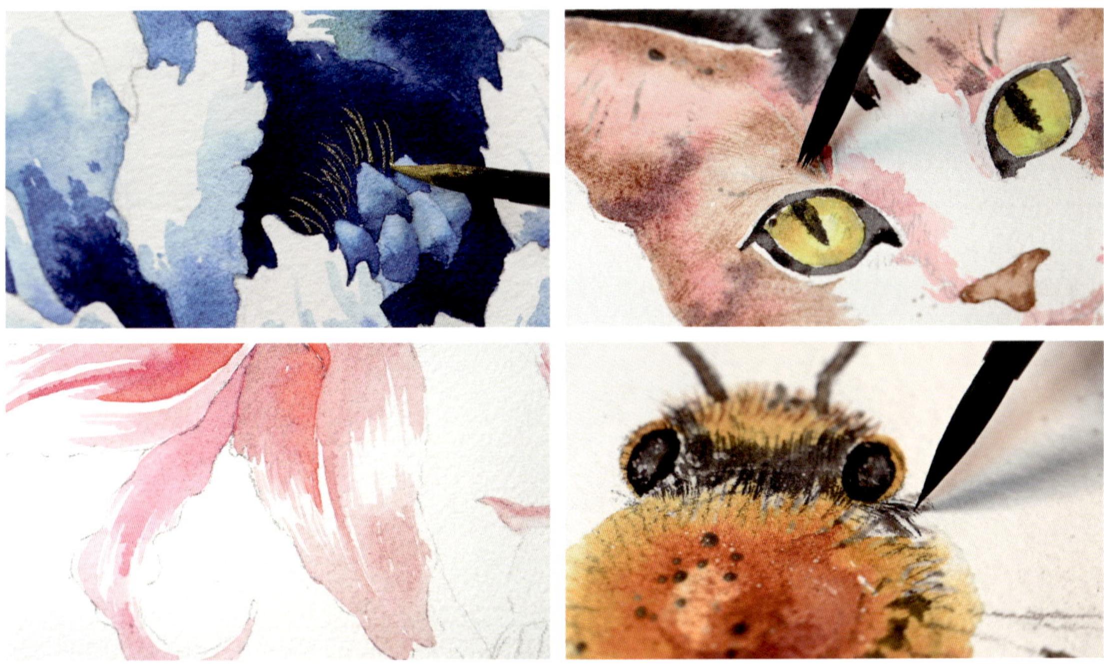

Characteristics of Wet-on-Dry Technique

1. Strong color coverage with clear layers, making it suitable for detailed depiction.

2. Brushstrokes are clearly visible, allowing for the creation of natural texture effects.

3. With less water content, it is less likely to produce accidental blending, making it easier to control the painting.

4. Ideal for depicting local details, it can also be combined with the wet-on-wet technique to add depth to the composition.

Steps of Wet-on-Dry Technique

1. Control moisture: Use a relatively dry brush, dip it into a small amount of undiluted paint, and gently remove excess moisture by wiping the brush on a palette or paper towel, leaving the brush semi-dry.

2. Apply brushstrokes: Use light, swift brushing motions on the paper surface, utilizing the dry state of the bristles to create natural granulation or "flying white" effect. The specific effect can be referred to in the "dry brush" technique mentioned in other common methods.

3. Layering: The dry painting technique is ideal for layering multiple colors. Let each layer dry thoroughly before adding another to enhance the three-dimensionality and richness of the artwork.

4. Combine with wet-on-wet technique: For a more layered effect, apply the wet-on-wet technique to lay down a base color, then use the wet-on-dry technique to add texture to the composition.

Wet-on-Wet Technique

This technique involves painting on a damp surface, where the paint is applied and allowed to spread and merge under the influence of water, creating soft, natural transitions. The wet-on-wet technique is commonly used for depicting scenes such as skies, clouds, lakes, mist, and flowers, where gentle color transitions or a dreamy atmosphere are needed. In the case tutorials of this book, the term "dabbing" refers to the wet-on-wet technique.

For example, in my projects, the soft background effects behind the daisy and king protea, the stormy cloud effect in the owl's background, and the butterfly's wings are all created using the wet-on-wet technique.

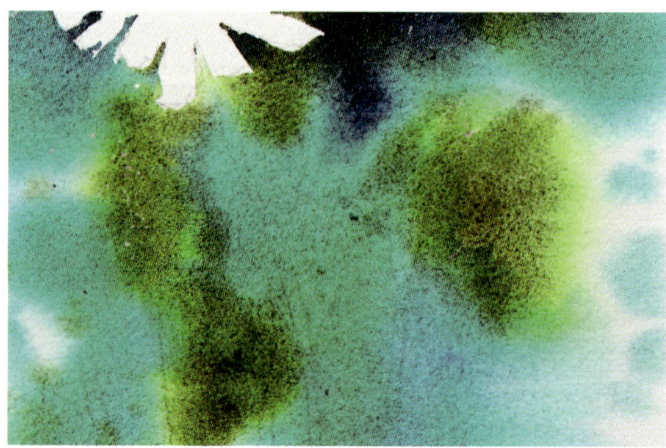

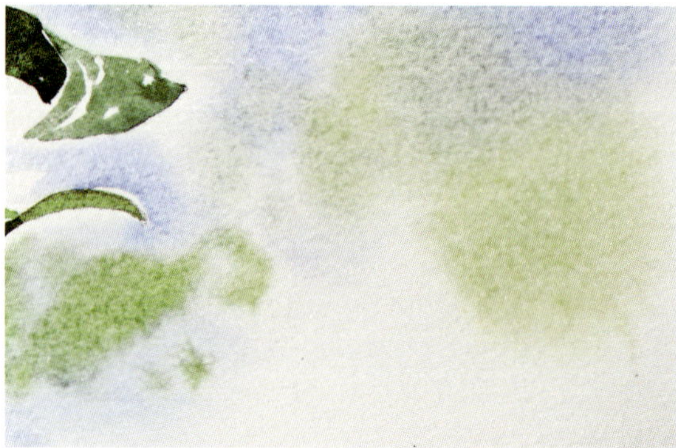

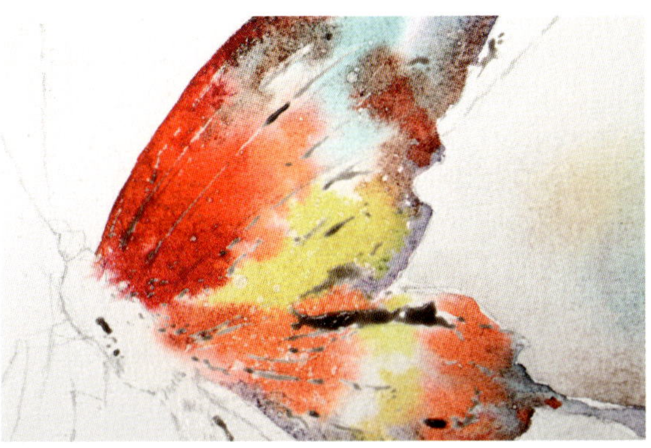

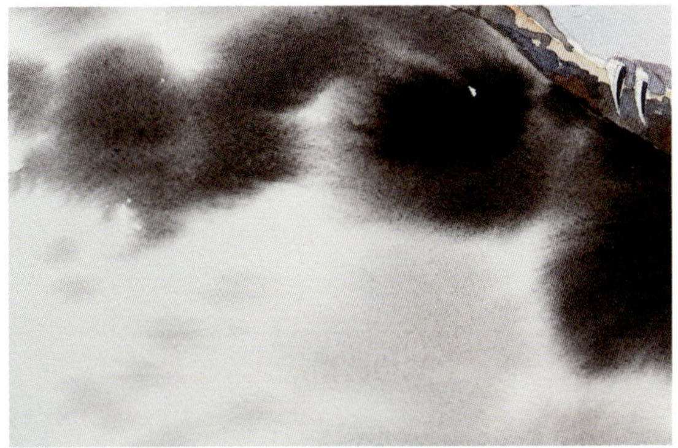

Characteristics of Wet-on-Wet Technique

1. Natural color transitions: Ideal for large areas of rendering and gradient effects.

2. Strong paint diffusion: Creates a sense of movement and unique textures.

3. Perfect for soft, dreamy atmospheres: Particularly effective for creating fog, halos, or water reflections.

4. Sensitive to water control: Requires some experience to manage the flow of paint.

Steps of Wet-on-Wet Technique

1. Moisten the paper surface: Begin by evenly applying clean water to the paper, ensuring it is damp but not saturated with excess water.

2. Apply color and blend: Gently add paint onto the dampened paper, allowing the colors to naturally spread and blend, creating a soft gradient effect.

3. Control diffusion: Adjust the amount of water and paint concentration to control the extent of diffusion. The more water used, the faster the color will spread and the softer the edges will be. Reducing water in certain areas will help maintain the clarity of the color.

4. Layering and adjustment: Wait until the first layer of color is semi-dry or completely dry before layering additional colors to create richer color depth and variation.

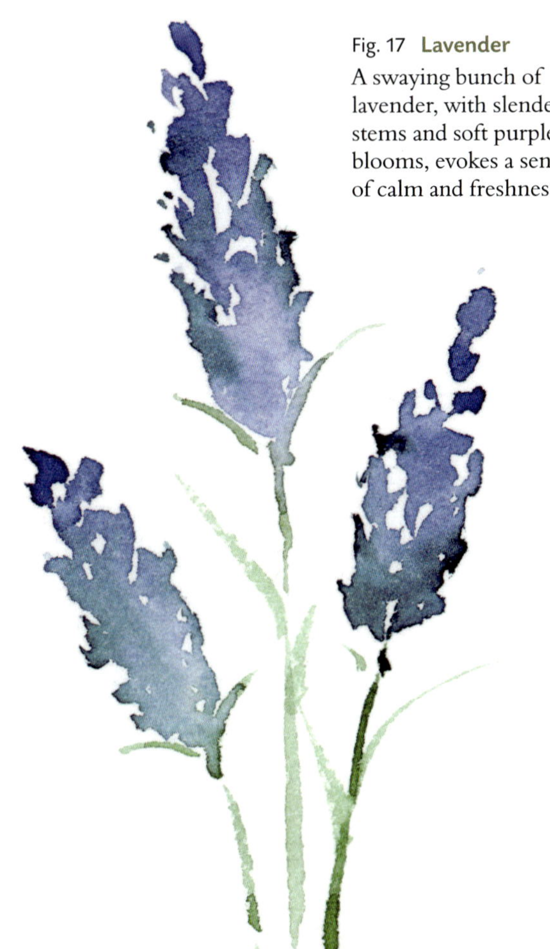

Fig. 17 **Lavender**
A swaying bunch of lavender, with slender stems and soft purple blooms, evokes a sense of calm and freshness.

Control of Brush Tip and Paper Moisture

In everyday painting, we often combine wet-on-dry and wet-on-wet techniques, as demonstrated in the examples throughout this book. Whether using wet-on-dry or wet-on-wet technique, it is essential to control both the moisture on the brush tip and the wetness of the paper. However, mastering the control of brush moisture and paper dampness is not something that can be achieved overnight. It requires long term practice, observation, and summarization to gradually perfect these skills.

The amount of moisture in the brush tip has a critical impact on the depth of the color. The more water in the brush, the more diluted the color will be, resulting in a lighter hue. Conversely, when the brush has less moisture, the color will be more concentrated and vivid.

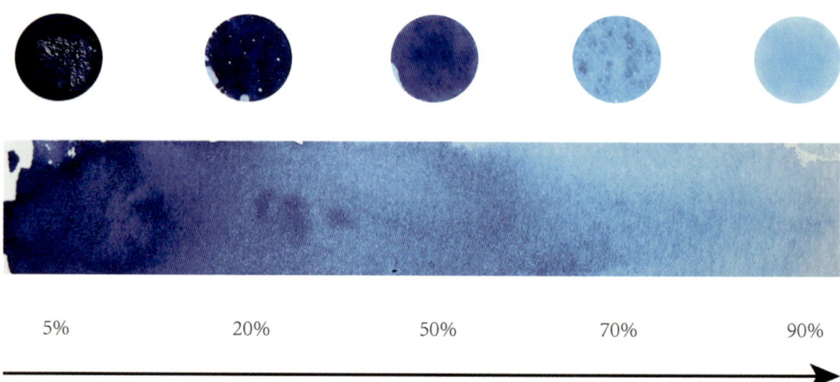

Fig. 18   The impact of different brush tip moisture levels on color depth.

How should we control the moisture level of the paper surface, and how can we determine if the moisture content of the paper is at the required level?

We can completely wet the surface of the paper. When viewed from the side, if there is strong reflection, it indicates that the paper is still very wet, with water remaining on the surface. At this stage, the colors applied will not hold their shape. When a large amount of color is applied, it will gradually spread and be absorbed by the paper, creating a large-area color penetration effect as the water spreads (see images below).

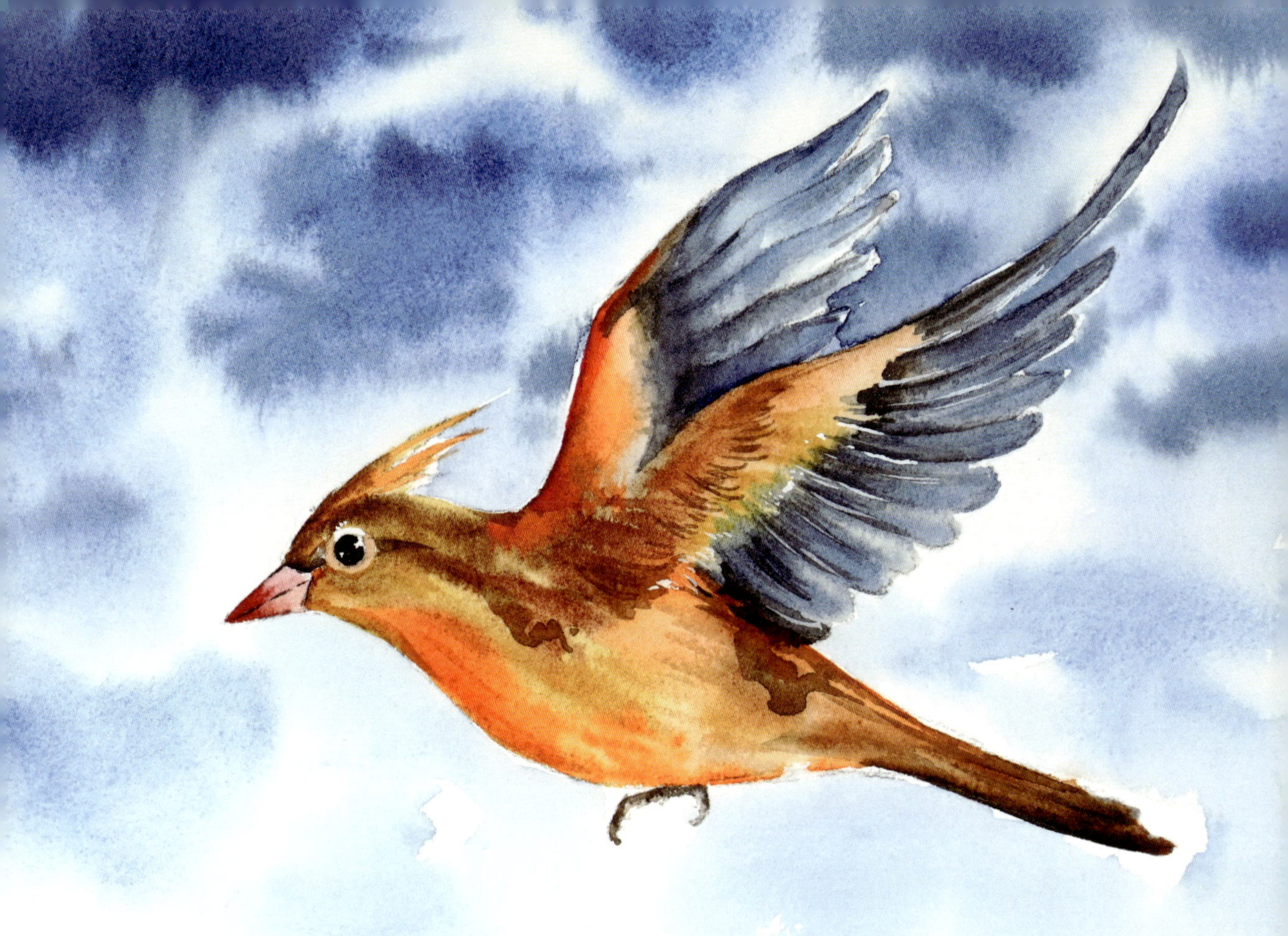

Fig. 19 **Bird Soaring in the Blue Sky**
A lone bird glides across a vast blue sky, embodying a sense of freedom and effortless grace.

When viewed from the side, if there is no reflection, but the paper feels damp and cool to the touch, it indicates that the surface of the paper is no longer wet, but the inner layers still contain moisture. At this stage, when color is applied, the edges won't be sharp, and the color will gradually spread outward with the moisture inside the paper, creating a soft, blurred effect (see images below).

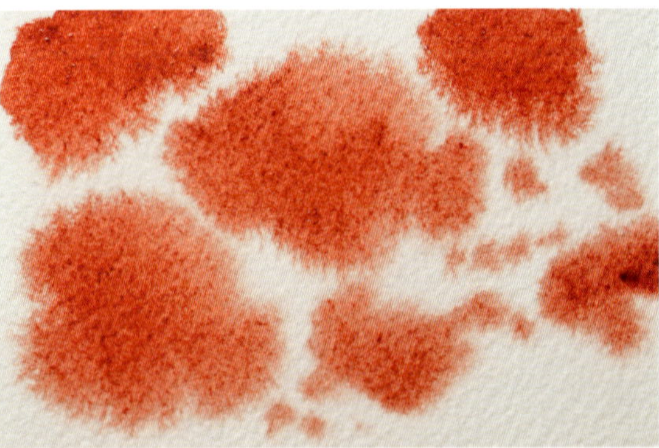

Other Common Techniques

Wet-on-dry and wet-on-wet techniques are the two fundamental methods in watercolor painting. However, when broken down further, there are various other techniques and some special methods. Below are the techniques commonly used in the projects presented in this book.

Gradient technique: Also known as the gradation technique. This involves adding water to the existing color to dilute and spread it, creating a gradient effect.

Blending technique: This involves applying a base color first, and while the surface is still wet, blending in other colors.

Merging technique: First, apply a layer of clean water, then gradually add two colors, allowing them to naturally blend and merge as they flow with the moisture.

Dropping water technique: Apply a color evenly on the paper, then while it's still wet, use a brush tip containing clean water to drop water onto the color. The water will spread outward, creating a natural effect.

Gradient technique

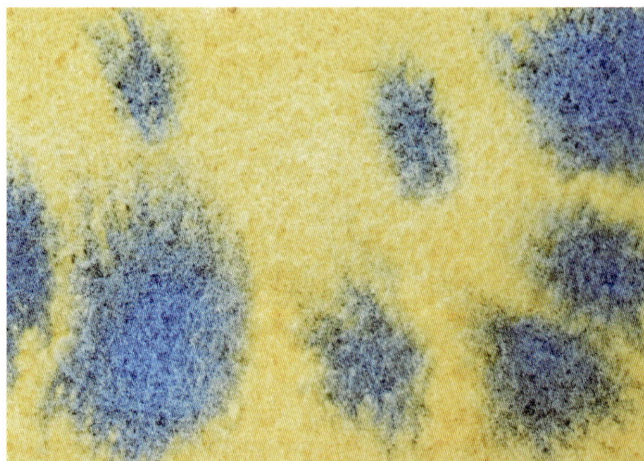

Blending technique

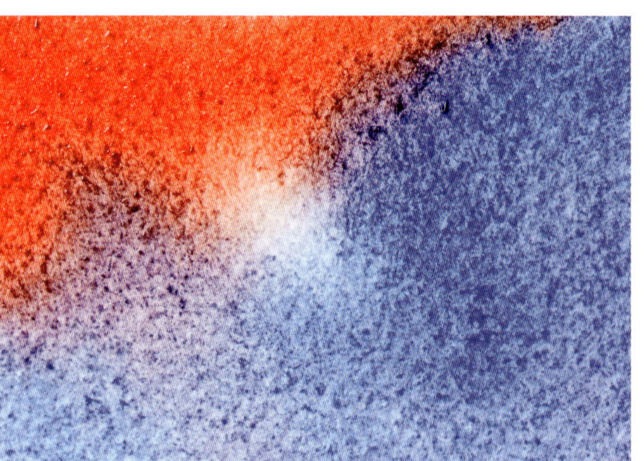

Merging technique

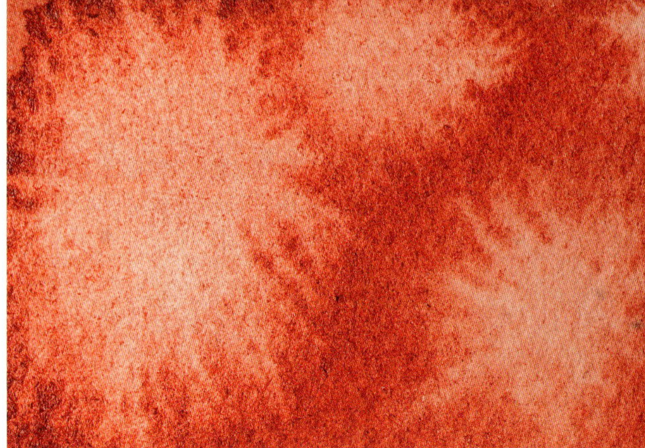

Dropping water technique

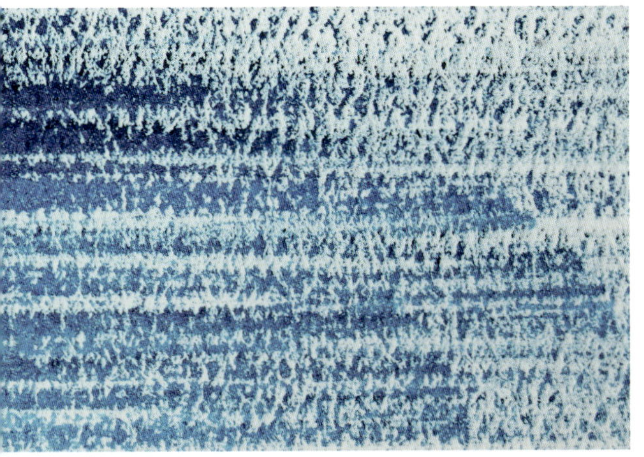

Dry brush technique

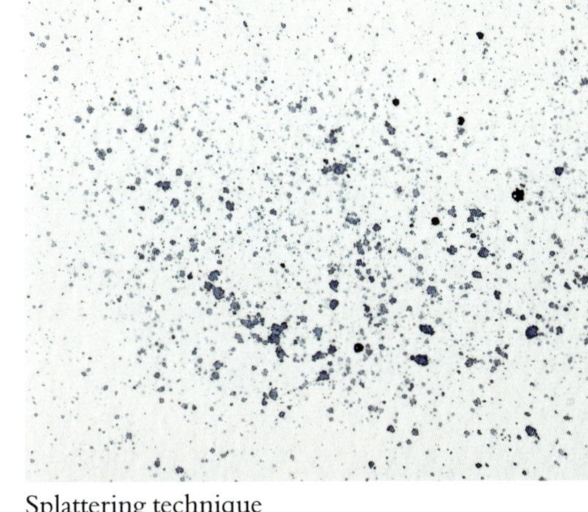

Splattering technique

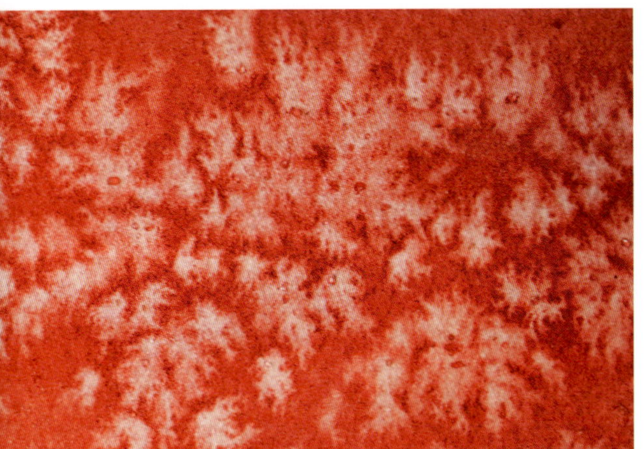

Sprinkling salt technique

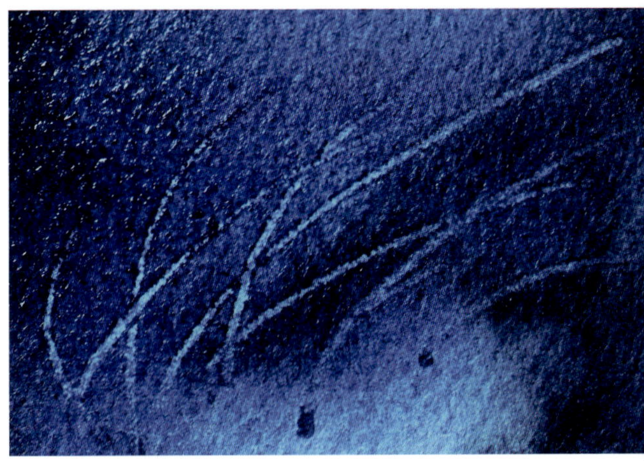

Scratching technique

Dry brush technique: On a dry paper surface, use a dry brush to pick up color and create dry brushstrokes.

Splattering technique: Use a slightly damp brush to pick up color, then flick the brush with your finger to create a texture effect.

Sprinkling salt technique: Apply a color with a higher water content on the paper, then sprinkle some fine salt on top. Once dry, it will create a texture effect like the one shown in the image. If you use coarse salt, the texture pattern will be larger.

Scratching technique: Apply a layer of color on the paper, and when the painting is about half dry, meaning the surface moisture no longer moves and the paper feels damp to the touch, use the barrel of a brush to scratch out shapes.

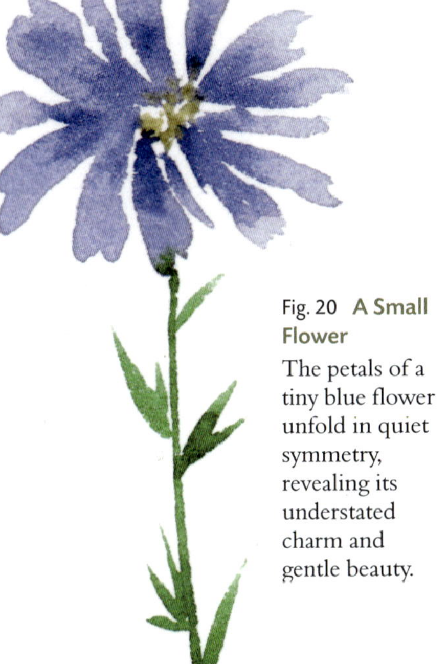

Fig. 20 **A Small Flower**
The petals of a tiny blue flower unfold in quiet symmetry, revealing its understated charm and gentle beauty.

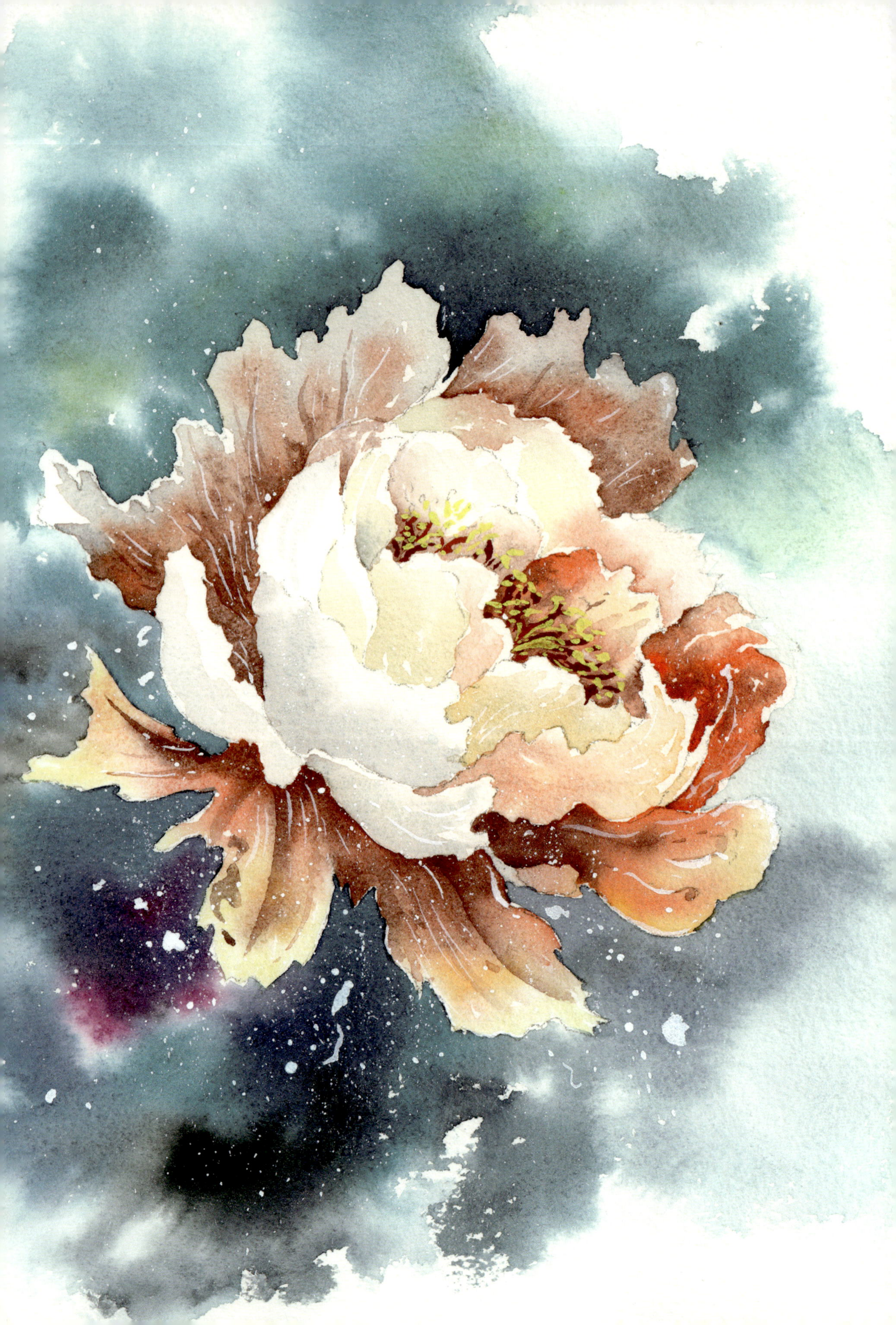

Chapter Three
Tutorials and Projects

After becoming familiar with the characteristics of watercolor tools and basic techniques, let us now turn our brushstrokes to a more vibrant stage. This chapter uses 16 natural creatures and flowers as examples to guide you in blending color, water, and brushwork through practice. Each project is a vivid interpretation of the techniques from Chapter Two, while quietly nurturing your ability to observe the world and capture its essence in your strokes.

Now, it's time to open the garden gate and let the colors bloom on the paper.

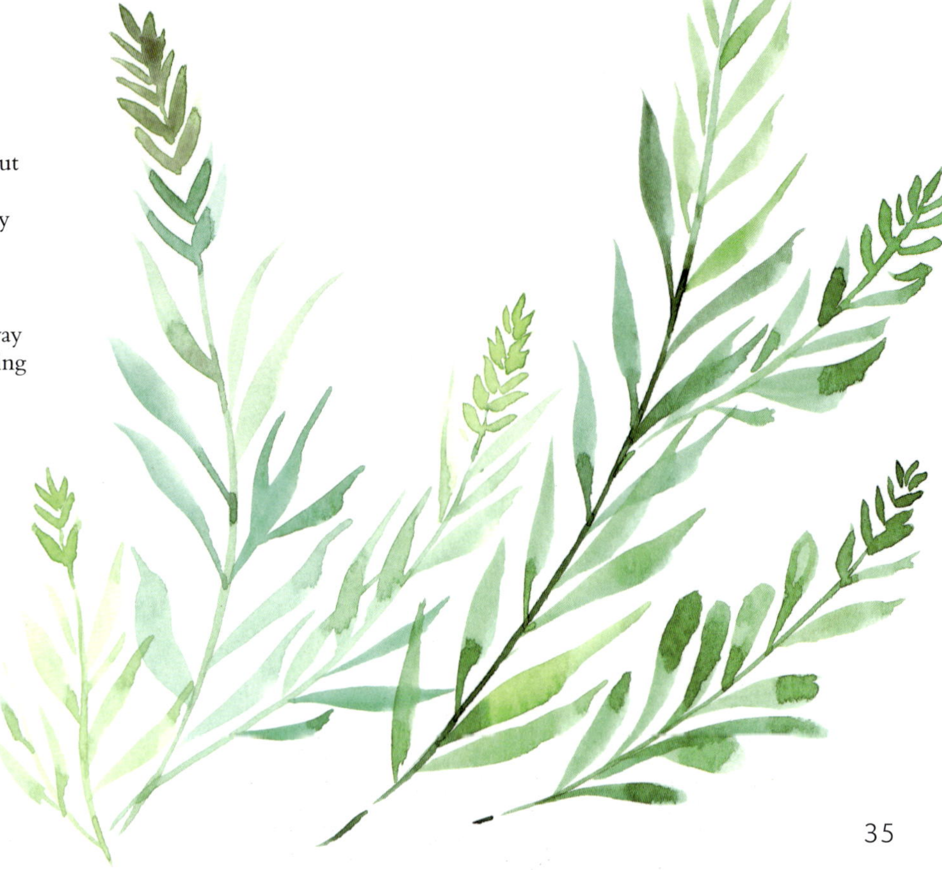

On the facing page
Fig. 21 **Peony in Bloom**
A stunning peony stands out against a bold, contrasting wash, radiating regal beauty and vibrant elegance.

Fig. 22 **Wild Grasses**
Clusters of wild grasses sway in quiet freedom, embodying nature's gentle resilience.

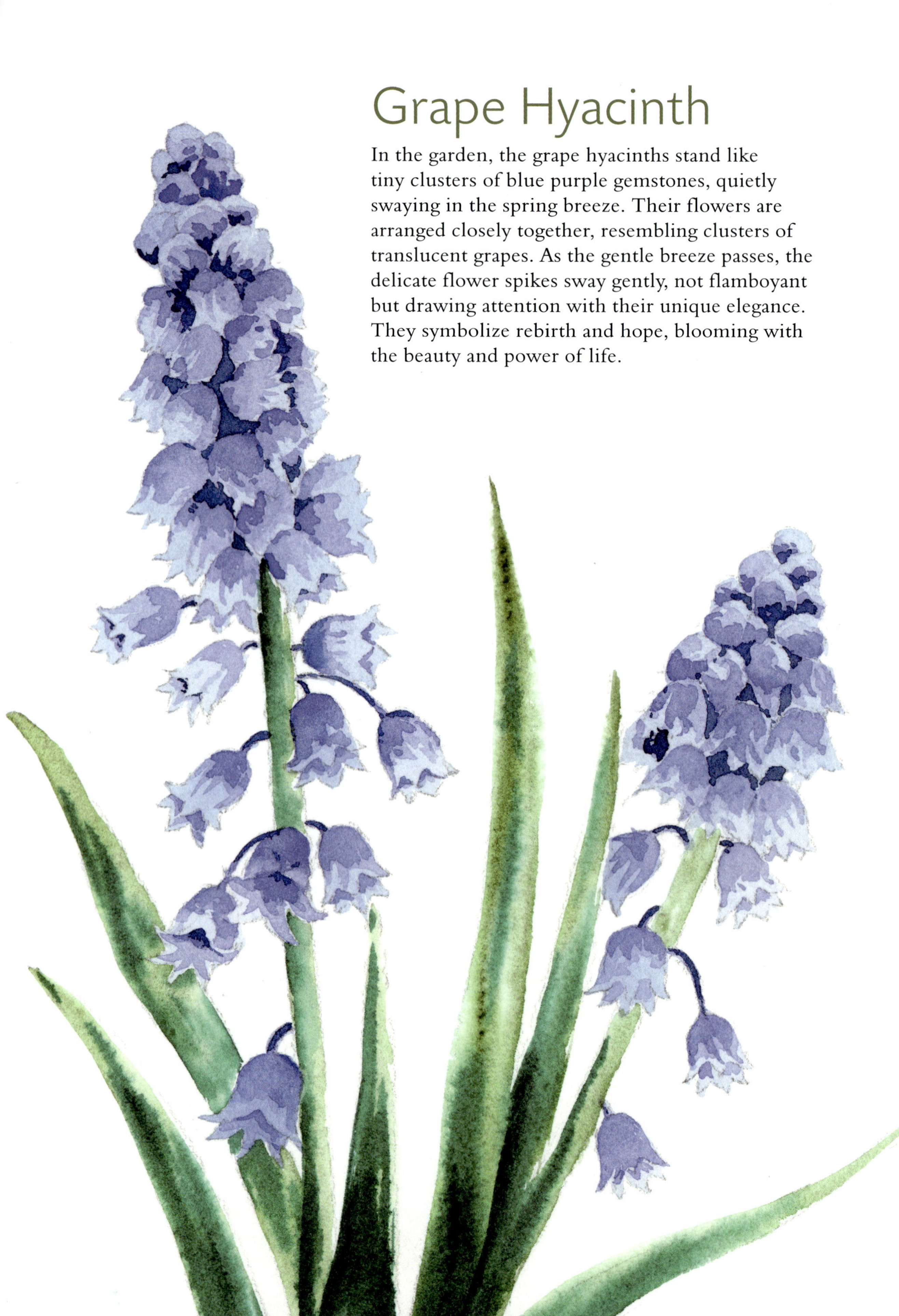

Grape Hyacinth

In the garden, the grape hyacinths stand like tiny clusters of blue purple gemstones, quietly swaying in the spring breeze. Their flowers are arranged closely together, resembling clusters of translucent grapes. As the gentle breeze passes, the delicate flower spikes sway gently, not flamboyant but drawing attention with their unique elegance. They symbolize rebirth and hope, blooming with the beauty and power of life.

Paint Brand
DANIEL SMITH

Color Codes
- 600021: Cerulean Blue, Chromium
- 600025: Cobalt Blue
- 600034: French Ultramarine
- 600082: Prussian Blue
- 600197: Green Apatite Genuine
- 600078: Phthalo Green (Blue Shade)

Recommended Watercolor Paper
ARCHES watercolor paper, cold pressed,
140 lb/300 g/m^2

Recommended Brush
Black Velvet 3000S brush for watercolor,
size 8

Key Challenges
1. How to paint small flower petals in clusters.
2. Using wet-on-wet technique for
painting leaves.

Steps

1

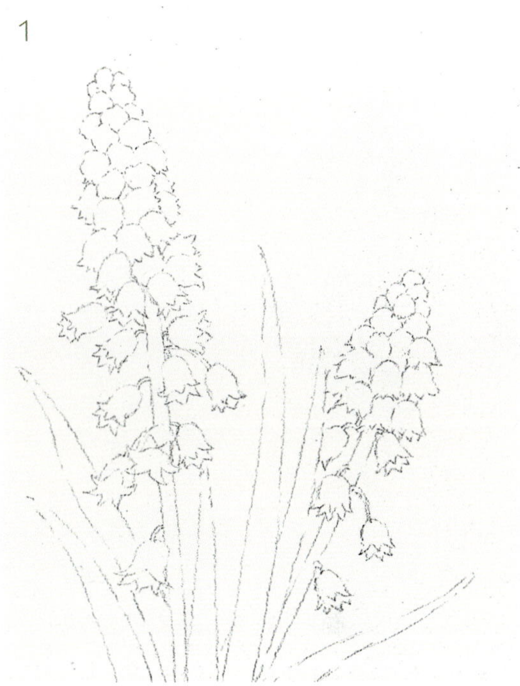

Lightly sketch the shape of the grape hyacinth with your
brush, paying attention to the spacing between the petals
and the positioning of the leaves relative to each other.

2

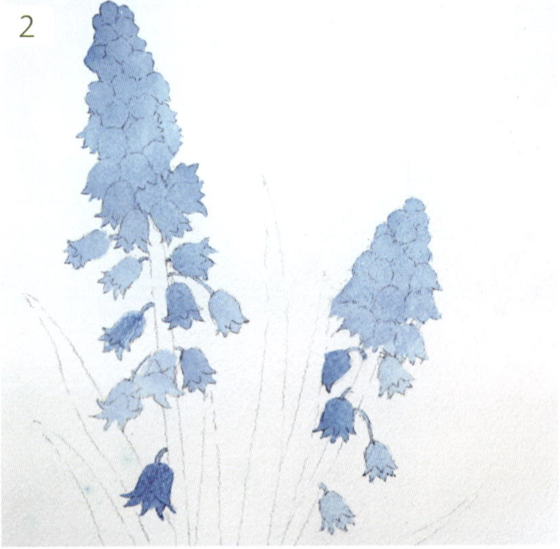

Fill the brush tip with water, and lightly apply a base
layer of color 600021 (Cerulean Blue, Chromium) along
the contour of the flowers. As you continue to paint,
the water in the brush will gradually decrease, creating
variations in the lightness and darkness of the same
color. If you notice that the brush tip is almost dry, you
should quickly dip it in water and add more paint before
continuing to paint. This way, the color will remain
moister and lighter.

3

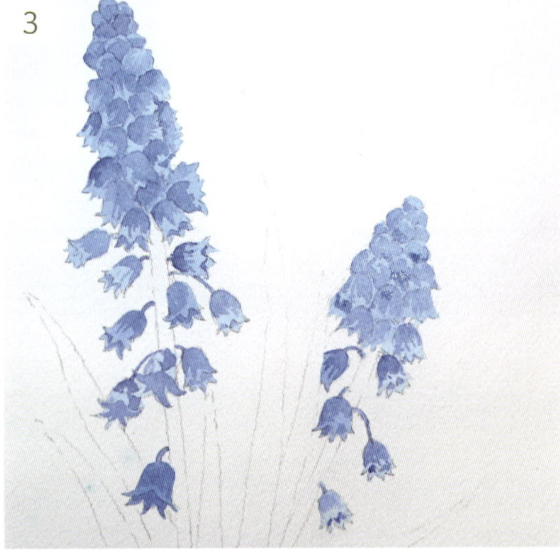

Wait for the first layer of color to dry completely.
Then, using a brush with plenty of water, dip into color
600025 (Cobalt Blue) to deepen the base of the flowers
and the open parts of the fully bloomed flowers. Pay
attention to the flower arrangement: the flowers in the
upper part of the bouquet that are not fully open yet
tend to grow upwards, while the fully bloomed flowers
droop towards the sides or downwards.

4

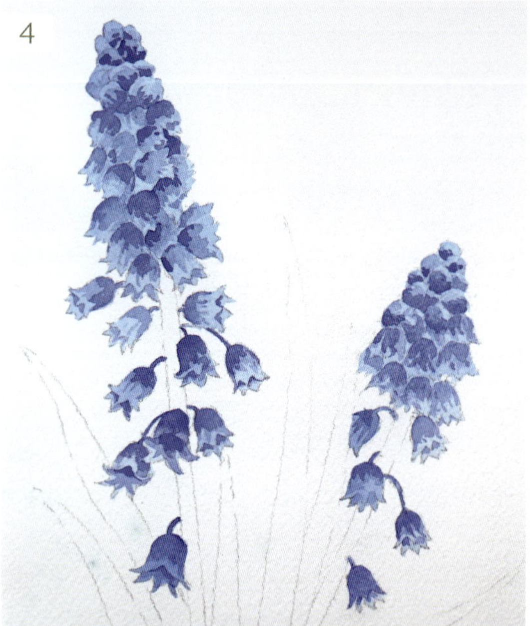

Continue using color 600034 (French Ultramarine) to deepen the base of the flowers.

5

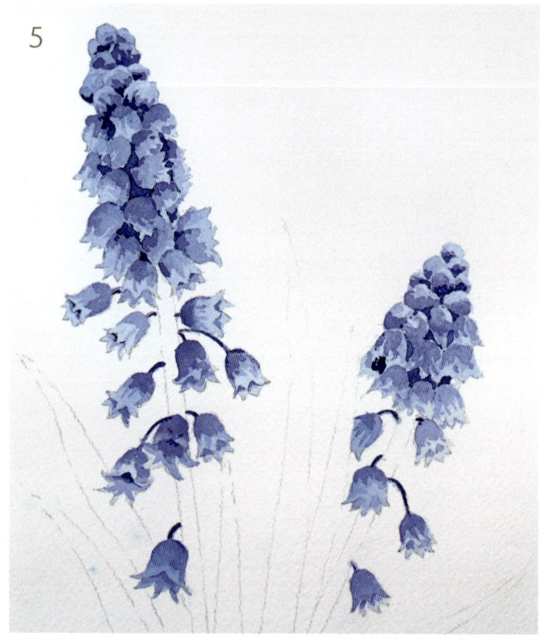

Use paint color 600082 (Prussian Blue) to fill in the gaps between the flowers. These areas represent the shadows between the flowers and the darker parts inside them. We only need to use a relatively deep blue color to represent it simply.

6

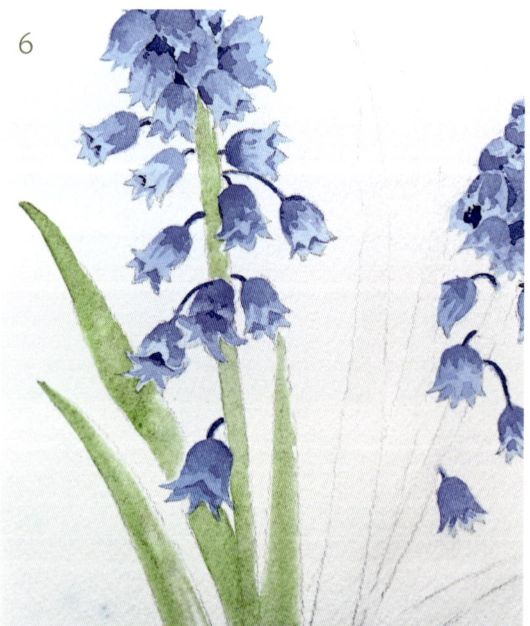

Start by painting the flower stems and leaves on the left half. Begin by moistening the area around the stems and leaves with clean water. Once the water has soaked into the paper, use color 600197 (Green Apatite Genuine) to apply the paint. Avoid using a flat wash. Instead, gently dab the color on, allowing it to spread and diffuse with the water, creating a gradient effect with varying shades of light and dark.

7

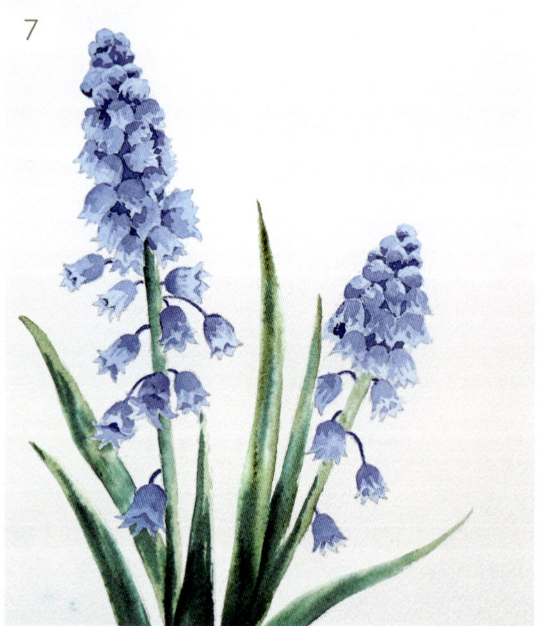

While the area is still wet, use color 600078 (Phthalo Green) to deepen the darker areas of the leaves and flower stems, adding details. With the same color and technique, paint the flower stems and leaves on the right half. This will complete the painting of the grape hyacinth in your garden.

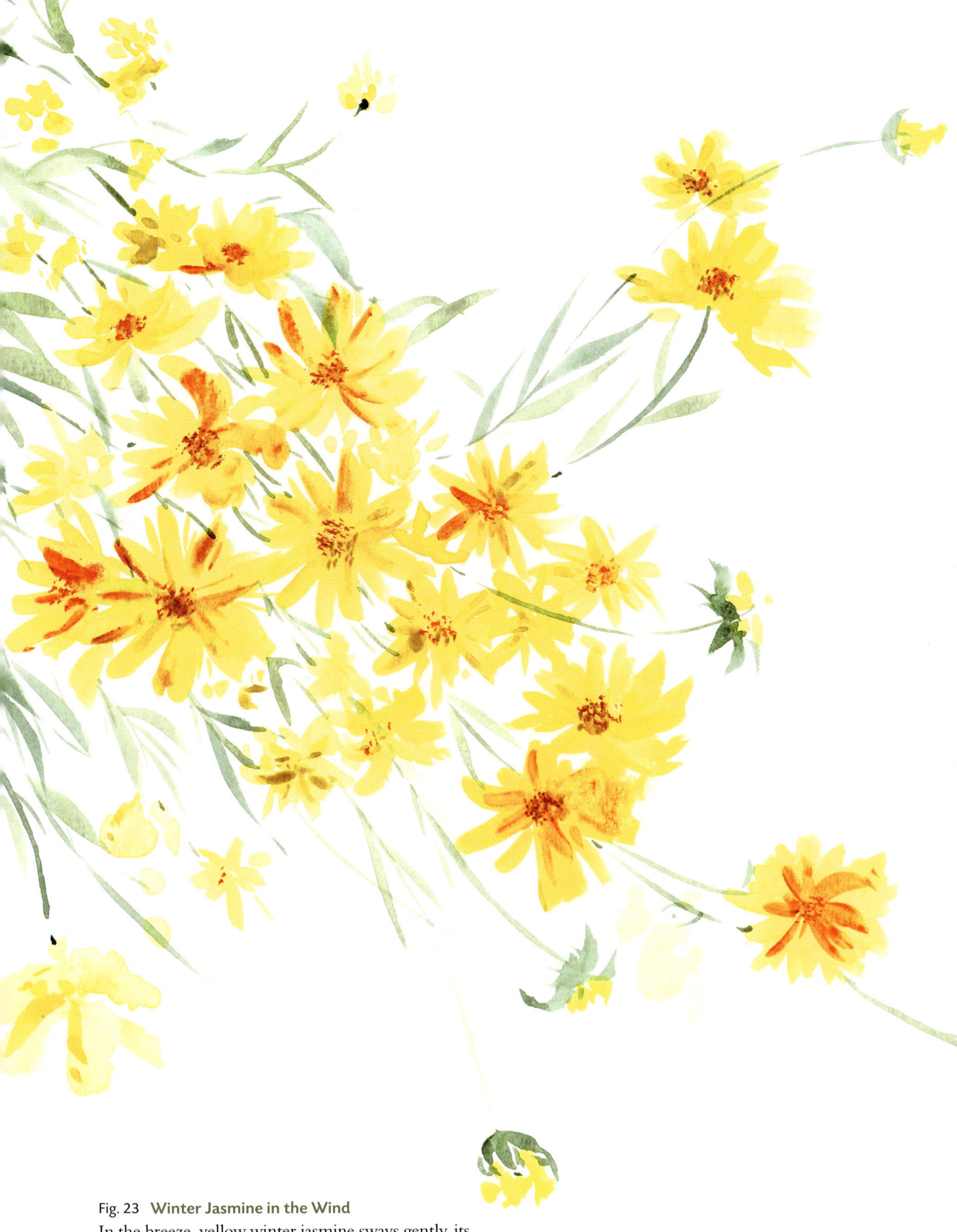

In the breeze, yellow winter jasmine sways gently, its
bright petals fluttering like sunlight in motion—light,
free, and full of early spring's breath.

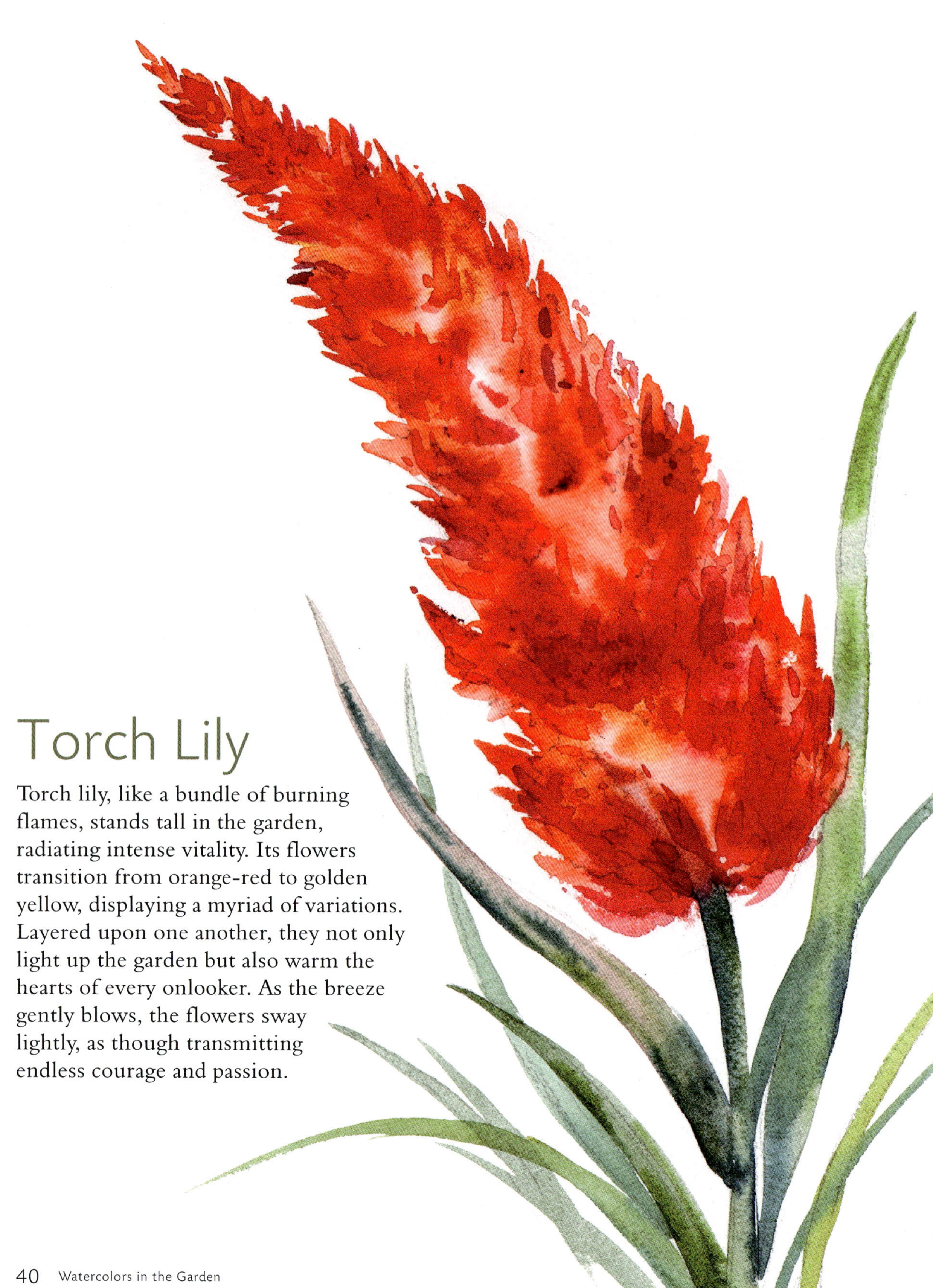

Torch Lily

Torch lily, like a bundle of burning
flames, stands tall in the garden,
radiating intense vitality. Its flowers
transition from orange-red to golden
yellow, displaying a myriad of variations.
Layered upon one another, they not only
light up the garden but also warm the
hearts of every onlooker. As the breeze
gently blows, the flowers sway
lightly, as though transmitting
endless courage and passion.

Paint Brand
DANIEL SMITH

Color Codes
- 600064: Organic Vermilion
- 600114: Yellow Ochre
- 600024: Chromium Green Oxide
- 600082: Prussian Blue
- 600033: Deep Scarlet
- 600005: Anthraquinoid Red
- 600197: Green Apatite Genuine

Recommended Watercolor Paper
ARCHES watercolor paper, cold pressed, 140 lb/300 g/m^2

Recommended Brush
Black Velvet 3000S brush for watercolor, size 8

Key Challenges
1. Combine wet-on-dry and wet-on-wet techniques to shape the flowers.
2. Use a freehand style to shape the flowers.

Steps

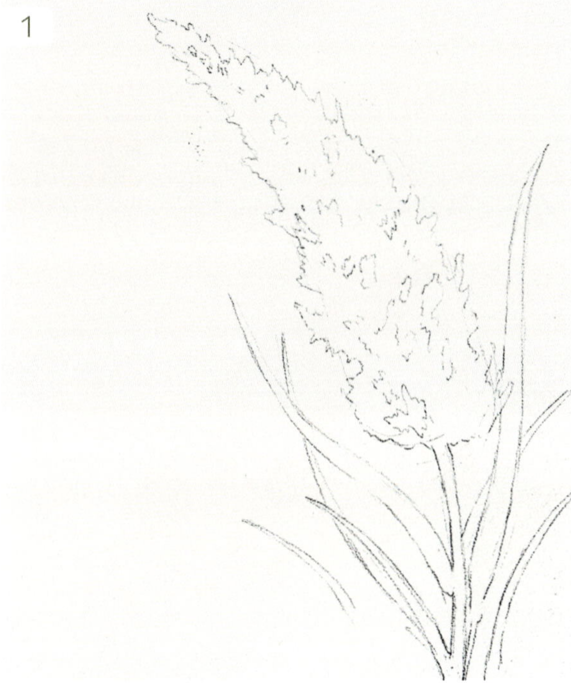

With a pencil, lightly sketch the general outline of the torch lily. Focus on capturing the overall shape and the layered structure of the flower cluster. Since the torch lily has numerous small flowers, it is not necessary to draw each flower in precise detail before painting. This requires us to roughly sketch the shape of the flower and depict it using a freehand style.

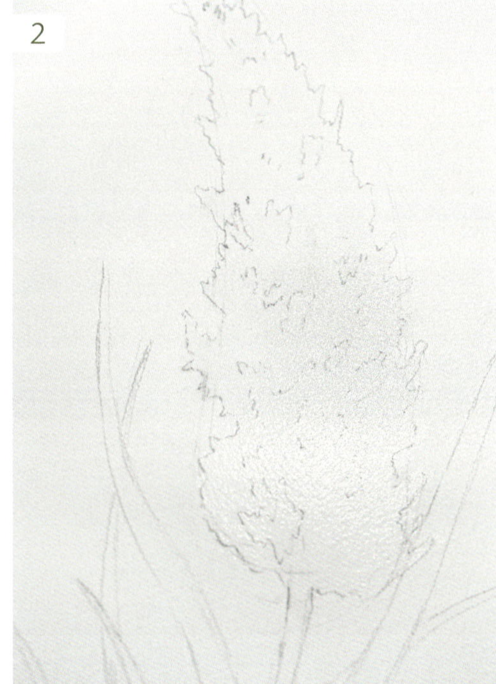

Start by wetting the entire flower cluster with clean water.

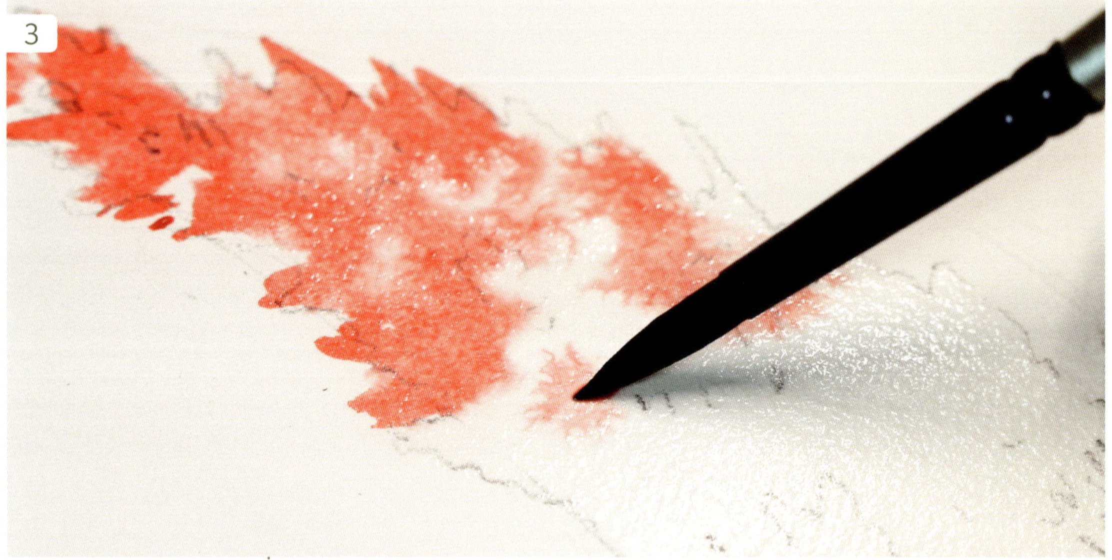

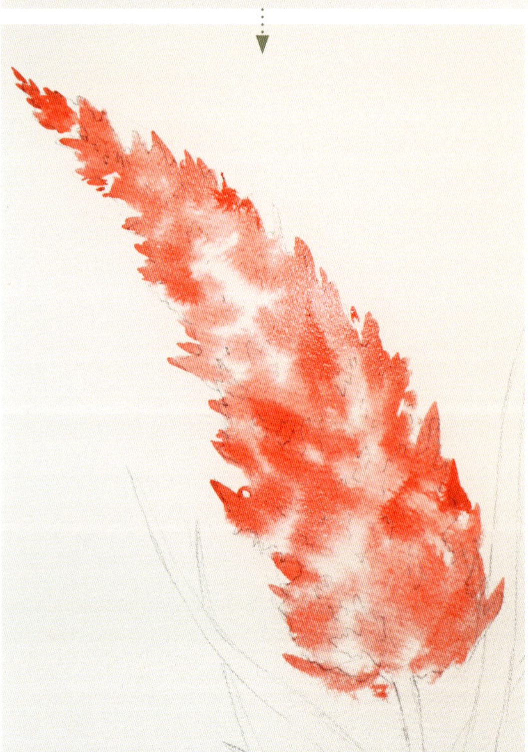

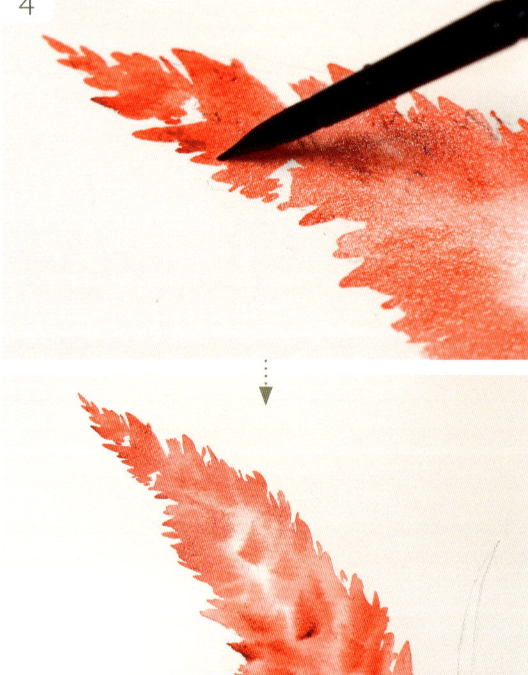

Once the water has sufficiently soaked into the paper, gently dab the flower areas with color 600064 (Organic Vermilion). Ensure that there is enough space between each brushstroke, so that when the colors penetrate each other with the flow of moisture, the colors between brushstrokes will not completely blend. This will create white gaps between strokes, allowing the painting to retain a breathable, light effect. Keep your strokes light and relaxed (varying the pressure of your brush, avoiding using a flat wash or rigidly defined shapes). This technique will allow the watercolor to show a beautiful range of light and dark tones, depending on the amount of moisture.

While the painting is still wet, use color 600033 (Deep Scarlet), a darker red, to deepen specific areas. Focus on enhancing the shadow regions of the flowers and the layers between petals to strengthen the sense of volume in the flowers.

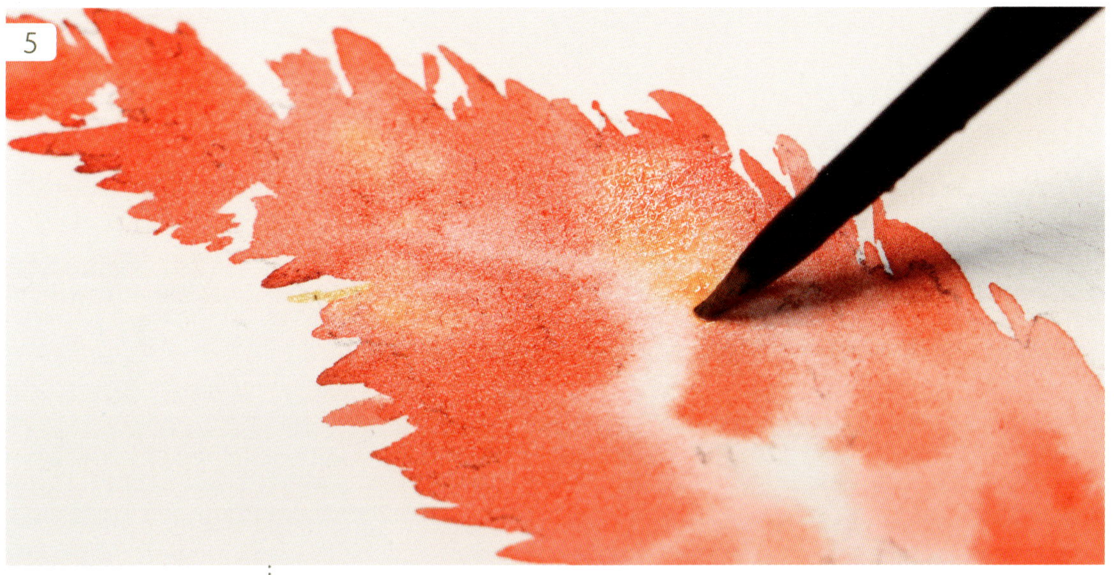

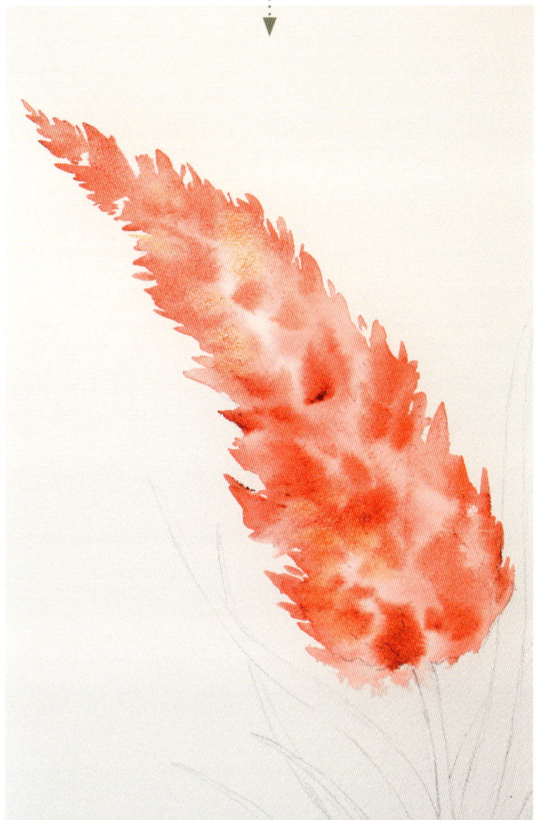

While the painting is still wet, use color 600114 (Yellow Ochre) to highlight certain areas. Since the flowers are being represented in a freehand style, the addition of yellow not only brings out the bright color of the torch lily's head but also enhances the layering of the entire flower through the blending of red and yellow, showcasing the natural gradation of the flower's colors from light to dark, enriching the expressiveness of the painting.

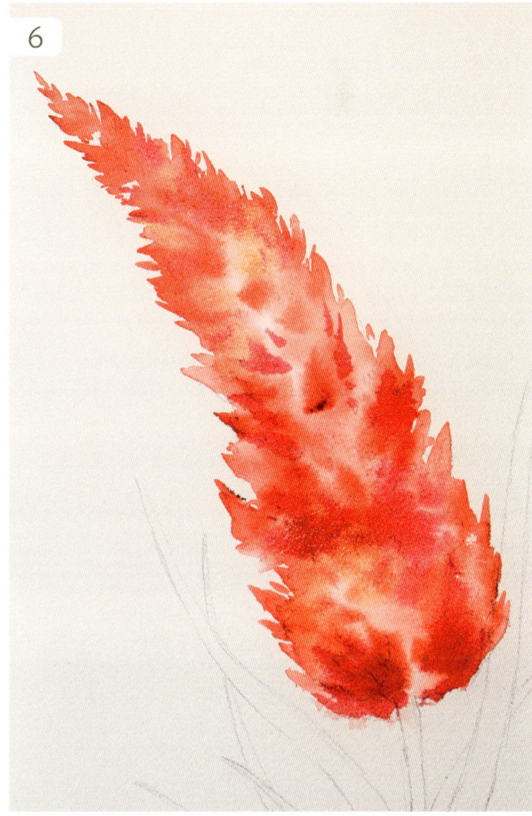

While the painting is still wet, continue to add color 600005 (Anthraquinoid Red) to strengthen the sense of volume in the flower petals. At this stage, the creation of the flower remains within the wet-on-wet technique, fully utilizing the flow of watercolor to produce a lively and dynamic color effect in the torch lily.

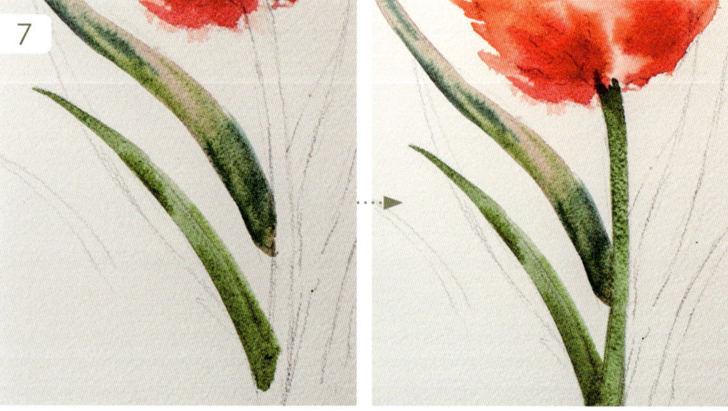

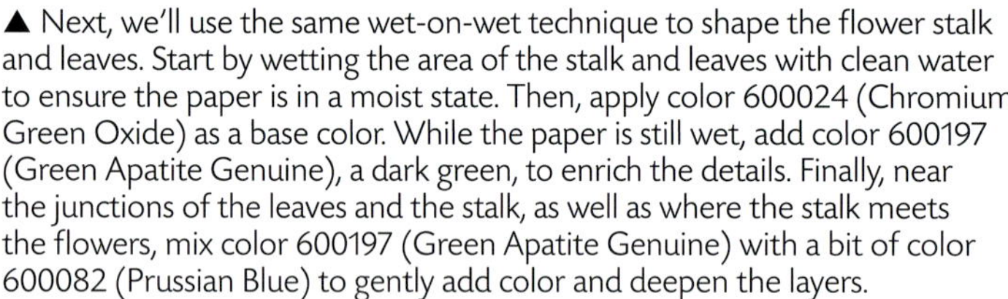

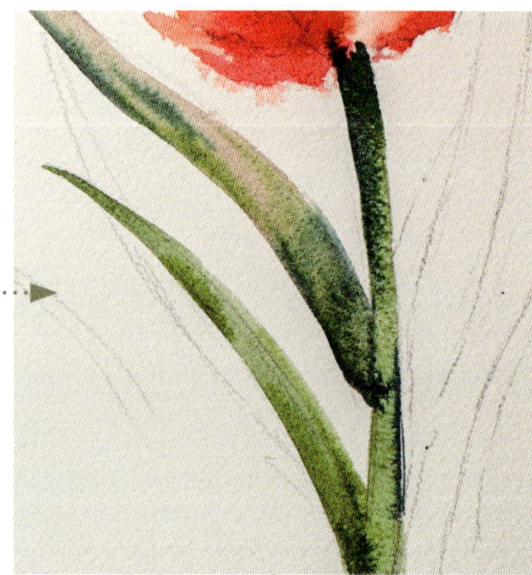

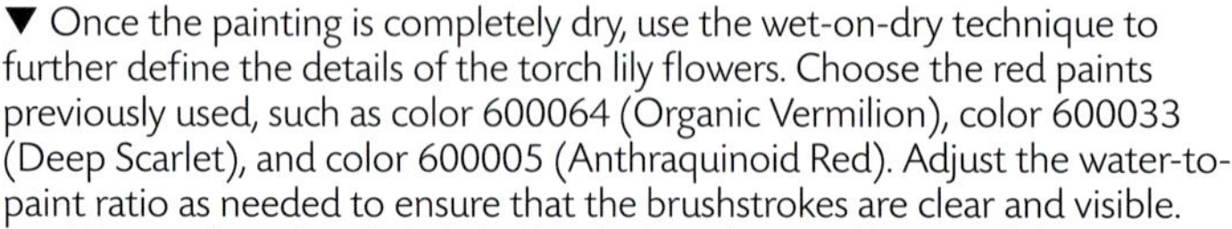

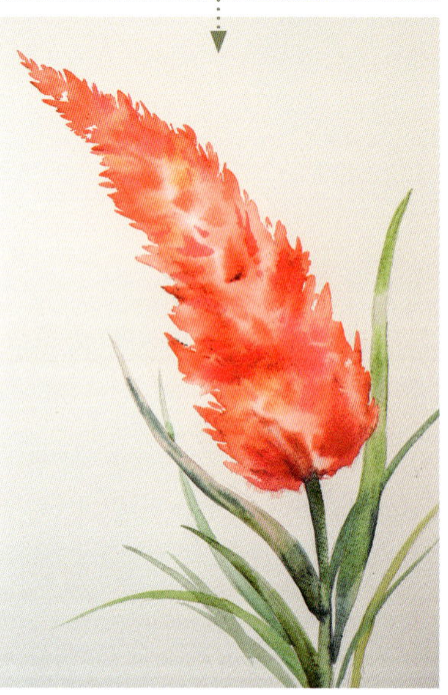

▲ Next, we'll use the same wet-on-wet technique to shape the flower stalk and leaves. Start by wetting the area of the stalk and leaves with clean water to ensure the paper is in a moist state. Then, apply color 600024 (Chromium Green Oxide) as a base color. While the paper is still wet, add color 600197 (Green Apatite Genuine), a dark green, to enrich the details. Finally, near the junctions of the leaves and the stalk, as well as where the stalk meets the flowers, mix color 600197 (Green Apatite Genuine) with a bit of color 600082 (Prussian Blue) to gently add color and deepen the layers.

▼ Once the painting is completely dry, use the wet-on-dry technique to further define the details of the torch lily flowers. Choose the red paints previously used, such as color 600064 (Organic Vermilion), color 600033 (Deep Scarlet), and color 600005 (Anthraquinoid Red). Adjust the water-to-paint ratio as needed to ensure that the brushstrokes are clear and visible.

Using a finer brush, lightly sketch the edges and layers of the flowers, paying attention to the flow and shape of the petals. Avoid stiff brushstrokes. By using varying concentrations of red and different brushstroke techniques, highlight the details and texture of the flowers, especially at the junctions where the flower heads and petals meet, to enhance the contrast of light and dark and emphasize the three-dimensional effect of the flowers.

Since watercolor paints are transparent, painting over the dried surface, even with the same color, will prevent the new color from blending with the previous one. The brushstrokes will remain visible, which adds richness to the flower details.

And with that, the torch lily in the garden is complete.

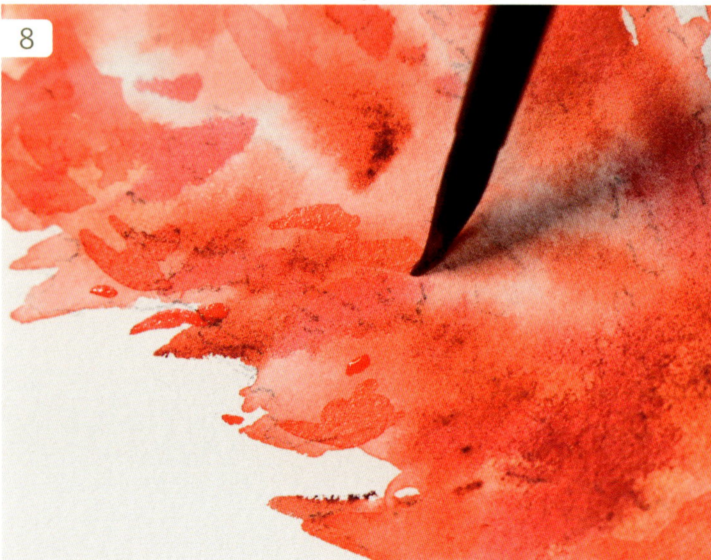

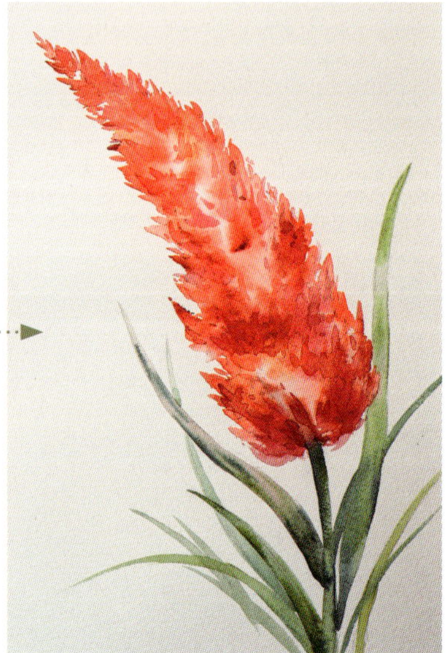

Bright clusters of red Nandina berries gleam among slender green leaves, adding a quite festive note to the scene.

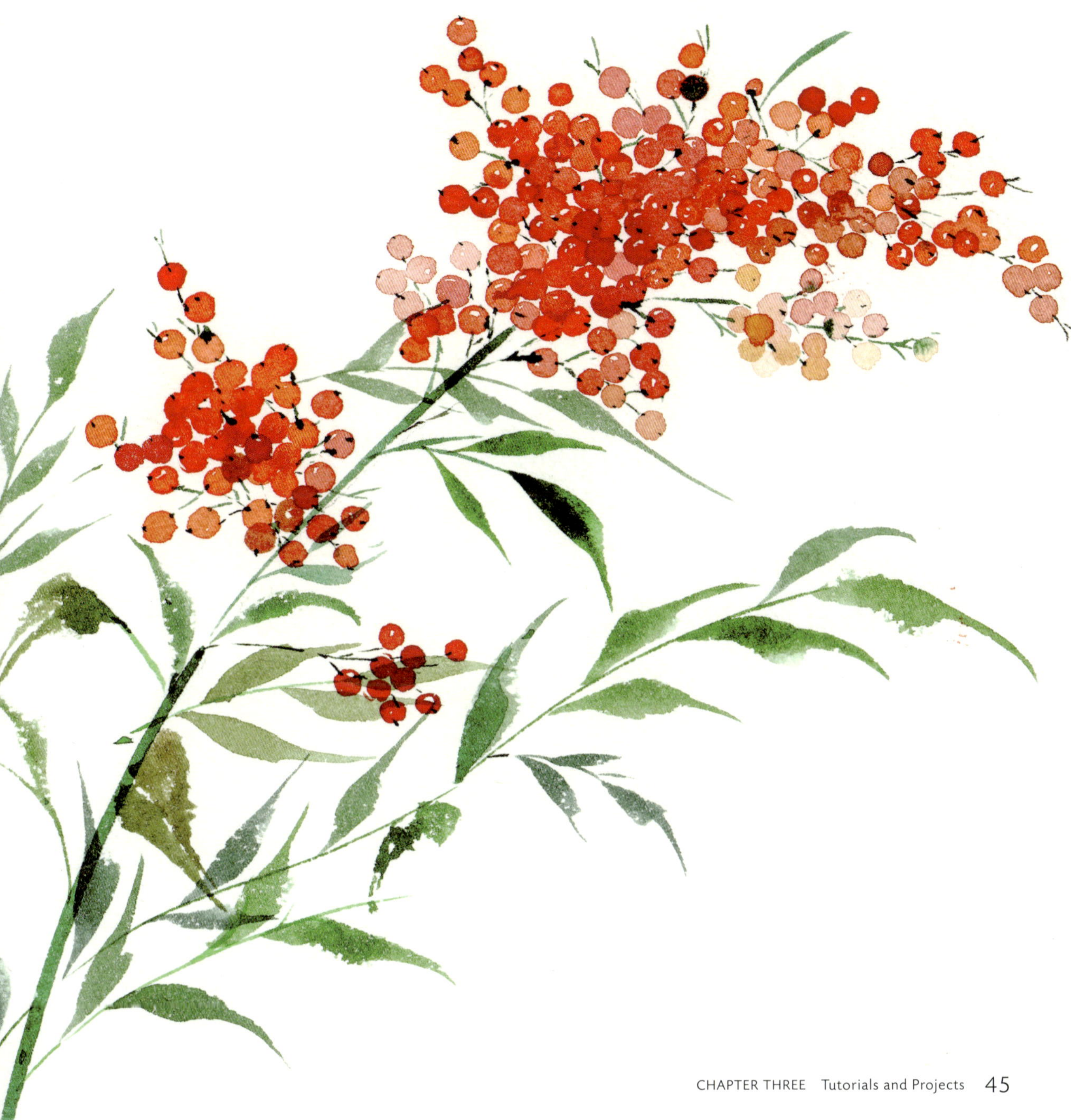

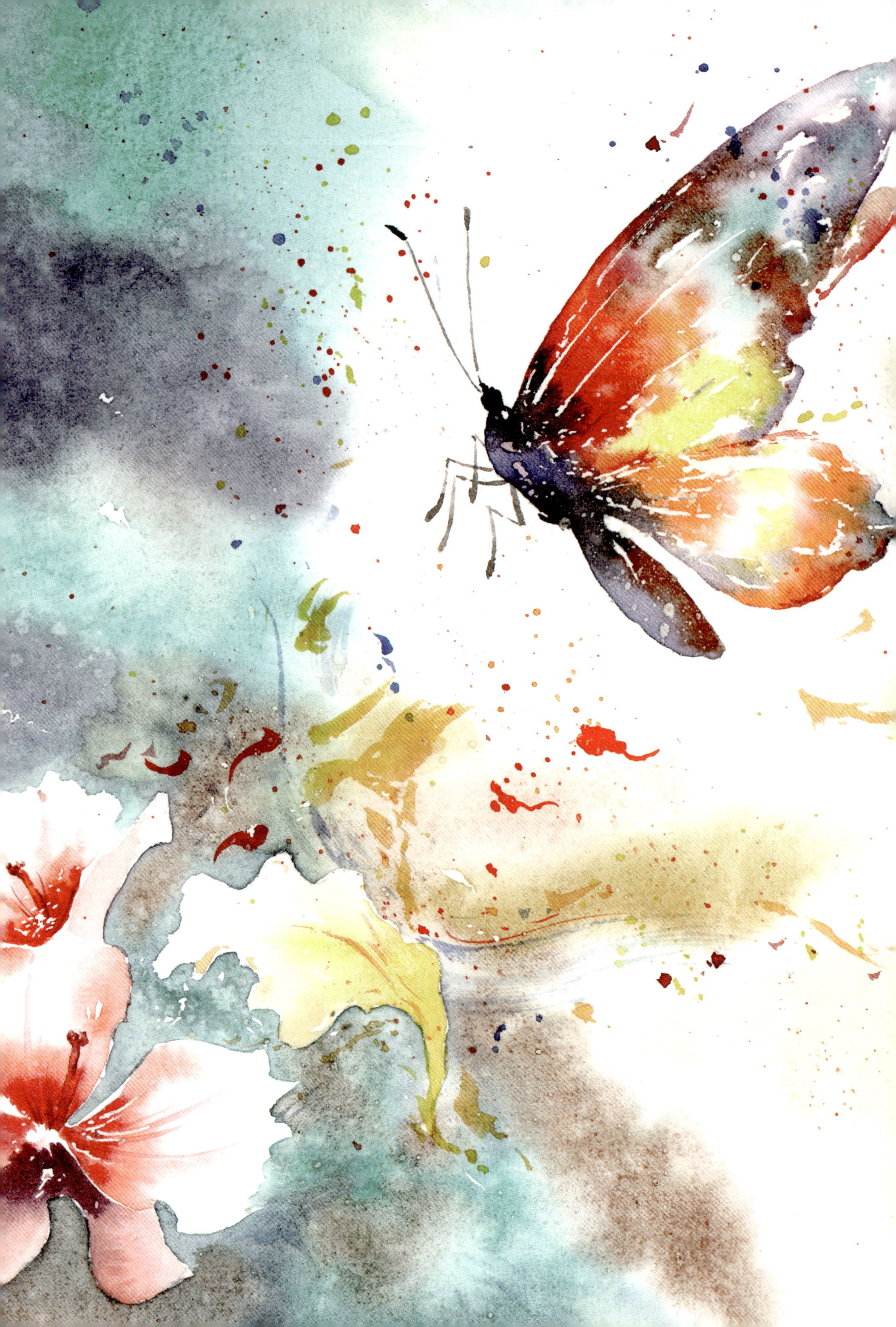

Butterfly

The butterflies in the garden are like brilliantly colored little spirits, dancing gracefully among the flowers. Their wings shimmer in the sunlight, like fragments of gold caught in the wind. With every delicate flutter, they speak of the mysteries of nature. As they weave through the petals, their elegant and free-spirited movements bring vibrant vitality and dreamlike colors to the garden.

Paint Brand
DANIEL SMITH

Color Codes
- 600242: Alvaro's Fresco Grey
- 600163: Amazonite Genuine
- 600010: Burnt Sienna
- 600056: Monte Amiata Natural Sienna
- 600057: Moonglow
- 600006: Aureolin (Cobalt Yellow)
- 600064: Organic Vermilion
- 600033: Deep Scarlet
- 600005: Anthraquinoid Red
- 600003: Lamp Black
- 600034: French Ultramarine

Auxiliary Materials
Masking fluid
Acrylic medium

Recommended Watercolor Paper
ARCHES watercolor paper, cold pressed, 140 lb/300 g/m^2

Recommended Brushes
Black Velvet 3000S brush for watercolor, size 8
Black Velvet 3000S brush for watercolor, size 6

Key Challenges
1. Use wet-on-wet technique to shape the background and butterfly wings.
2. Create an intense, romantic atmosphere.

Steps

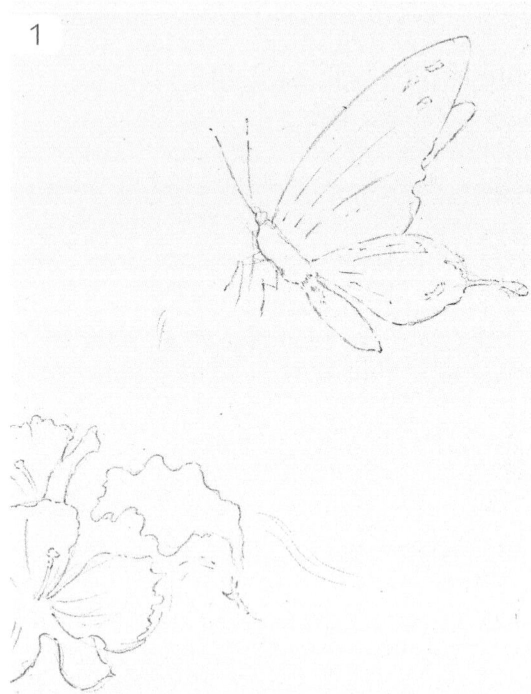

Roughly sketch the outlines of the butterfly and flowers, paying attention to their proportional relationship in the composition.

Apply masking fluid to reserve the highlight areas on the butterfly, the flowers, and the background.

Use a fan brush or a toothbrush to load acrylic medium and flick it evenly across the paper. The opaque to semi-transparent textures created by the acrylic medium appear at the spots indicated by the arrows.

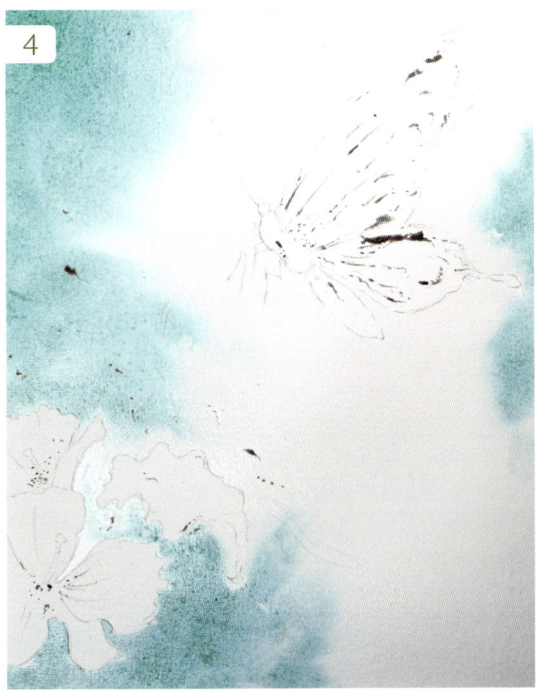

Wet all areas except the butterfly and flowers with clean water, then use color 600242 (Alvaro's Fresco Grey) to wash in the background. Because the paper holds a lot of moisture, the paint will naturally spread along the texture, creating a soft gradation effect. To keep the butterfly as the focal point, confine the wash to the area immediately surrounding it.

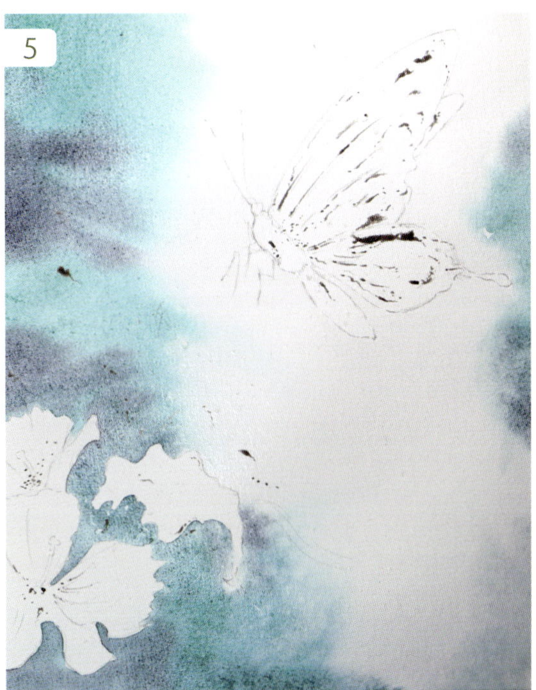

While the surface is still wet, deepen selected areas using color 600163 (Amazonite Genuine). Since the paper is still quite moist, this layer will blend with the first wash, creating a natural and beautiful gradation effect.

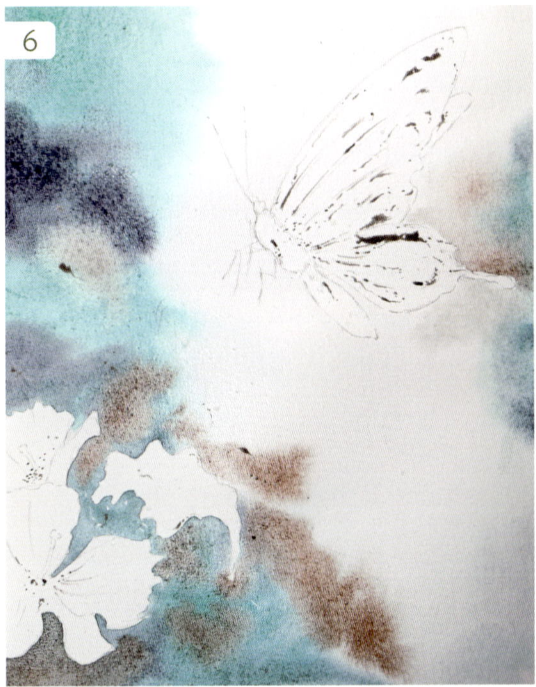

While the paper is still wet, continue to paint the background using color 600010 (Burnt Sienna).

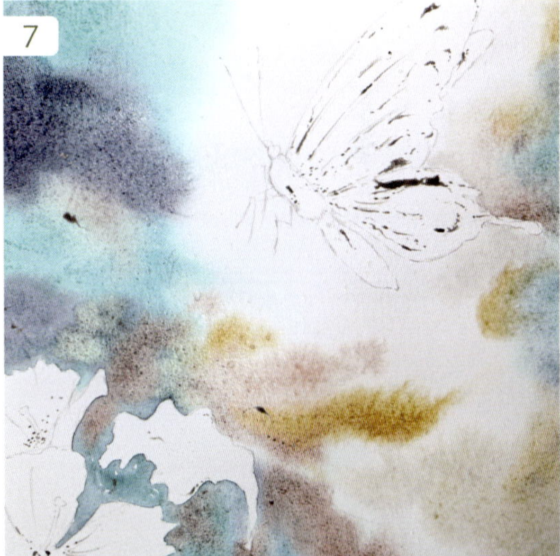

Next, use color 600056 (Monte Amiata Natural Sienna) to brighten parts of the background. The four colors used in steps 4 to 7 can be blended based on your personal preference and aesthetic sense, but be sure to limit the washes to the area around the butterfly to maintain it as the focal point. This stage mainly uses the wet-on-wet technique to create a vibrant, colorful garden atmosphere.

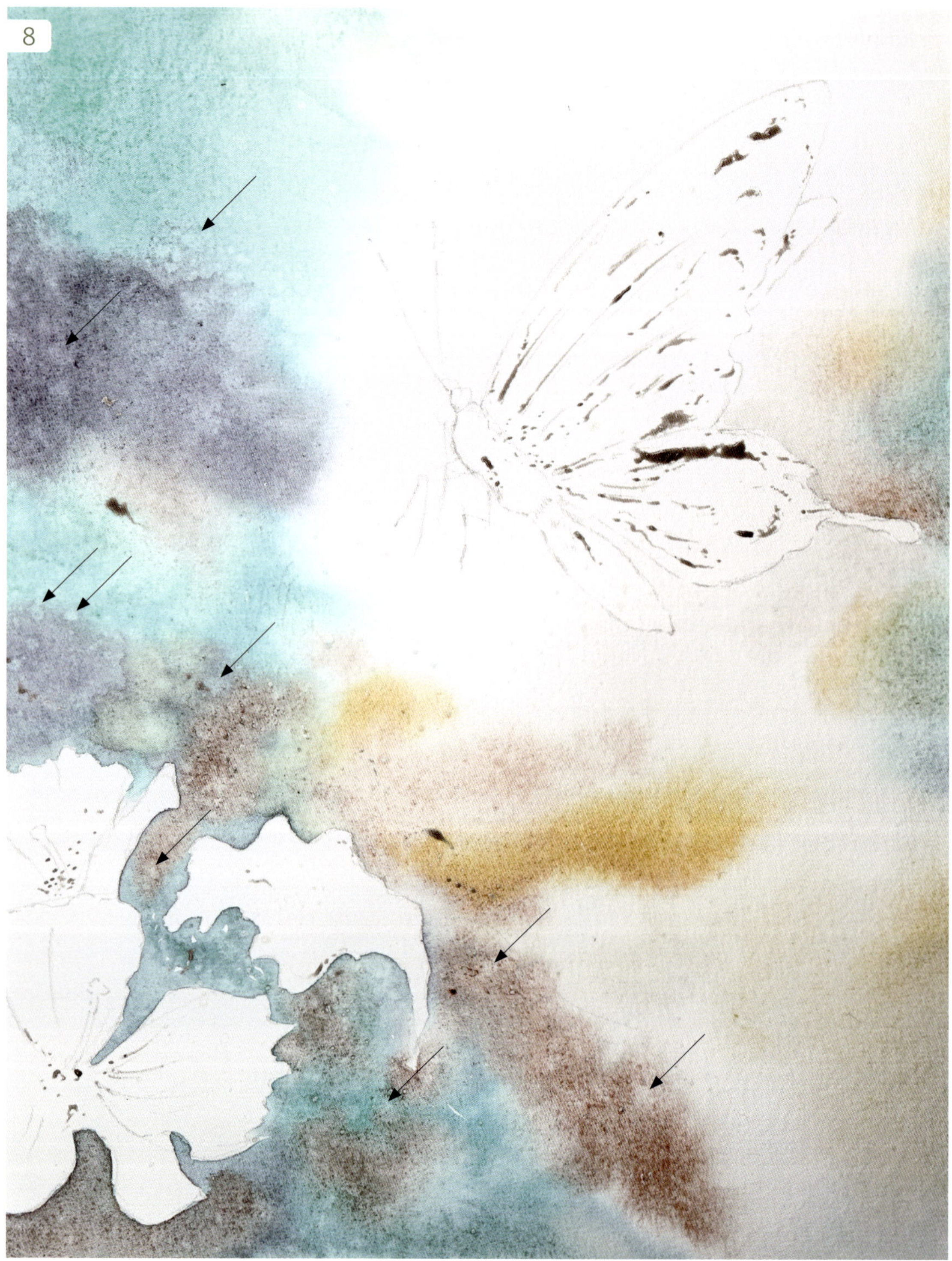

8

Finally, use a small spray bottle to mist water over the painting. The droplets will create beautiful, snowflake like speckled textures on the surface (as shown in the areas indicated by the arrows in the image).

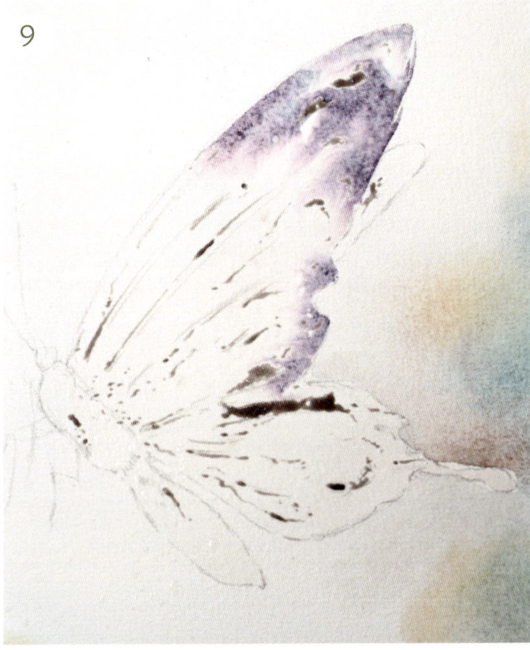

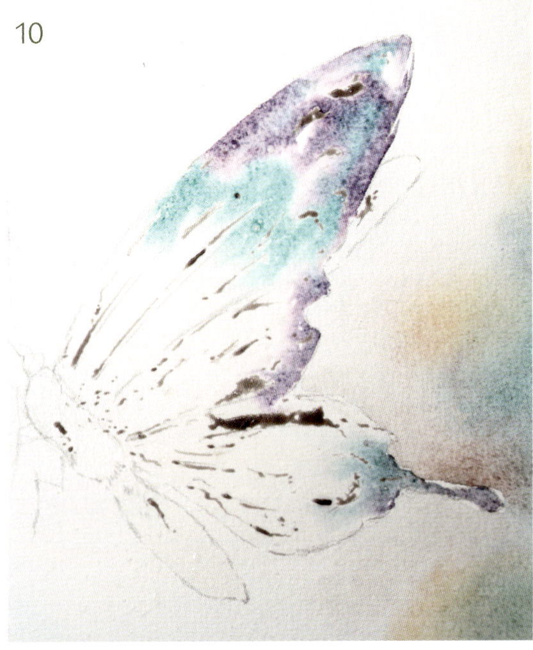

Next, paint the butterfly wings. When coloring the wings, apply the colors starting from the outer edges and gradually work toward the base of the wings. Once the background is completely dry, wet the entire surface of the butterfly wings with clean water. While the paper is still wet, use color 600057 (Moonglow) to paint the outer edges of the wings, allowing the color to spread naturally with the moisture. Note that all subsequent coloring of the wings should be done while the wings remain damp.

Continue working inward using color 600163 (Amazonite Genuine), allowing it to blend with the previous color through the moisture on the paper.

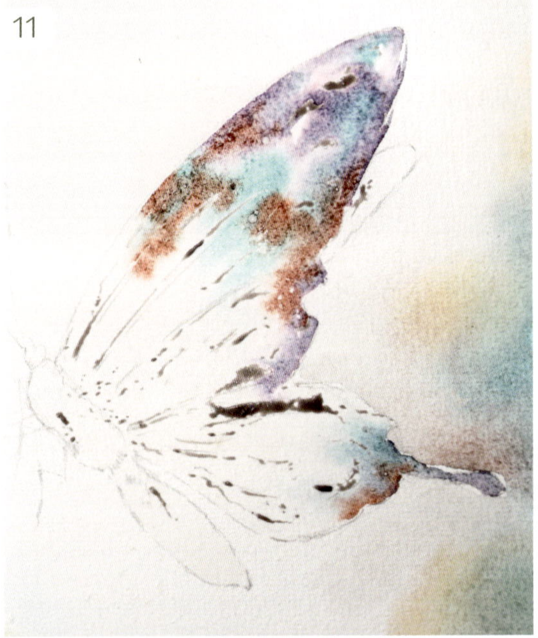

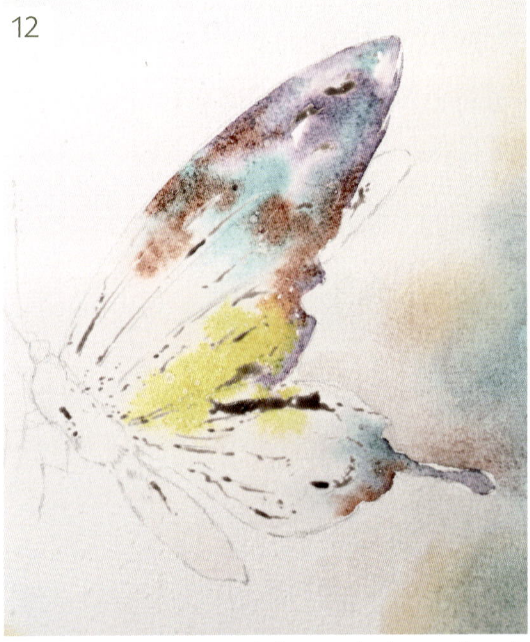

Keep working inward using color 600010 (Burnt Sienna), allowing it to blend with the previous color.

With color 600006 (Aureolin), paint the lower edge of the upper wing.

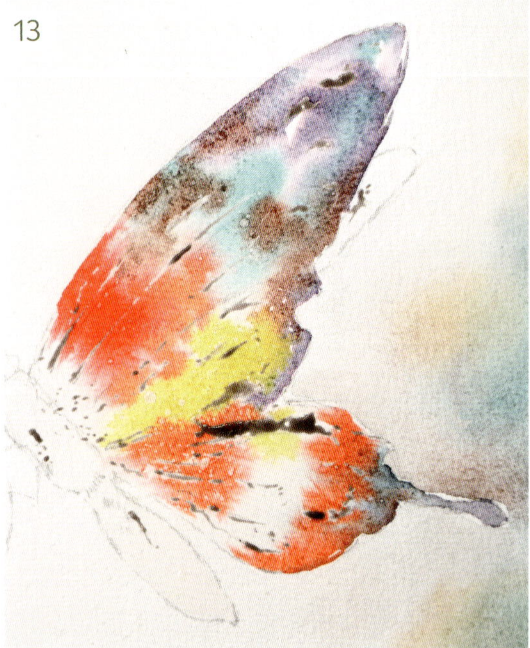

13

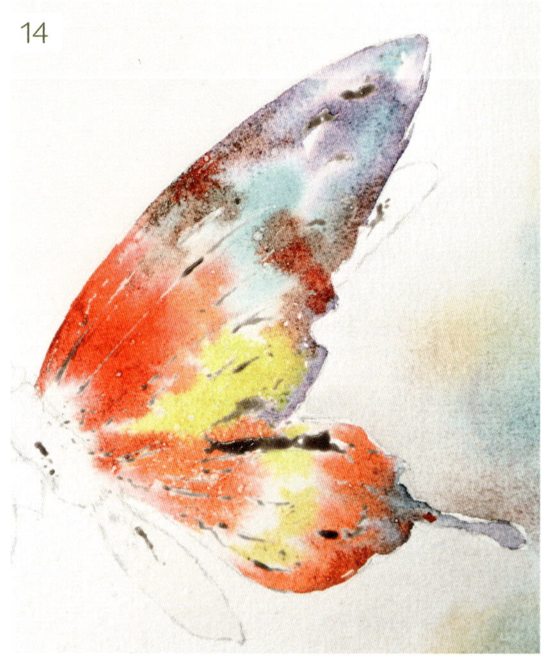

14

Continue using color 600064 (Organic Vermilion) to paint the base of the upper wing, as well as the outer edge and base of the lower wing. Let it blend naturally with the previous colors through the moisture on the paper.

Use color 600033 (Deep Scarlet) to deepen the red at the base of the wings from the previous step and to define some of the edges of the wings.

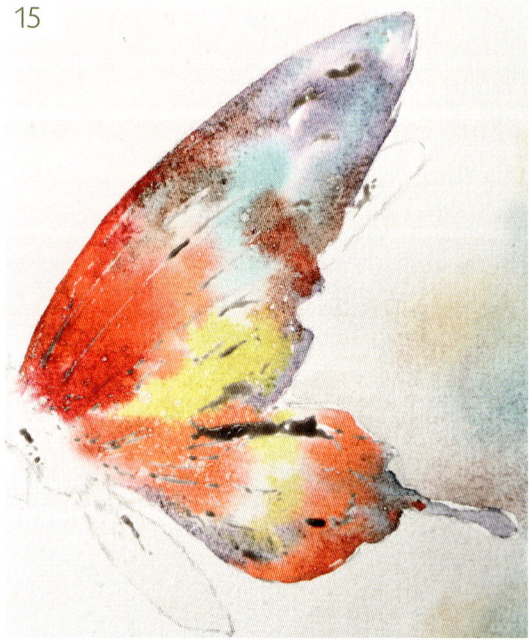

15

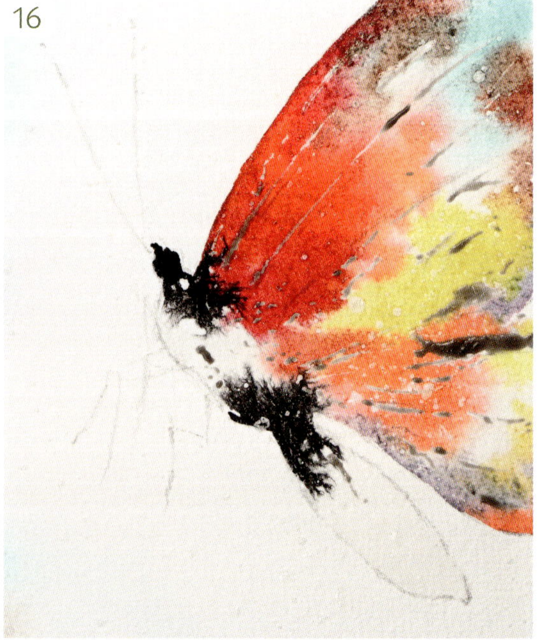

16

Continue using color 600005 (Anthraquinoid Red) to deepen the color at the base of the wings.

Use color 600003 (Lamp Black) to paint the butterfly's head, as well as the junction between the body and tail. While the paper is still damp (if it has dried, re-wet this area to ensure the moisture is still there), let the color spread naturally with the water.

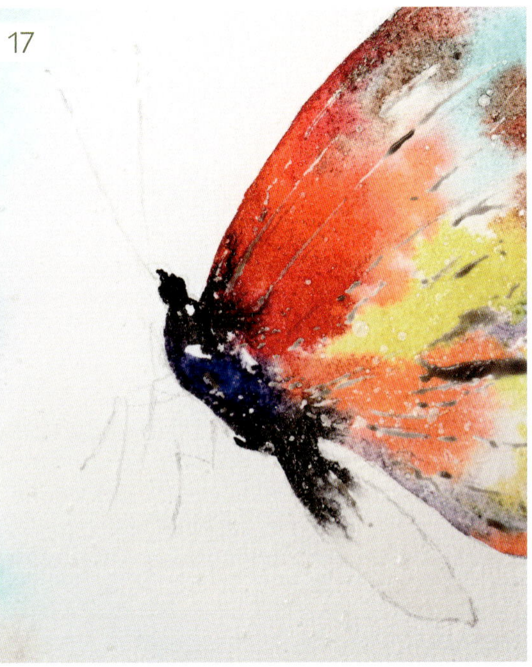

Mix color 600242 (Alvaro's Fresco Grey) and color 600034 (French Ultramarine) in a 1:2 ratio to create a gray-blue color. Use this mixture to paint the butterfly's abdomen.

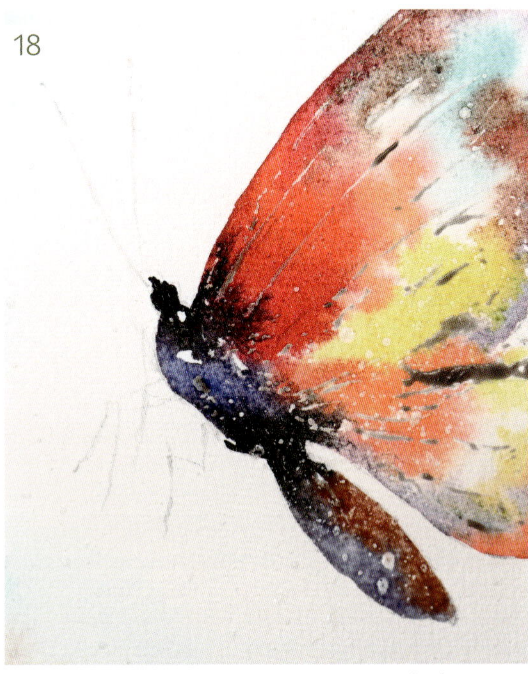

Use the gray-blue color in step 17 to paint the lower edge of the tail, while using color 600010 (Burnt Sienna) to paint the upper edge of the tail where it connects.

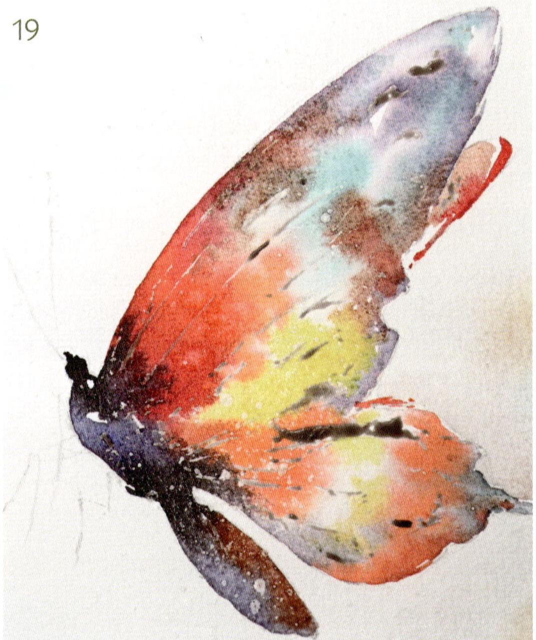

With color 600010 (Burnt Sienna) and color 600033 (Deep Scarlet), lightly outline the tip of the wing hidden behind the back wing.

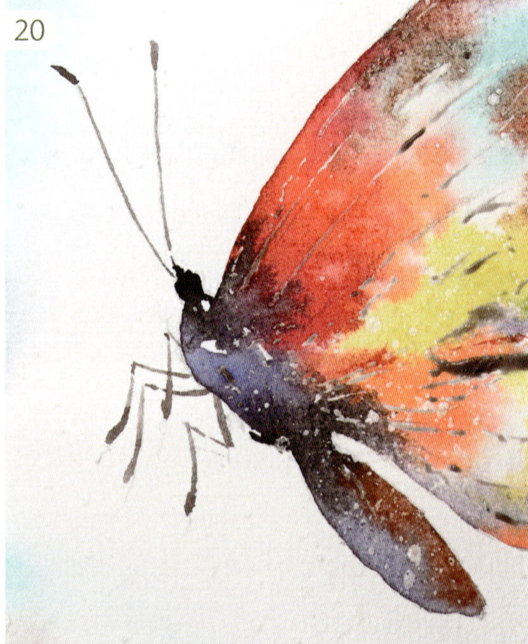

Finally, mix color 600010 (Burnt Sienna) and color 600003 (Lamp Black) in a 2:1 ratio to outline the antennae and legs. Use a light touch with a quick brushstroke to ensure smooth, natural lines, avoiding any jerky movements that might occur from moving too slowly. The main body of the butterfly is now complete.

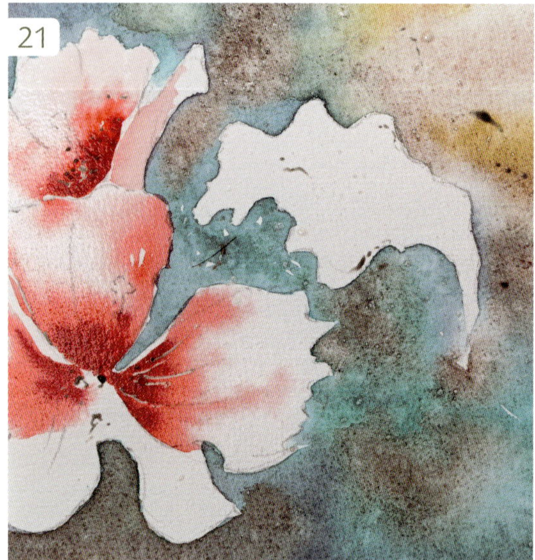

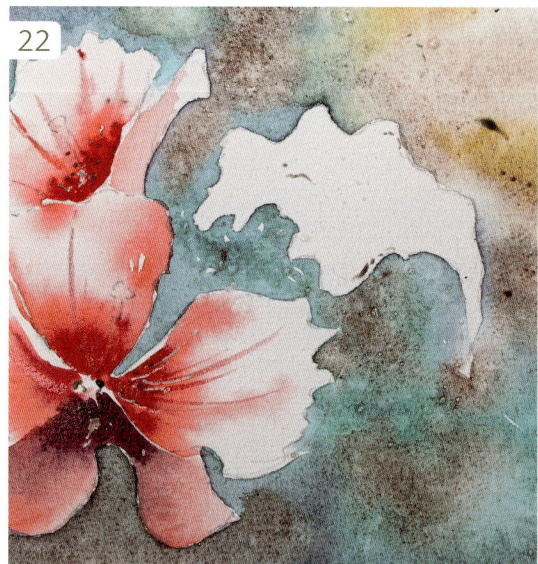

Next, paint the flowers. Begin by wetting the petals, then use color 600064 (Organic Vermilion) to color from the center, allowing the color to naturally spread outward with the moisture. While the petals are still wet, use color 600005 (Anthraquinoid Red) to deepen the center.

Mix color 600064 (Organic Vermilion) and color 600242 (Alvaro's Fresco Grey) in equal proportions and use this mixture to paint the two petals at the lower half of the flower. First, apply a base layer, then, while the paper is still wet, use color 600242 (Alvaro's Fresco Grey) to deepen the base of the petals.

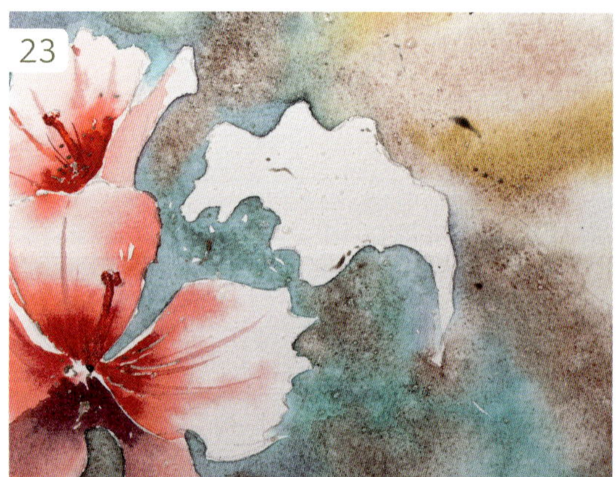

Use color 600033 (Deep Scarlet) to outline the flower's stamen.

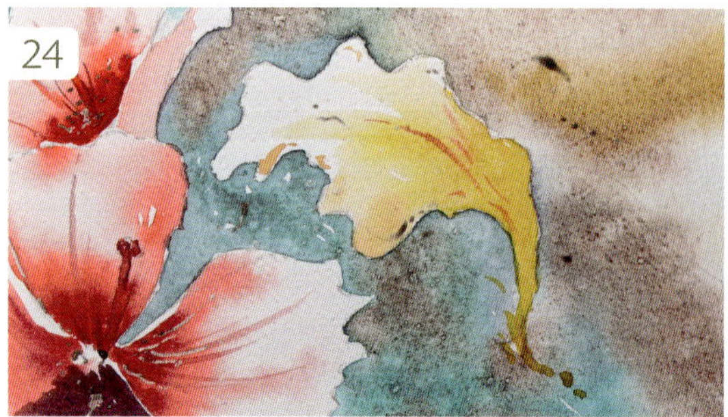

Wet the yellow flower petal with clean water, then use color 600006 (Aureolin) at the base, allowing the color to naturally spread outward with the moisture.

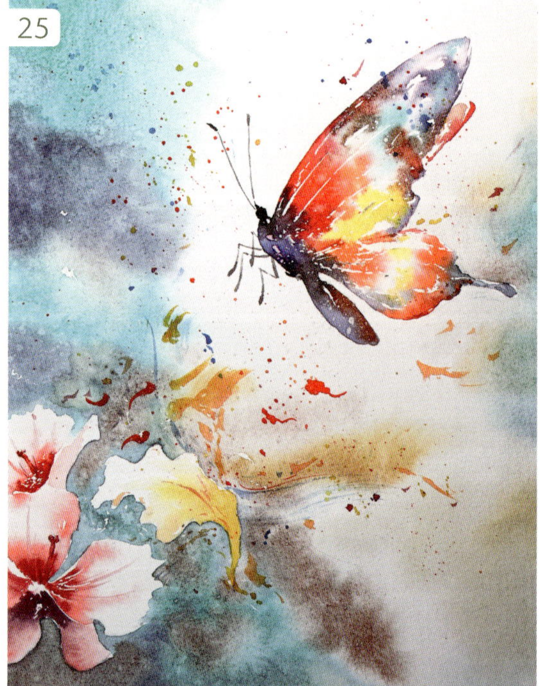

Erase the masking fluid to reveal the highlighted areas. Finally, based on personal preference, feel free to add some freehand shapes using different colors, applying decisive brushstrokes. Also, load a brush with paint and flick some colorful dots onto the paper, adding dynamic energy and vibrancy, creating a lively atmosphere. With that, the butterfly in the garden is complete.

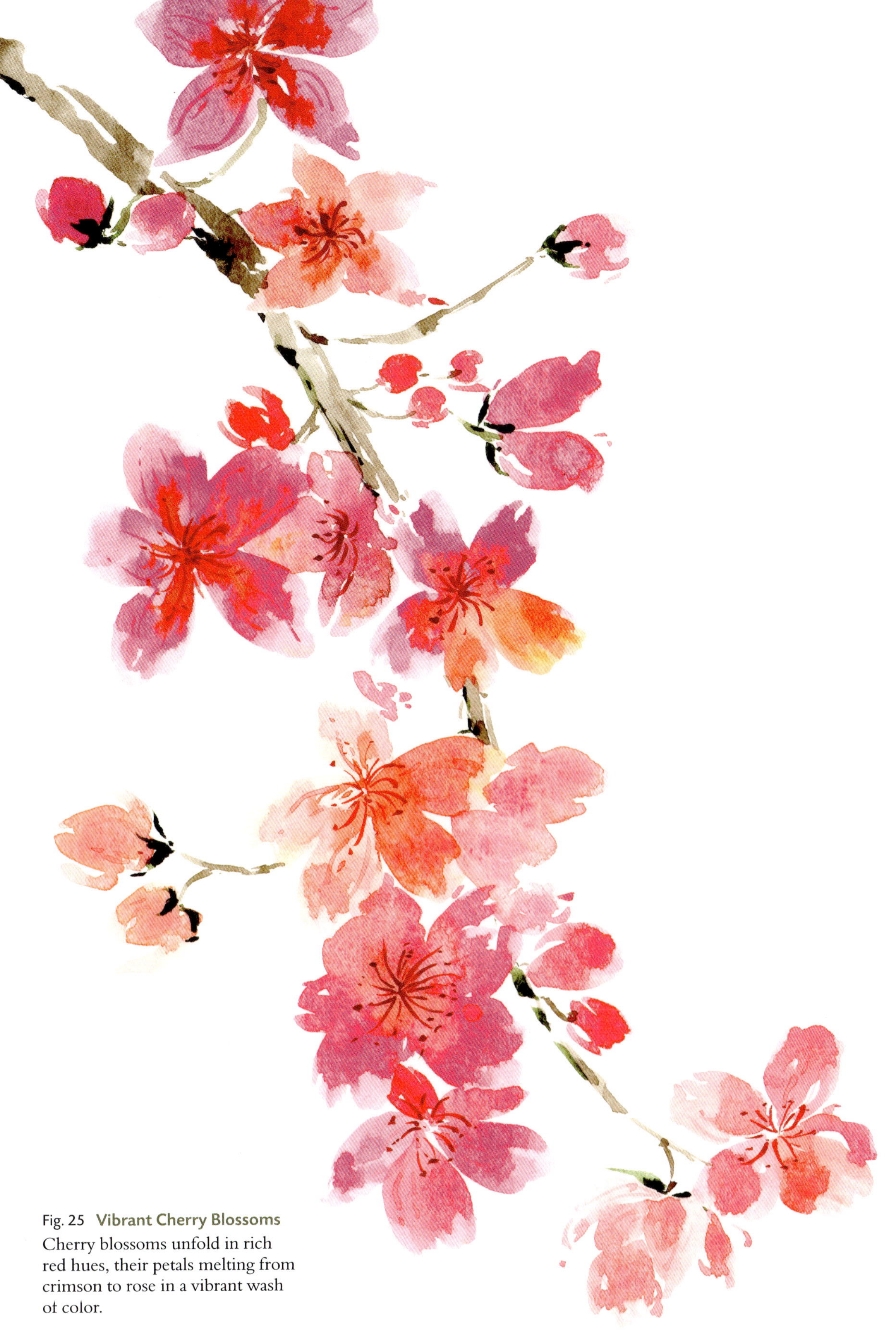

Fig. 25 **Vibrant Cherry Blossoms**
Cherry blossoms unfold in rich red hues, their petals melting from crimson to rose in a vibrant wash of color.

Cherry Blossom

In the spring garden, the cherry blossoms bloom like a dream, their delicate petals gently falling in the breeze, as if a soft pink rain is showering down. Light and shadow intertwine, and the air is filled with a faint, sweet fragrance. The beauty of the cherry blossoms is fleeting, yet it exudes a captivating romance, as if time itself pauses in this moment, leaving only the fluttering petals behind, whispering the poetry of the season and the tenderness of life.

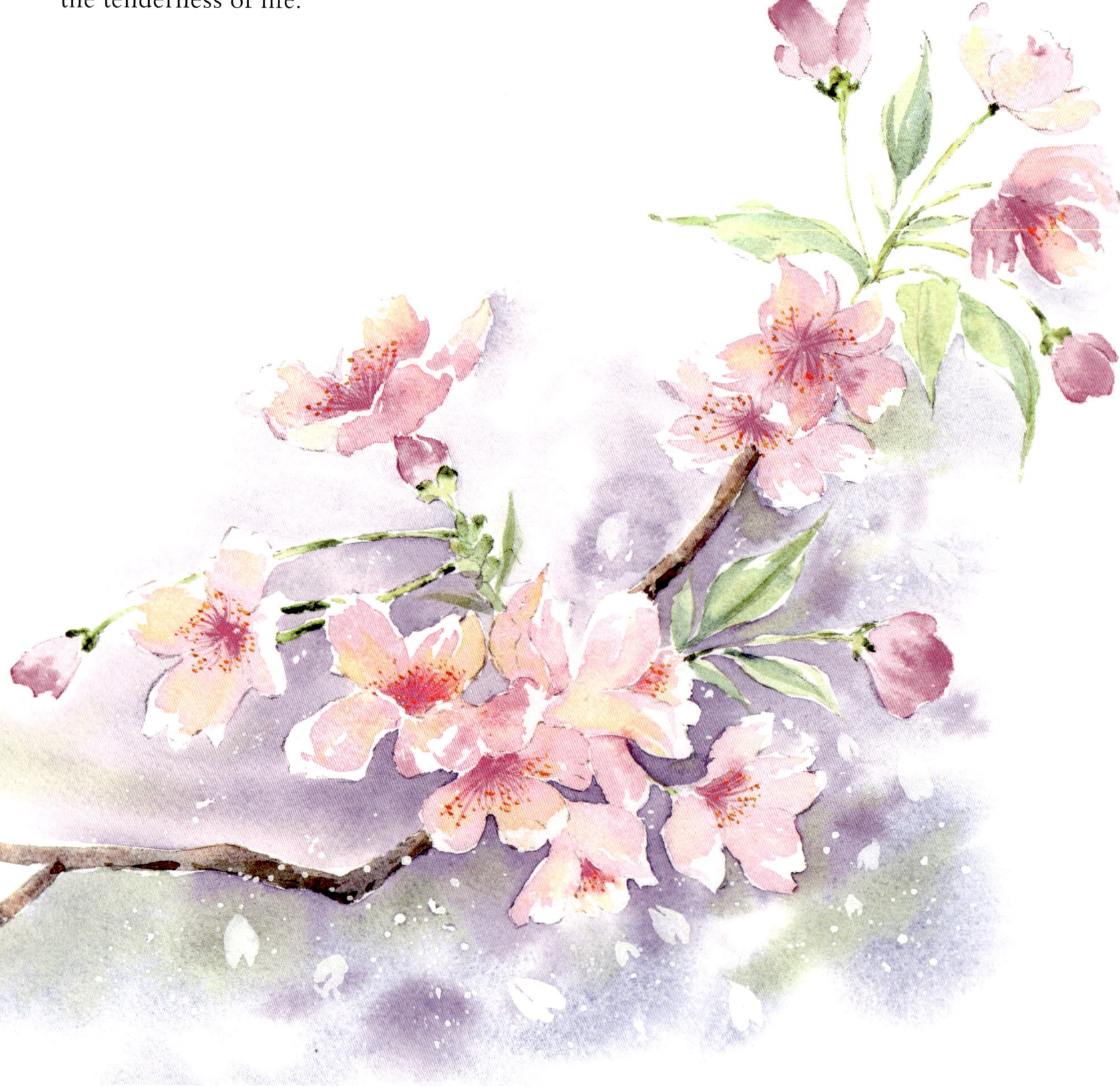

Paint Brand
DANIEL SMITH

Color Codes
- 600198: Opera Pink
- 600197: Green Apatite Genuine
- 600010: Burnt Sienna
- 600234: Aussie Red Gold
- 600019: Carbazole Violet
- 600006: Aureolin (Cobalt Yellow)
- 600029: Cobalt Turquoise
- 600034: French Ultramarine
- 600232: Lavender

Auxiliary Materials
NICKER opaque white gouache
Masking fluid

Recommended Watercolor Paper
ARCHES watercolor paper, cold pressed, 140 lb/300 g/m^2

Recommended Brushes
Black Velvet 3000S brush for watercolor, size 6
Black Velvet 3000S brush for watercolor, size 8

Key Challenges
1. The shape and structure of cherry blossom petals.
2. Creating a dreamy, romantic atmosphere with soft and hazy effects typical of cherry blossoms.

Steps

1

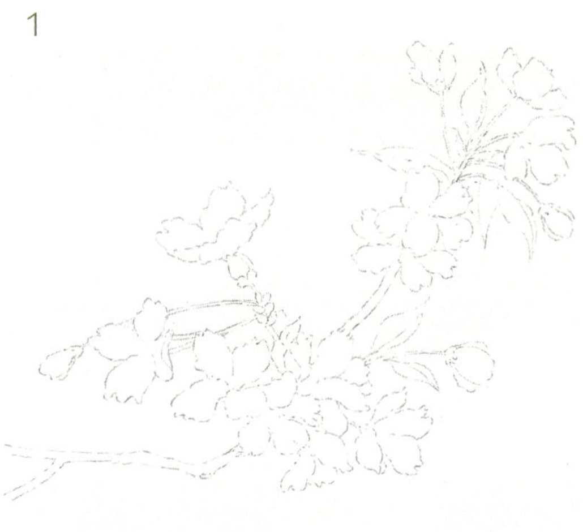

Lightly sketch the outline with a pencil, paying attention to the shapes of the cherry blossoms and branches. In particular, note that the tips of the cherry blossom petals have notches, they are not smooth curves.

2

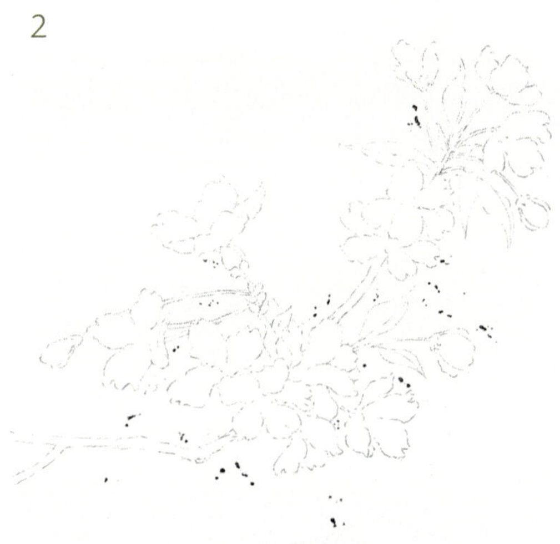

Dab masking fluid sporadically around the cherry blossoms in a loose, random manner to prepare for creating the effect of scattered cherry blossom petals later.

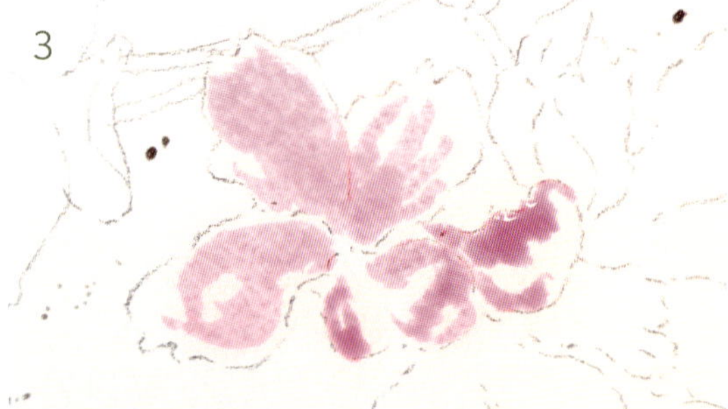

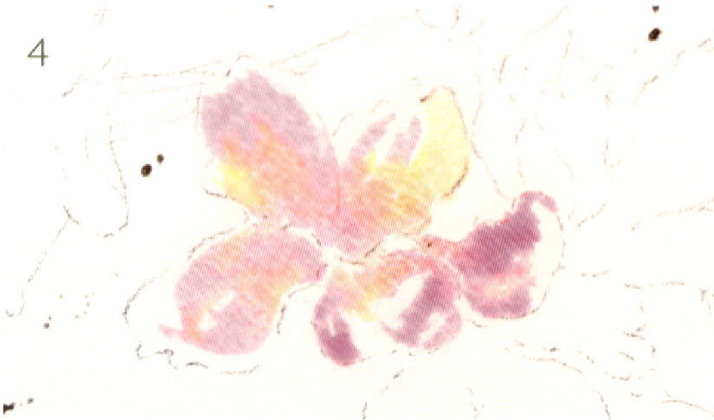

First, apply a base layer of color to the petals using color 600198 (Opera Pink). Make sure to dilute the paint well with plenty of water so the color appears lighter, helping to create a romantic atmosphere. Be careful not to fill in the entire petal with color, leaving some areas white at random, especially along the edges, since in real life, the edges of cherry blossom petals are often the lightest part of the flower.

While the paint is still wet, mix in color 600006 (Aureolin). Make sure it's well diluted with enough water so the color stays light. Let the two colors naturally blend into each other. Cherry blossom petals are delicate and pale, and under natural light, they're easily influenced by surrounding colors, often reflecting subtle hints of other hues. Here, we use the fusion of these two colors to create a soft, natural gradient effect.

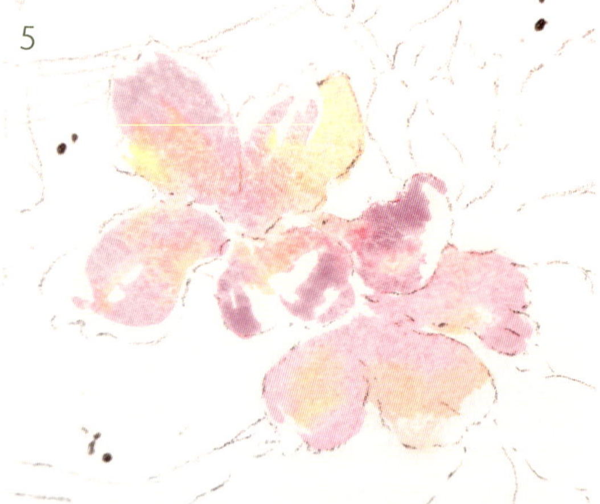

Use the same technique from steps 3 to 4 to paint the flower in the lower right corner.

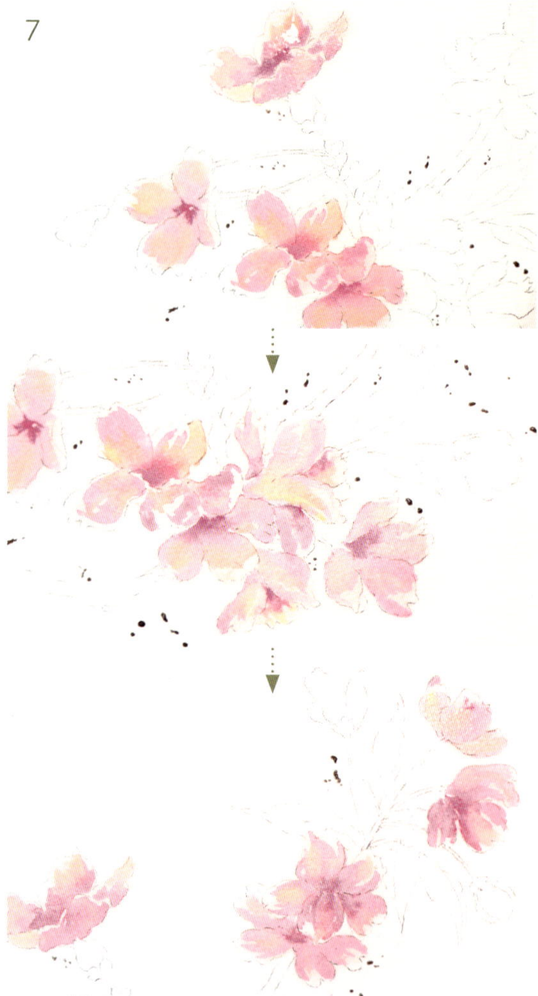

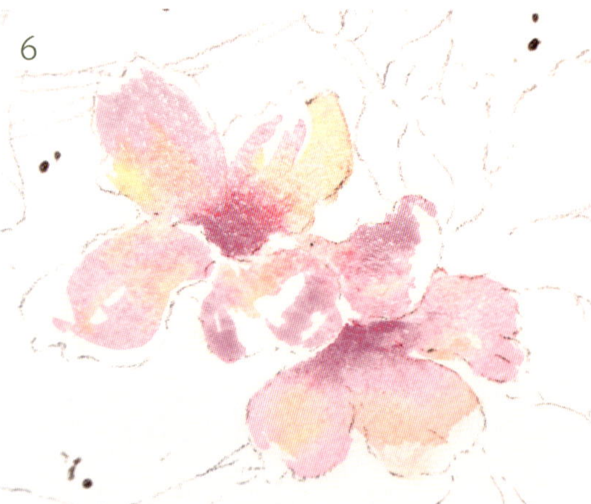

While the surface is still wet, dab the centers of the two flowers with 600198 (Opera Pink) using a more concentrated mix of pigment to water in a 2:1 ratio.

Use the same technique and key points from steps 3 to 6 to paint the remaining flowers.

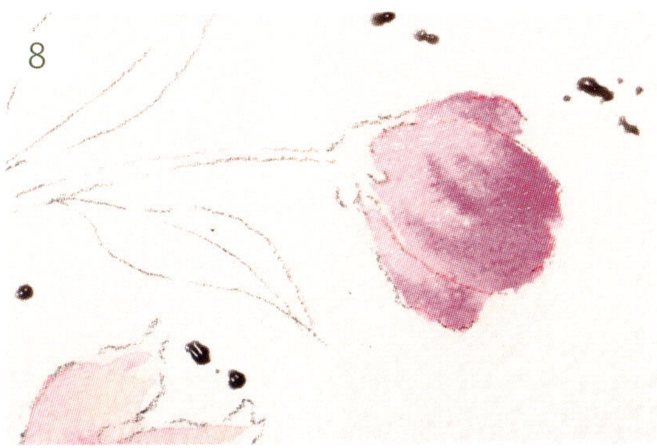

Next, paint the cherry blossom buds. Start by applying a light layer of color 600198 (Opera Pink) as the base color. While it's still wet, use a slightly deeper mix (less diluted) of the same color to dab the top of the buds, creating a natural transition effect.

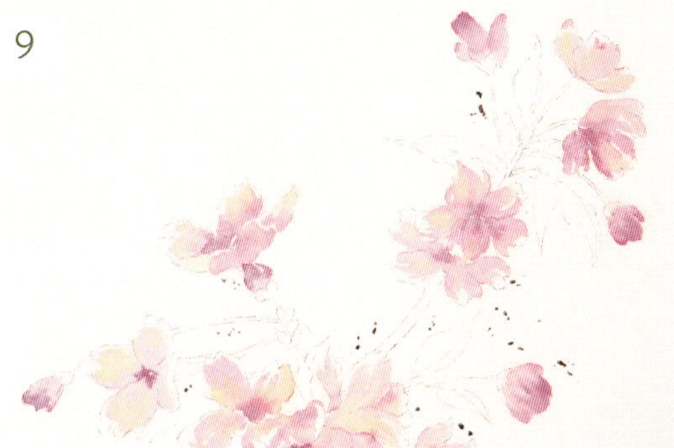

Use the same technique from step 8 to paint the remaining flower buds.

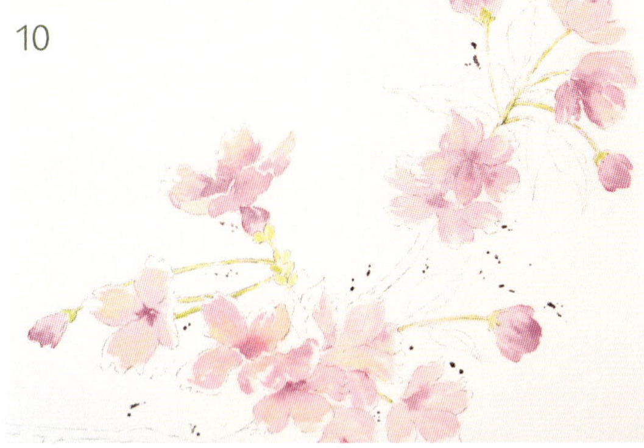

Mix color 600006 (Aureolin) and color 600197 (Green Apatite Genuine) in equal proportions to create a soft green color. Then, with plenty of water, use this color to paint the flower stems and sepals.

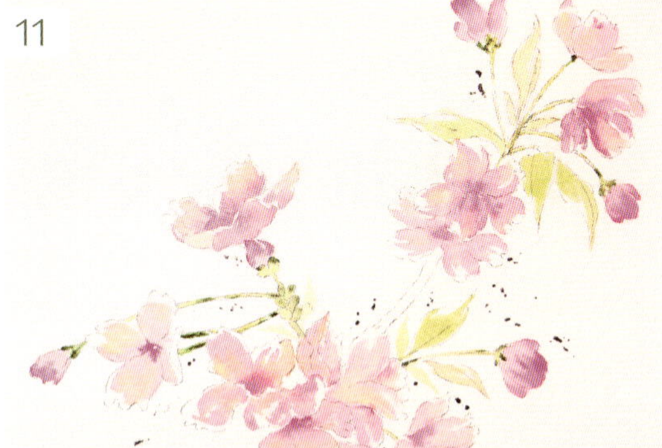

While still wet, use color 600197 (Green Apatite Genuine) to add color to the tips of the flower stems and sepals. Then, use the soft green color mixed in step 10 to color the leaves.

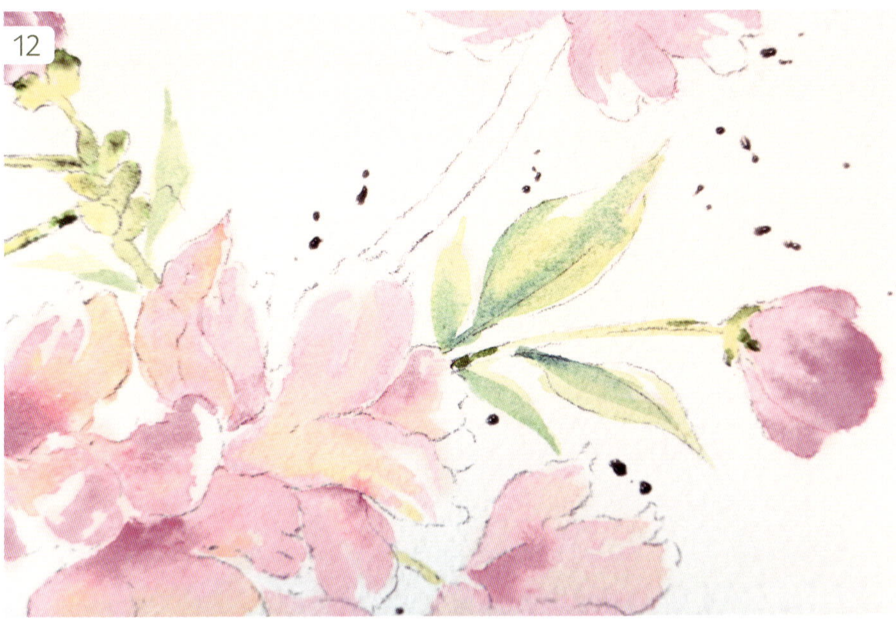

While still wet, use color 600029 (Cobalt Turquoise) to color along the base and the central main veins of all the leaves. Allow the two colors to merge with the moisture, enhancing the leaves' sense of layers.

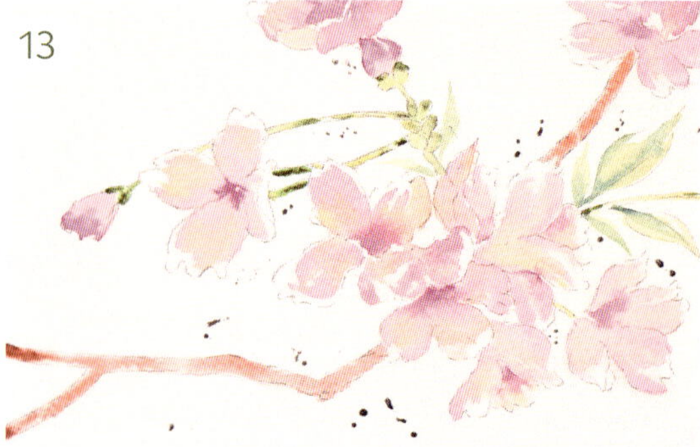

13

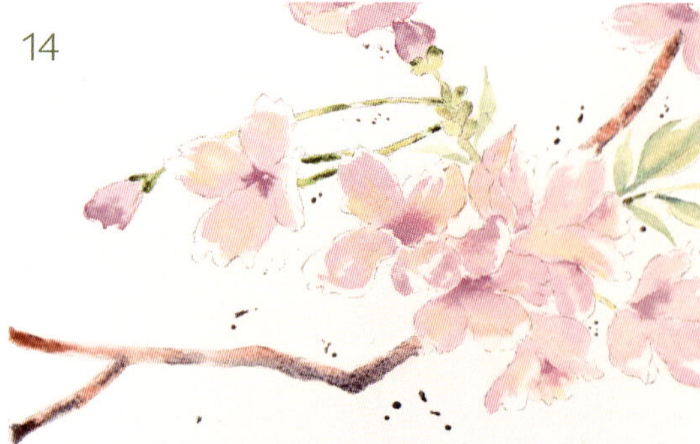

14

Apply clear water to the main branch first. While still wet, dot in color 600010 (Burnt Sienna).

Mix color 600010 (Burnt Sienna) with color 600034 (French Ultramarine) in a 2:1 ratio. While still wet, gently dab the shadowed areas of the branch to create a sense of volume. Take note that the key areas to dab are the bends and the lower edges of the branch.

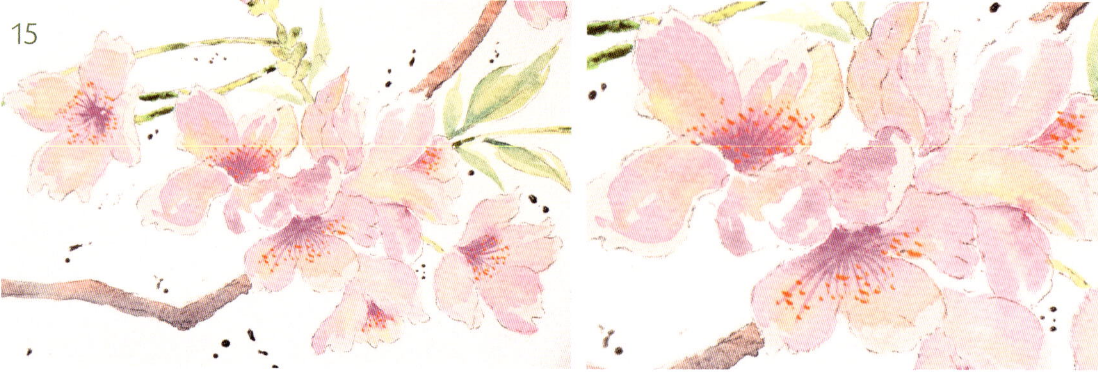

15

Use color 600198 (Opera Pink) to carefully outline the pistils. Then, use color 600234 (Aussie Red Gold) to paint the stamens (A close–up of the detail is in the right image).

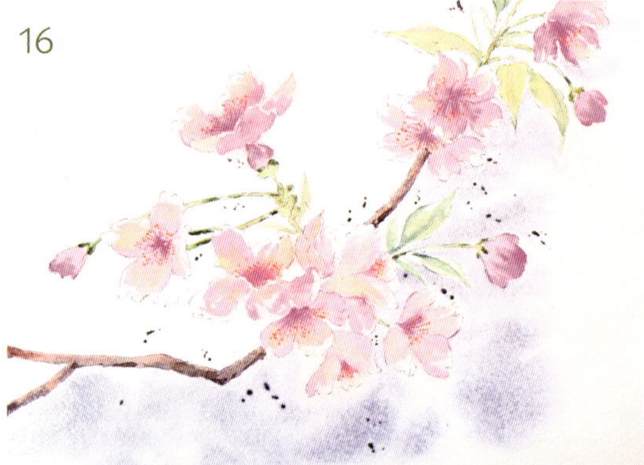

16

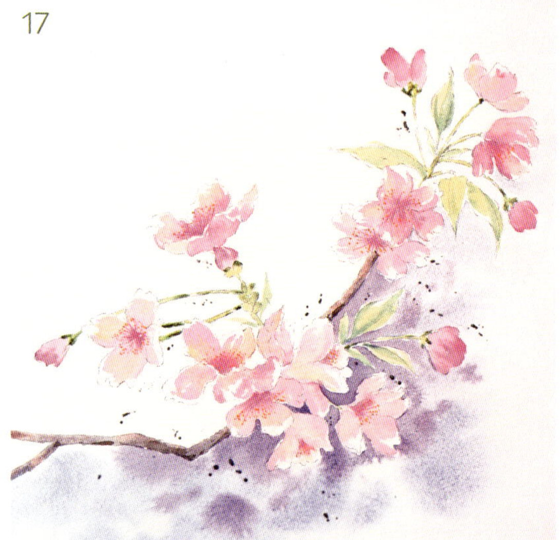

17

Begin rendering the surrounding environment to enhance the romantic atmosphere. First, apply clean water to the lower part of the painting, ensuring a smooth transition where the water meets the subject. Be careful not to mix the water into the flowers or branches, as the background colors may spread into these areas and disturb their shapes. While the paper is still wet, dab with color 600232 (Lavender), using varying sizes of color blocks and leaving some areas blank. Once the color spreads, it will create a natural, airy effect.

While the paper is still wet, dab the denser areas of the flowers with color 600019 (Carbazole Violet) to enhance the depth and contrast of the background color.

18

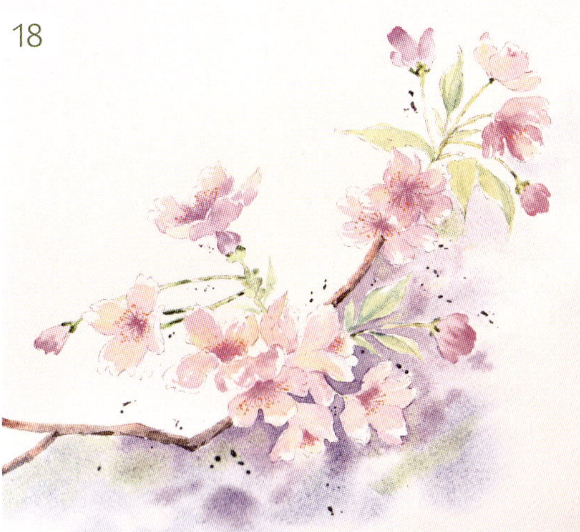

Continue to dab with color 600197 (Green Apatite Genuine) while the paper is still wet, creating soft, subtle hints of leaves.

19

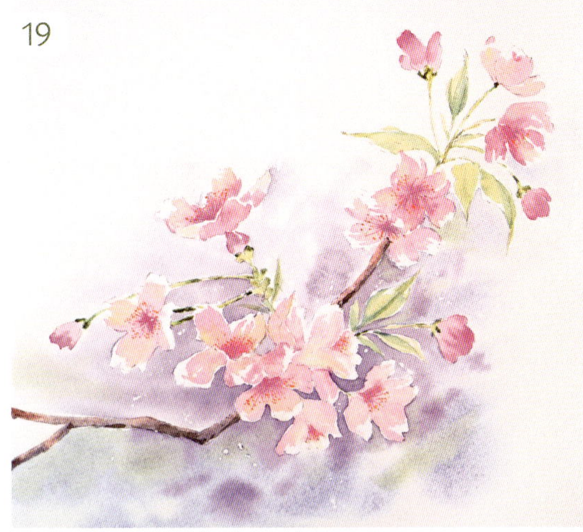

Use the same methods and colors from steps 16 to 18 to render the upper part of the painting.

20

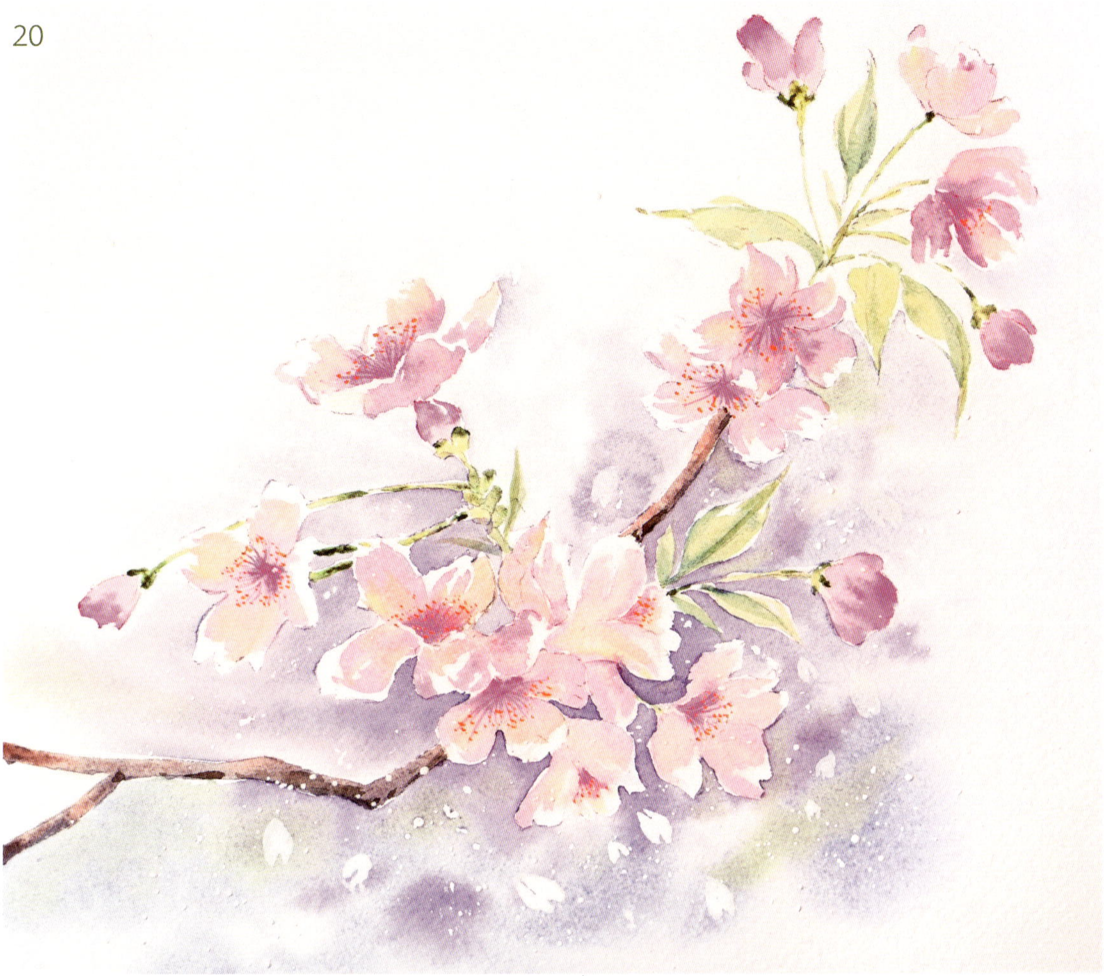

Finally, use NICKER opaque white gouache to randomly paint some scattered petals, then remove the masking fluid. This completes the romantic cherry blossoms of spring.

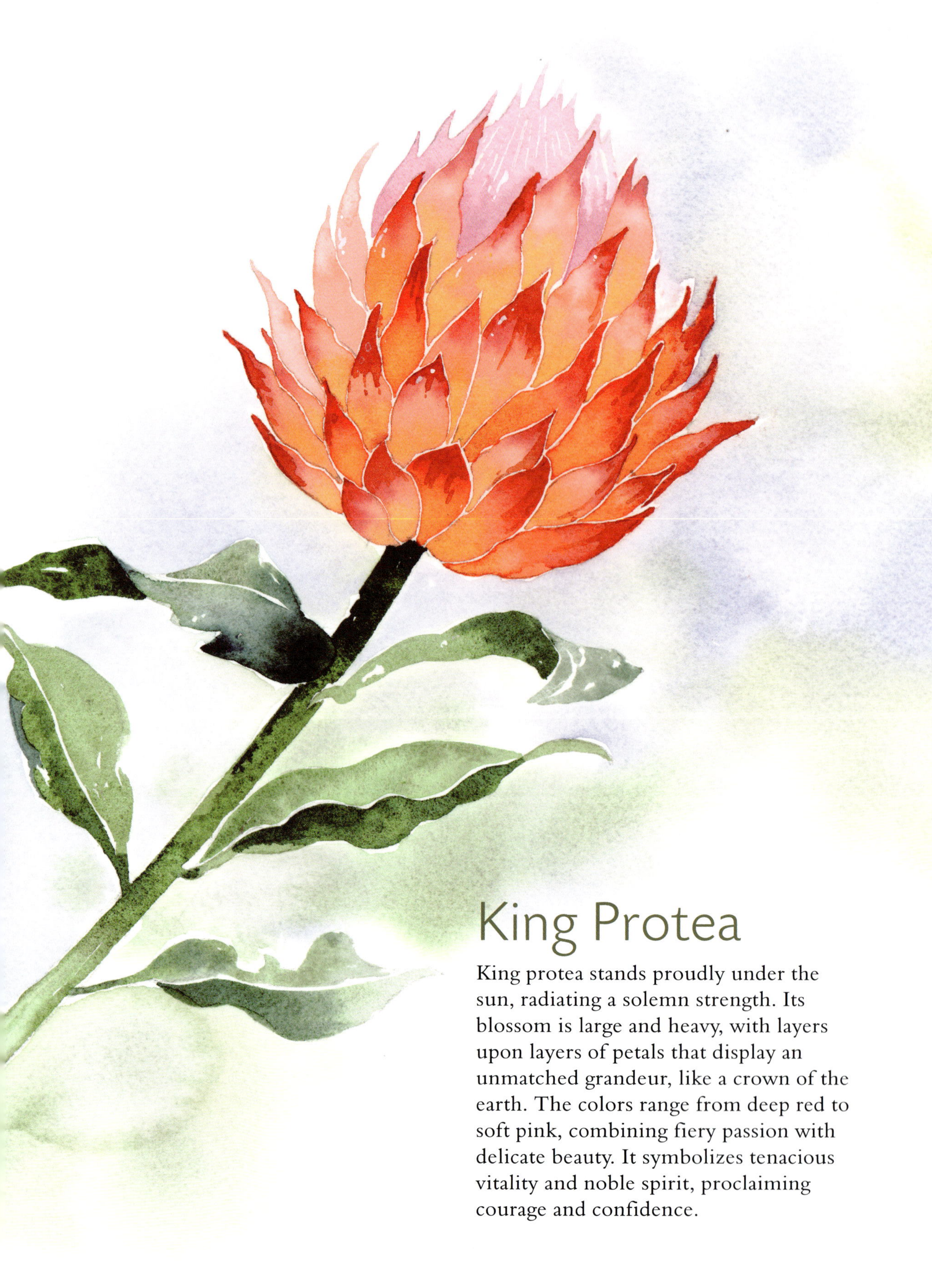

King Protea

King protea stands proudly under the sun, radiating a solemn strength. Its blossom is large and heavy, with layers upon layers of petals that display an unmatched grandeur, like a crown of the earth. The colors range from deep red to soft pink, combining fiery passion with delicate beauty. It symbolizes tenacious vitality and noble spirit, proclaiming courage and confidence.

Paint Brand
DANIEL SMITH

Color Codes
- 600198: Opera Pink
- 600009: Buff Titanium
- 600064: Organic Vermilion
- 600005: Anthraquinoid Red
- 600006: Aureolin (Cobalt Yellow)
- 600033: Deep Scarlet
- 600197: Green Apatite Genuine
- 600082: Prussian Blue
- 600024: Chromium Green Oxide
- 600232: Lavender

Auxiliary Materials
NICKER opaque white gouache
Masking fluid

Recommended Watercolor Paper
ARCHES watercolor paper, cold pressed,
140 lb/300 g/m^2

Recommended Brush
Black Velvet 3000S brush for watercolor, size 8

Key Challenges
1. How to prevent color bleeding between petals.
2. How to transition the colors smoothly on each petal.
3. Using water marks to create a soft, blurred background effect.

Steps

1

Outline the shape of the king protea with a pencil, paying attention to clearly define each petal. This tutorial mainly teaches how to color a multi-petaled flower, ensuring that the colors of each petal do not bleed into each other.

2

Apply masking fluid to the flower head and leaves, leaving the highlight areas.

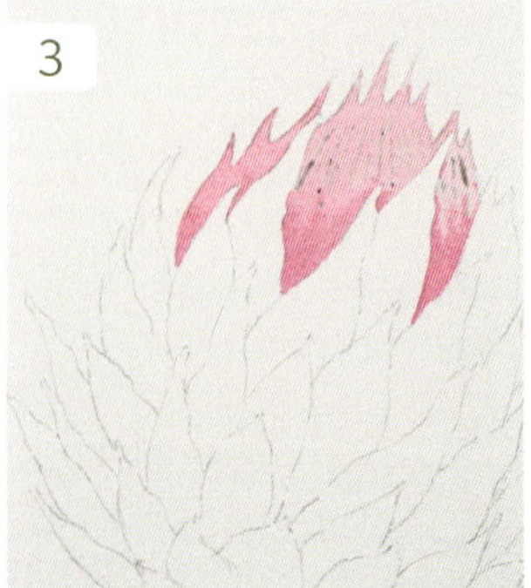

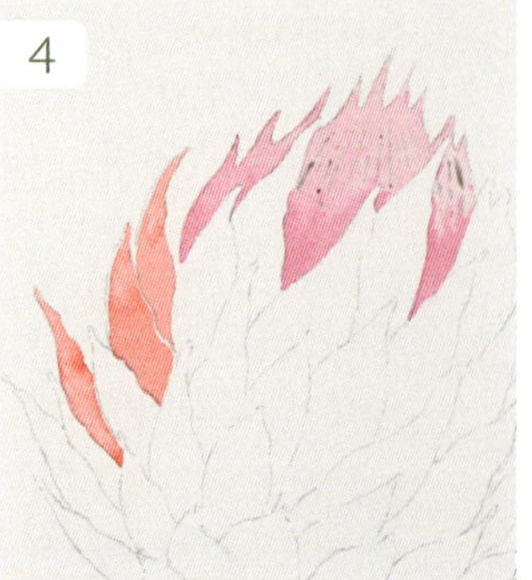

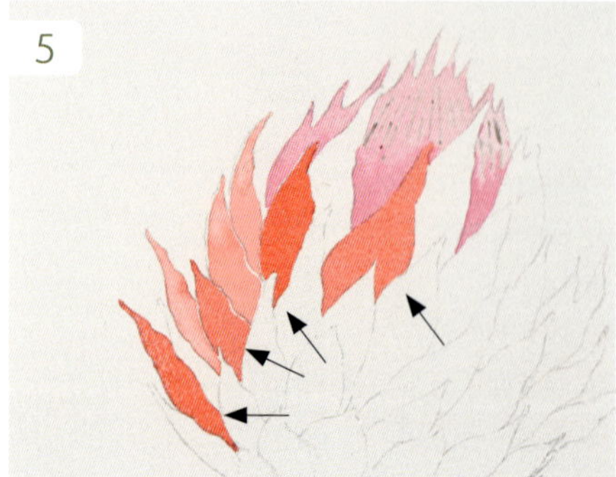

Mix equal parts of color 600198 (Opera Pink) and color 600009 (Buff Titanium) to create a lighter pink. Apply this color to the softest part of the flower head, then, while the area is still wet, use color 600198 (Opera Pink) to deepen the base.

Use color 600064 (Organic Vermilion) to apply a layer of color to the three petals on the left side that are exposed to light. Add more water to dilute the color, making it lighter.

Next, we can alternate applying color to the petals. As shown in the picture, use color 600064 (Organic Vermilion) to apply a layer of color to the four petals indicated by the arrows. Be careful to leave a small white gap between each petal to prevent the colors from blending into each other.

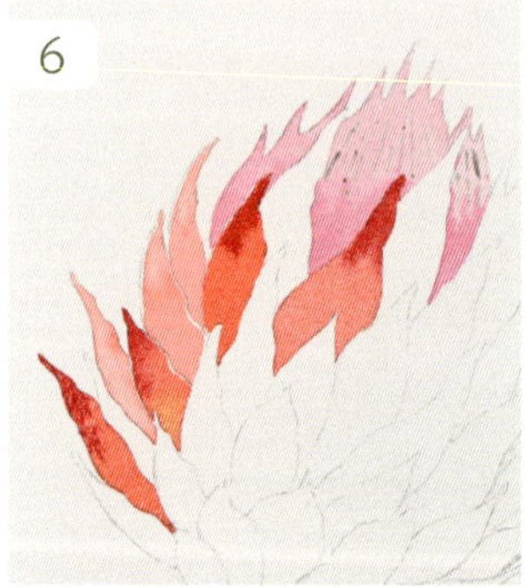

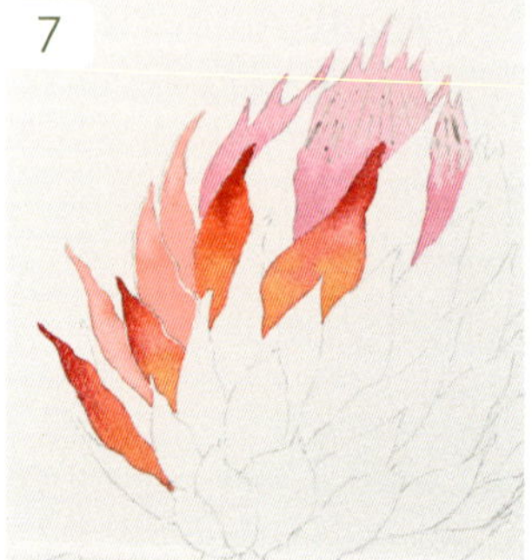

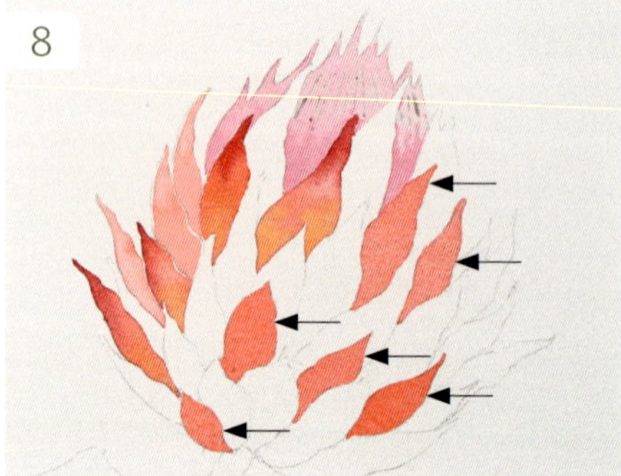

While still wet, use color 600005 (Anthraquinoid Red) to paint the tips of the four petals from step 5, allowing it to naturally merge with color 600064 (Organic Vermilion).

While still wet, use a deeper shade of color 600006 (Aureolin) with less dilution to paint the bases of the four petals, allowing it to naturally merge with color 600064 (Organic Vermilion). Once the moisture dries, this will create a natural transition effect between the three colors.

We selectively choose several petals as indicated by the arrows and repeat steps 5 to 7 for painting the petals. Start by applying color 600064 (Organic Vermilion). The purpose of selecting petals at intervals is to help beginners have better control. This is because if the previously painted petals are not completely dry, coloring the petals right next to them can cause the colors to easily bleed onto the adjacent petals due to the moisture.

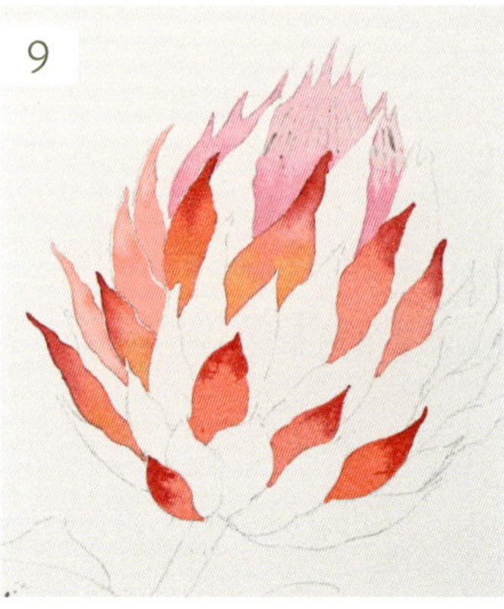

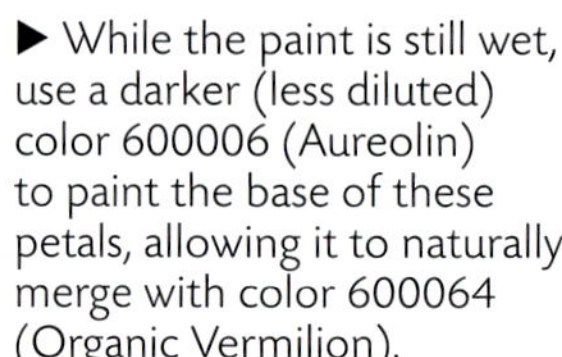

◀ While the paint is still wet, use color 600005 (Anthraquinoid Red) to paint the tips of these petals, allowing it to naturally blend with color 600064 (Organic Vermilion).

▶ While the paint is still wet, use a darker (less diluted) color 600006 (Aureolin) to paint the base of these petals, allowing it to naturally merge with color 600064 (Organic Vermilion).

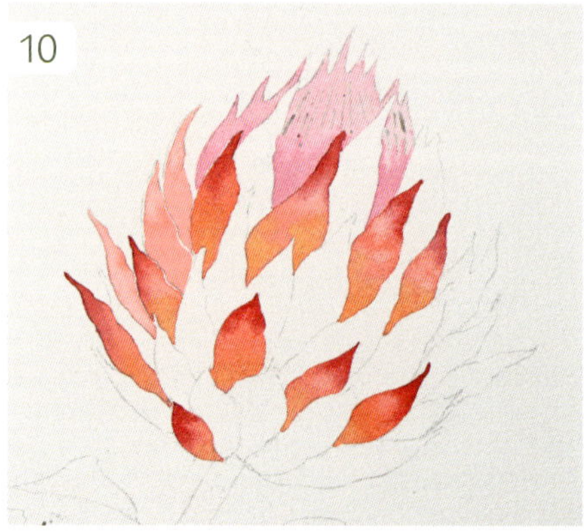

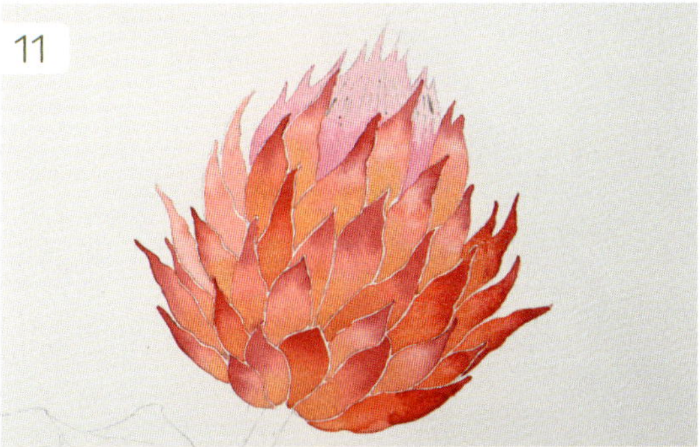

Use the same colors and the same technique from steps 5 to 7 to color the remaining petals. Be sure to leave a small white gap between the petals. The purpose is twofold, to prevent the colors from bleeding into each other, and to give the flower a sense of airiness. Without this, the flower will appear too solid and stifled.

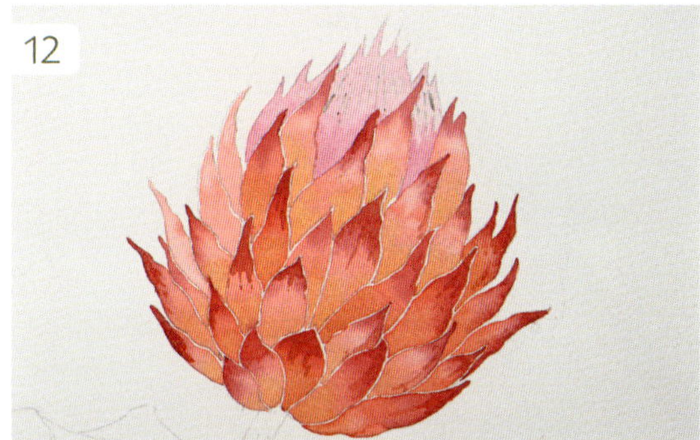

To add depth to the petals, we can use color 600033 (Deep Scarlet) and apply it sparingly to the tips of some petals, adding finer details.

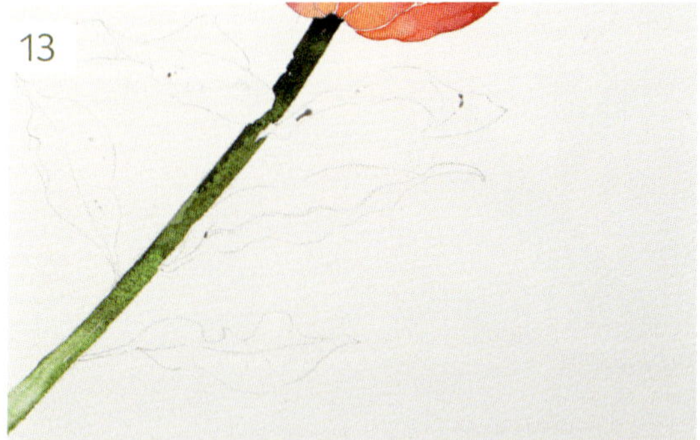

Start painting the flower stem. First, apply a layer of base color using paint color 600197 (Green Apatite Genuine). Then, mix color 600197 (Green Apatite Genuine) and color 600082 (Prussian Blue) in a 3:1 ratio to create a deeper green. Use this color to paint the part of the stem near the flower, as this area is shaded by the flower, creating a shadow, so the color should be darker.

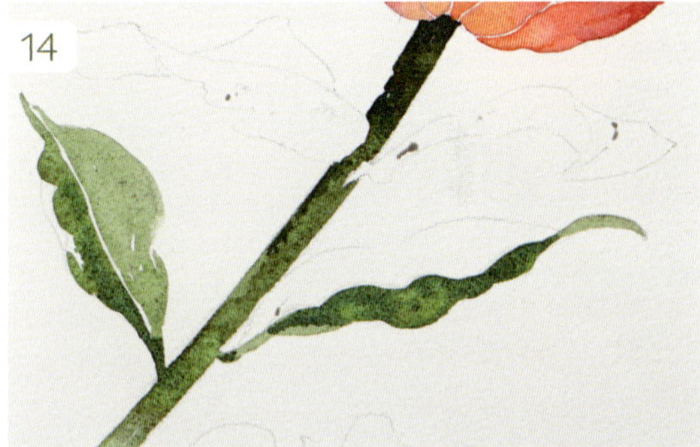

Similarly, use color 600197 (Green Apatite Genuine) to paint two leaves. Control the amount of water to create a slight variation in color depth. Note that for the left leaf, leave a gap in the center to form the leaf vein. For the right leaf, use a lighter green on the folded side.

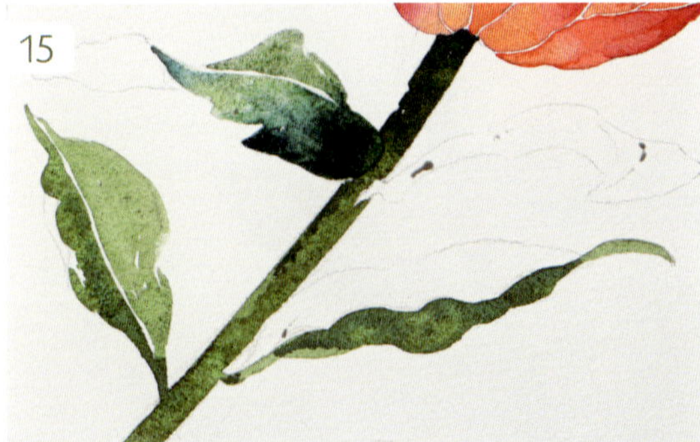

Use color 600024 (Chromium Green Oxide) to apply a base color on the upper leaf, leaving a white gap in the center to form the leaf vein. At the same time, mix color 600024 (Chromium Green Oxide) and color 600082 (Prussian Blue) in a 2:1 ratio to create a darker green. Use this to detail the darker parts of the leaf, giving it more dimension.

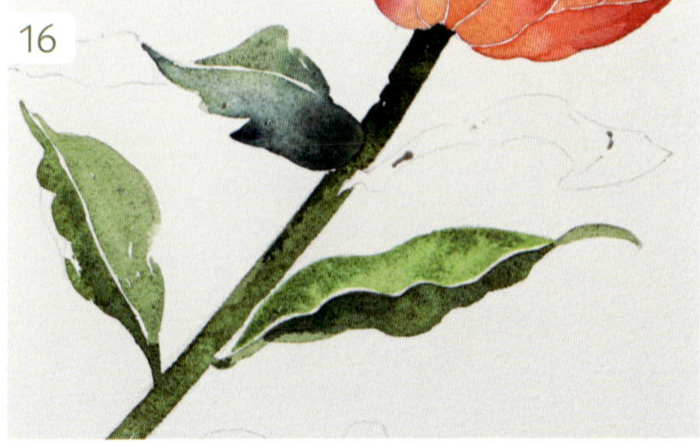

Use color 600197 (Green Apatite Genuine) to paint the upper half of the leaf on the right. Then, use a more concentrated (less diluted) color 600197 (Green Apatite Genuine) to dab it, creating the mottled effect on the leaf. Be sure to leave a gap in the center to form the leaf vein.

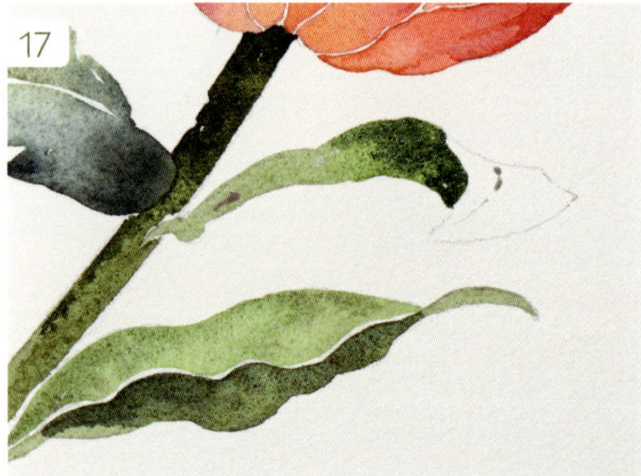

For the backside of the leaf on the upper right, first use color 600197 (Green Apatite Genuine) to lay down the base color. Then, while still wet, mix color 600197 (Green Apatite Genuine) and color 600082 (Prussian Blue) in a 3:1 ratio to create a darker green and use it to paint the shadowed areas.

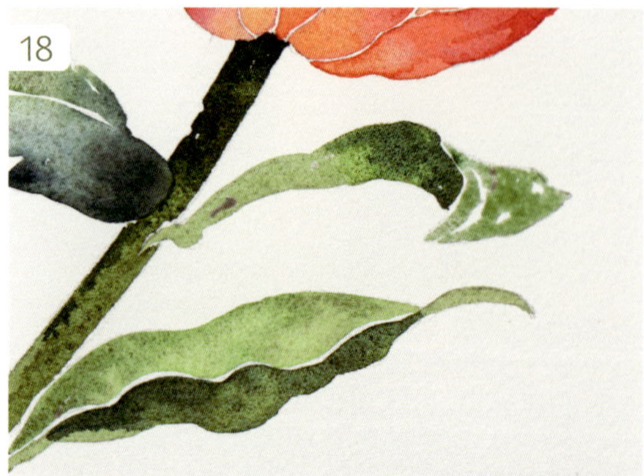

Use color 600024 (Chromium Green Oxide) to paint the upward folded surface of the leaf on the upper right.

Use color 600024 (Chromium Green Oxide) to fill in the bottommost leaf, leaving a gap in the middle to represent the leaf vein.

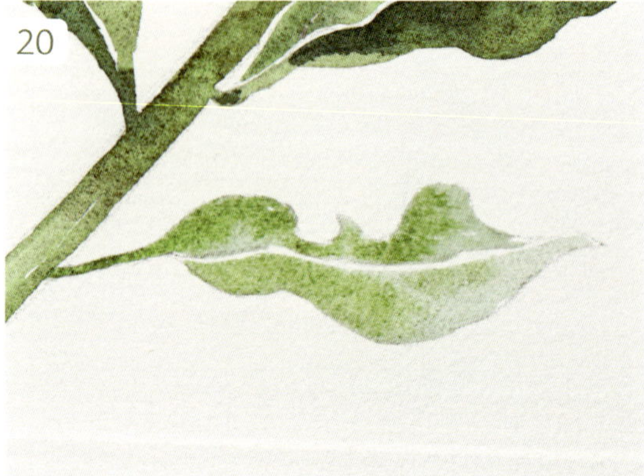

Use color 600197 (Green Apatite Genuine) to dab the darker areas.

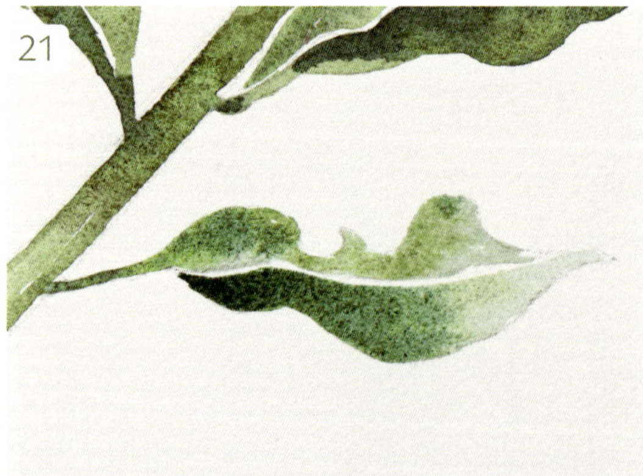

Mix color 600197 (Green Apatite Genuine) and color 600082 (Prussian Blue) in a 3:1 ratio to create a darker green, and continue dabbing the shadowed areas at the bottom to give the entire leaf a sense of dimension.

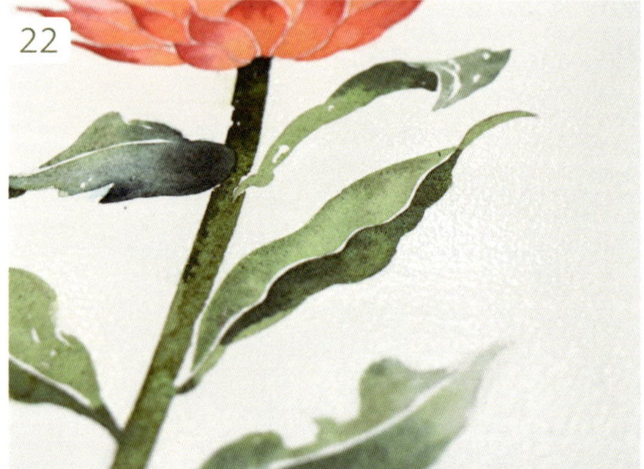

Quickly apply clean water to the areas outside the entire flower stem. Be especially careful when reaching the areas where the flower, stem, and leaves meet, ensuring that you do not touch the areas that have already been painted.

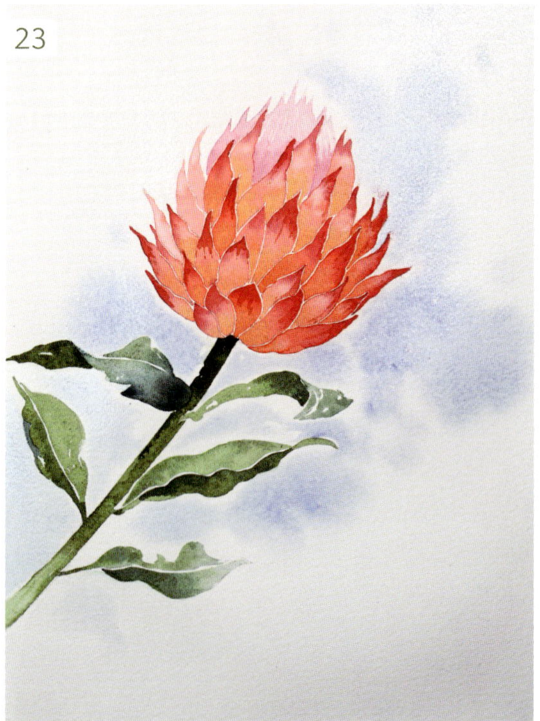

23

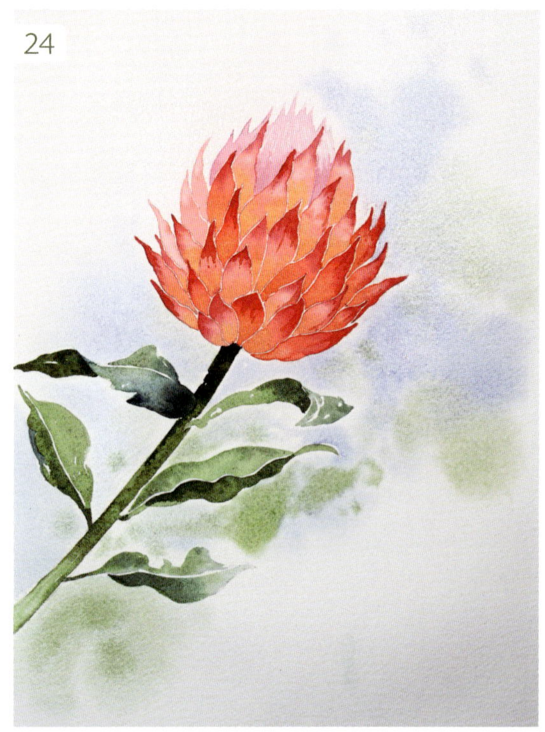

24

While still wet, use color 600232 (Lavender) to lightly apply around the main flower. Be sure to leave some space between each stroke, as the color will naturally spread outward with the moisture. The further out the color goes, the lighter it becomes, creating a misty, smoky effect.

Similarly, while still wet, lightly apply color 600197 (Green Apatite Genuine).

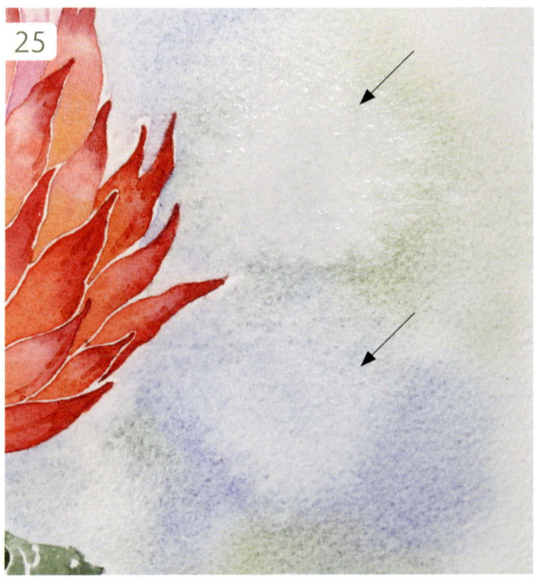

25

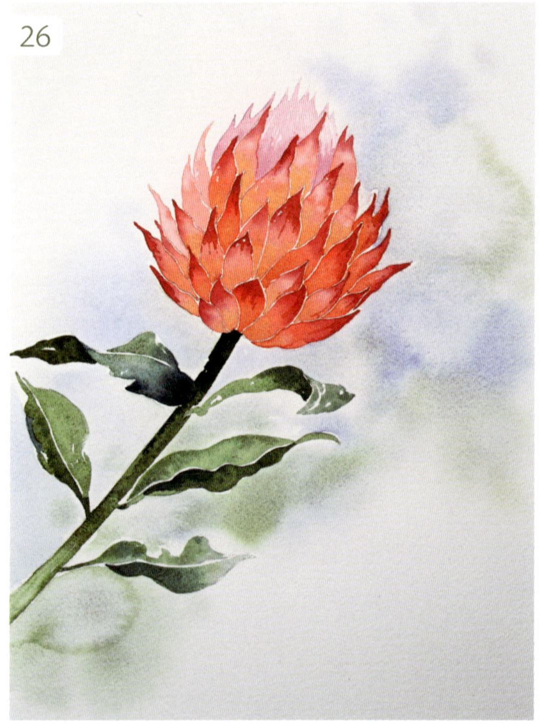

26

When the paper is about 70% dry, meaning the surface no longer reflects light but still feels damp and cool to the touch, use a clean brush to dip into plenty of clean water. Then, drop the water onto the areas indicated by the arrows in the image to create water marks, enhancing the atmospheric effect.

Use NICKER opaque white gouache to add some highlight details to the flowers, and erase the masking fluid with an eraser. The king protea in the garden is now complete.

Praying Mantis

In the garden, a green praying mantis quietly rests on a stone, as if it is the guardian of this garden. It remains silent and alert, occasionally turning its head, seemingly sensing the movements around it.

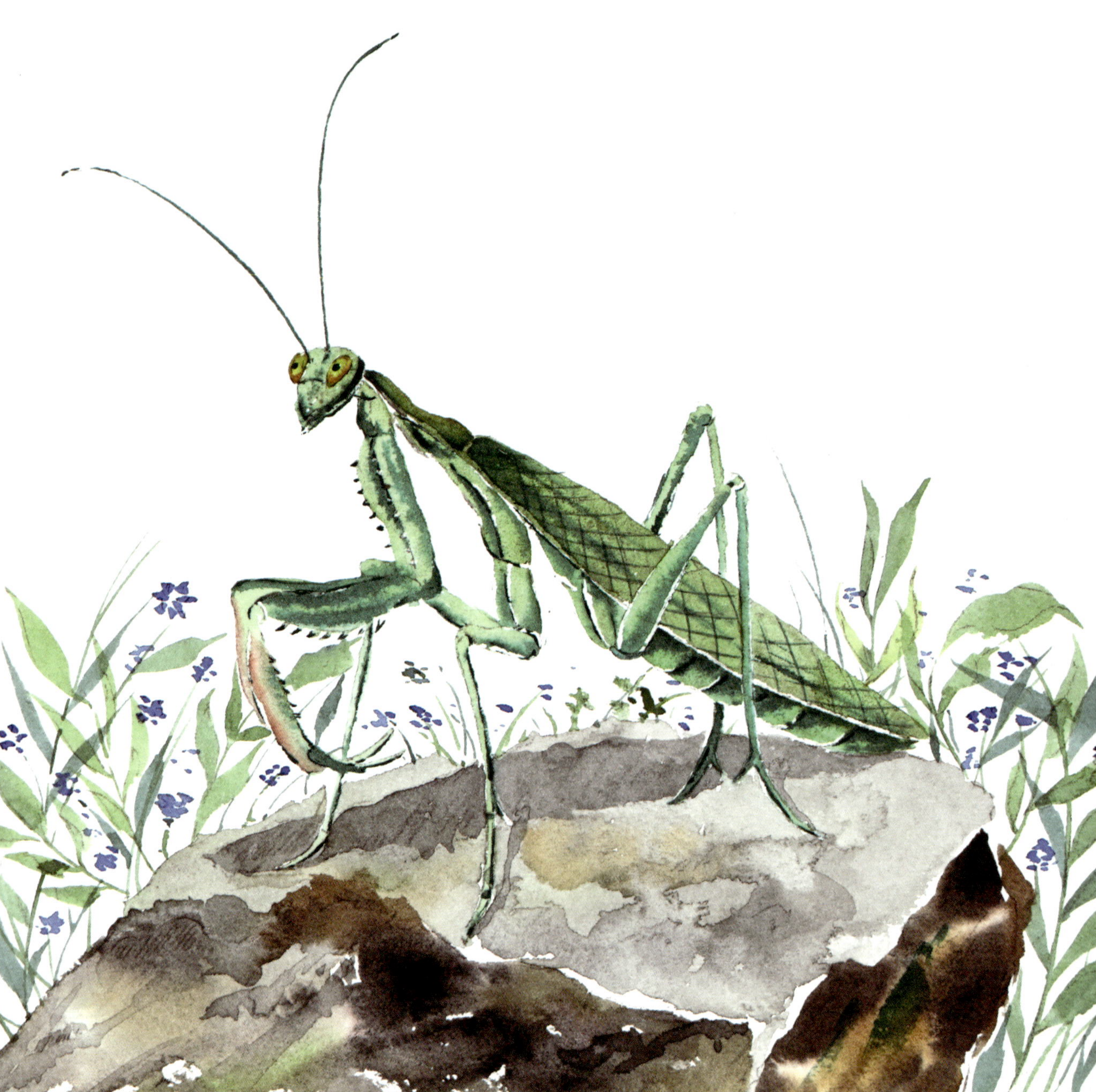

Paint Brand
DANIEL SMITH

Color Codes
- 600197: Green Apatite Genuine
- 600033: Deep Scarlet
- 600114: Yellow Ochre
- 600188: Shadow Violet
- 600041: Hansa Yellow Light
- 600078: Phthalo Green (Blue Shade)
- 600006: Aureolin (Cobalt Yellow)
- 600233: Raw Sienna Light
- 600244: Joseph Z's Neutral Grey
- 600173: Verditer Blue

Auxiliary Material
Masking fluid

Recommended Watercolor Paper
ARCHES watercolor paper, cold pressed, 140 lb/300 g/m^2

Recommended Brush
Black Velvet 3000S brush for watercolor, size 8

Key Challenges
1. Rendering the form and structure of the praying mantis.
2. Depicting the stone.
3. Painting the leaves in a single brushstroke.

Steps

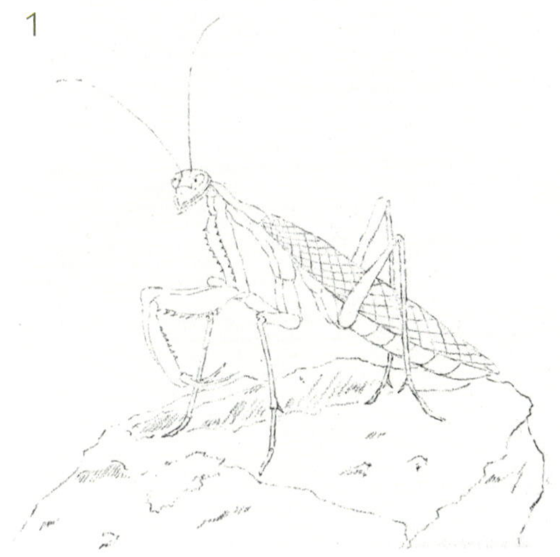

1

Use a pencil to sketch the shapes of the praying mantis and the stone. Pay close attention to their spatial relationship, the texture of the wing on the mantis's back, and the shadow the mantis casts onto the stone.

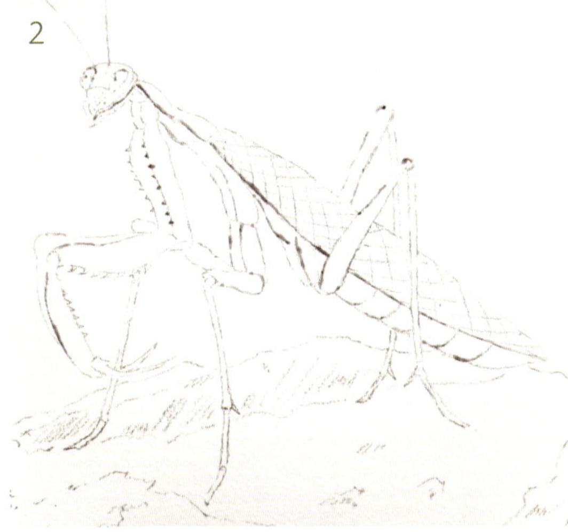

2

Apply masking fluid along the edges of the praying mantis's body (where the outline appears dark gray in the image).

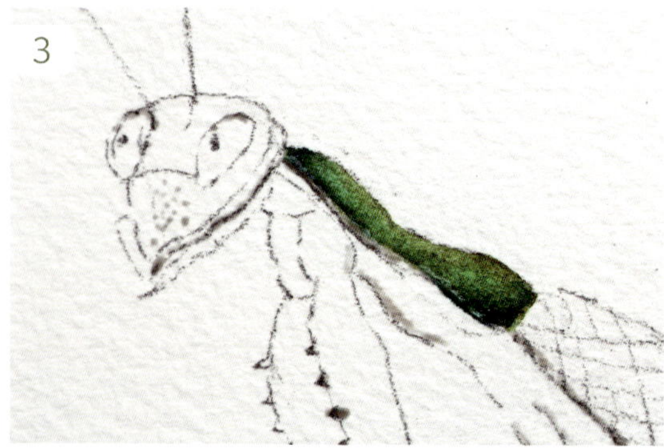

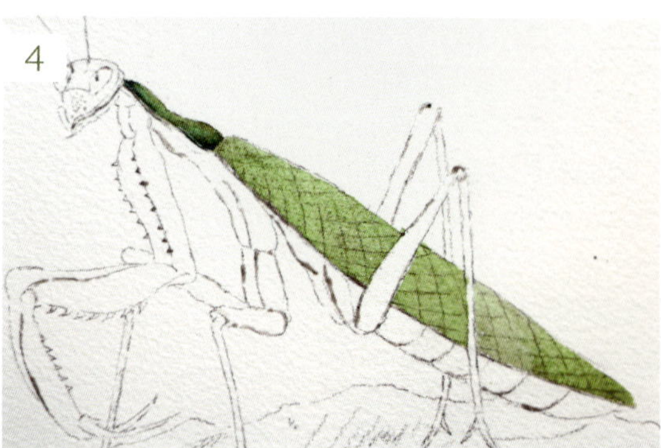

Near the head area of the mantis, first apply a base layer using color 600197 (Green Apatite Genuine). While the area is still wet, deepen the lower edge by blending in a dark green color 600078 (Phthalo Green).

Paint the mantis's wing by first laying down a base color using color 600197 (Green Apatite Genuine).

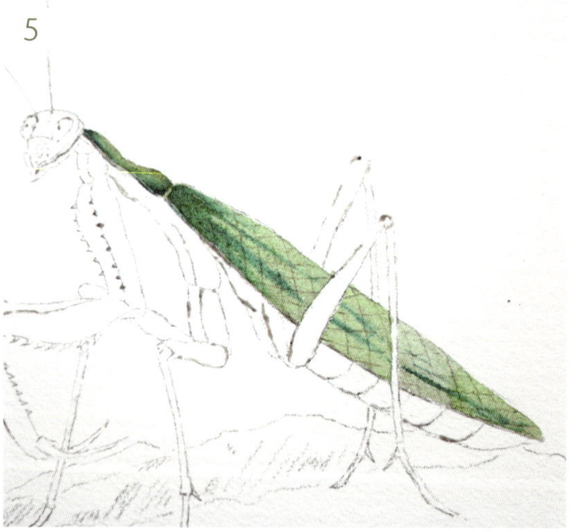

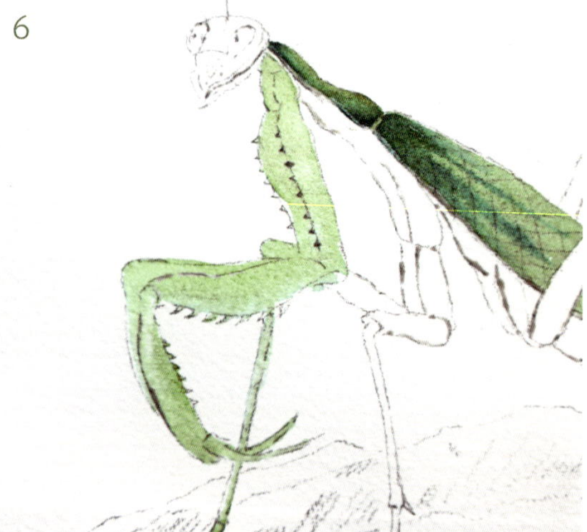

While the surface is still wet, use color 600078 (Phthalo Green) to darken the edges and enhance the texture on the wing.

Paint the forelegs by first laying down a base layer using color 600197 (Green Apatite Genuine).

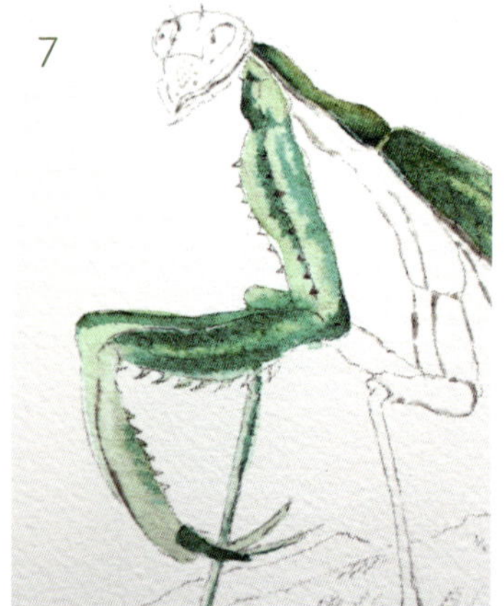

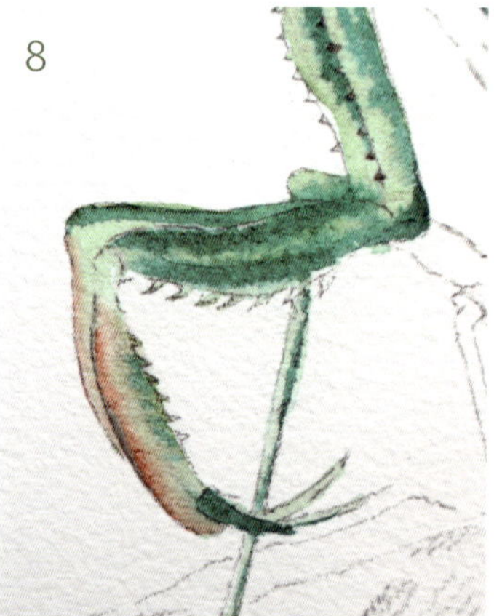

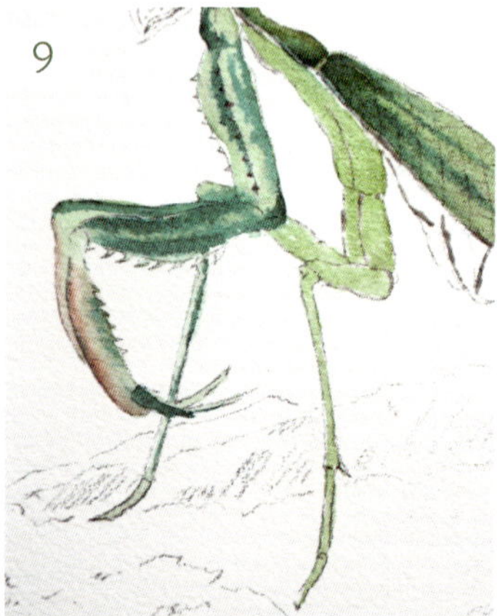

While the surface is still wet, use color 600078 (Phthalo Green) to darken the edges and define details and shadows.

While the surface is still wet, lightly dab a shade with color 600033 (Deep Scarlet) on the front ends of the forelegs.

Similarly, use color 600197 (Green Apatite Genuine) to lay the base color for the middle legs of the mantis.

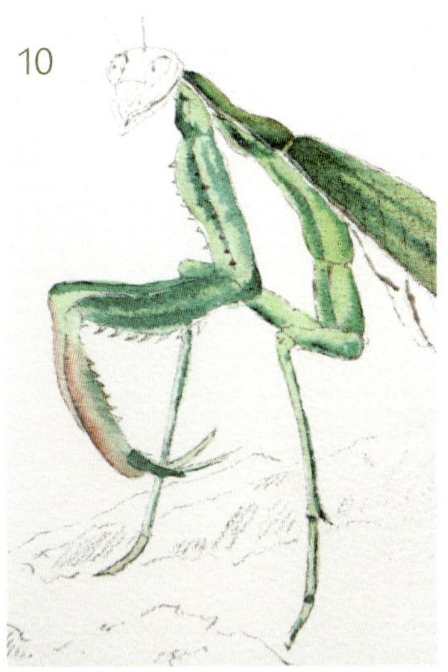

While still wet, use color 600078 (Phthalo Green) to darken the edges and joints of the middle legs, adding details and shadows.

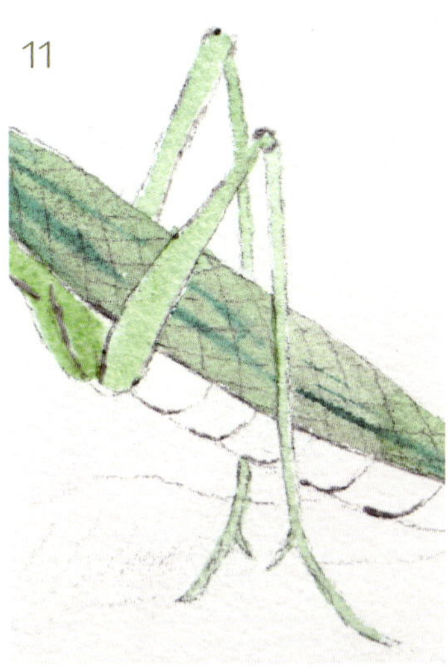

Paint the hind legs, using color 600197 (Green Apatite Genuine) to lay down the base color.

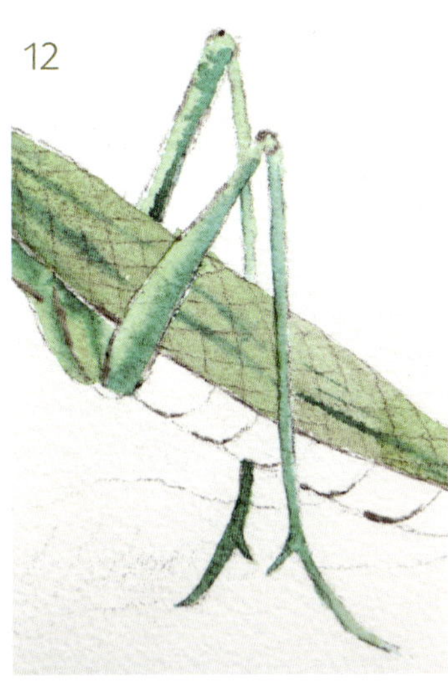

While the paint is still wet, use color 600078 (Phthalo Green) to deepen the edges and joints, adding details and shadows.

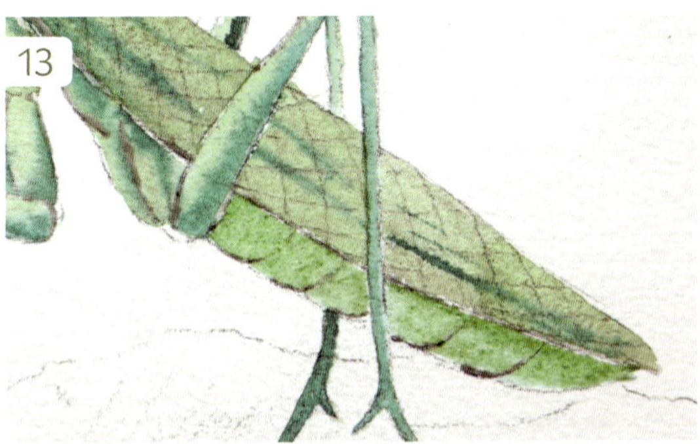

Paint the abdomen by applying a base layer of color 600197 (Green Apatite Genuine).

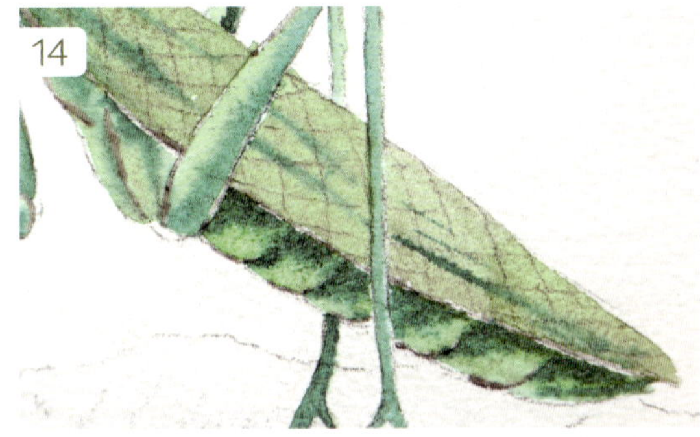

While the area is still wet, use color 600078 (Phthalo Green) to deepen the edges of the mantis's abdomen. Dab the color along the segmented structure of the abdomen to depict the layered relationship and create a sense of volume.

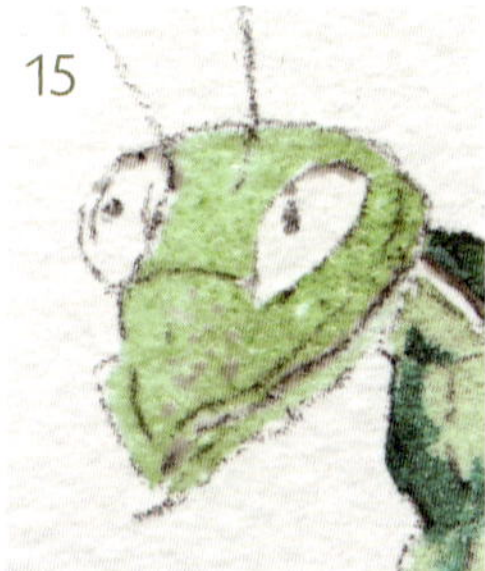

Avoiding the mantis's eyes, use color 600197 (Green Apatite Genuine) to lay down the base color for the entire head.

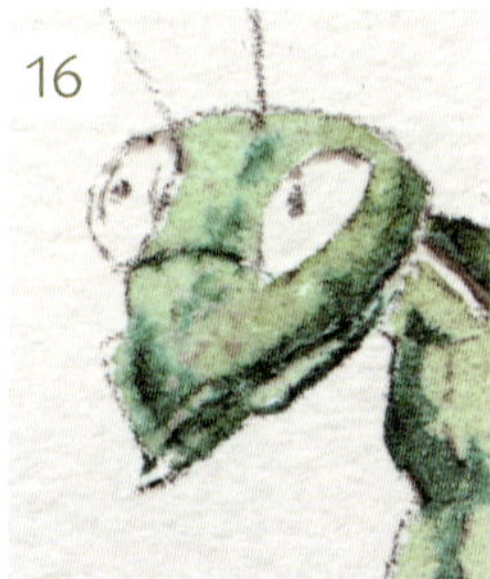

While still wet, use color 600078 (Phthalo Green) to darken the edges of the head, enhancing the shadow details and shaping the sense of volume.

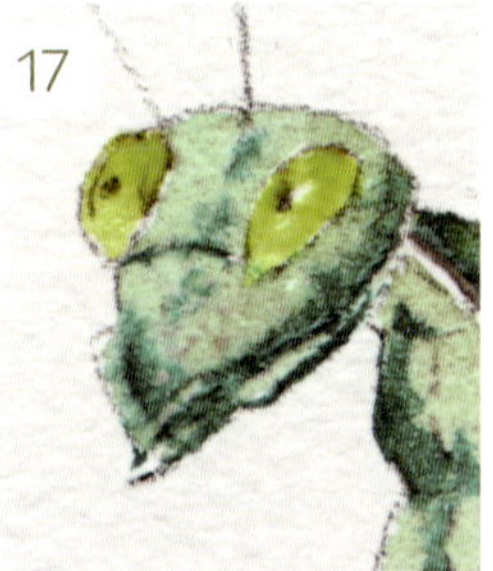

Draw the mantis's eyes, treating them as a spherical shape with both highlighted and shadowed areas. Start by using color 600006 (Aureolin) to fill in the eyes.

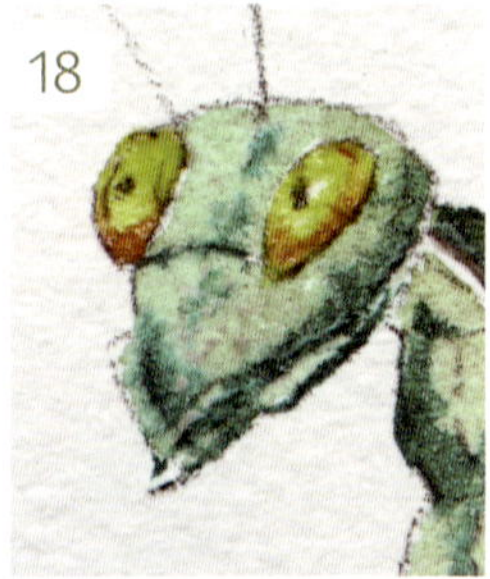

Use color 600114 (Yellow Ochre) to paint the transition between light and shadow, shaping the volume of the eyes.

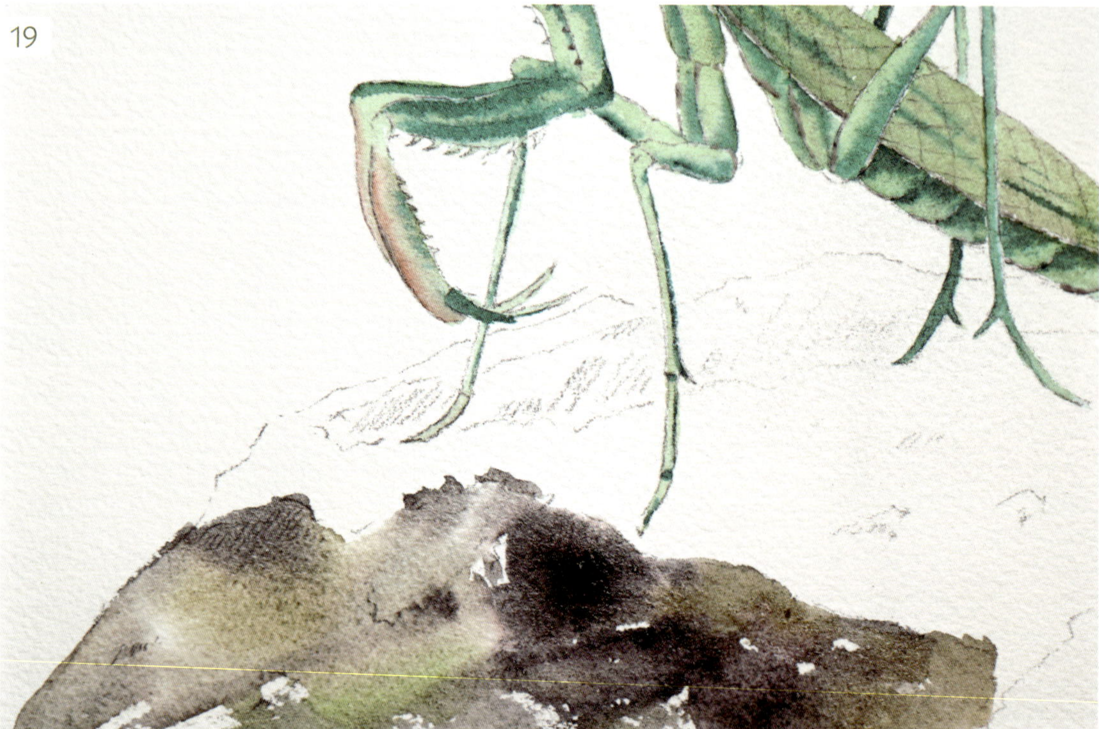

Start painting the stone, first distinguishing between the light-facing side and the shadowed side. The top of the stone is the light-facing side, while the two sides are in shadow. Therefore, in terms of light and dark, the color of the top should be lighter than that of the sides.

Start by painting the left side of the stone. First, apply clean water to the area as a base. Once the paper is fully saturated, while the paper is still wet, use color 600233 (Raw Sienna Light), color 600188 (Shadow Violet), and color 600244 (Joseph Z's Neutral Grey) to add color. Be light-handed with the brush. There's no need to be too precise with any specific area or color. Allow the three colors to naturally blend, creating a rich and layered color effect.

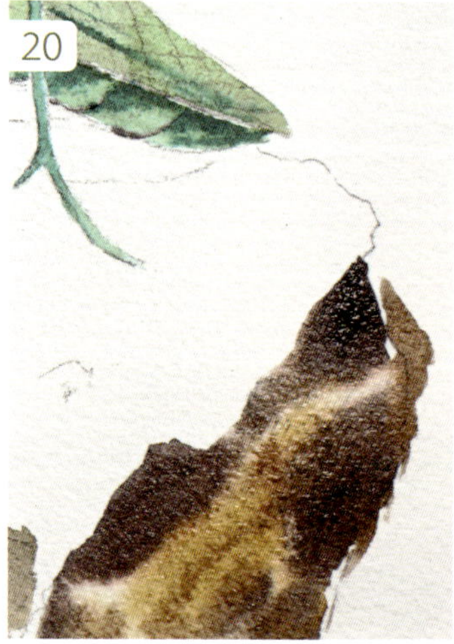

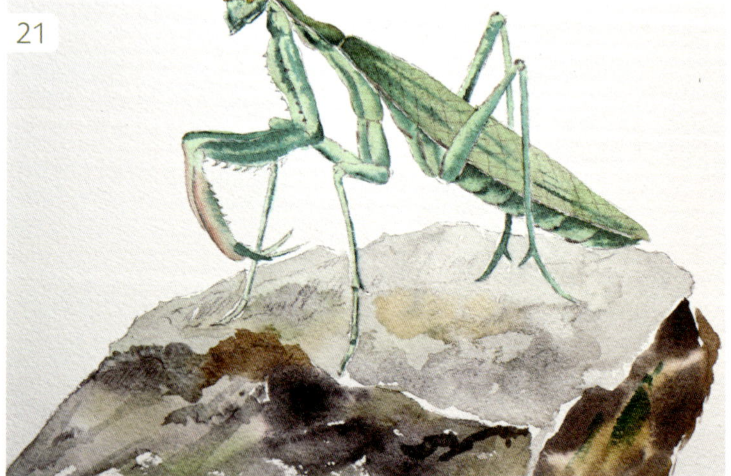

Use the same method and colors as in step 19 to paint the right side of the stone. Again, don't worry about sticking to a specific color ratio or defined areas. Use the wet-on-wet technique here as well, allowing the three colors to blend freely into each other.

Wet the top surface of the stone with clean water. Once the water has fully soaked into the paper, apply color 600244 (Joseph Z's Neutral Grey) and color 600233 (Raw Sienna Light), letting the two colors blend naturally into each other. You can dilute both colors with more water than usual to create a lighter effect. Be sure to leave a thin white line at the edge where the top of the stone meets the sides. This mimics the reflective highlights typically found on sharp stone edges, enhancing the stone's three dimensionality and texture.

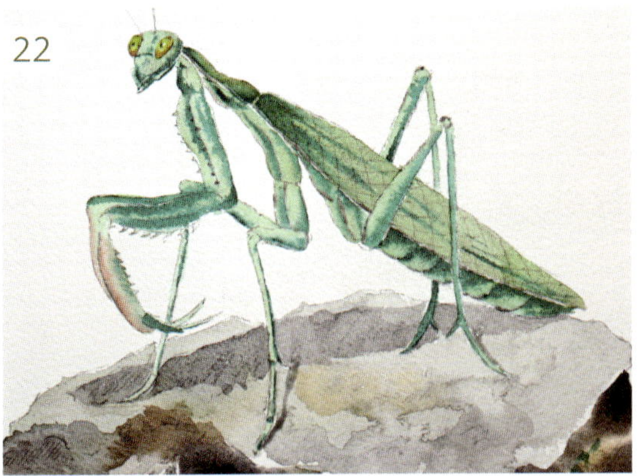

Use a very light wash of color 600244 (Joseph Z's Neutral Grey) to paint the shadow cast by the mantis onto the stone.

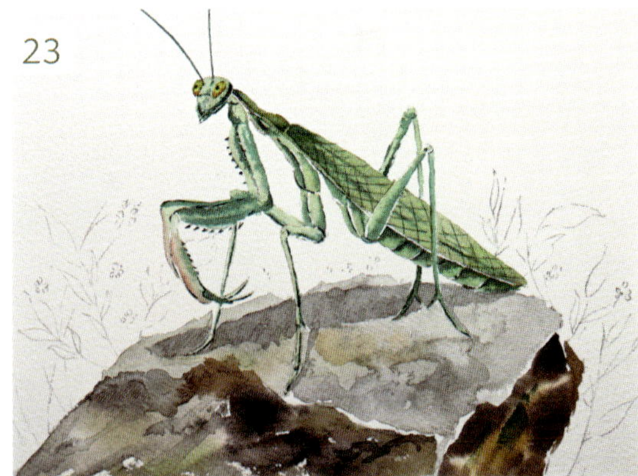

Lightly sketch the shapes of the leaves and weeds in the background using a pencil.

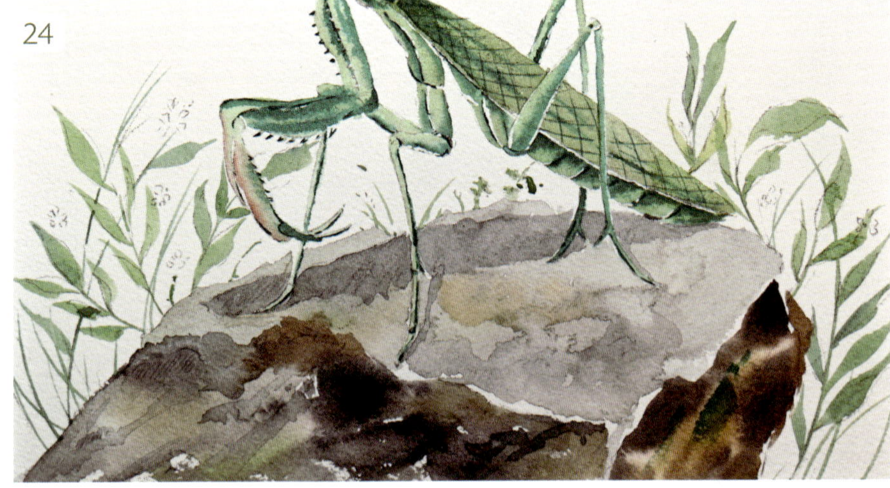

Mix color 600041 (Hansa Yellow Light) and color 600173 (Verditer Blue) in equal parts to create a light green, and use it to paint the leaves and weeds.

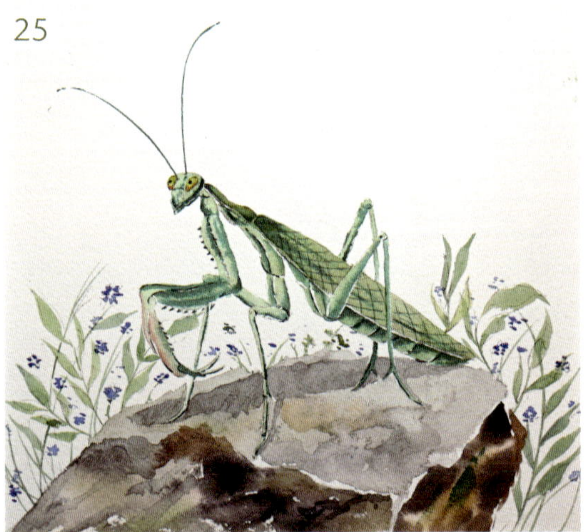

Use any blue color you like to scatter and dot in some small flower petals.

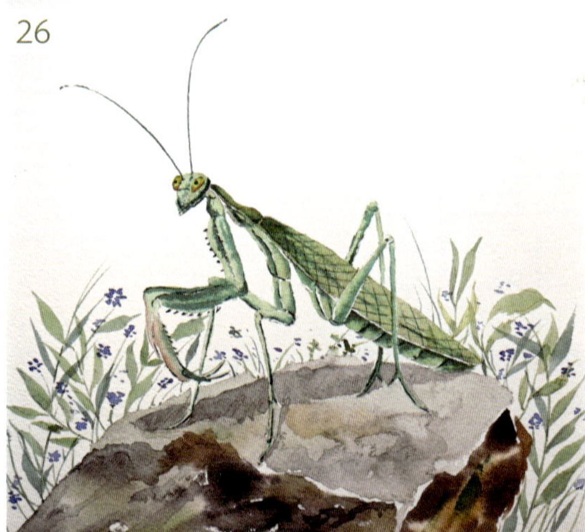

Then, use any green you like to paint a few more leaves, adding richness and depth to the layers. Finally, remove the masking fluid from the mantis's body, and your mantis is complete.

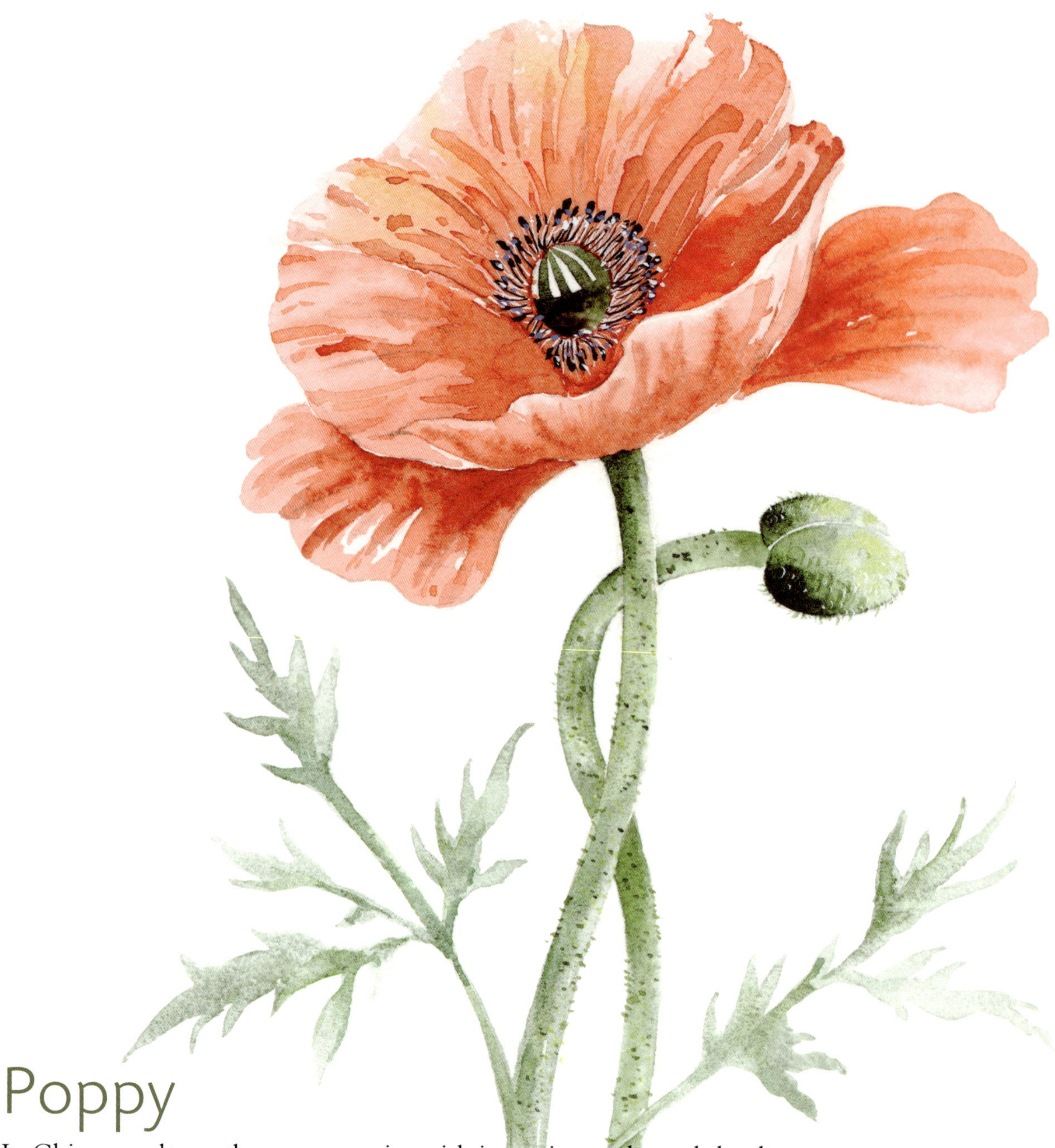

Poppy

In Chinese culture, the poppy carries with it a poignant legend that has
endured for over a thousand years. It is said to be tied to Yu Ji, the beloved
consort of Xiang Yu (c. 232–c. 202 BC), the Hegemon-King of Western Chu
(206–202 BC). When Xiang Yu was defeated, Yu Ji took her own life out
of loyalty and love. The blood-soaked earth where she fell is said to have
bloomed into vivid red poppies. Because of this, the poppy is often imbued
with the symbolism of tragic beauty and unwavering devotion. Its bloom is
brilliant yet fleeting, its fall resolute. Though its flowering period is brief, it
burns a vivid red, like a farewell that gives everything. For generations, poets
and scholars have used it to express themes of life and death, parting, and
lingering sorrow.

Paint Brand
DANIEL SMITH

Color Codes
- 600064: Organic Vermilion
- 600033: Deep Scarlet
- 600006: Aureolin (Cobalt Yellow)
- 600080: Phthalo Turquoise
- 600232: Lavender
- 600024: Chromium Green Oxide
- 600197: Green Apatite Genuine

Auxiliary Material
NICKER opaque white gouache

Recommended Watercolor Paper
ARCHES watercolor paper, cold pressed,
140 lb/300 g/m^2

Recommended Brushes
Black Velvet 3000S brush for watercolor, size 8
Black Velvet 3000S brush for watercolor, size 6

Key Challenges
1. Shaping the petals.
2. Detailing the stems and flower buds.

Steps

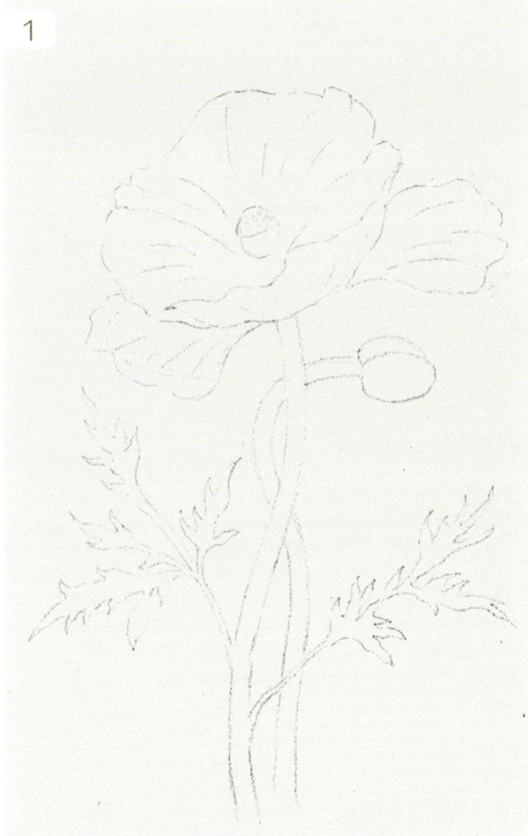

Lightly draw the shape of the poppy with a pencil. The shape of the flower is similar to an oval. Pay attention to the curvature of the flower stem, making sure the stem is aligned with the flower's center. Although part of it is covered, if the position is incorrect, it will appear as though the flower and the stem are separate. The lines of the flower stem should be smooth, and the thickness should remain consistent.

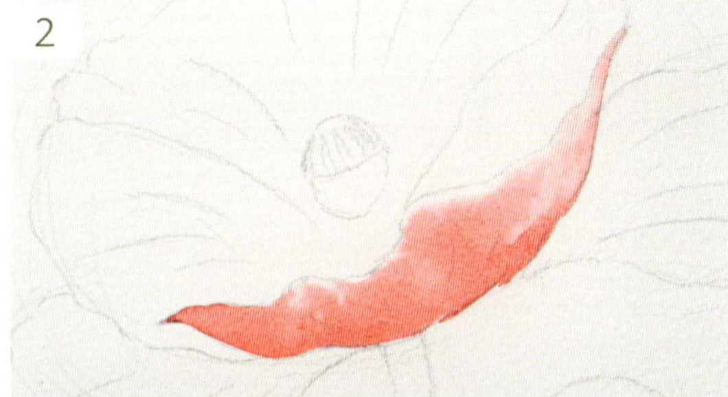

Start by painting the petal that faces outward. Wet the paper within the outline of this petal using clean water. Then, lightly apply color 600064 (Organic Vermilion) to lay down a base layer. Leave a small amount of white space along the top edge of the petal, allowing the color to spread and blend with the moisture on the paper. Keep the brushstrokes light and flexible, and be careful not to apply flat wash.

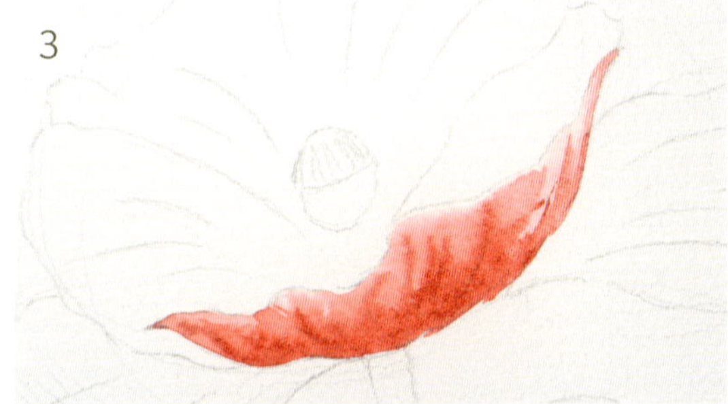

When the paper is about 70% dry, meaning the surface no longer reflects light but still feels damp and cool to the touch, quickly use a more concentrated (less diluted) color 600033 (Deep Scarlet) to outline the texture of the petal. At this stage, the paper's moisture allows you to create both soft, blurred edges and sharper, more defined lines, making the petal appear livelier.

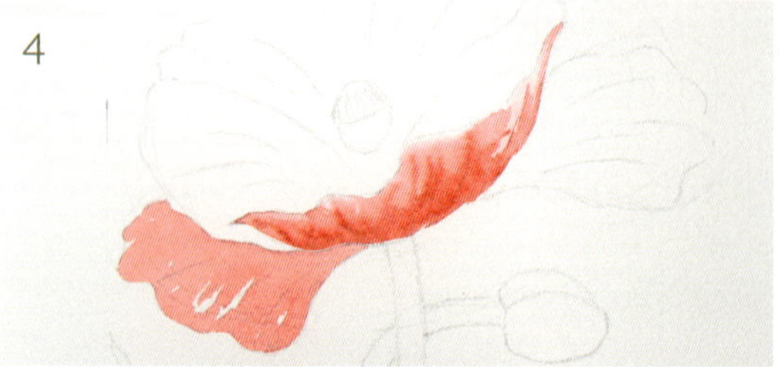

Next, paint the petal on the left that is folding outward. Make sure the brush is well-loaded with water and apply lightly a more diluted color 600064 (Organic Vermilion) to create a soft base. Be mindful of leaving some white space to give the painting a sense of airiness.

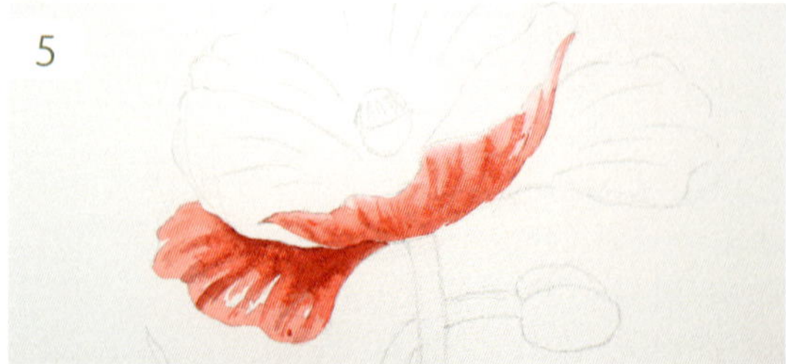

Before the paper dries completely, quickly use color 600033 (Deep Scarlet) to outline the texture and deepen the base of the petal.

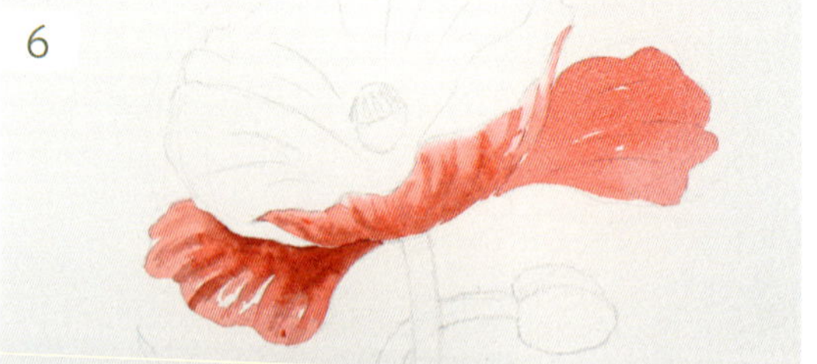

For the petal on the right that is flipping outward, similarly, ensure the brush has enough moisture. Lightly apply a diluted layer of color 600064 (Organic Vermilion), leaving some areas blank.

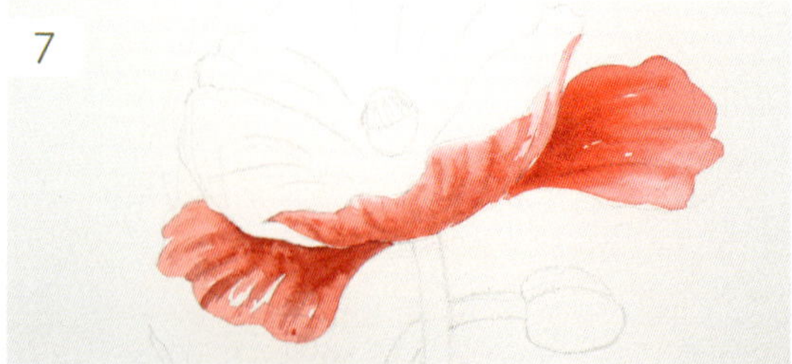

While the paper is still wet, use color 600033 (Deep Scarlet) to outline the texture and deepen the base of the petals.

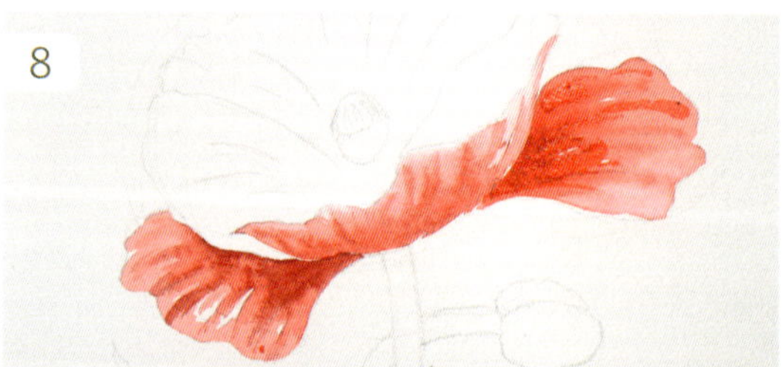

Continue to use color 600033 (Deep Scarlet) to enhance the texture of the petals and depict the details.

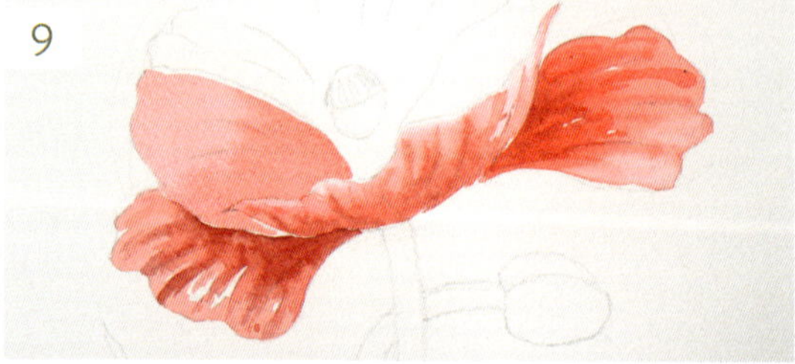

Paint the petal on the left side of the center. The brush should be well-loaded with water, using a lighter wash of color 600064 (Organic Vermilion) to gently lay down the base color. Unlike in the previous steps, here, you should not leave any white spaces, but apply a flat wash across the entire petal. To create depth and variations in tone, you can use a tissue to blot and lift the color from the top of the petal while it is still wet.

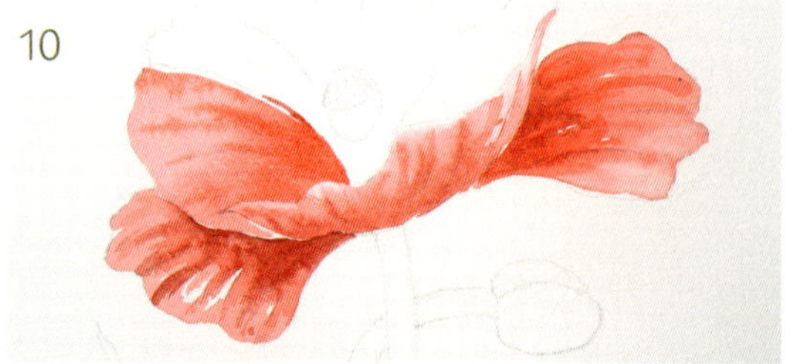

While the surface is still wet, use color 600033 (Deep Scarlet) to outline the petal's texture and deepen the base of the petal.

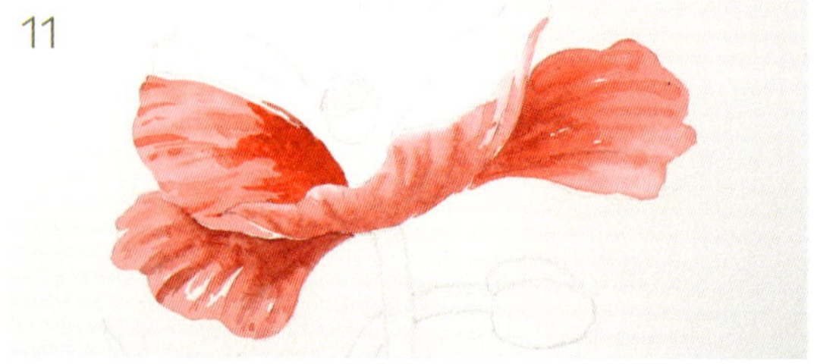

Continue using color 600033 (Deep Scarlet) to enhance the petal's texture and depict the details.

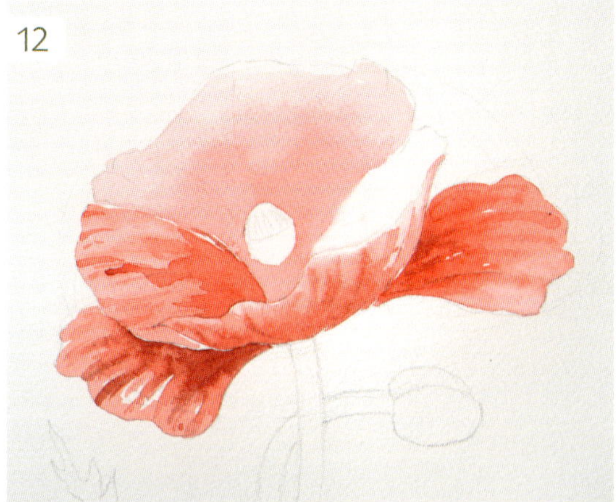

12

Use the same method as in step 9 to paint the center petal.

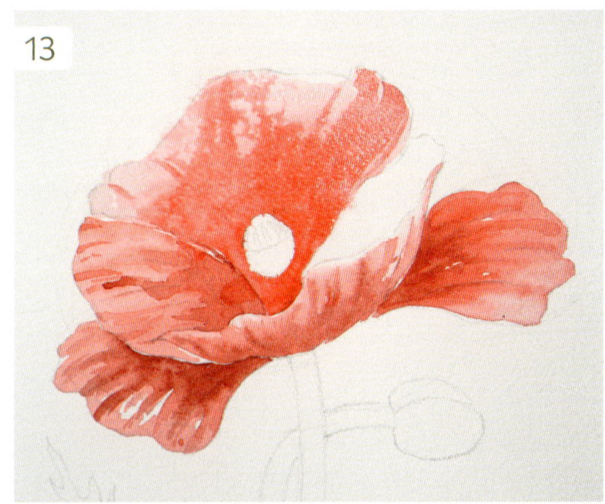

13

While the paper is still wet, use color 600033 (Deep Scarlet) to outline the texture and deepen the base of the petal.

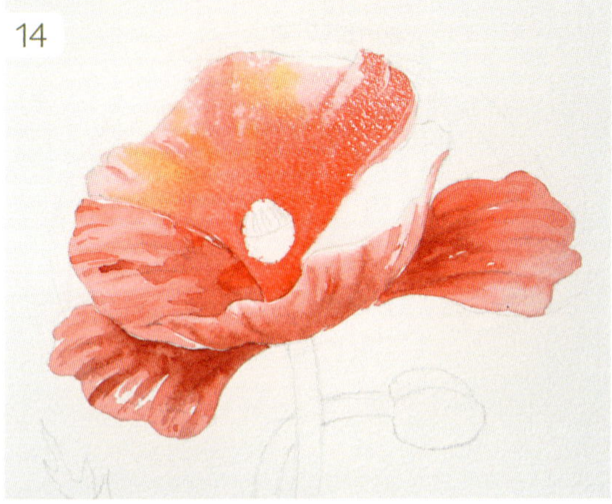

14

While still wet, blend in color 600006 (Aureolin) at the top of the petal to enrich the coloration.

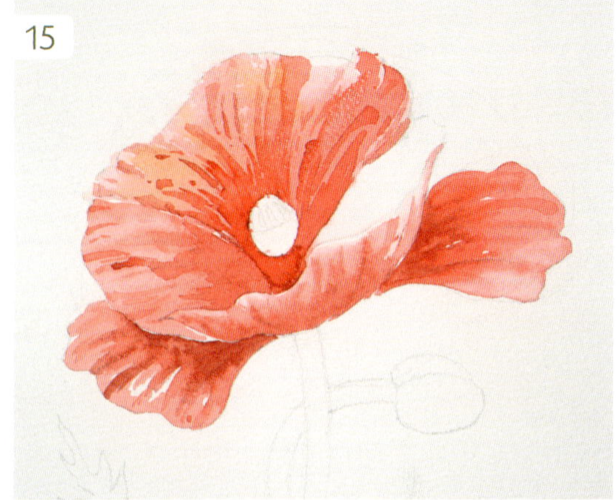

15

Once the painting is completely dry, use a well moistened brush loaded with color 600033 (Deep Scarlet) to paint texture on some petals from the base outward, adding detail.

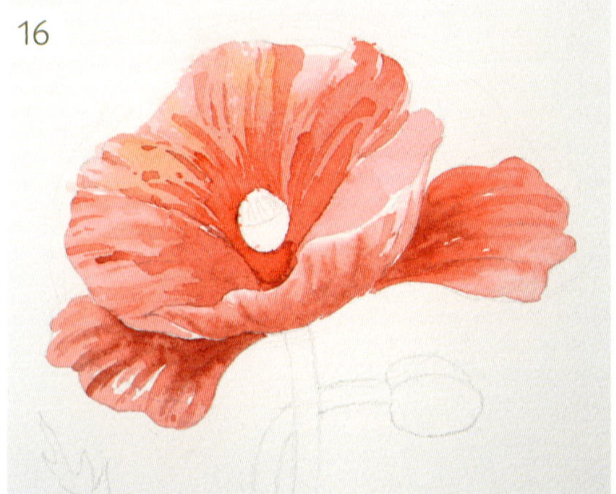

16

Following the same method as in step 9, paint the middle right petal.

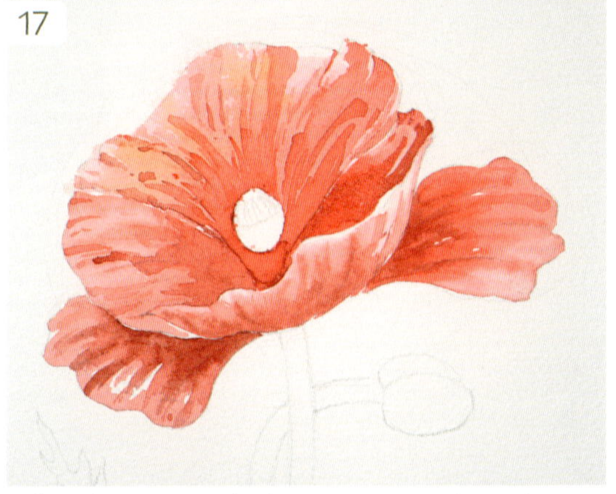

17

Follow the same method as in step 15 to depict the details.

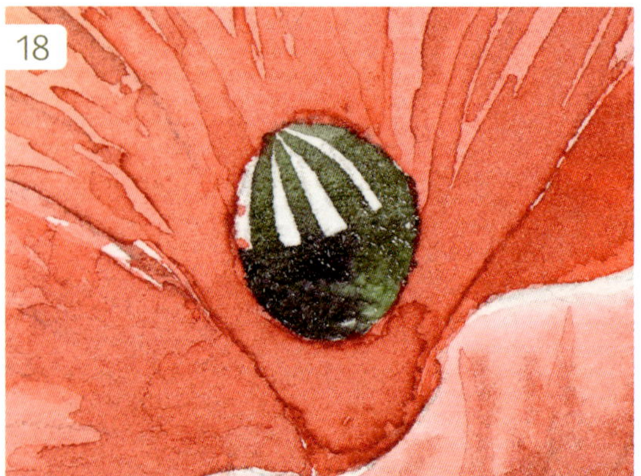

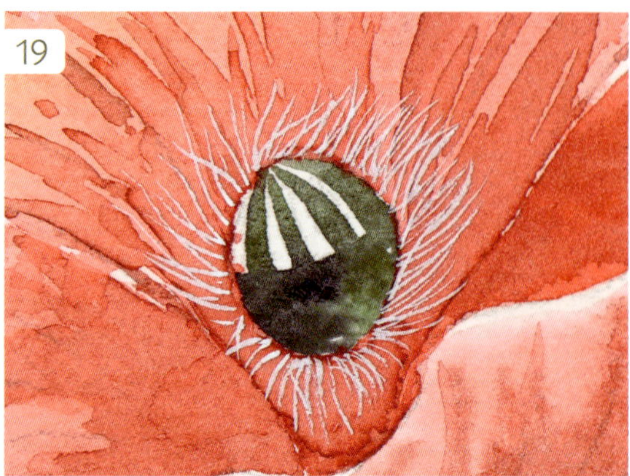

Apply color 600024 (Chromium Green Oxide) along the edge of the flower center's contour, creating stripe-like patterns. While still wet, dab in color 600080 (Phthalo Turquoise) to enhance the shadows.

Use the Black Velvet 3000S brush for watercolor, size 6 to dip into NICKER opaque white gouache, and outline the filaments. Pay attention to the direction of the filaments. They should radiate outward in all directions.

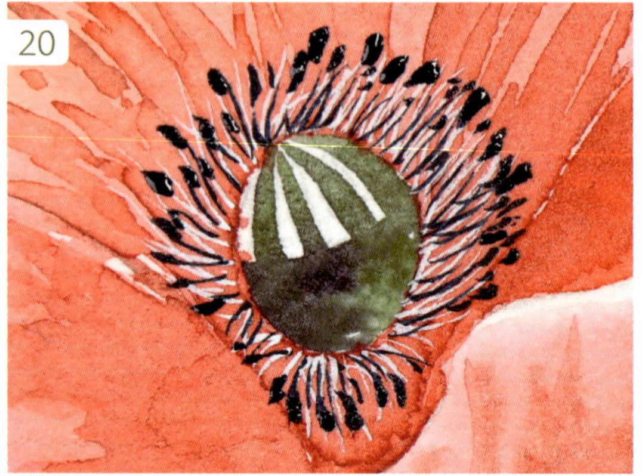

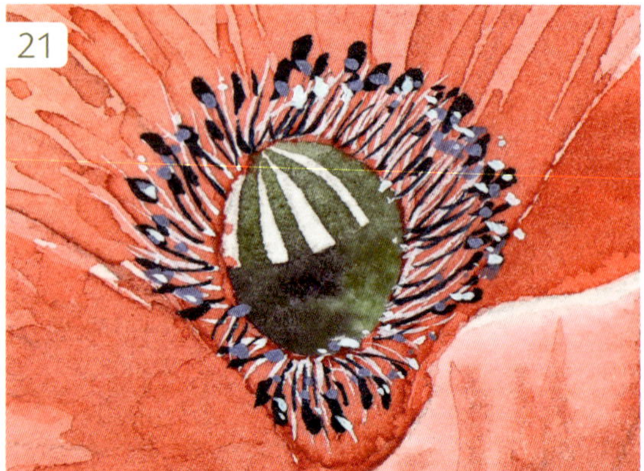

Use color 600080 (Phthalo Turquoise) to outline the dark-colored filaments and dot in the anthers.

Then, use color 600232 (Lavender) and NICKER white opaque gouache to add the light-colored anthers.

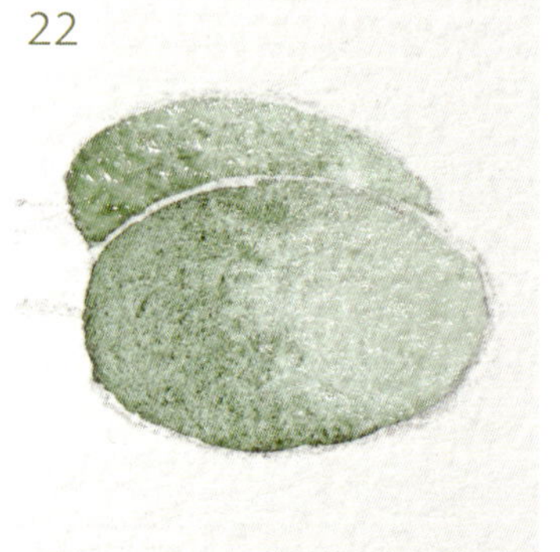

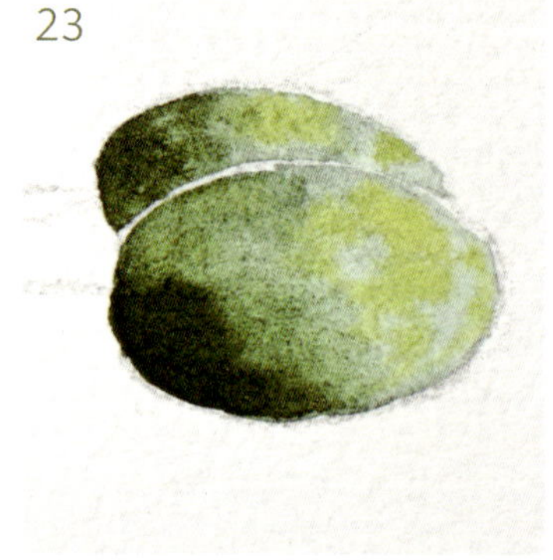

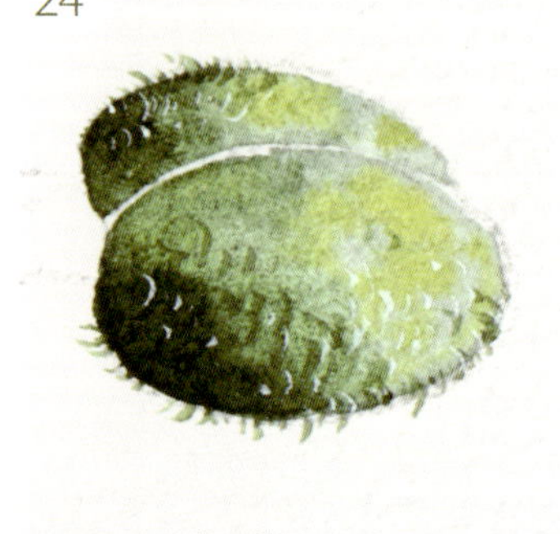

Use a brush with plenty of water to dip into color 600024 (Chromium Green Oxide) and apply a flat wash to the bud, making sure to leave a white line in the middle to prevent colors from bleeding into each other. While still wet, use a tissue to blot the top of the bud, creating a gradient of light and dark.

While still wet, blend in yellow color 600006 (Aureolin) at the top of the bud, and green color 600197 (Green Apatite Genuine) at the base.

Use color 600197 (Green Apatite Genuine) and NICKER opaque white gouache to paint the silk hairs, paying attention to the variation in density and length.

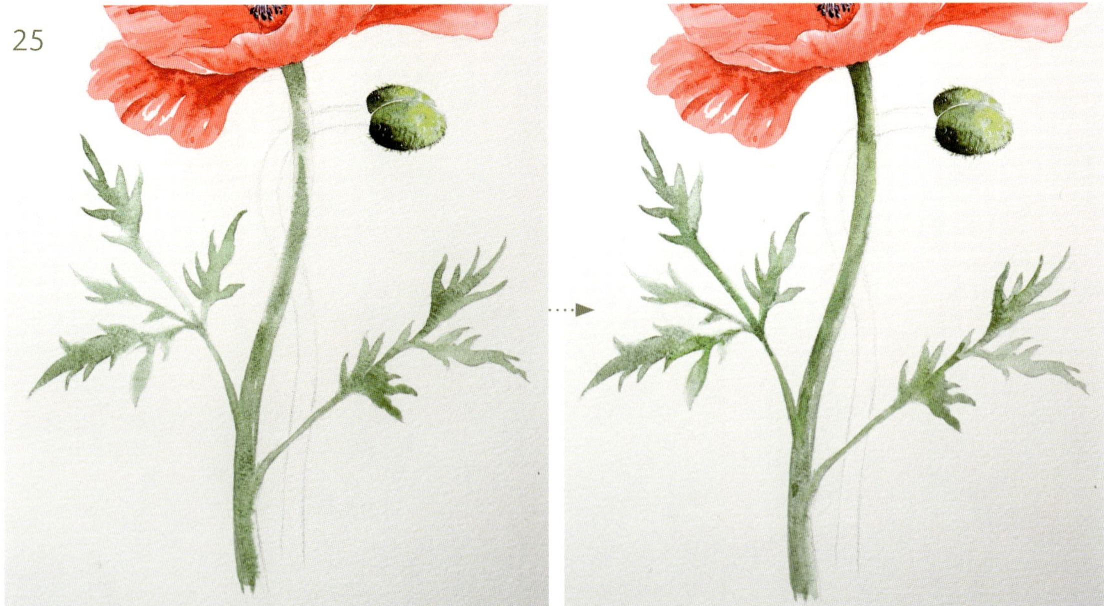

▲ First, lightly lay down a base of color 600024 (Chromium Green Oxide) on the stem and leaves. While still wet, add touches of color 600197 (Green Apatite Genuine), applying deeper green along one side of the stem and on the stem near the flower, and randomly dabbing the leaves.

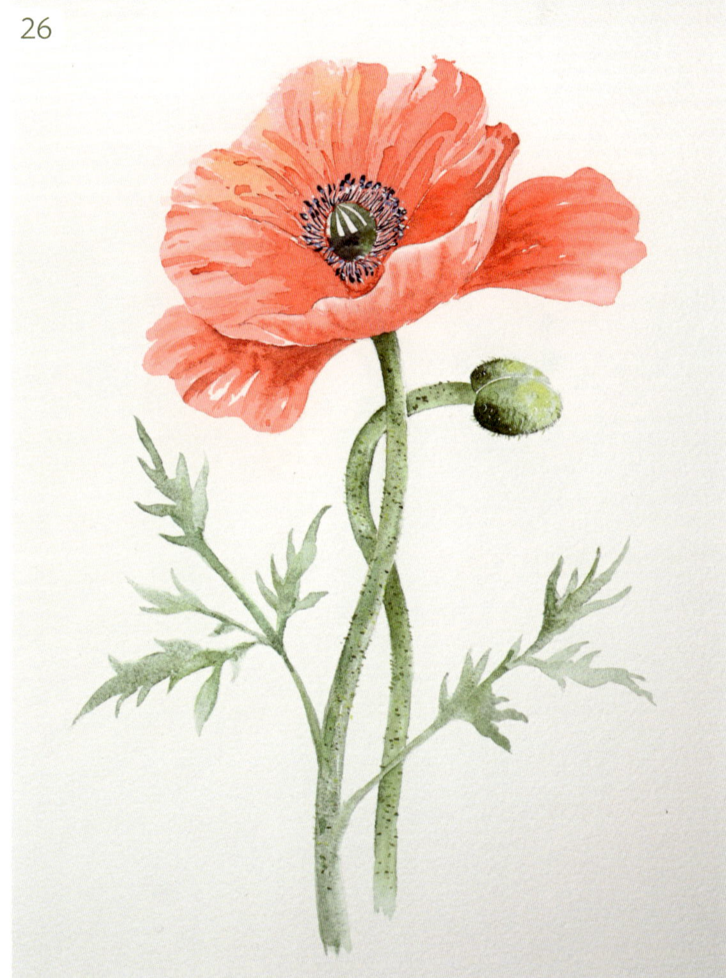

26

▶ Using the same colors and method from step 25, paint the flower stem of the bud. Once the painting is completely dry, randomly dot some silk hairs with color 600197 (Green Apatite Genuine) on the stems. This completes the garden's poppy.

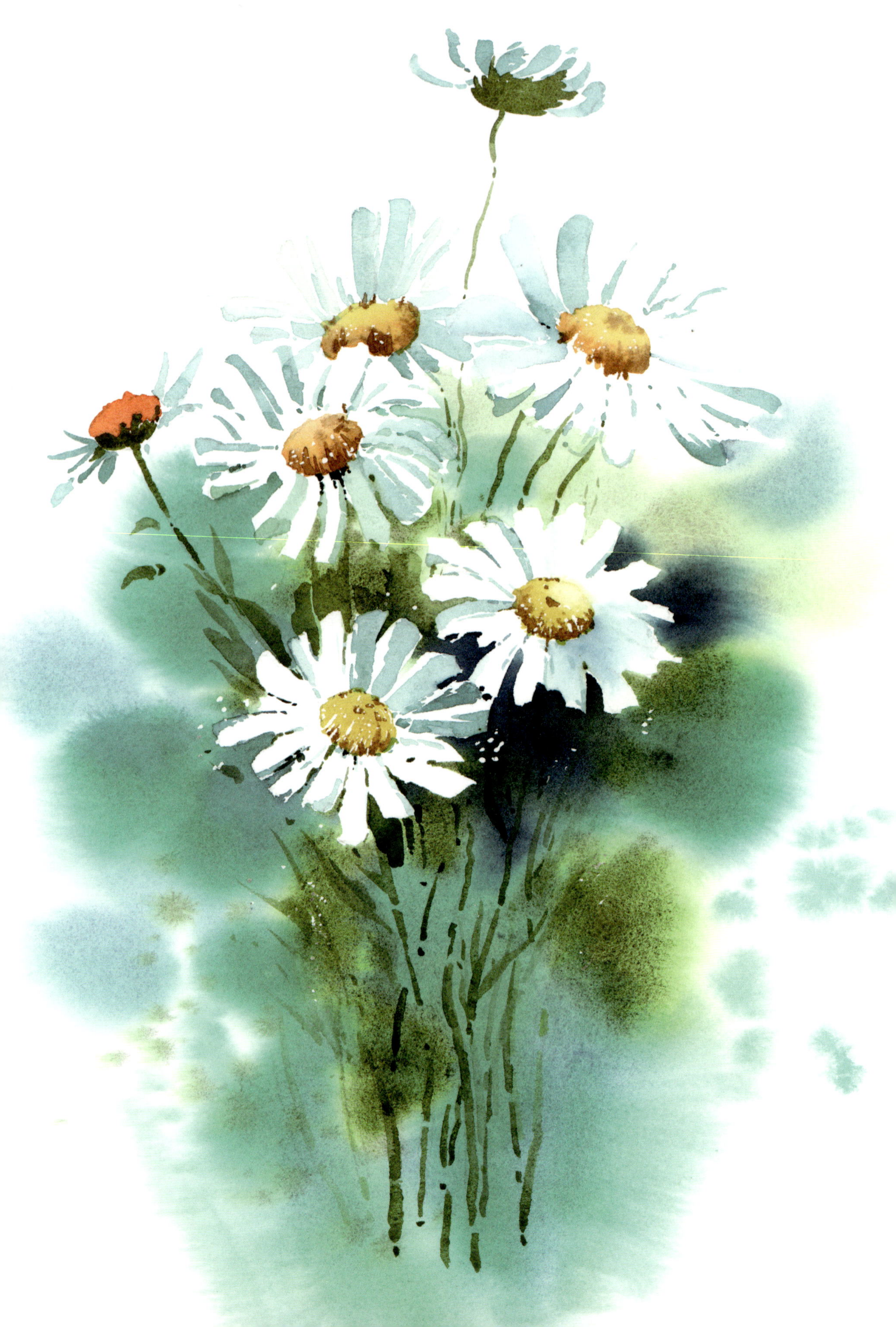

Daisy

The meaning of daisies is "hidden love" or "eternal protection." Their delicate and adorable appearance evokes a sense of tenderness, and they often bloom in my garden during spring, symbolizing hope and rebirth as the earth awakens. Whenever I prepare to give someone a bouquet, I always bend down to gather a few daisies. What they convey is a pure and selfless emotion, as well as silent care and eternal companionship.

Paint Brand
DANIEL SMITH

Color Codes
- 600197: Green Apatite Genuine
- 600080: Phthalo Turquoise
- 600078: Phthalo Green (Blue Shade)
- 600232: Lavender
- 600163: Amazonite Genuine
- 600006: Aureolin (Cobalt Yellow)
- 600011: Burnt Umber
- 600024: Chromium Green Oxide
- 600064: Organic Vermilion

Auxiliary Material
Masking fluid

Recommended Watercolor Paper
ARCHES watercolor paper, cold pressed, 140 lb/300 g/m^2

Recommended Brush
Black Velvet 3000S brush for watercolor, size 8

Key Challenges
1. How to portray the white petals of the daisy.
2. Handling the background gradation effect.

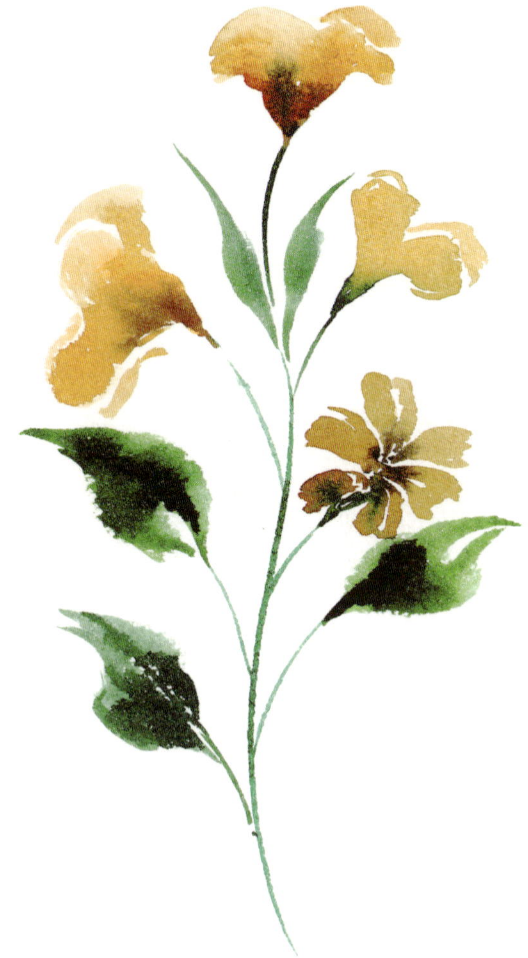

Fig. 26 **Yellow Wildflowers**
Perhaps there's a small, nameless wildflower in your garden—unnoticed, yet reaching in its own way toward your bright, blooming world.

Steps

1

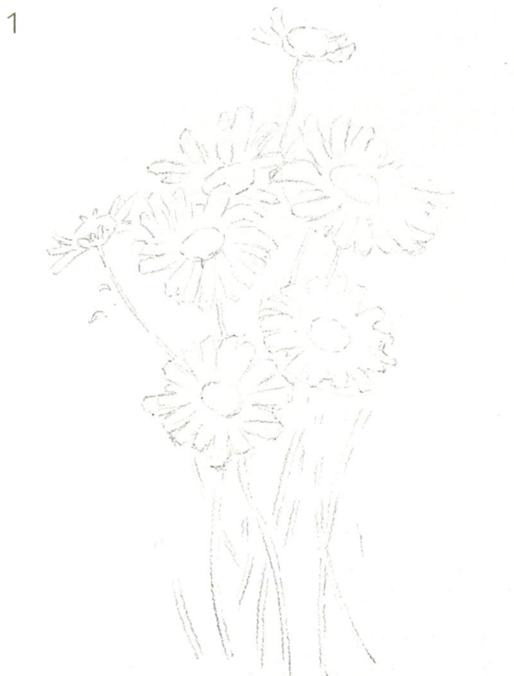

First, lightly sketch the outline of the daisies and the flower stems with a pencil. Pay attention to the delicate, winding shape of the stems, and carefully consider the spatial relationship between each flower, which ones are in front and which are behind.

2

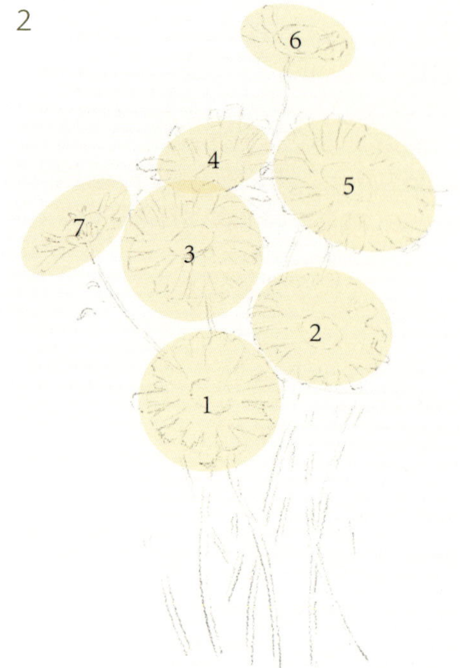

For the sake of teaching clarity, I have numbered each daisy. The following steps will refer to these numbers for easy identification.

3

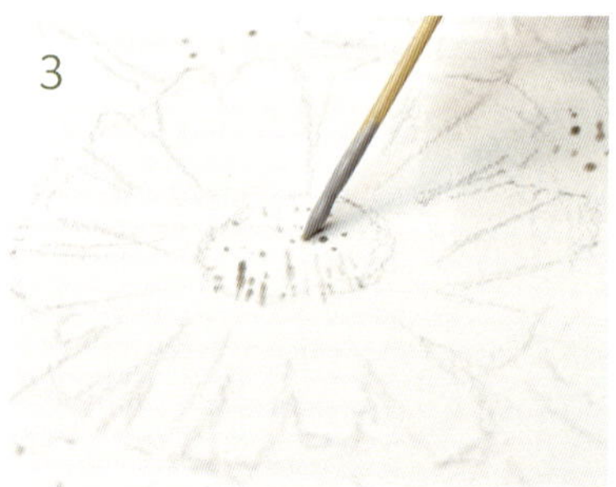

Use a toothpick to gently apply masking fluid to the center of each daisy and the blank areas in the background to represent the highlight regions.

4

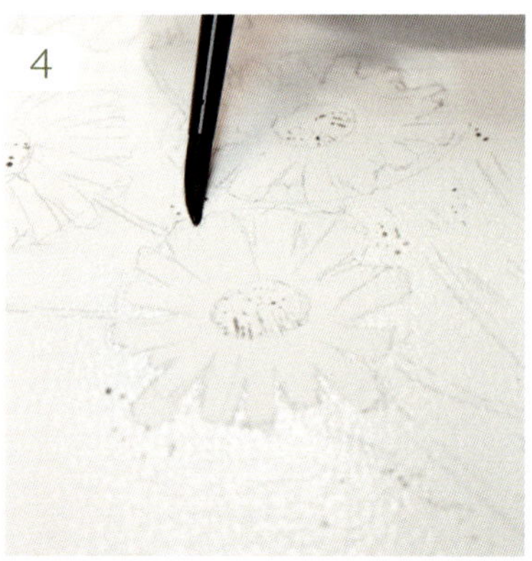

Brush clean water over all areas outside the flowers, paying special attention to the gaps between the petals. Ensure there is enough water in these areas, as insufficient water can cause these gaps to dry quickly, making it harder for the color to blend smoothly.

5

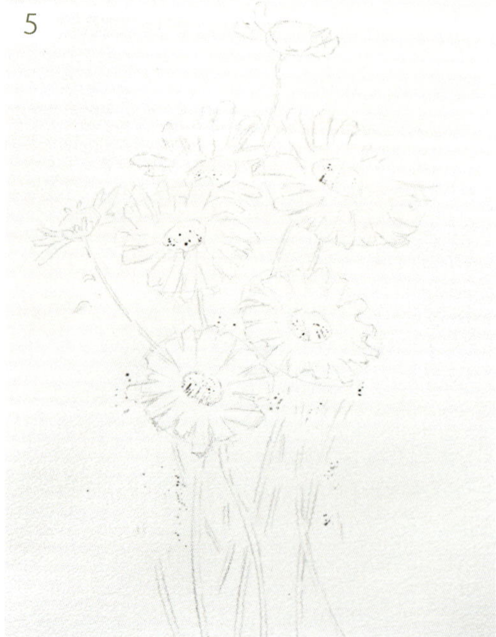

The image shows the overall effect after applying masking fluid and brushing clean water on the paper.

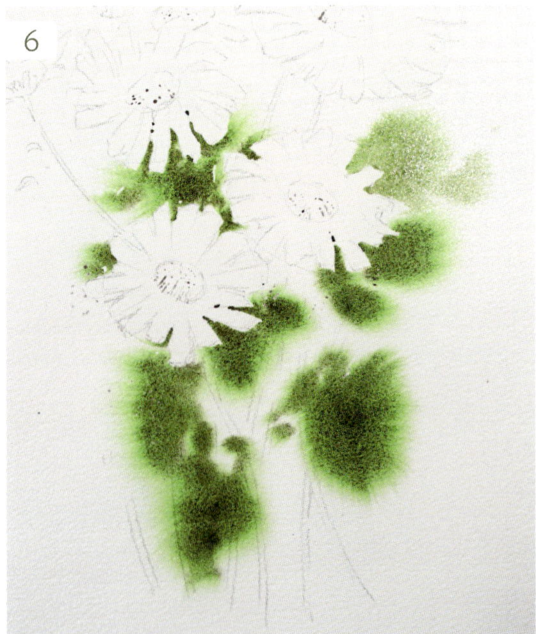

6

Since the lower half of the composition primarily features leaves, we won't focus on detailed leaf shapes. Instead, we'll use the gradient technique to create a sense of lushness. First, while the paper is still wet, apply color 600197 (Green Apatite Genuine) around the lower part of the flower bouquet, allowing the color to naturally spread and blend, representing the base color of the leaves.

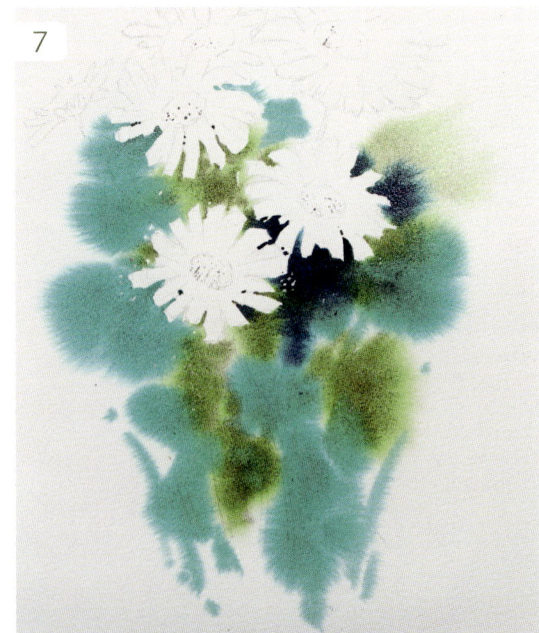

7

Use a more concentrated (less diluted) color 600080 (Phthalo Turquoise) to paint the darker shadows beneath the flowers. Then, immediately use color 600078 (Phthalo Green) to paint the surrounding area. Compared to color 600197 (Green Apatite Genuine), color 600078 (Phthalo Green) has a lower saturation and brightness, so a gradation of light and dark tones is formed between the two.

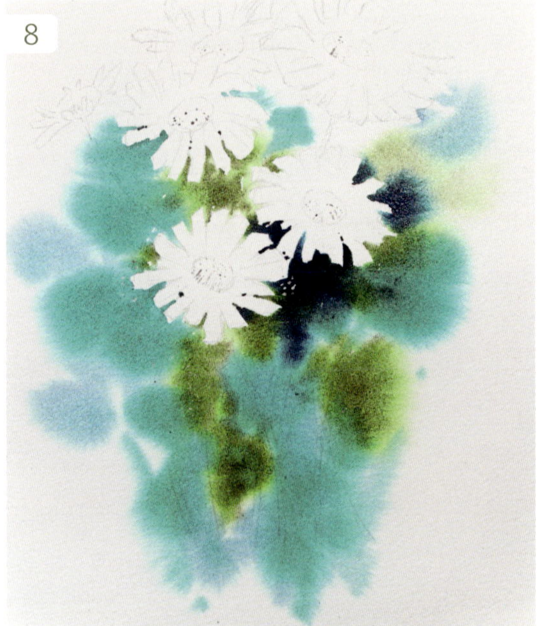

8

Use a highly diluted light color 600232 (Lavender) to paint the outermost area, creating a colorful atmosphere for the flower cluster. This is only an auxiliary tone, applied lightly, to maintain the overall harmony with green as the dominant color.

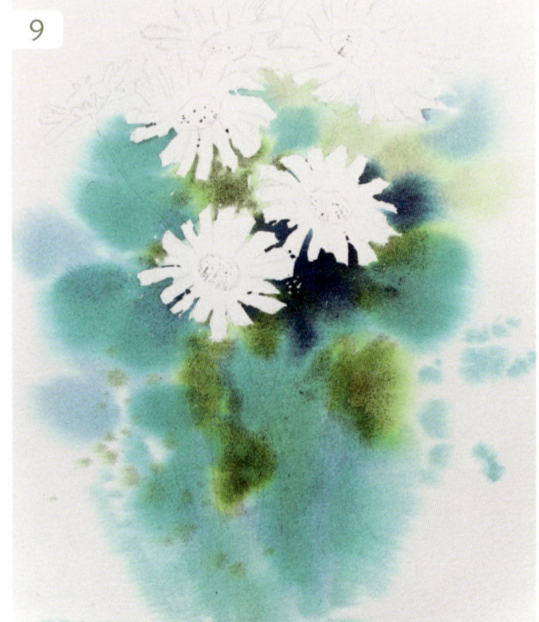

9

Use highly diluted color 600197 (Green Apatite Genuine) and color 600078 (Phthalo Green) to scatter and dot the outer edges. Note that steps 6 to 9 should be done while the background paper still has moisture and is not fully dry.

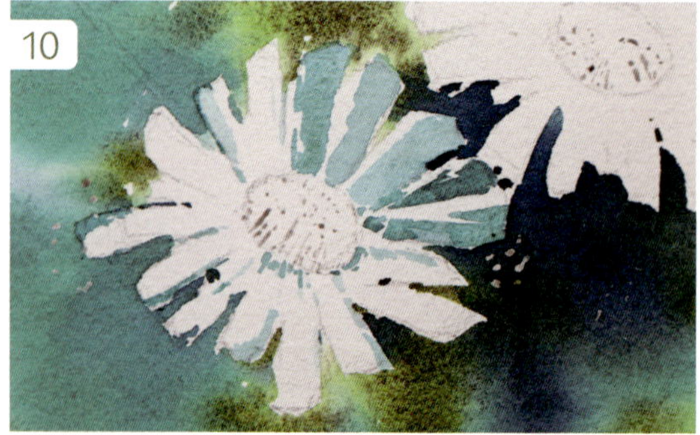

Wait for the painting to dry completely, then use color 600163 (Amazonite Genuine) to paint the shadow of flower 1. Keep the brush relaxed and apply the shadow mainly along the edges of the petals, avoiding covering the whole petal. Additionally, due to the varying water content in the brush, the same color may appear in different shades, which is why the shadow of flower 1 is created using a single color, yet the result has varying degrees of light and dark.

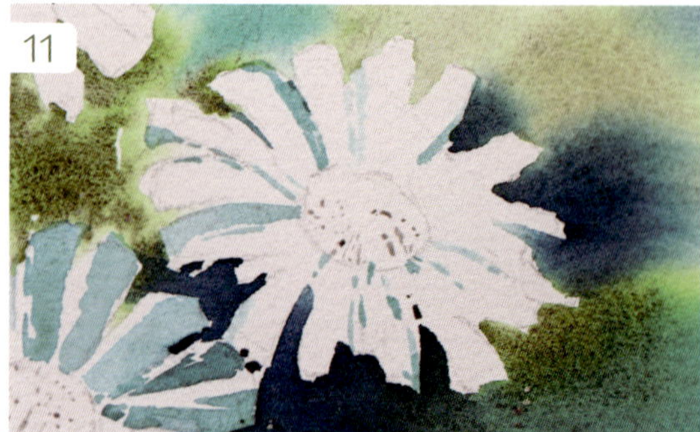

Use the same method and colors from step 10 to paint the shadow of flower 2.

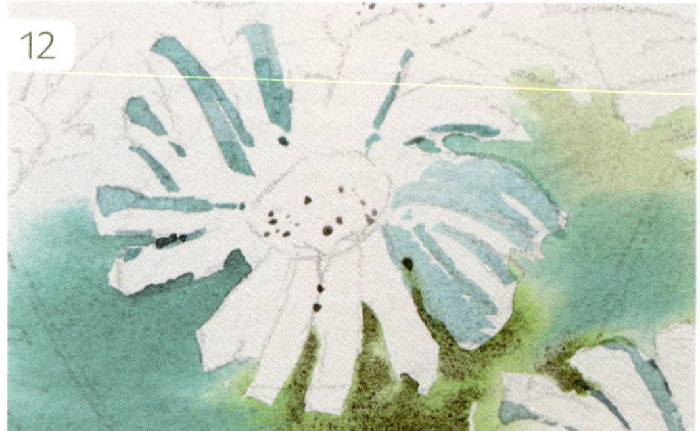

Use the same method and colors from step 10 to paint the shadow of flower 3.

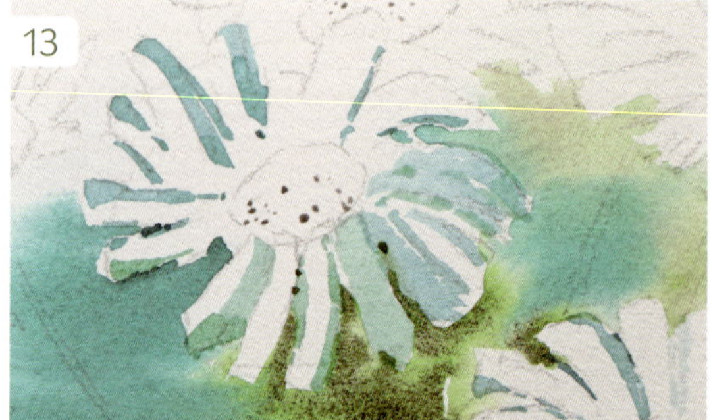

When painting flower 3, we can mix color 600163 (Amazonite Genuine) and color 600197 (Green Apatite Genuine) in a 2:1 ratio to paint the shadow on the lower part of the petals. Since this flower has a strong green background underneath, adding some color 600197 (Green Apatite Genuine) will help reduce the influence of the surrounding color.

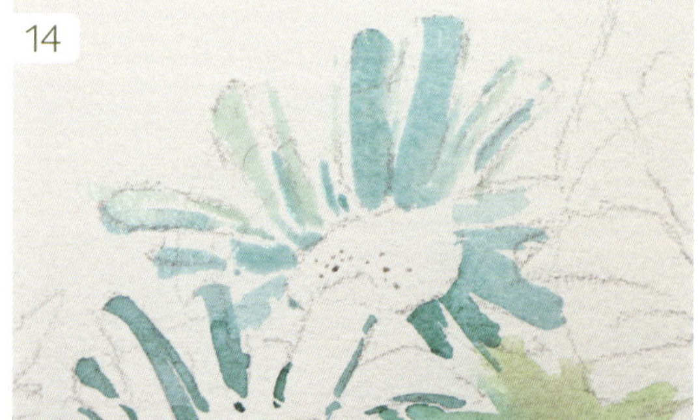

Use diluted color 600197 (Green Apatite Genuine) and color 600163 (Amazonite Genuine) to paint the shadow on flower 4. The area where it connects with flower 3 should be slightly darker due to the overlap between the flowers.

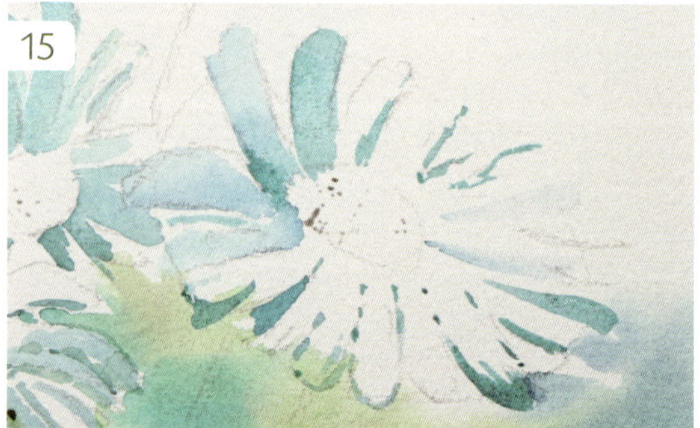

To add variation to the painting, in addition to continuing to use color 600163 (Amazonite Genuine), use color 600080 (Phthalo Turquoise) and color 600197 (Green Apatite Genuine) to paint the shadow of flower 5. Be sure to keep the colors light, and you can even mix the three colors together in pairs to apply.

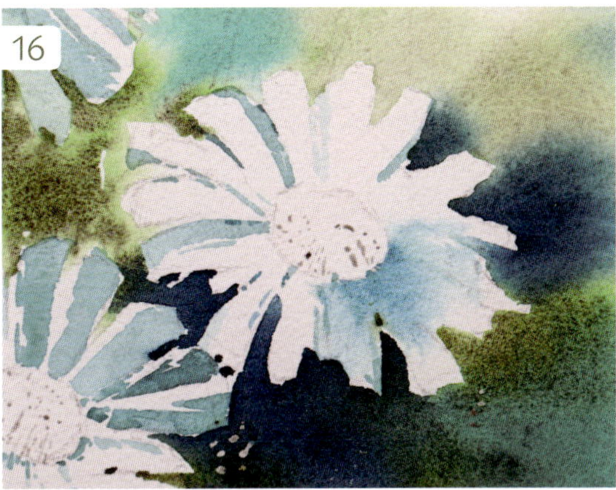

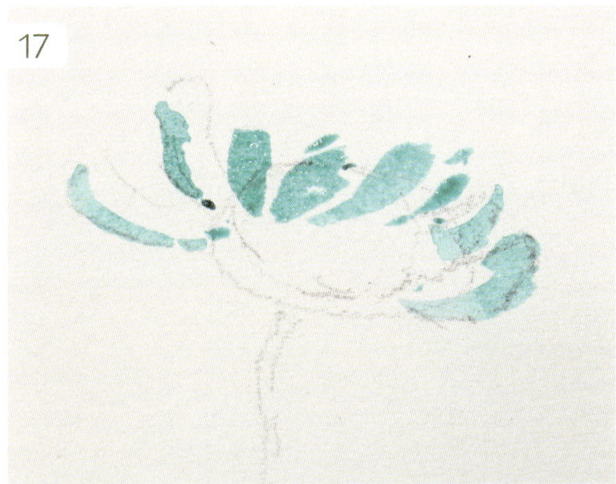

As we mentioned earlier, the shadows on the petals are influenced by the surrounding colors. Now, we can go back and lightly add a layer of shadow to the petals on flower 2 with color 600080 (Phthalo Turquoise).

Use the same method from step 10 and color 600163 (Amazonite Genuine) to paint the shadow of flower 6. Since this flower only shows its back, every petal needs to be painted. However, be careful not to fill in all the petals completely, as it's important to maintain a sense of airiness in the painting.

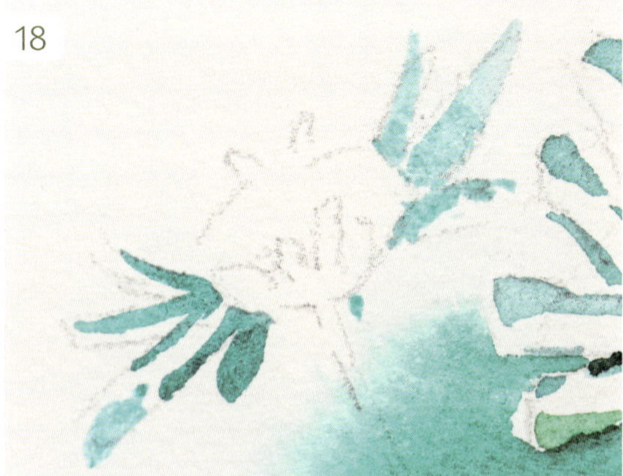

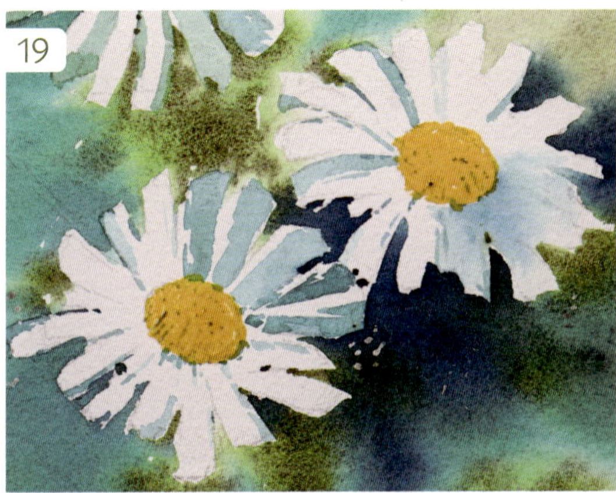

Use the same color, method, and key points as in step 17 to paint the shadow of flower 7.

Use a relatively concentrated color 600006 (Aureolin) to paint the stamens of flowers 1 and 2.

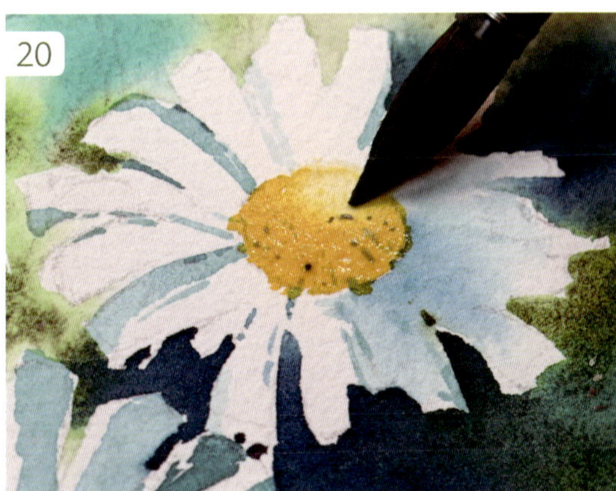

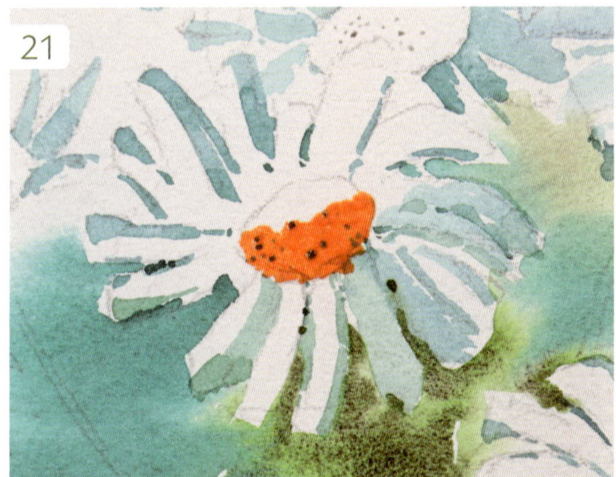

Use a clean, dry brush to gently wipe the stamen of flower 2, using a color-lightening technique to create highlights.

Mix color 600006 (Aureolin) and color 600064 (Organic Vermilion) in a 2:1 ratio to create an orange color, and use this to paint the darker area of the stamen in flower 3.

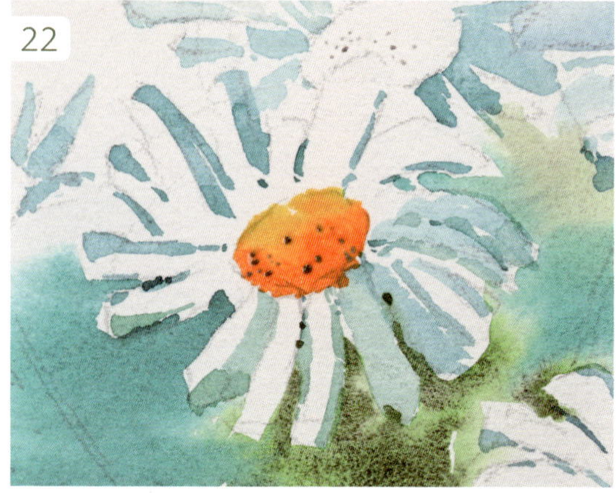

Use color 600006 (Aureolin) to paint the lighter area of the stamen in flower 3, merging it naturally with the darker areas.

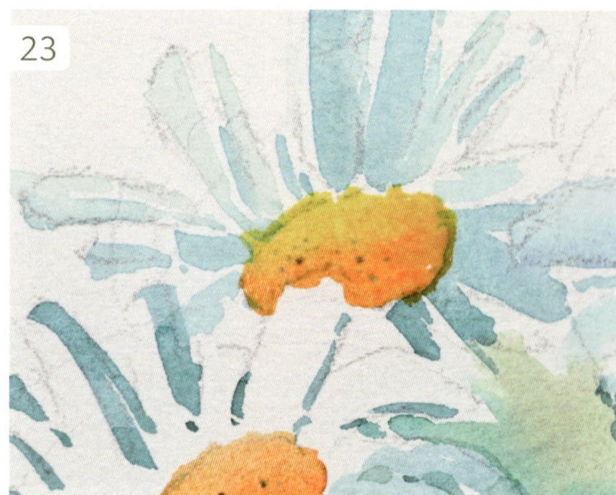

Use the same colors and method as in steps 21 and 22 to paint the stamen of flower 4.

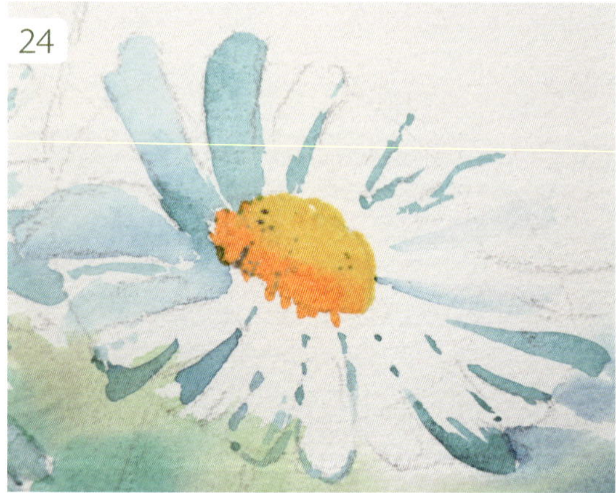

Use the same colors and method as in steps 21 and 22 to paint the stamen of flower 5.

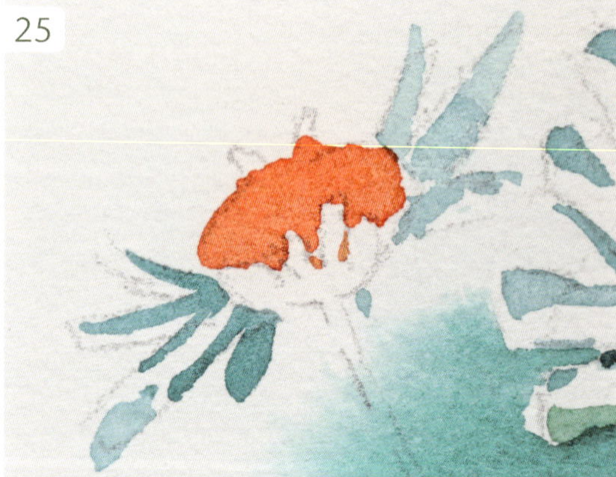

Lightly paint the stamen of flower 7 using color 600064 (Organic Vermilion).

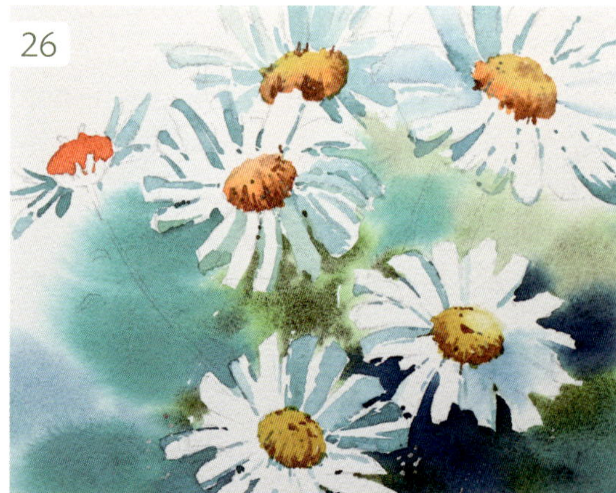

After completing the base color of all the stamens, use color 600011 (Aureolin) to paint the texture of the stamens. Note that the stamens are semi-spherical in shape, so our brushstrokes should follow the curvature of the surface, with the tips of the lines naturally converging towards the center.

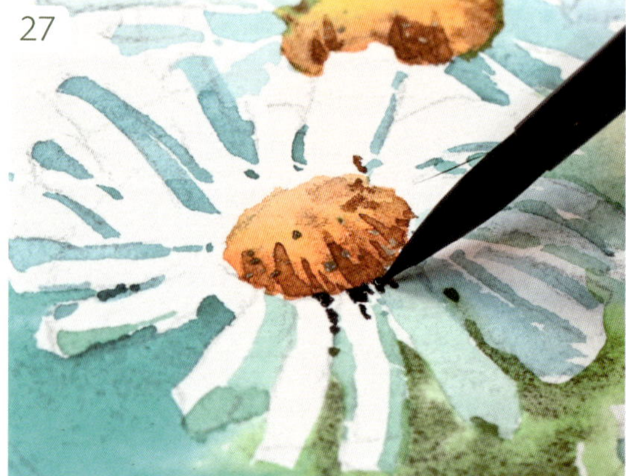

Mix equal parts of color 600011 (Aureolin) and color 600080 (Phthalo Turquoise), and delicately dot the areas where the petals meet with this deeper tone to enhance the details.

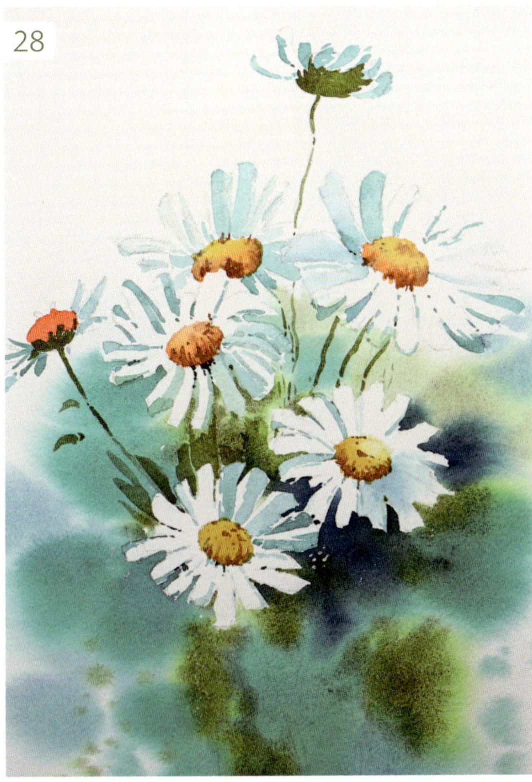

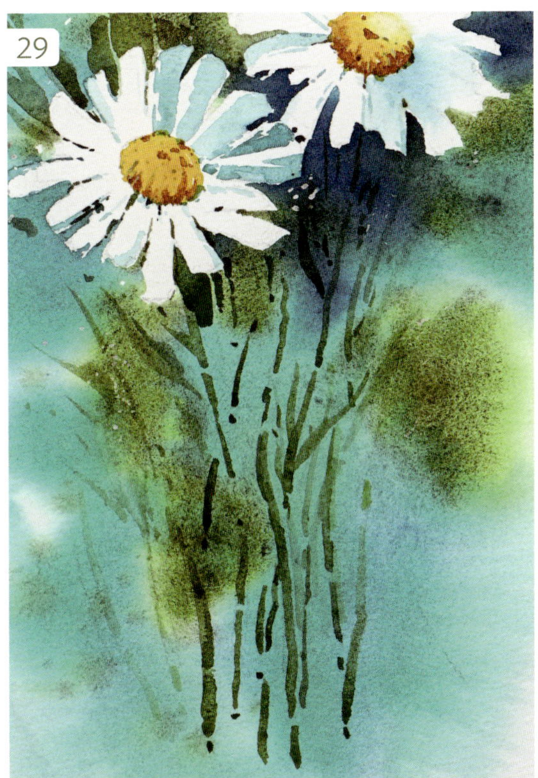

Use color 600197 (Green Apatite Genuine) to paint the flower receptacles and the flower stems on the upper part of the picture. The daisy's stem is thin and flexible, so we can use curved, broken, and intermittent brushstrokes to depict it. The upper part should be relatively sparse, only a few stems are needed. Then, with color 600011 (Aureolin), deepen some of the darker areas.

Use color 600197 (Green Apatite Genuine) and color 600024 (Chromium Green Oxide) to paint the lower part of the flower stems. Pay attention to the variation in color depth and the spacing of the stems. At this point, relax your brushwork and feel free to loosely sketch a few leaves. Then, use color 600011 (Aureolin) to darken some of the shadowed areas.

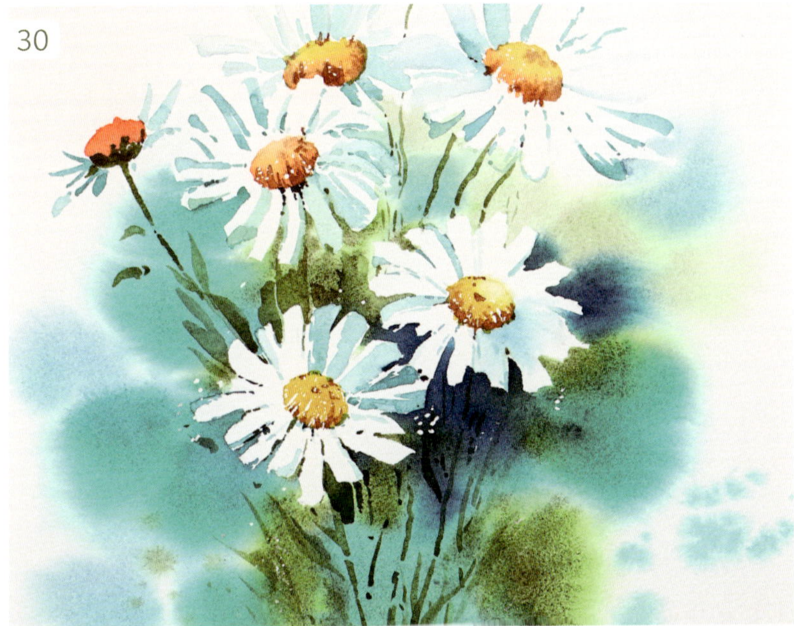

Erase the masking fluid and any noticeable pencil marks. The daisies are now complete.

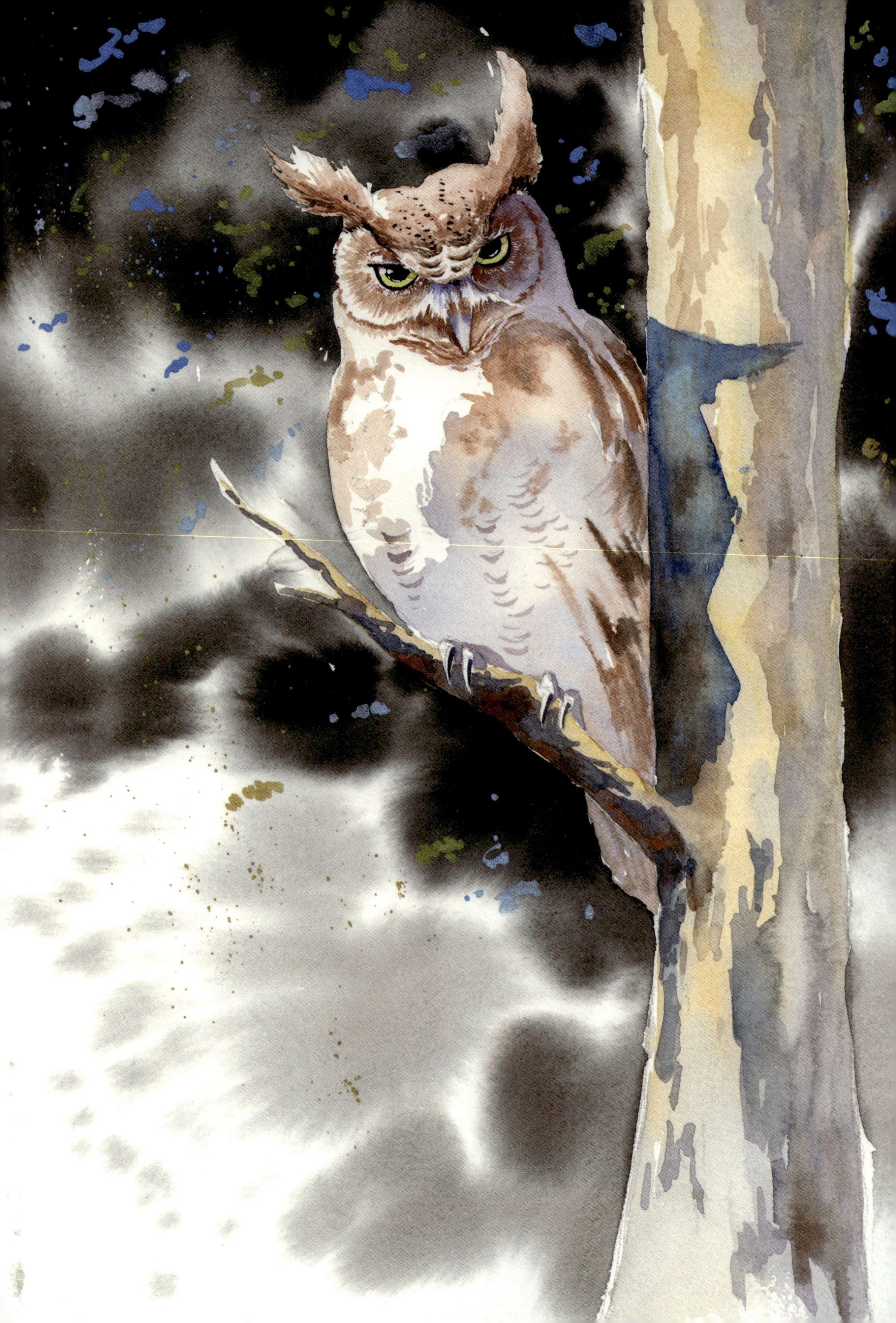

Owl

As the night deepens, the garden falls into slumber, with only the owl standing silently on a branch, becoming the guardian of the night. Its eyes shine like starlight, piercing through the darkness, watching the rustling movements in the grass. In this moment, the garden is no longer a place of daytime bustle, but its domain—silent, mysterious, yet brimming with hidden vitality.

Paint Brand
DANIEL SMITH

Color Codes
- 600010: Burnt Sienna
- 600003: Lamp Black
- 600057: Moonglow
- 600173: Verditer Blue
- 600006: Aureolin (Cobalt Yellow)
- 600009: Buff Titanium
- 600233: Raw Sienna Light
- 600011: Burnt Umber
- 600082: Prussian Blue

Auxiliary Materials
NICKER opaque white gouache
DANIEL SMITH pearlescent paints

Recommended Watercolor Paper
ARCHES watercolor paper, cold pressed,
140 lb/300 g/m^2

Recommended Brush
Black Velvet 3000S brush for watercolor,
size 8

Key Challenges
1. Depicting feathers.
2. Rendering the texture of tree.
3. Handling the relationship between the subject and background.

Steps

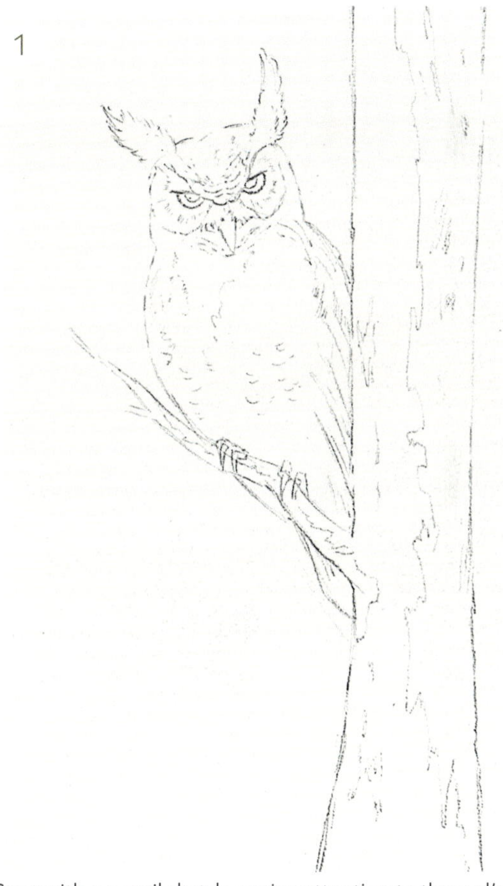

Start with a pencil sketch, paying attention to the owl's facial features and its spatial relationship with the tree trunk in the composition.

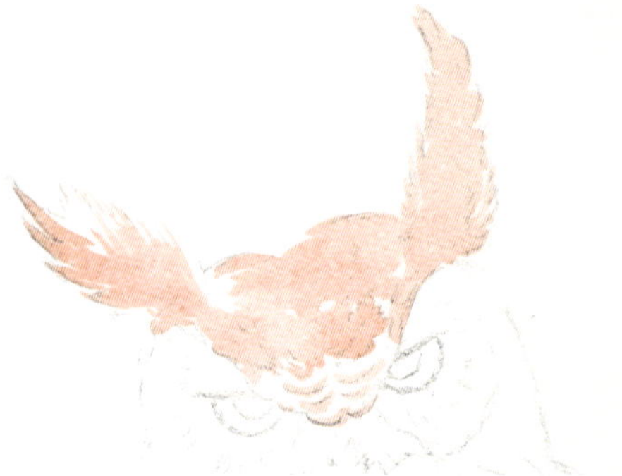

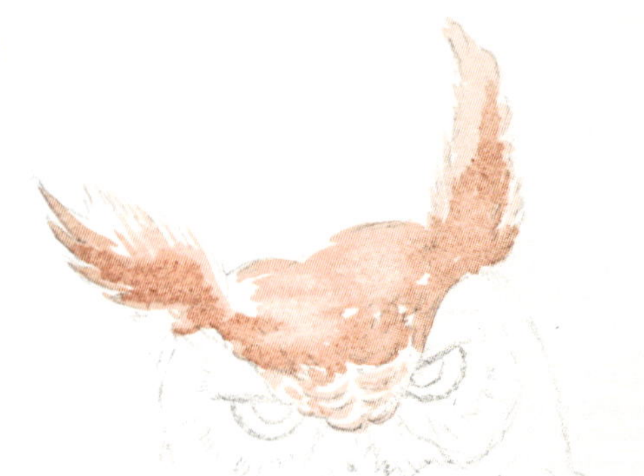

Before applying color, let's first determine the areas of light and shadow in the composition. Even at night, the owl would be affected by the garden's lighting. We assume the light is coming from the left side of the composition, so both the owl and the tree trunk will have the left side as the lit area and the right side as the shadowed area. With this in mind, we begin adding color. Start by using color 600010 (Burnt Sienna) to lightly lay a base color on the top of the owl's head, making sure to paint individual feathers along the edges.

While the previous layer is still wet, use a less diluted version of color 600010 (Burnt Sienna) to deepen the shadowed areas. This will create the basic contrast between light and dark.

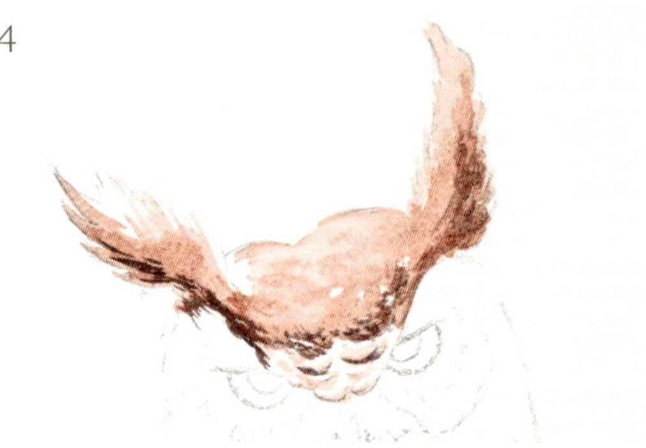

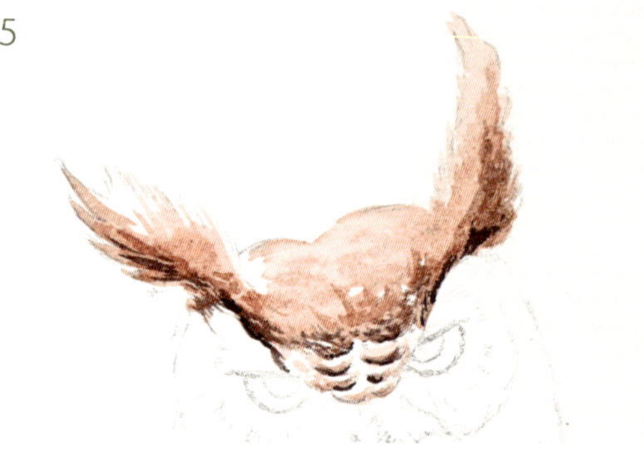

Once the painting is completely dry, mix color 600010 (Burnt Sienna), color 600003 (Lamp Black), and color 600057 (Moonglow) in a 5:1:3 ratio. Use light, short brushstrokes to outline the dark feathers. This will delicately show the texture and shadows of the feathers, enhancing the layers of the painting.

Continue mixing color 600010 (Burnt Sienna) and color 600003 (Lamp Black) in a 3:1 ratio to create the darkest shade. With a few decisive brushstrokes, outline the deepest areas. Be sure to apply the paint firmly and avoid overworking the strokes.

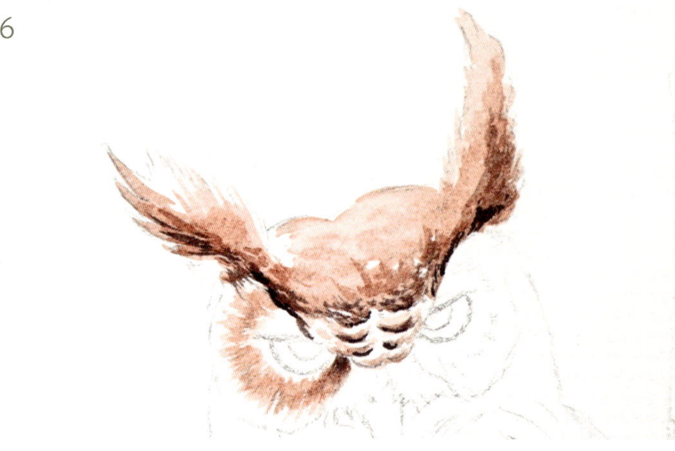

Next, paint the fur around the eyes. At this point, you can dry the brush by blotting the moisture on a tissue, then gently rub the brush with your fingers to splay the bristles. Pick up some color 600010 (Burnt Sienna) and lightly sweep to create the texture of the fur. The color near the center of the eye socket should be deepened to portray the shadows.

The purpose of drying the brush is to prevent excess moisture from gathering, allowing for a more precise depiction of fine, natural fur textures.

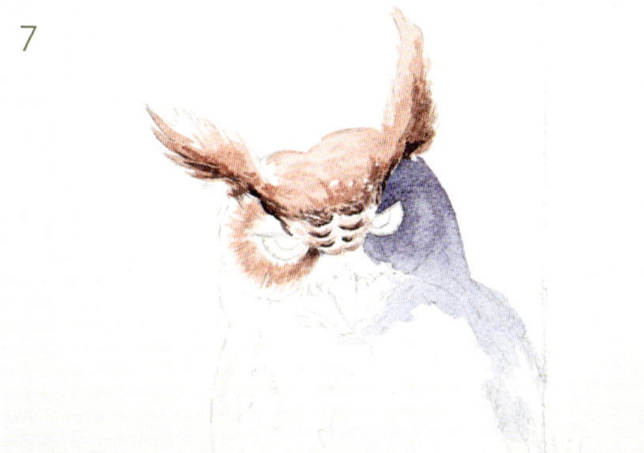

7

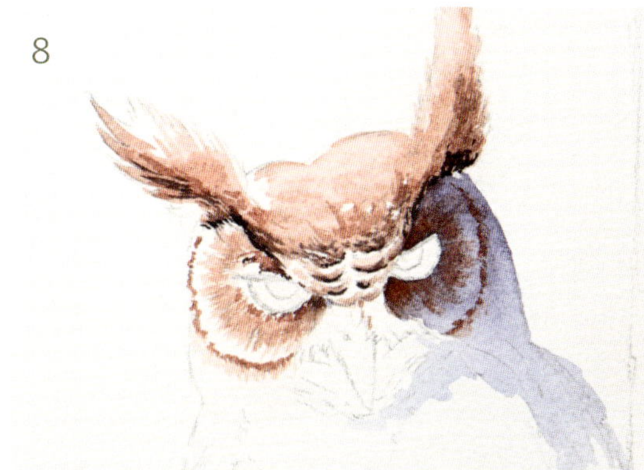

8

Mix color 600173 (Verditer Blue) and color 600057 (Moonglow) in a 2:1 ratio, and gently apply a light layer of color to the owl's face and back in the backlit area.

Using the same method as in step 6, use color 600010 (Burnt Sienna) to gently brush out the fine feathers around the owl's eye in the backlit area, and also outline the ring of feathers around both sides of the cheeks. Take note that the feathers around the cheeks and eyes vary in length.

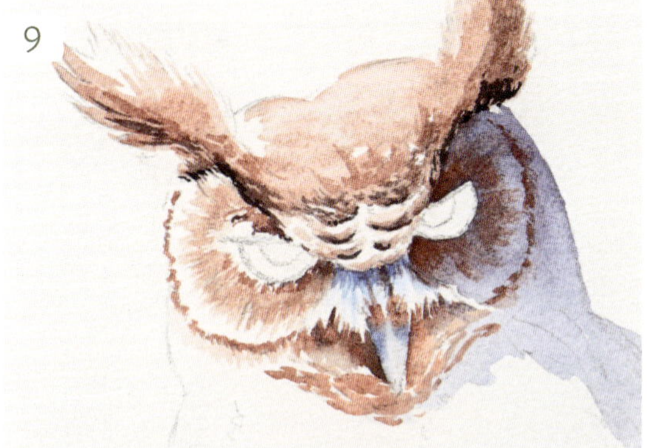

9

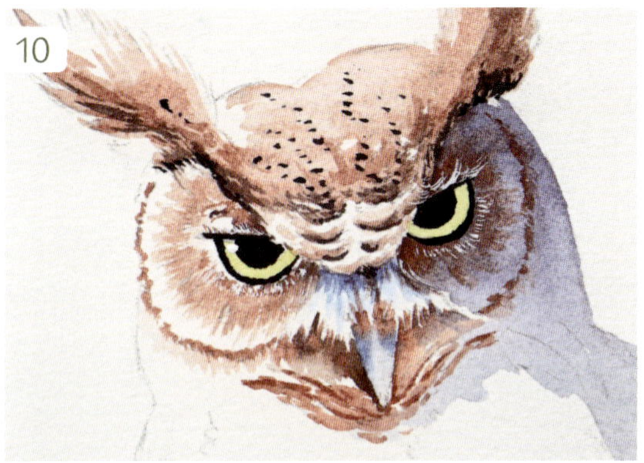

10

Use color 600173 (Verditer Blue) to outline the blue feathers above the owl's beak. Then, mix color 600010 (Burnt Sienna) and color 600173 (Verditer Blue) to paint the shape of the beak. Keep in mind that the beak has a conical shape, with the center as the highlight area, which should be left blank. Finally, use color 600010 (Burnt Sienna) to sketch out the texture of the feathers on the owl's neck.

First, mix color 600006 (Aureolin) and color 600009 (Buff Titanium) in equal proportions to create a light yellow color. Use this to paint the iris of the eyes. Then, use color 600003 (Lamp Black) to outline the eyelids, pupils, and the markings on the top of the head. Be mindful of the spacing and density of the markings on the top of the head. Finally, use opaque white gouache to carefully paint the white feathers around the eyes.

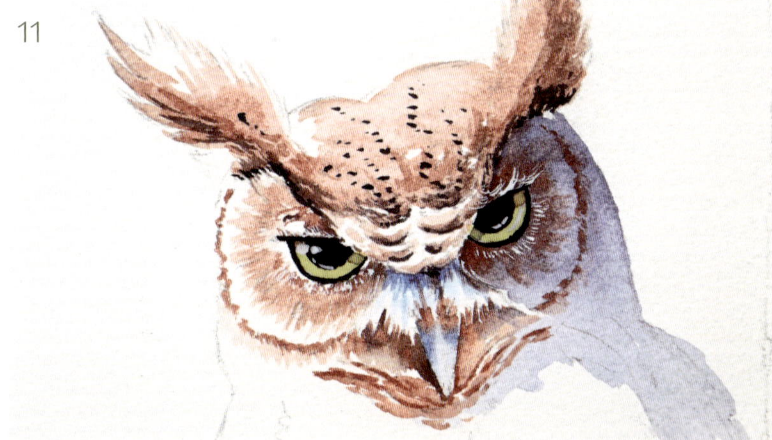

11

Finally, lightly paint the shadow of the eyelids above the yellow iris using color 600010 (Burnt Sienna). Then, use NICKER opaque white paint to add highlights to the eyes.

12

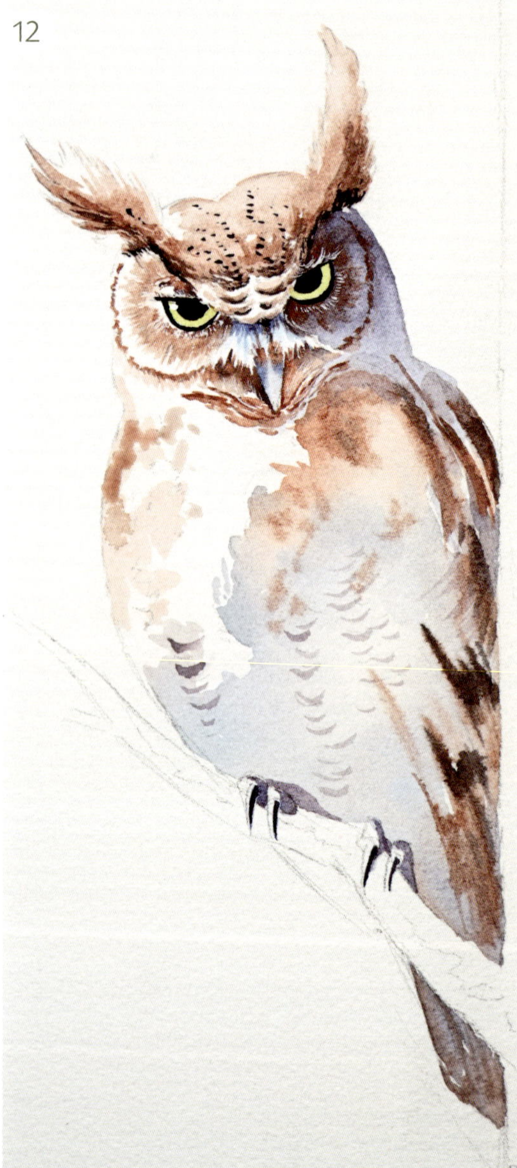

13

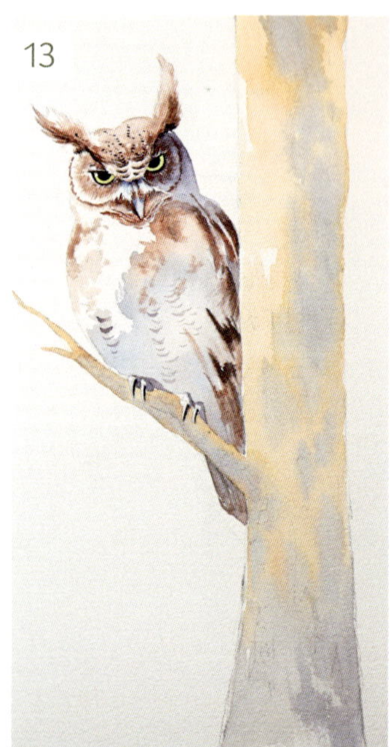

Moisten the tree trunk and branch with clean water. While it's still wet, mix color 600233 (Raw Sienna Light) and color 600011 (Burnt Umber) in equal parts to create a light yellow-brown color and apply it evenly to the trunk and branch. Then, use a highly diluted mix of color 600173 (Verditer Blue) to paint the backlit area of the tree, establishing the initial light and shadow contrast.

14

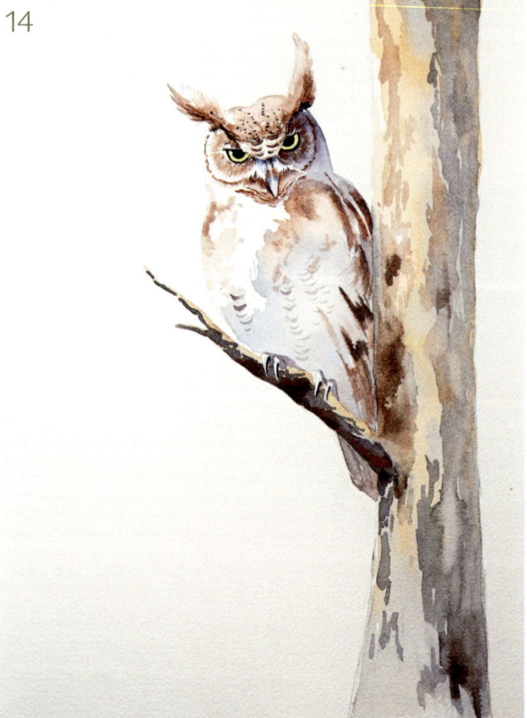

Next, let's work on the abdomen, wings, and tail feathers. Start by moistening the areas that need to be colored with clean water, but be careful to leave the highlight areas dry. While the paper is still wet, apply highly diluted color 600010 (Burnt Sienna) and color 600173 (Verditer Blue), allowing the colors to naturally merge and create a soft color transition. Once the paper is about 70% dry (the surface no longer reflects light, but it feels damp and cool to the touch), use the darker color 600010 (Burnt Sienna) to outline the shape of the wings and tail feathers, paying attention to the direction of the feathers. Then, use color 600057 (Moonglow) to depict some darker soft feather textures on the abdomen and the shadow cast by the claws on the abdomen. Finally, mix color (Moonglow) and color 600003 (Lamp Black) in a 5:1 ratio to depict the claws' tips, making sure to capture the contrast between light and shadow on the claws.

Mix color 600173 (Verditer Blue), color 600003 (Lamp Black), and color 600233 (Raw Sienna Light) in a 4:1:4 ratio to create a light gray color. Use this mix to continue painting the backlit areas of the tree. Use brushstrokes of different shapes—dots, lines, and planes, to depict the texture, creating a mottled bark effect. While still wet, use color 600010 (Burnt Sienna) to deepen the shadows, focusing particularly on the smaller, finer branches.

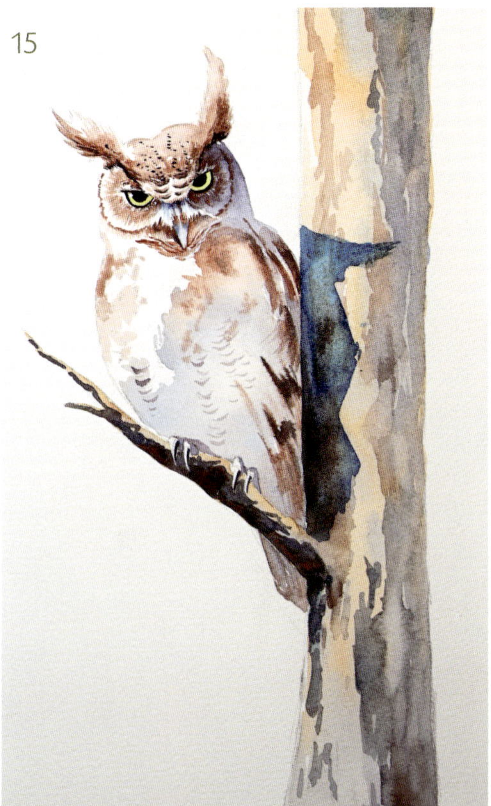

15

Mix color 600082 (Prussian Blue) and color 600010 (Burnt Sienna) in a 3:1 ratio, and gently paint the owl's shadow on the tree.

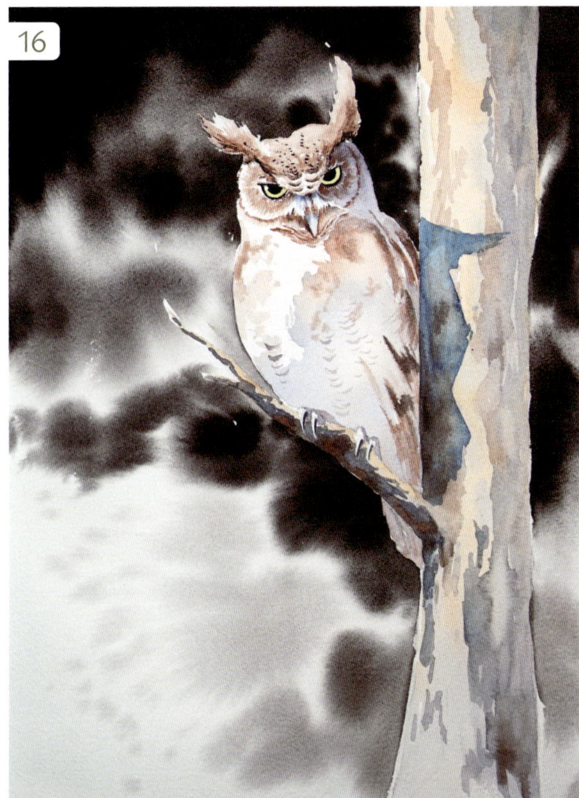

16

Wet the background with clean water, making sure to keep the edges of the owl and tree dry to maintain clear contours. Mix color 600003 (Lamp Black) to create a rich black, and apply the black background flexibly. Vary the size of the color blocks, leaving some blank spaces between them. Allow the colors to naturally spread and blend into the background, creating a natural sense of breathability.

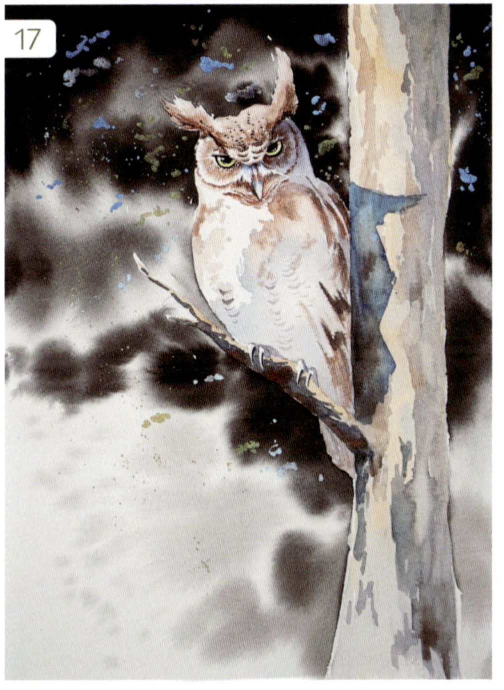

17

Once the background is fully dry, use some pearlescent paints to add speckles (you can choose specific color numbers based on your preference). This will add a lively touch, making the painting more engaging. And with that, the owl is complete.

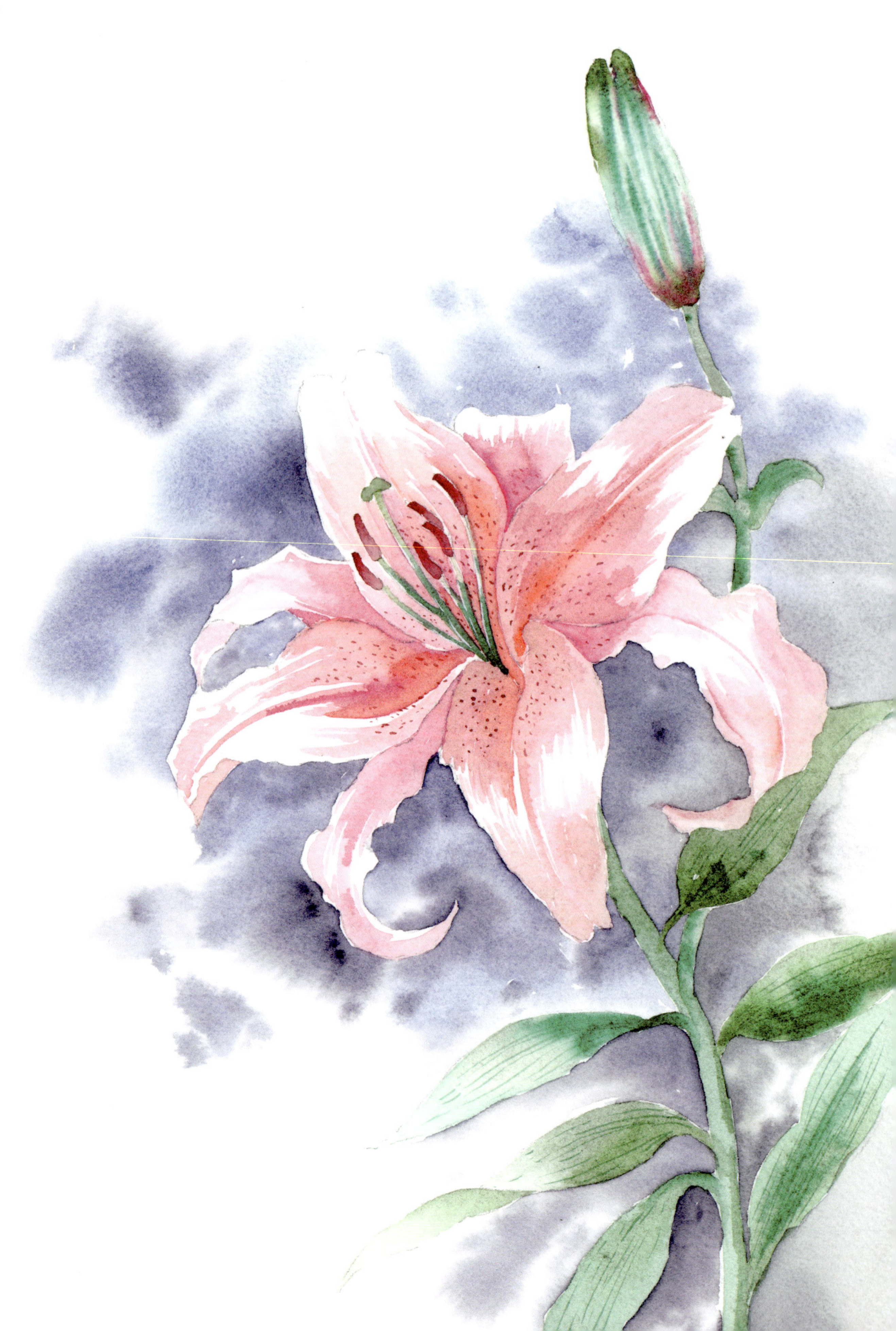

Lily

In the garden, the lily blooms for the first time, its petals as smooth as silk, with a soft pink hue that exudes a sense of tranquility and elegance. She holds the wish of "a hundred years of harmony," the most beautiful blessing from the East for marital bliss. She also resembles a sage, isolated from the world, untouched by mundane affairs. In the morning light, she lowers her head gracefully, transforming a thousand years of purity and good fortune into a subtle, lingering fragrance.

Paint Brand
DANIEL SMITH

Color Codes
600198: Opera Pink
600009: Buff Titanium
600064: Organic Vermilion
600197: Green Apatite Genuine
600078: Phthalo Green (Blue Shade)
600005: Anthraquinoid Red
600024: Chromium Green Oxide
600173: Verditer Blue
600242: Alvaro's Fresco Grey

Recommended Watercolor Paper
ARCHES watercolor paper, cold pressed, 140 lb/300 g/m²

Recommended Brush
Black Velvet 3000S brush for watercolor, size 8

Key Challenges
1. Use the wet-on-dry technique to depict the petals.
2. Shaping the flower form and presenting a subtle effect in the composition.
3. Apply segmented background rendering.

Steps

1

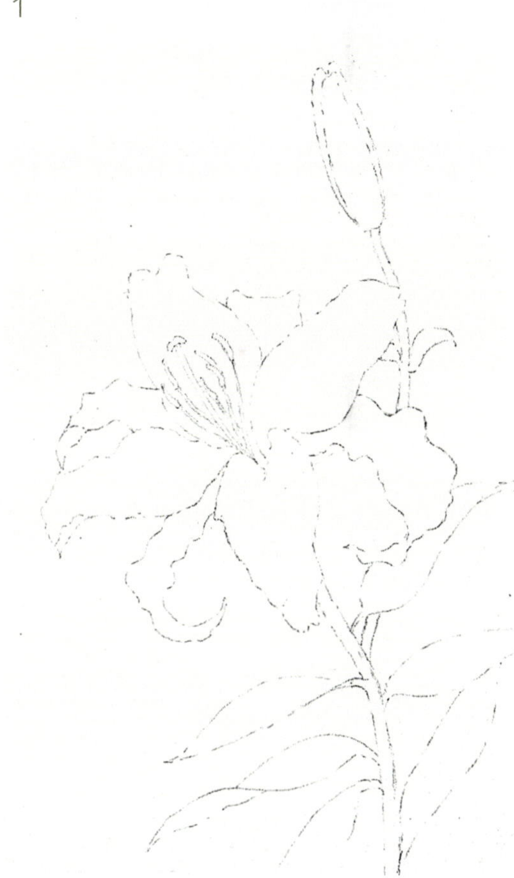

Lightly sketch the shape of the lily with a pencil, paying attention to the graceful spread of the lily petals and the folding relationship between the petals and leaves.

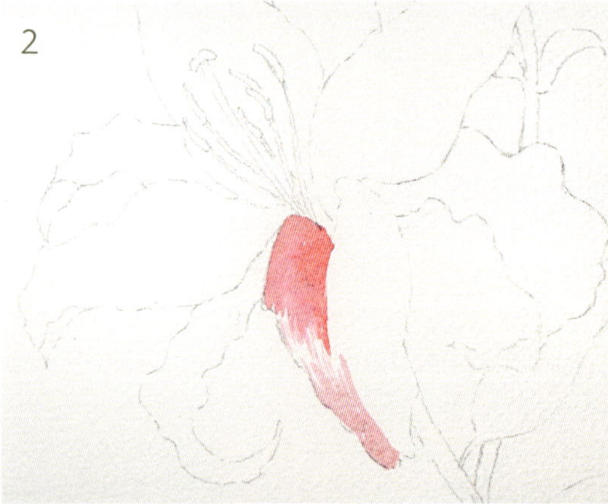

2

Mix color 600198 (Opera Pink) with color 600009 (Buff Titanium) in equal proportions, adding more water to create a light pink shade. Use the wet-on-dry technique to paint the base and tips of the petals, paying attention to the brushstrokes, and leaving white space in the center of the petal. The strokes should be finer near the white areas to depict the texture and pattern of the lily petals. While still wet, gently blend color 600064 (Organic Vermilion) into the base of the petal to create a three-dimensional effect that transitions from light to dark.

Note: The wet-on-dry technique used for the lily refers to painting with a brush that has enough moisture, where the paper is dry, and the color is applied without the brush being completely dry. This method results in visible water marks, but the boundaries are clear, unlike the wet-on-wet technique where the surface is moistened first, and the paint blends with the water for a more diffused boundary.

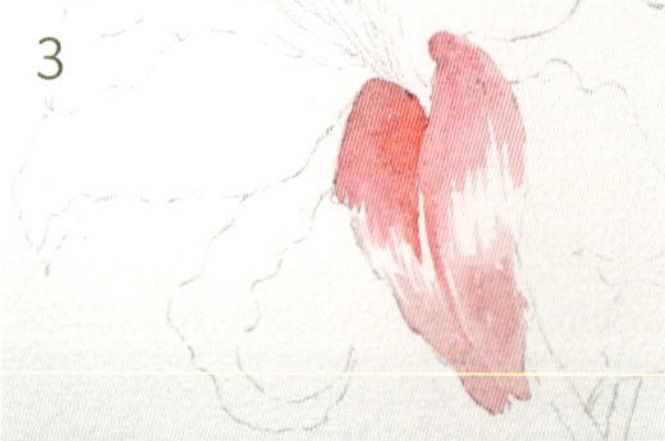

3

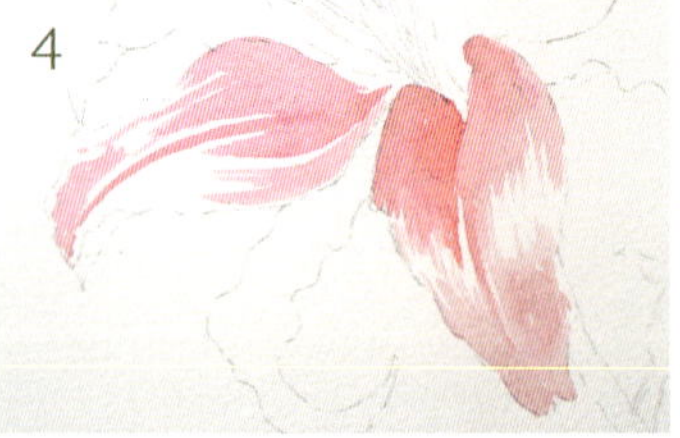

4

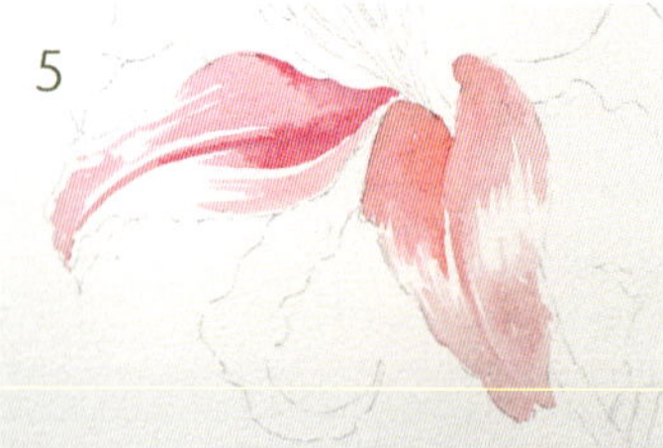

5

Use the same method as in step 2 to paint the right half of the petal. Note that there is no need to darken the base of the petal, as the right half is positioned higher than the left half and receives more light, so the color will naturally be lighter compared to the left half.

Similarly, use the light pink mixture prepared in step 2 to paint the left petal. Be sure to pay attention to the brushstrokes, just as you did for the previous petals.

Directly use color 600198 (Opera Pink) to deepen the base of the petal, creating a sense of dimension.

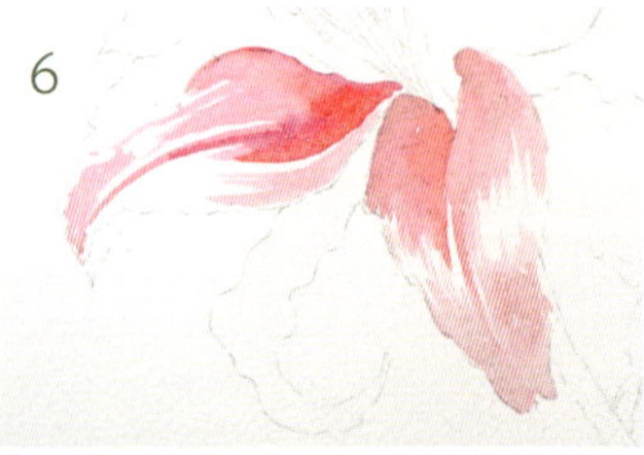

6

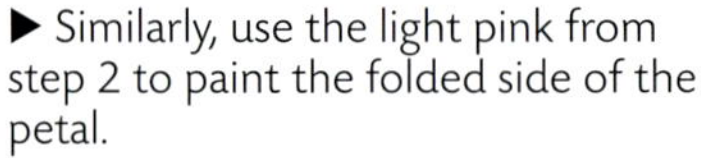

◀ While still wet, mix in an appropriate amount of color 600064 (Organic Vermilion) at the base of the petal.

▶ Similarly, use the light pink from step 2 to paint the folded side of the petal.

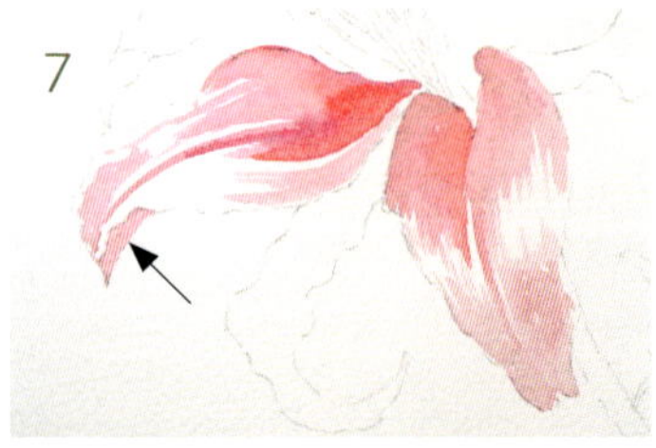

7

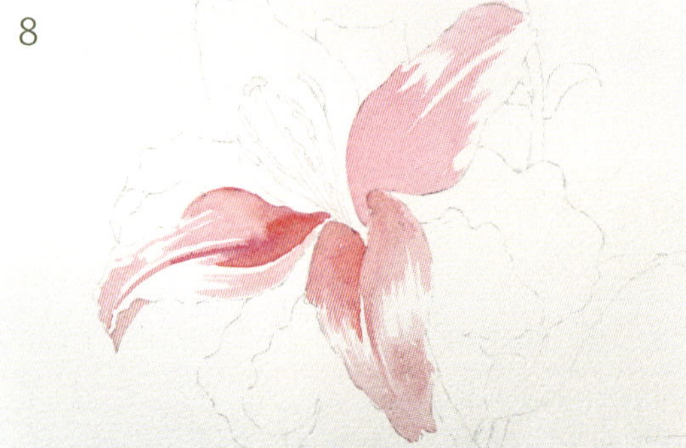

8

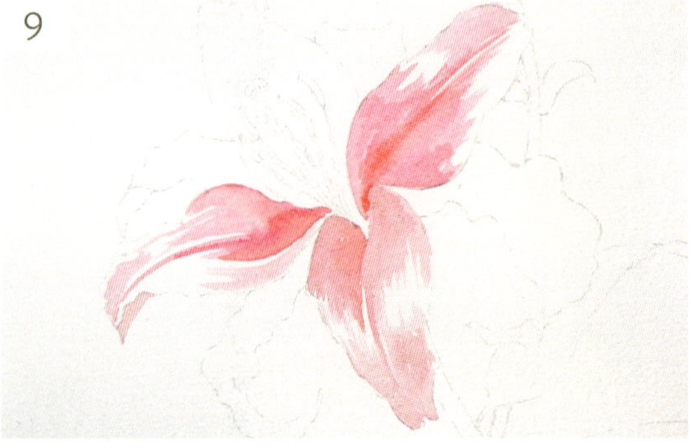

9

Use the same color and technique as in step 2 to paint the higher right petal, making sure to leave some white space.

While the area is still wet, mix in color 600198 (Opera Pink) and color 600064 (Organic Vermilion).

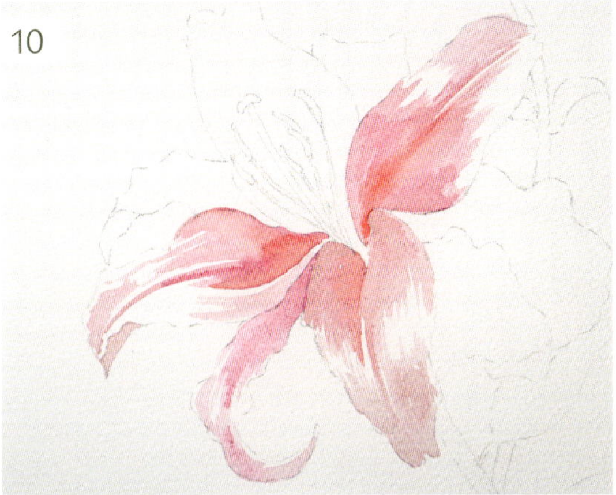

Using the same method from step 2, paint the curved flower petal at the lower left corner, ensuring to leave white space in the center of the petal. While it's still wet, mix in color 600198 (Opera Pink) at the base to create a sense of volume.

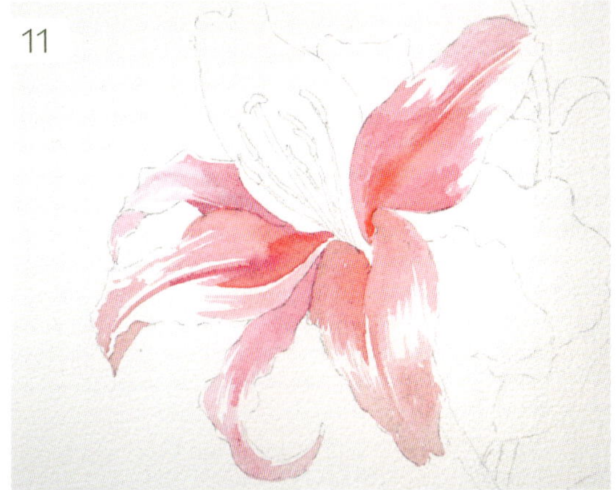

Using the same method as in step 10, paint the flower petal located towards the upper left and further back.

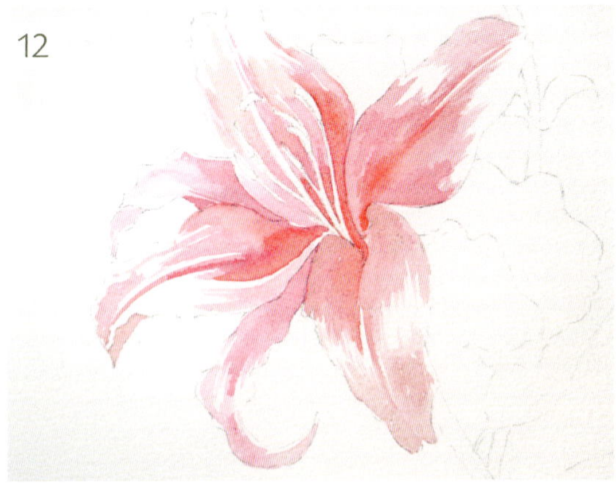

Begin painting the upper middle petal using the light pink mixture prepared in step 2. Use the wet-on-dry technique to render the texture of the petal. Leave the top part of the petal white because it is illuminated. While still wet, use color 600198 (Opera Pink) and color 600064 (Organic Vermilion) to darken the root area. When painting, be careful to leave the thin and long stamen and anther areas unpainted. (Alternatively, you can pre-paint the stamens using masking fluid, which makes coloring easier later. If you don't use masking fluid, you'll need to be extra careful when painting to manually preserve the white areas.)

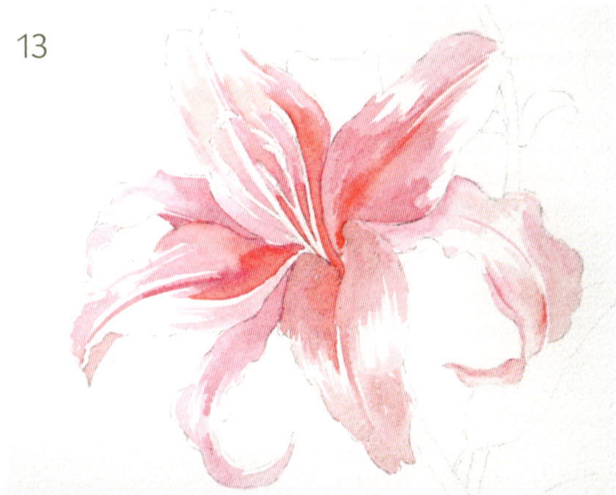

Use the same method and colors as in step 12 to paint the petal at the lower right corner. Start by painting the root and top of the petal with the light pink mixture, leaving the center white. Then, use color 600198 (Opera Pink) to darken the root area and gently outline the central crease and edges of the petal.

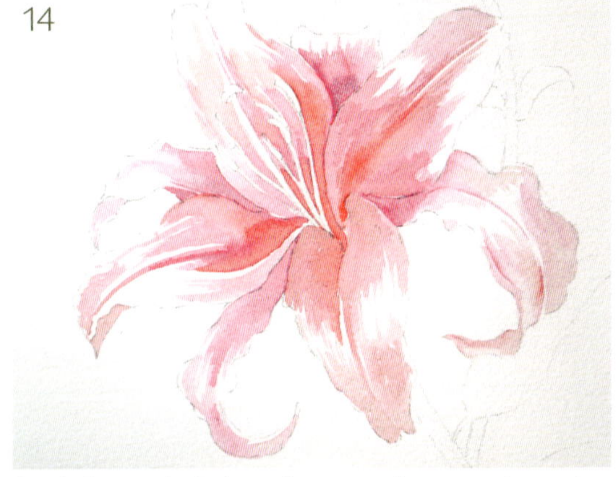

Similarly, use the light pink mixture from step 2 to paint the petal at the top, hidden behind the others. Since this petal is folded, the folded area is the lighted part, so leave it white. Pay attention to the brushstrokes. While it's still wet, use color 600198 (Opera Pink) to darken the root area.

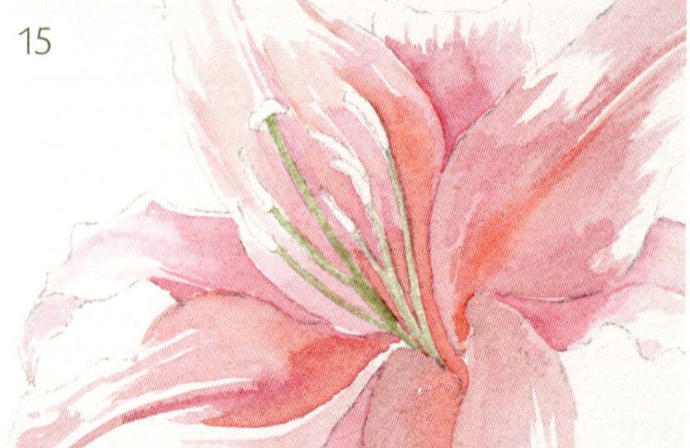

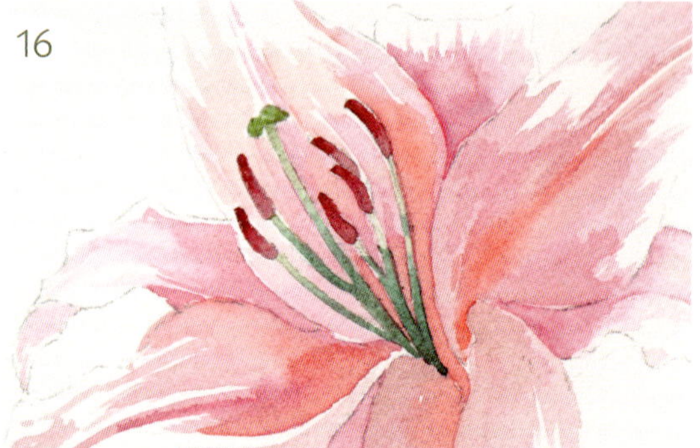

Color the filaments. Even the fine filaments have light and shadow. Start by lightly painting the filaments with color 600197 (Green Apatite Genuine), and while it's still wet, blend in color 600078 (Phthalo Green) at the base of the filaments to depict the shadowed areas.

Use color 600005 (Anthraquinoid Red) to paint the anthers. Start by applying color to the top of the anthers, then use clean water to diffuse the color, creating a gradient effect where the top is darker and the bottom is lighter. Next, use color 600197 (Green Apatite Genuine) to directly paint the stylus.

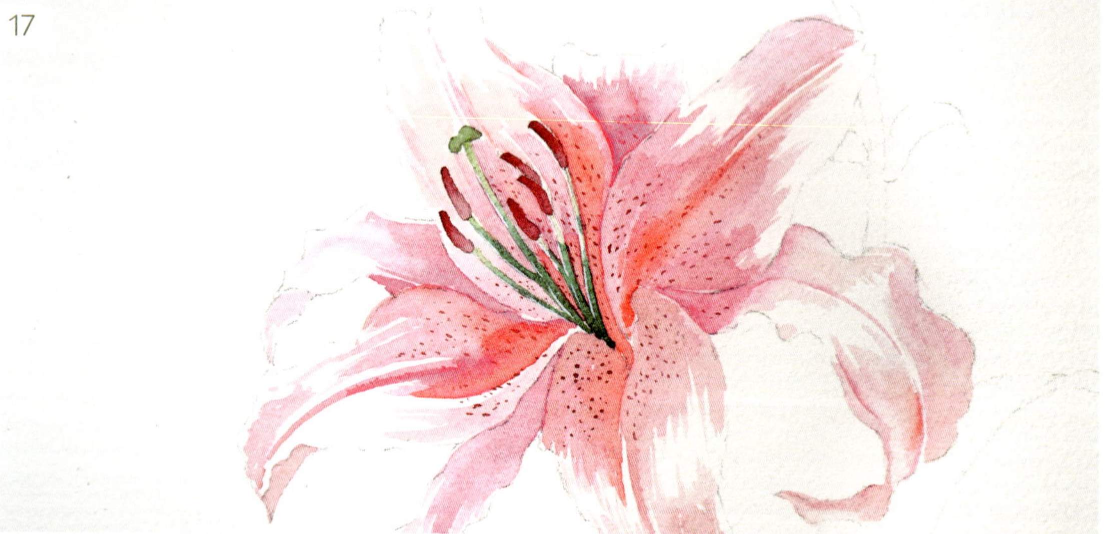

Use the tip of the brush to pick up color 600005 (Anthraquinoid Red) and randomly dot the petals with small spots.

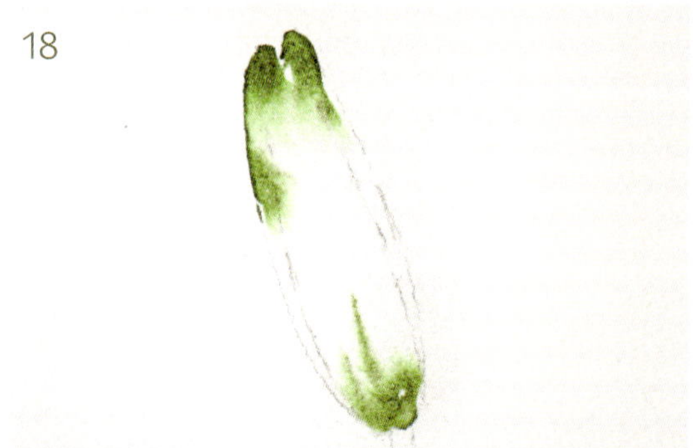

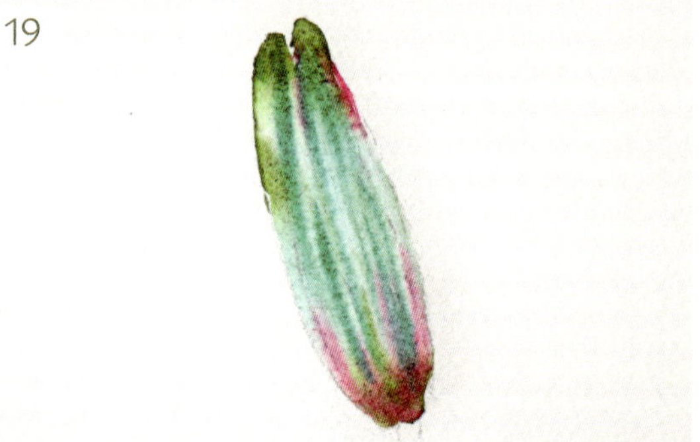

Next, paint the flower bud on the right side of the composition. First, apply clean water to cover the entire flower bud. While still wet, use color 600197 (Green Apatite Genuine) to add color to the top and bottom of the bud, allowing the color to naturally spread with the moisture.

Continue while the area is still wet by gently mixing in color 600198 (Opera Pink), as this is to depict a bud that is about to bloom, where the pink of the flower starts to show. Finally, use a dark green to outline some of the textures on the flower bud.

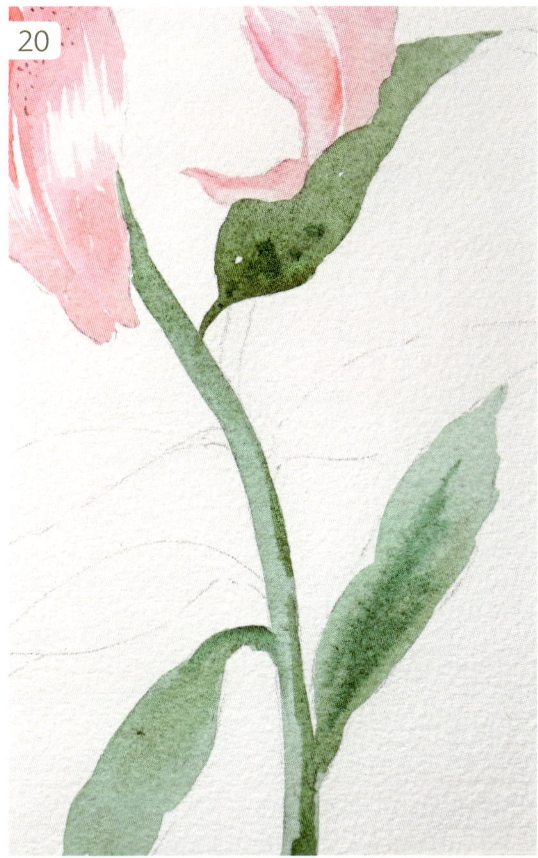

Start by applying a light layer of color 600024 (Chromium Green Oxide) to the flower stem and leaves. While still wet, mix in color 600197 (Green Apatite Genuine) and color 600078 (Phthalo Green) at the base of the leaves and along the edges of the flower stem to create a sense of volume.

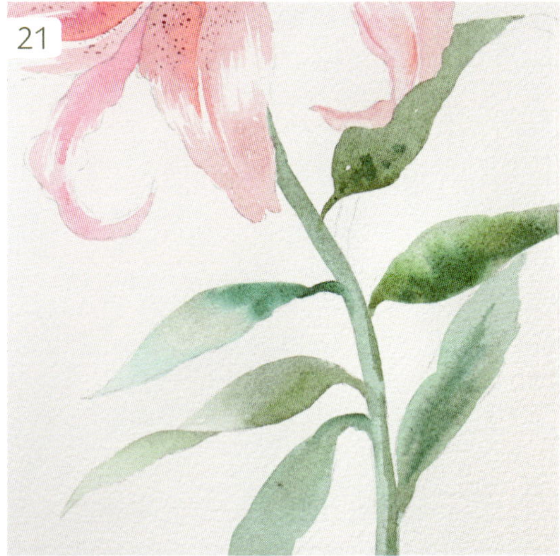

Use the same method as in step 20 to paint the two leaves on the upper left and the leaf in the middle on the right.

Note: If there are many leaves in the painting, applying the base color all at once can be difficult for beginners to manage the wetness properly. If painted too slowly, the base color will dry, making it hard to achieve the two-tone blending effect typical of wet-on-wet technique. In this case, you can either work in sections as I do or use the wet-on-wet technique to paint each leaf one at a time.

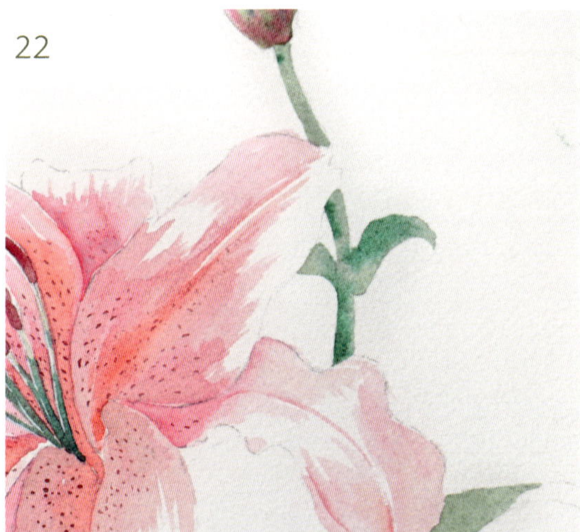

Use the same method as in step 20 to paint the flower stalk and small leaves of the flower bud.

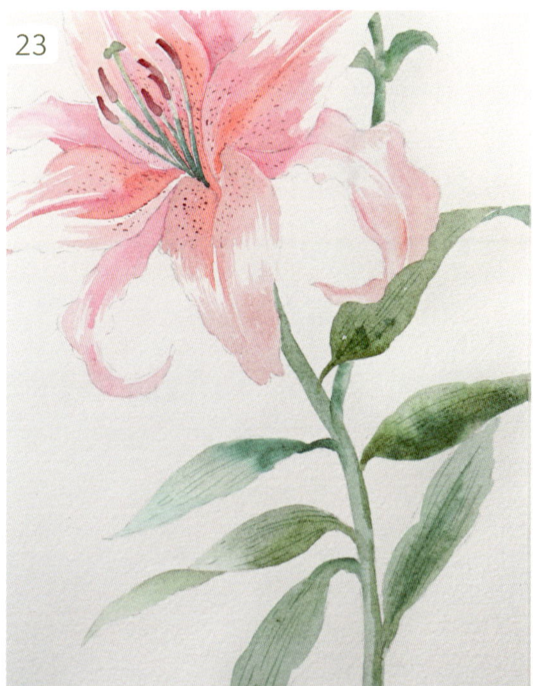

Use color 600024 (Chromium Green Oxide) to gently and delicately outline the veins on the leaves. Be sure to keep your hand light, and avoid making the lines too orderly, as this could make them look stiff.

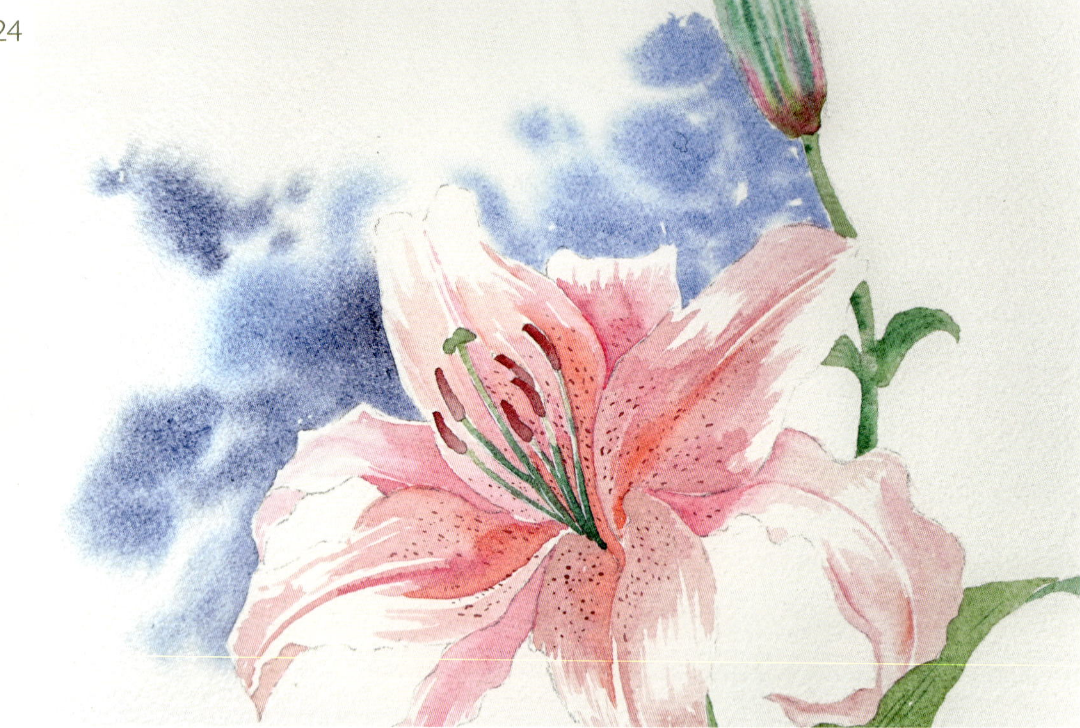

Begin the segmented background rendering. We use a segmented approach because when rendering the background, we need to wet all areas except for the flowers, leaves, and stems, especially the tiny gaps between the flowers and leaves. This requires careful work, and it can take a lot of time to wet these small areas. During this process, the previously wetted areas may dry, causing the water and colors to have difficulty blending, which results in harsh transitions.

So, start by wetting the area above the flowers with clean water, ensuring that the flower contours remain clear. While still wet, use color 600173 (Verditer Blue) and apply it flexibly to create a blue background, setting a fresh and elegant atmosphere. The color blocks can vary in size, and leave some blank spaces where necessary. Once the color spreads, it will naturally form a breathable effect. For the area near the flowers, you can appropriately mix in color 600242 (Alvaro's Fresco Grey).

25

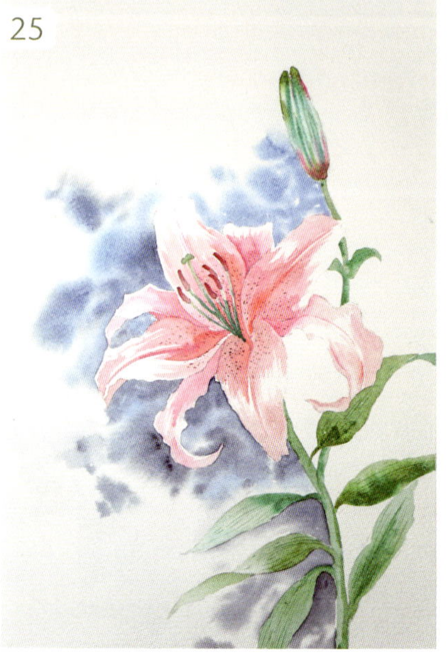

◀ Use the same method and colors from step 24 to render the background on the left side of the flowers.

26

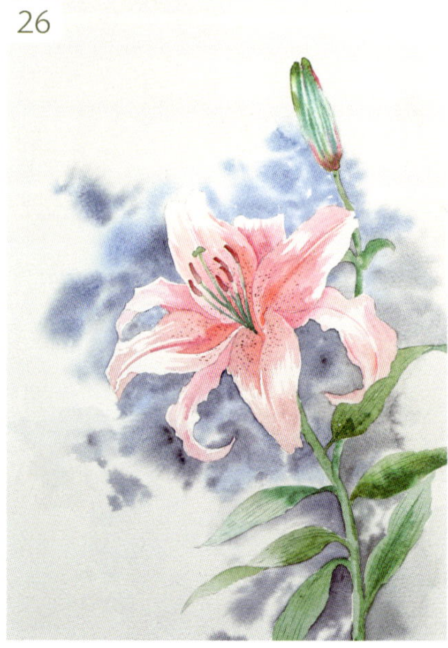

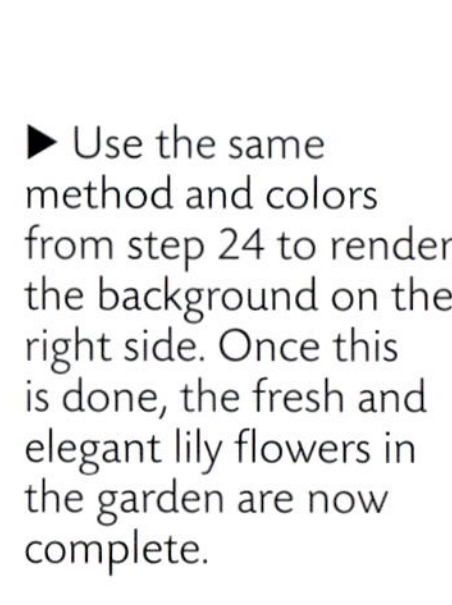

▶ Use the same method and colors from step 24 to render the background on the right side. Once this is done, the fresh and elegant lily flowers in the garden are now complete.

Fig. 27 A Plump Red Bird
A plump red bird sits in stillness, its rounded form
exuding quiet warmth and gentle charm.

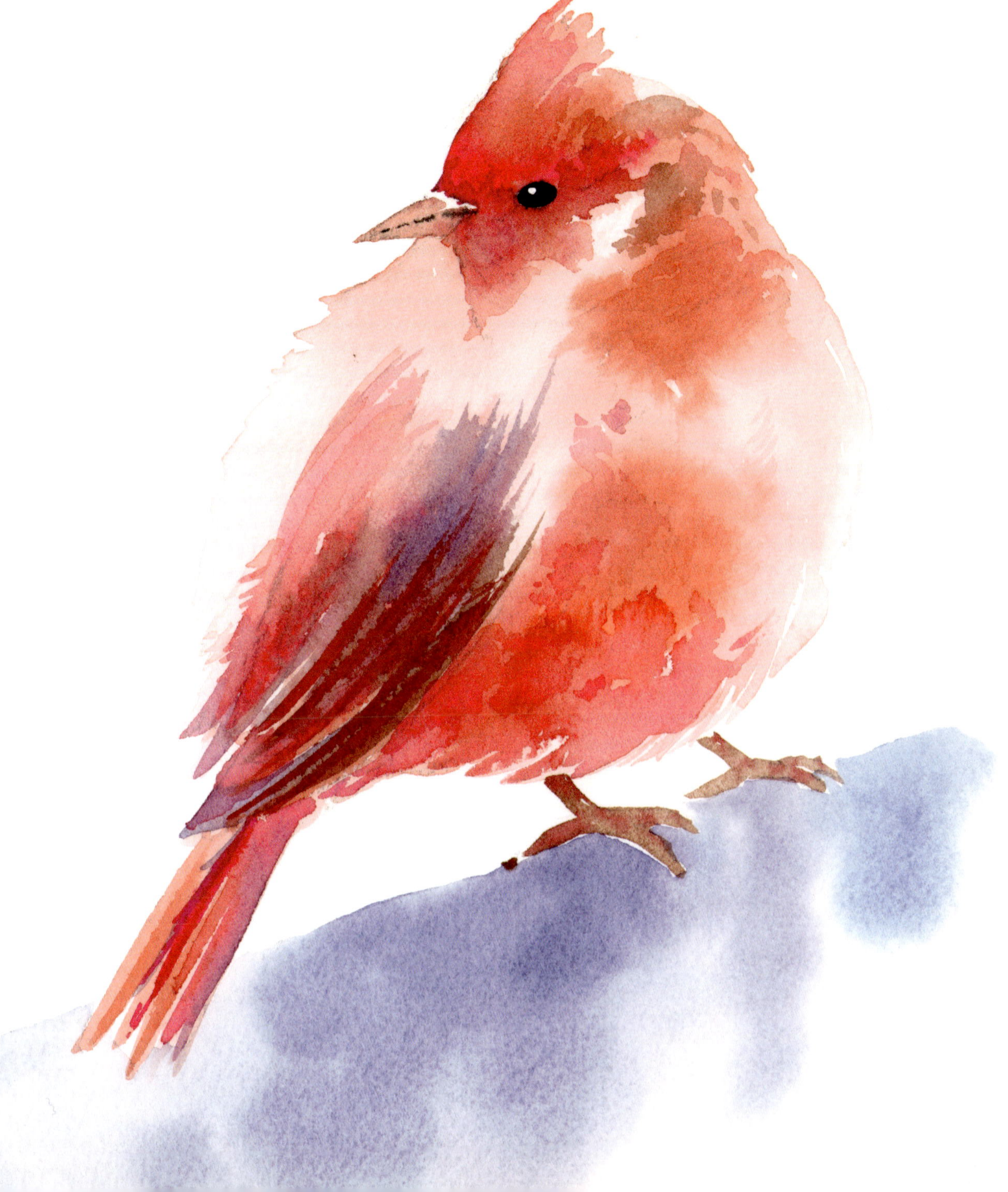

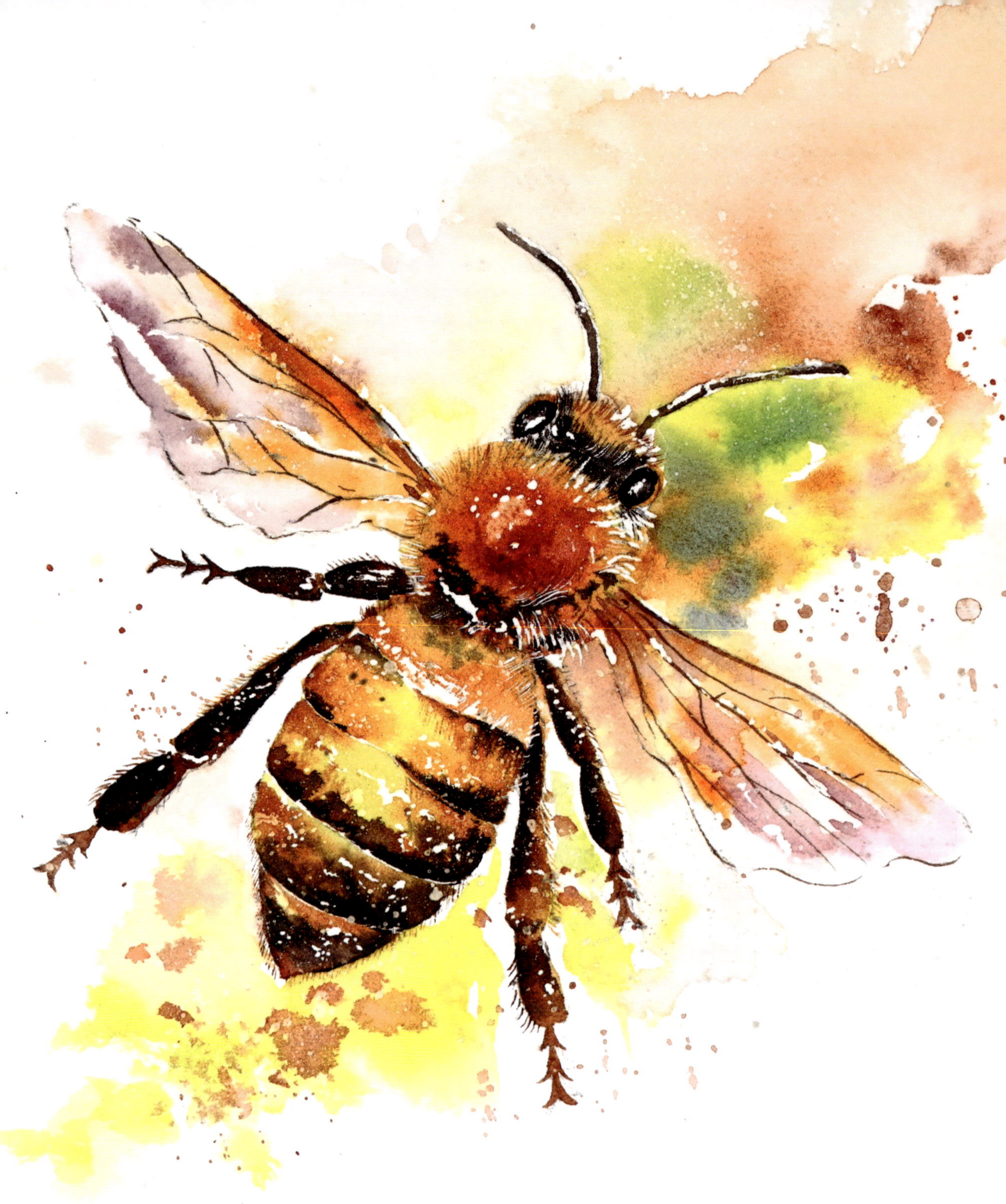

Bee

In the garden, bees busily flit among the blossoms. These little artisans are
diligently gathering nectar. Their wings hum with a rhythmic buzz, as if
composing a symphony of nature. Dancing in the sunlight, they bring wafts
of sweetness through the air, as though declaring with every graceful flight
that life is made abundant through tireless effort.

Paint Brand
DANIEL SMITH

Color Codes
- 600056: Monte Amiata Natural Sienna
- 600073: Permanent Violet
- 600064: Organic Vermilion
- 600003: Lamp Black
- 600041: Hansa Yellow Light
- 600010: Burnt Sienna

Auxiliary Materials
Masking fluid
Acrylic medium
NICKER opaque white gouache

Recommended Watercolor Paper
ARCHES watercolor paper, cold pressed,
140 lb/300 g/m^2

Recommended Brushes
Black Velvet 3000S brush for watercolor,
size 8
Black Velvet 3000S brush for watercolor,
size 4

Key Challenges
1. Depicting the fuzziness of the bee's fur.
2. Managing the transparency of the
wings.
3. Background treatment.

Steps

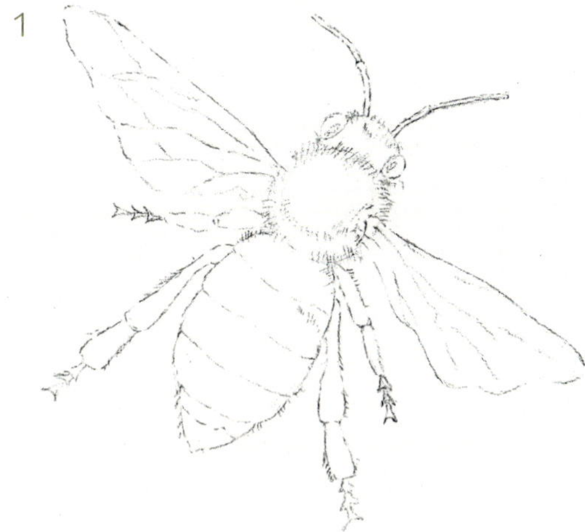

Lightly sketch the bee's flight posture with a pencil,
paying attention to the proportional relationships of its
various parts.

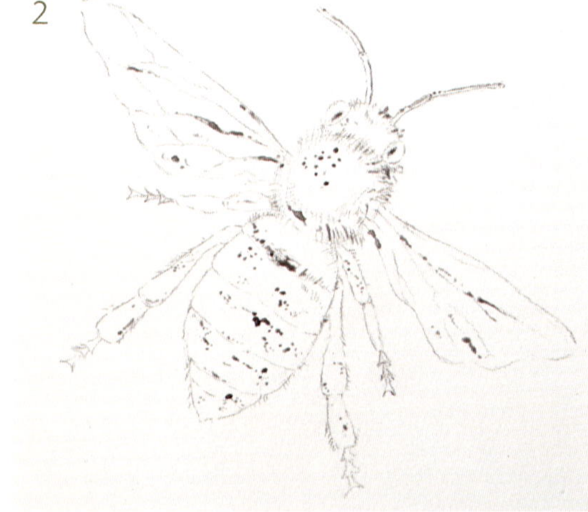

Use masking fluid to apply on the areas of the bee that
need to remain white, including the antennae, eyes,
wings, thorax, abdomen, and legs.

3

Use a fan brush or toothbrush to dip into acrylic medium and evenly splatter it onto the paper. Focus on the areas indicated by the arrows in the image, which should have a semi-transparent texture created by the splattered acrylic medium.

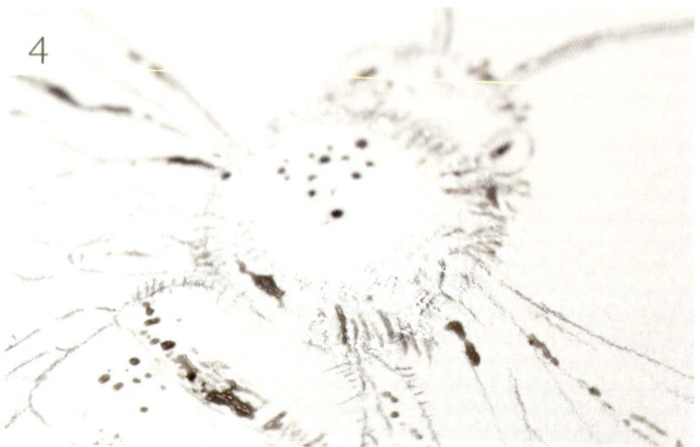

4

Wet the chest area with clean water, ensuring that the wet area slightly extends beyond the outline. This will allow the colors to spread more easily in the next steps.

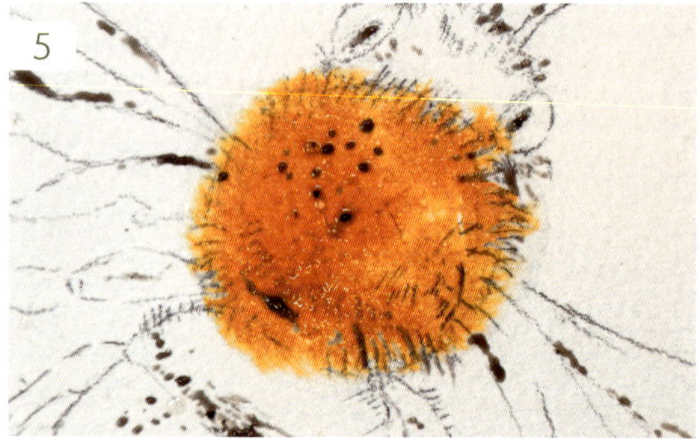

5

While the area is still wet, evenly apply color 600056 (Monte Amiata Natural Sienna). Be mindful not to cover the entire wet area with color. As you approach the waterline, stop applying color to allow it to spread and blend naturally, creating a soft, fuzzy effect.

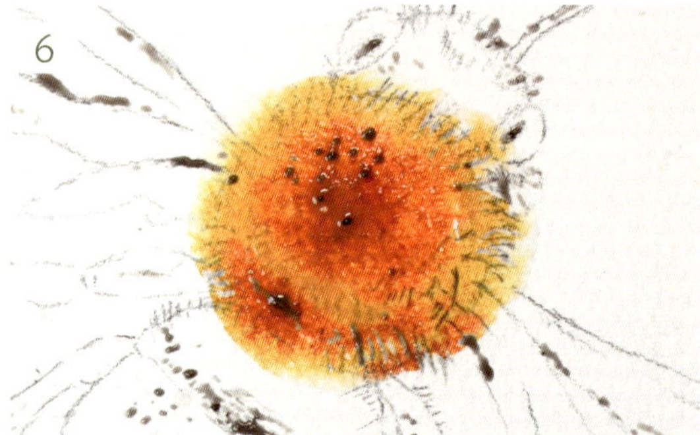

6

Mix color 600056 (Monte Amiata Natural Sienna), color 600073 (Permanent Violet), and color 600064 (Organic Vermilion) in equal proportions to create a deep purplish red hue. Use this color to paint the central raised portion of the chest and the area where the chest connects with the abdomen. This will help sculpt the rounded, three-dimensional form of the bee's chest.

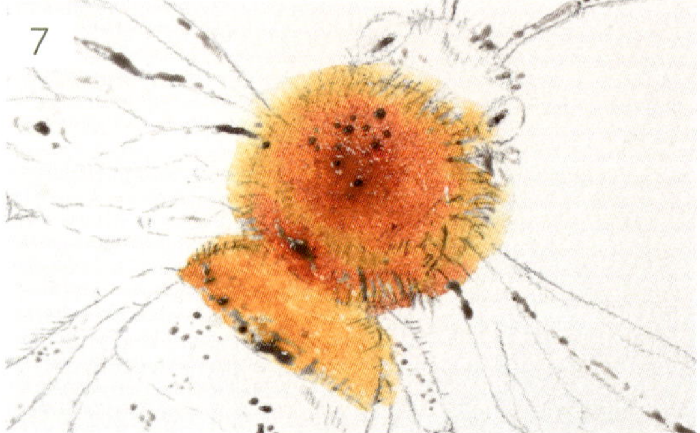

7

While the chest color is still wet, continue to use color 600056 (Monte Amiata Natural Sienna) to paint the first section of the bee's abdomen. Allow the color of this section to naturally blend with the chest color.

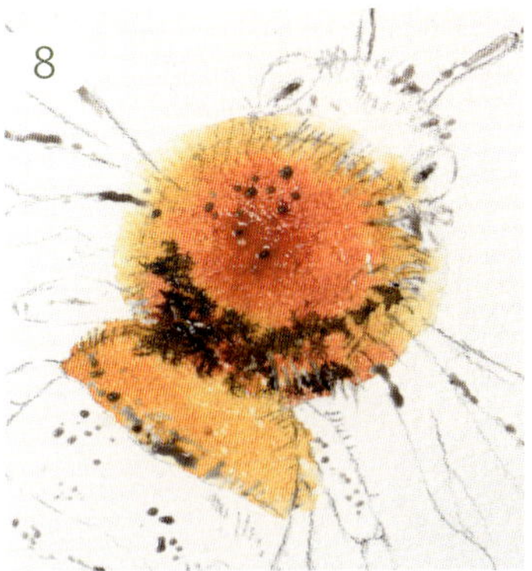

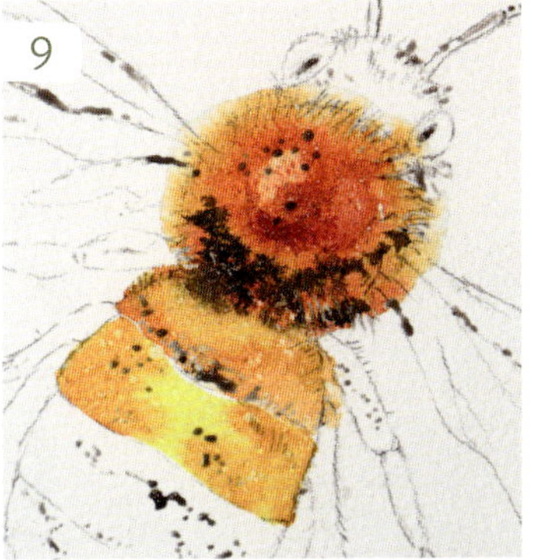

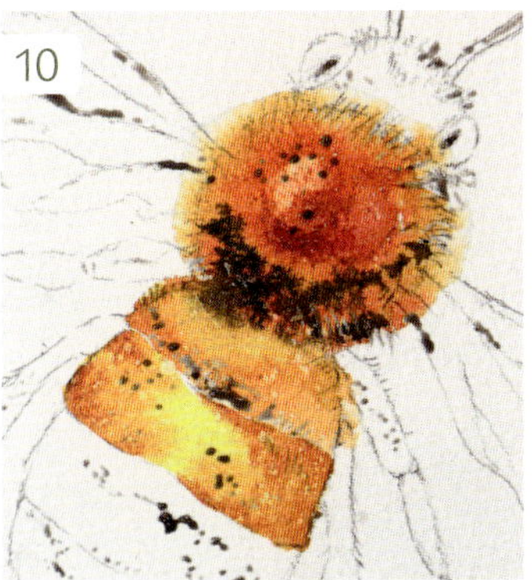

8 While the paint is still wet, use color 600003 (Lamp Black) to deepen the junction between the chest and abdomen. Allow the color to naturally blend and seep into the surrounding areas.

9 Use color 600041 (Hansa Yellow Light) to paint the second section of the abdomen. While the area is still wet, dab color 600056 (Monte Amiata Natural Sienna) on both sides to create a sense of dimensionality.

10 While the second section of the abdomen is still wet, use color 600010 (Burnt Sienna) to deepen the colors on both sides of this section.

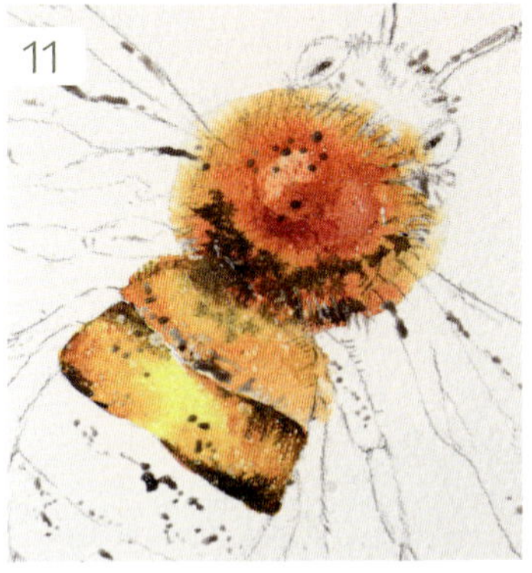

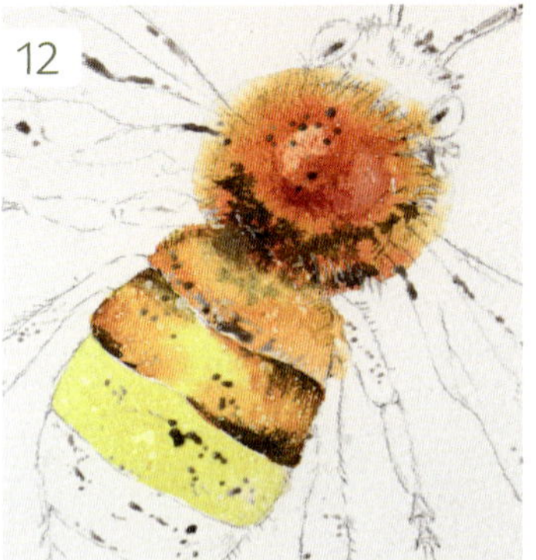

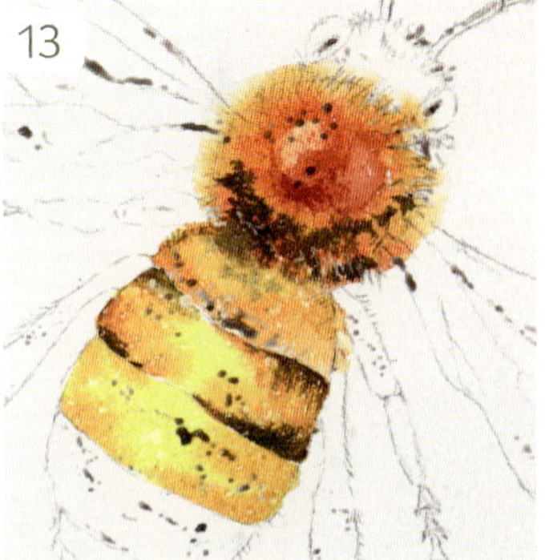

11 While the second section of the abdomen is still wet, use color 600003 (Lamp Black) to darken its edges.

12 Use color 600041 (Hansa Yellow Light) to evenly fill in the third section of the abdomen.

13 While the third section of the abdomen is still wet, gently apply color 600056 (Monte Amiata Natural Sienna) to the sides to create a sense of dimensionality.

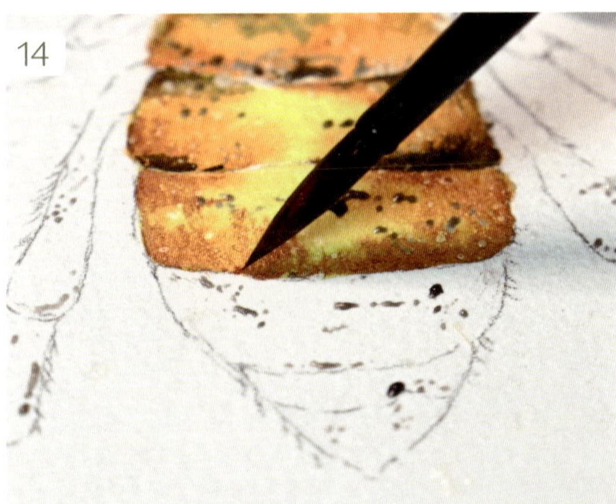

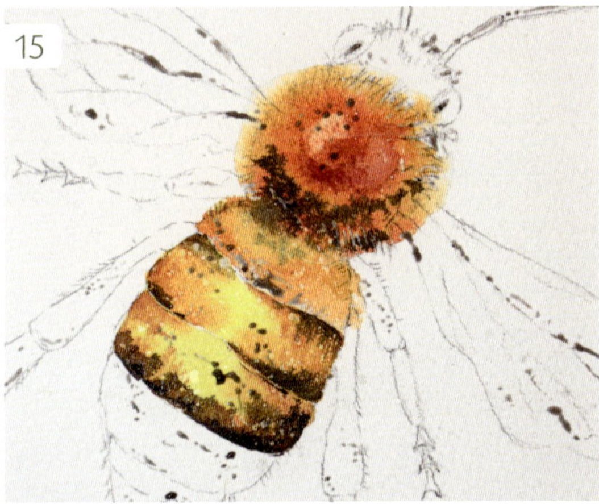

14 Use color 600010 (Burnt Sienna) to depict some details.

15 While still wet, apply color 600003 (Lamp Black) along the edges of the third section of the abdomen to enhance the three-dimensional effect.

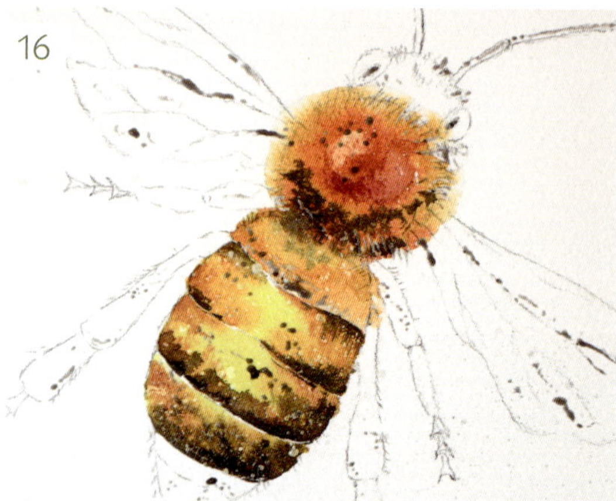

Use the same method and colors as in steps 12 to 15 to paint the fourth section of the abdomen.

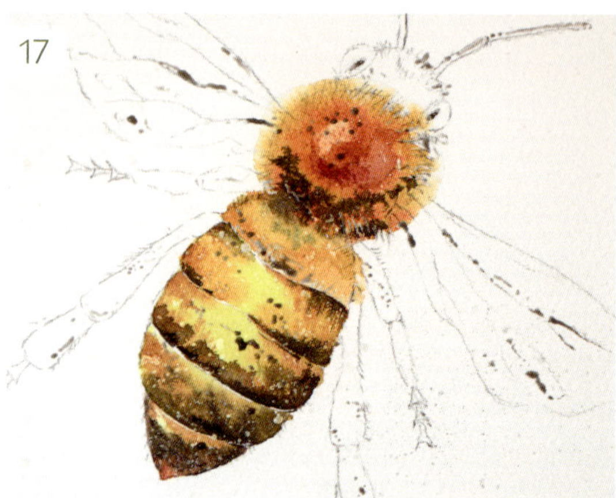

Use the same method and colors as in steps 12 to 15 to paint the fifth section of the abdomen.

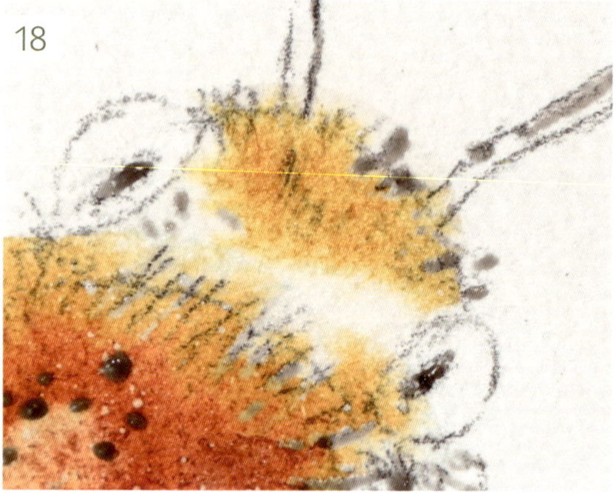

Next, start painting the head area. Begin by laying down a base layer with color 600056 (Monte Amiata Natural Sienna).

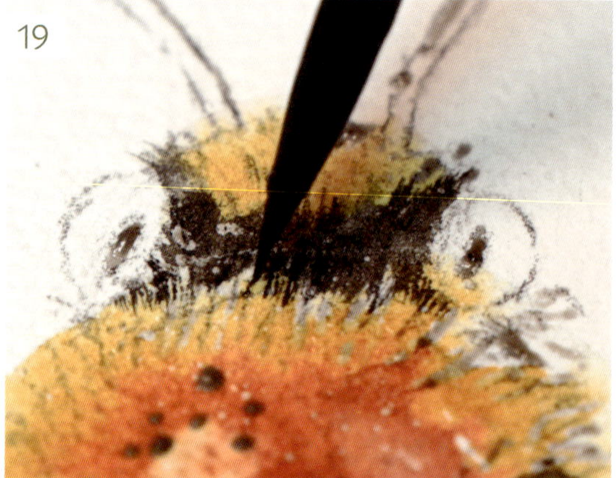

Lightly apply the darker areas of the head using color 600003 (Lamp Black). Use fine, linear brushstrokes to create a smooth transition between the head and thorax.

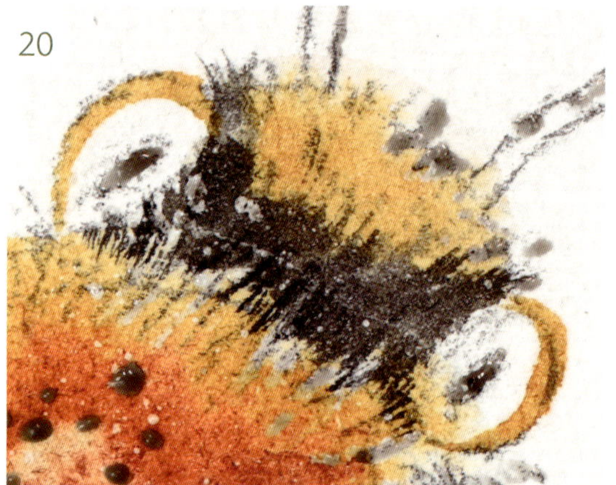

Paint the outer rim of the eyes using color 600056 (Monte Amiata Natural Sienna).

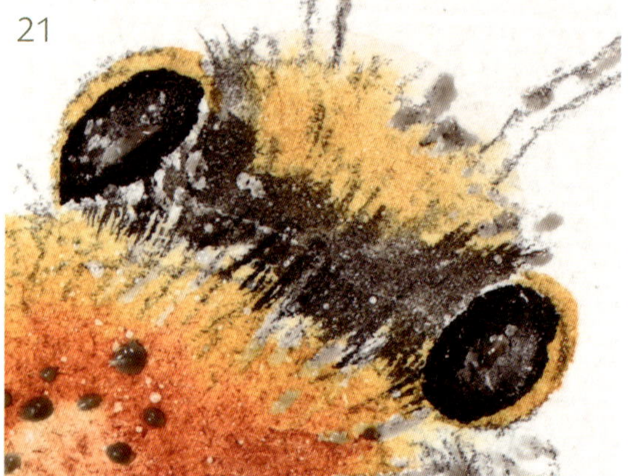

Paint the eyes using color 600003 (Lamp Black), making sure the center is slightly lighter. To achieve this effect, first fill in the entire eyes with black, then use a tissue to lift some paint from the center. This creates a naturally lighter black tone, giving the eyes a three-dimensional appearance.

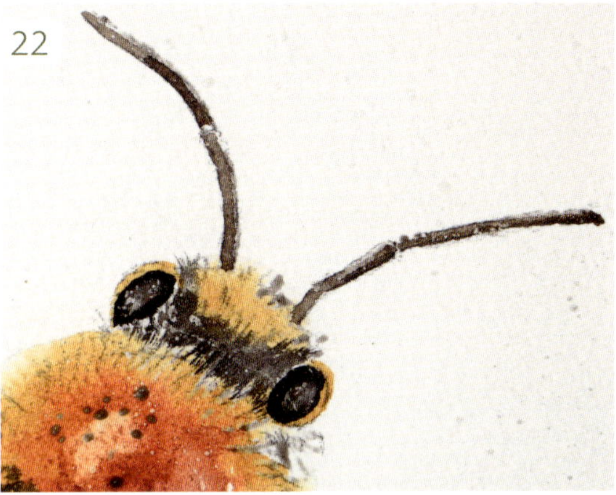

22

Paint the antennae using color 600010 (Burnt Sienna).

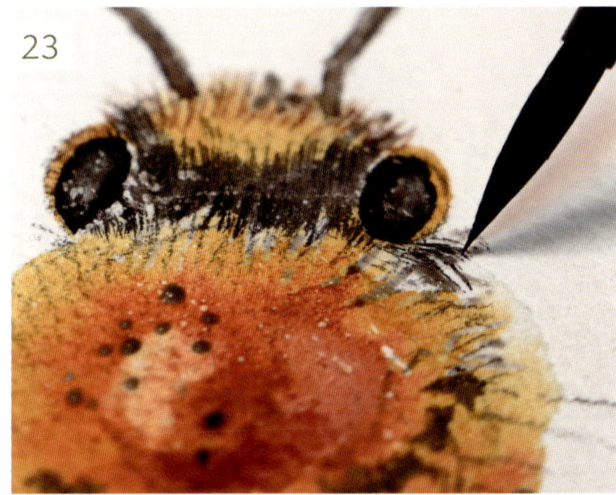

23

Use the Size 4 brush to lightly outline some of the fine hairs around the eyes, adding detailed texture.

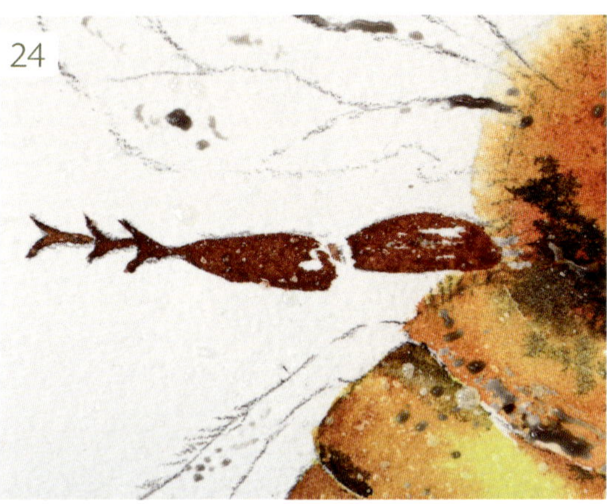

24

Next, paint the bee's middle leg. Start by laying down a base with color 600010 (Burnt Sienna). Be sure to leave highlight areas and where joints intersect appropriately unpainted to enhance the three-dimensional effect of the leg.

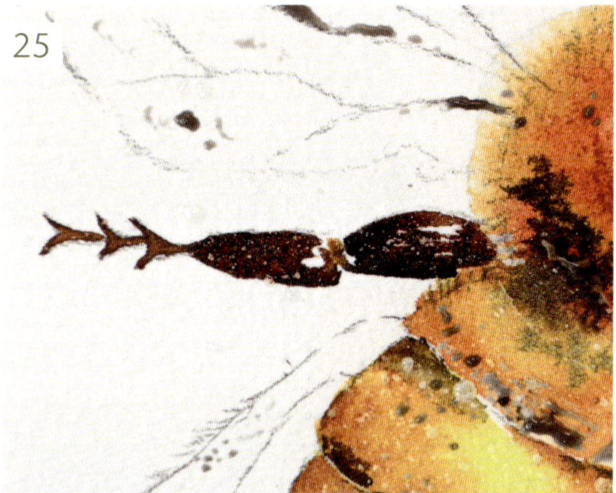

25

While the paint is still wet, use color 600003 (Lamp Black) to deepen the shadows.

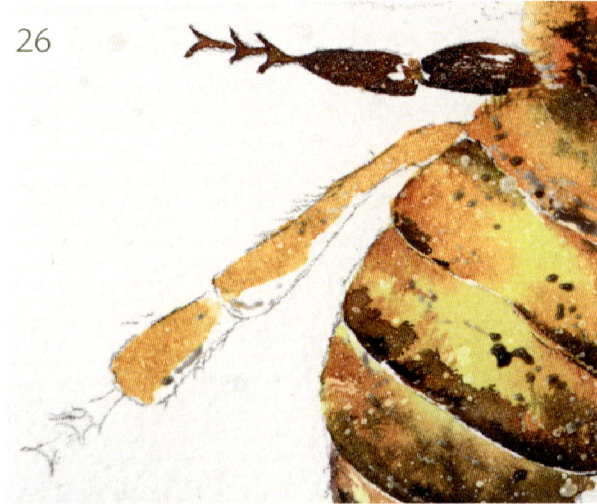

26

Use color 600056 (Monte Amiata Natural Sienna) to paint the hind leg, leaving out the highlight areas.

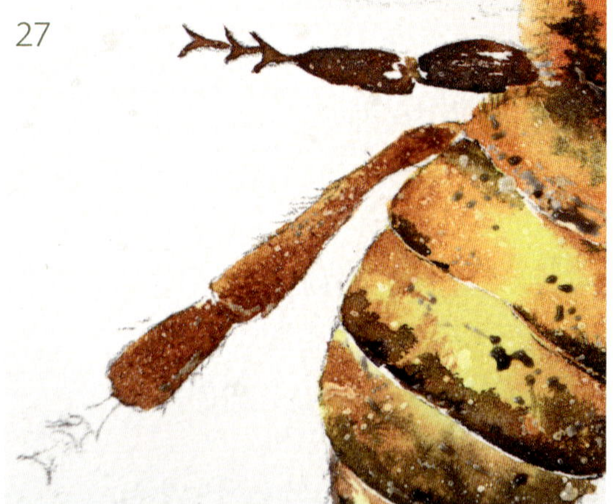

27

While the area is still wet, dab color 600010 (Burnt Sienna) onto the joints. The paint will naturally flow and blend with the moisture.

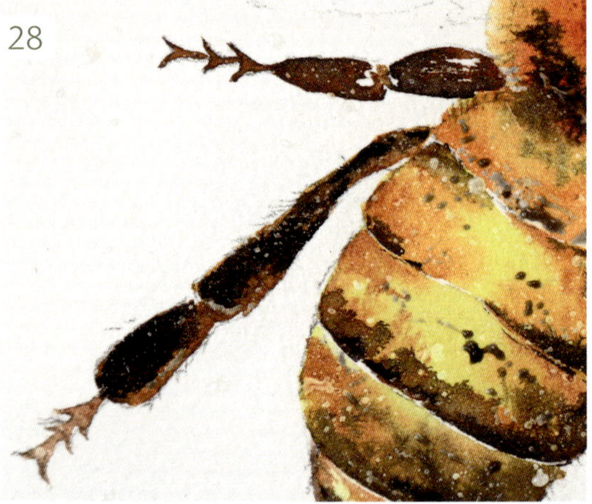

Finally, use color 600003 (Lamp Black) to enhance the sense of volume.

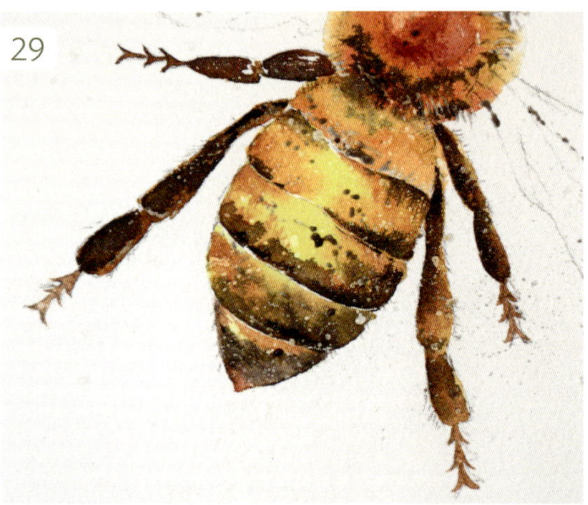

Use the same colors and method as in steps 24 to 28 to paint the middle and hind legs on the right side.

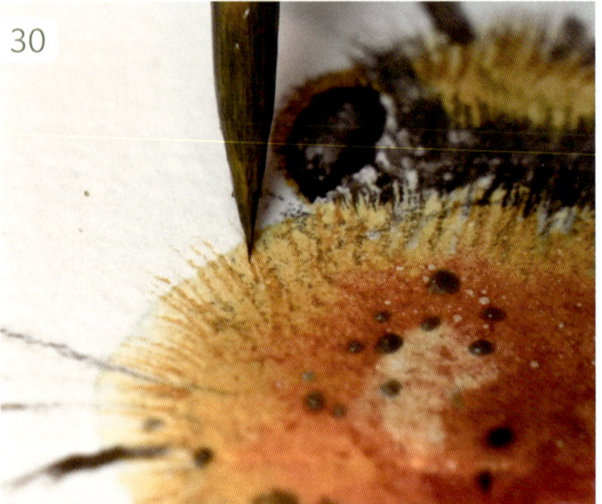

In steps 30 to 33, we will use a finer Size 4 brush to outline the details. Start by using color 600056 (Monte Amiata Natural Sienna) to outline the fuzz around the chest area.

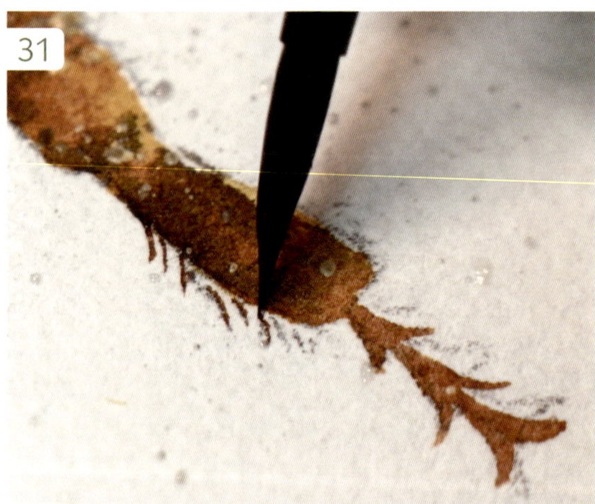

Similarly, use color 600010 (Burnt Sienna) to outline the fuzz on all the legs.

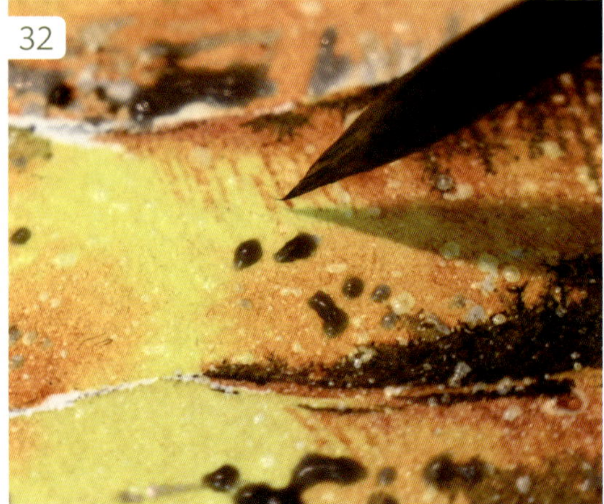

Use color 600056 (Monte Amiata Natural Sienna) to outline some of the textural details on the abdomen.

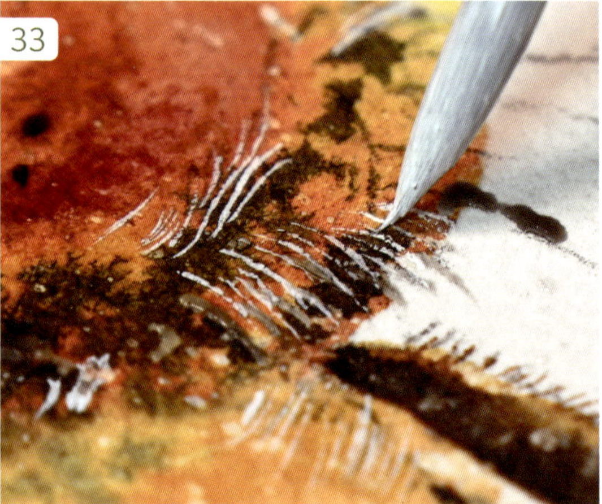

Use NICKER opaque white gouache to continue detailing the fuzz on the bee.

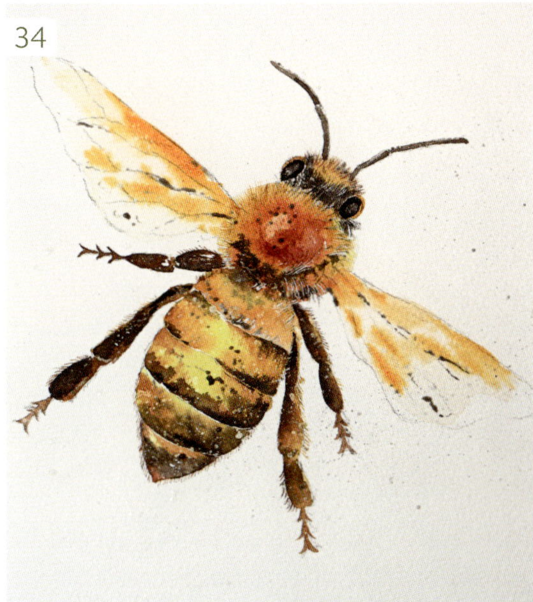

Switch back to the Size 8 brush. First wet the wings with clean water. While still wet, dab color 600056 (Monte Amiata Natural Sienna) in scattered spots. Be sure to leave large areas of blank space between the colors, allowing the colors to naturally diffuse with the water, creating a light and airy effect for the wings.

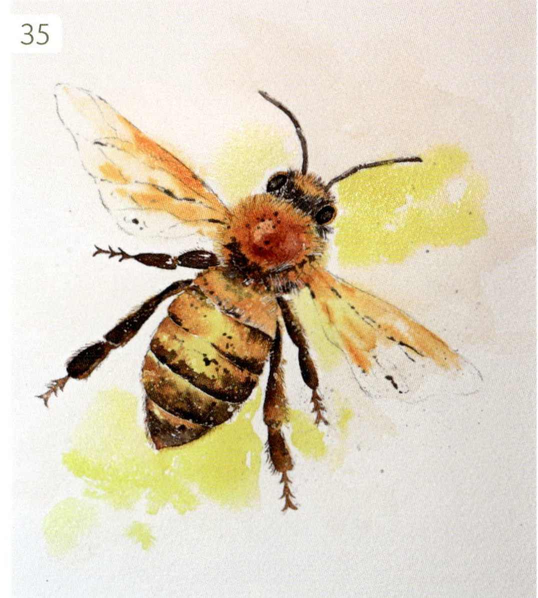

Wet the background area around the bee with clean water. While still wet, evenly dab color 600041 (Hansa Yellow Light) in scattered spots to create the background. At the same time, you can lightly apply this color to the wings as well, to enhance their transparent nature. This allows the background color to subtly show through the wings, enhancing the natural feel of the painting.

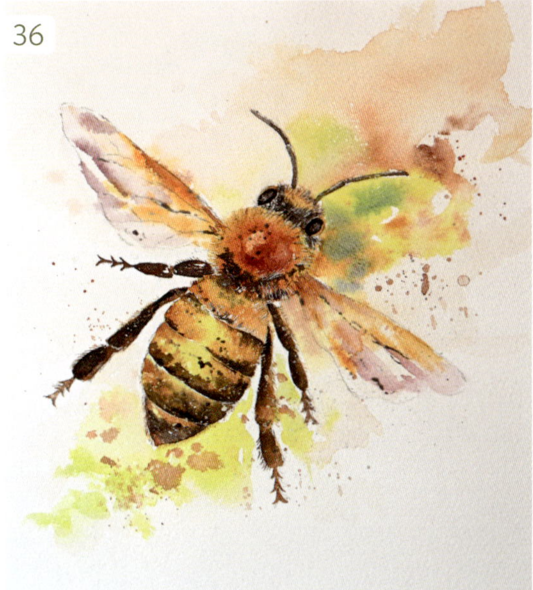

Continue to add some light purple and orange yellow to the background. Feel free to choose color shades to create the atmosphere of a blooming garden. Let the colors naturally blend together in the wet areas, while the dry areas naturally form watermarks. By using a combination of the wet-on-wet and wet-on-dry painting techniques, you will enrich the layers of the painting, enhancing the liveliness of the background.

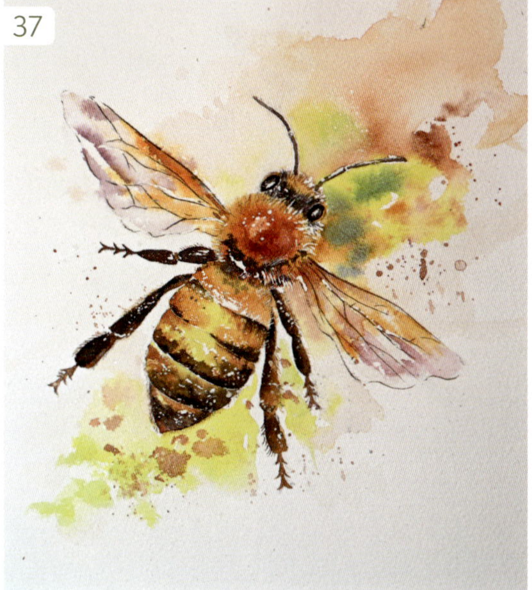

Finally, use color 600010 (Burnt Sienna) to outline the veins on the wings. Once the entire painting has dried, gently remove the masking fluid, and your little bee is complete.

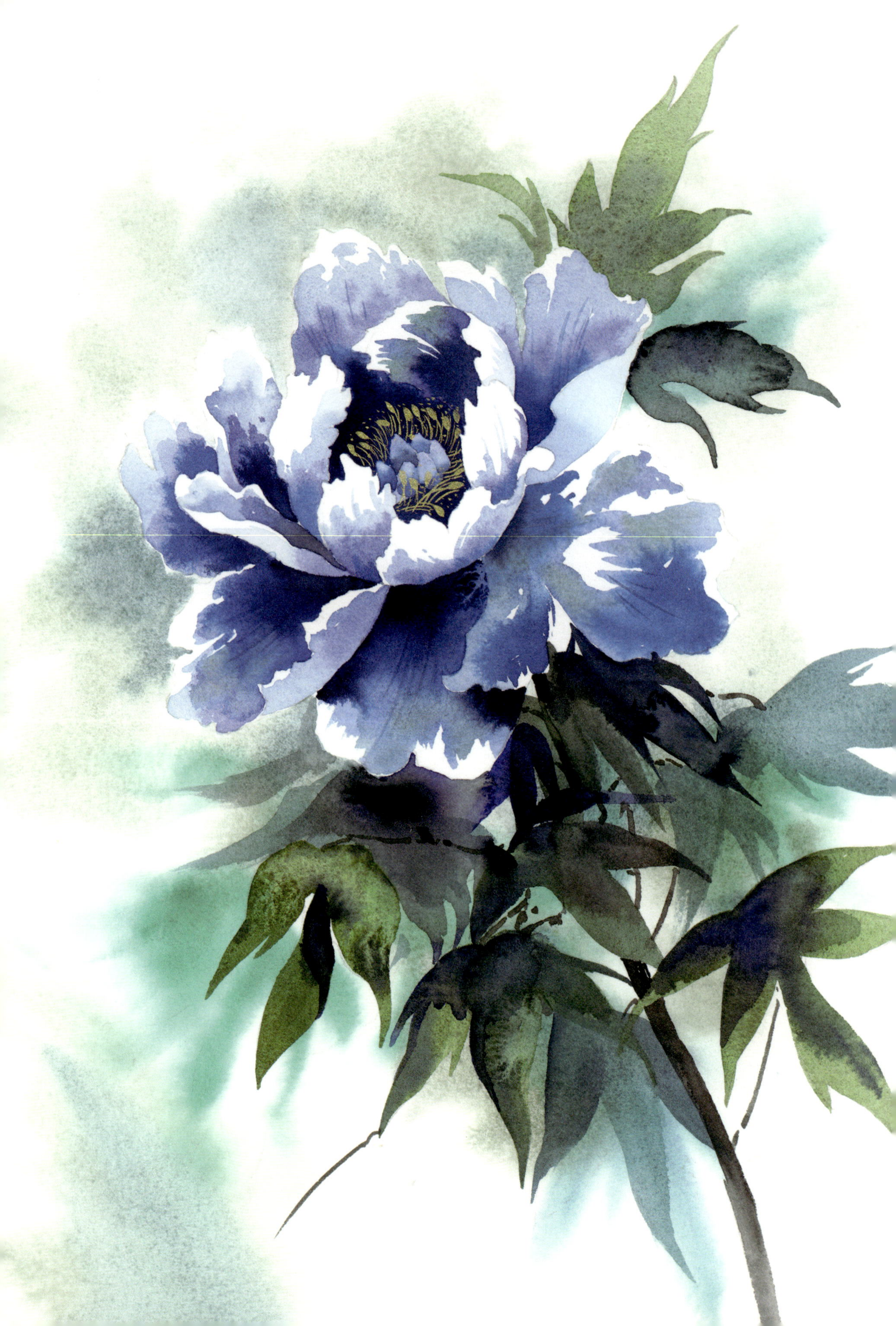

Peony

In the spring breeze, the peony unfurls its layered, brocade-like petals, resembling a beauty gently lowering her head with folded sleeves. This is the thousand-year romance behind the line "I present you with peonies" from the oldest collection of Chinese poems *The Book of Songs*, containing the most subtle love words of the Chinese people. It was once the "flower of wealth and honor" in the gardens of the Tang and Song dynasties (618–1279), with its full blooms carrying people's hopes for completeness. It is also the "Goddess of May Flowers" blooming alone in late spring, still holding onto the last faint fragrance after the other flowers have faded.

Paint Brand
DANIEL SMITH

Color Codes
- 600021: Cerulean Blue Chromium
- 600025: Cobalt Blue
- 600077: Phthalo Blue (Green Shade)
- 600082: Prussian Blue
- 600003: Lamp Black
- 600142: Cascade Green
- 600024: Chromium Green Oxide
- 600029: Cobalt Turquoise
- 600078: Phthalo Green (Blue Shade)
- 600197: Green Apatite Genuine
- 600034: French Ultramarine
- 640017: Iridescent Gold

Recommended Watercolor Paper
ARCHES watercolor paper, cold pressed, 140 lb/300 g/m^2

Recommended Brush
Black Velvet 3000S brush for watercolor, size 8

Key Challenges
1. Shaping the form of the flower blooming.
2. Depicting the color of the petals from light to dark.
3. The relationship between the solid and translucent layers of the leaves.

Steps

1

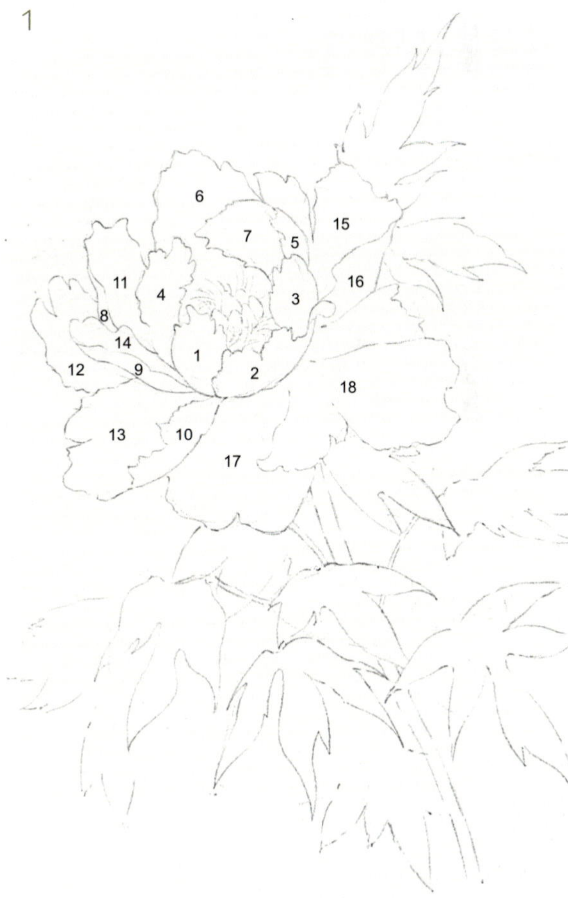

Use a pencil to sketch the shape of the flower and leaves, paying particular attention to the blooming state of the flower, the wrapping of the petals, the relationship between the front and back sides of the petals, and the form of the folded petals. To facilitate later instruction, each petal is labeled for reference.

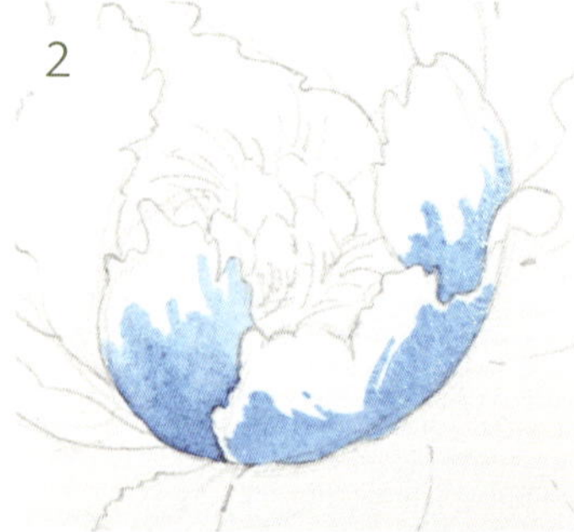

2

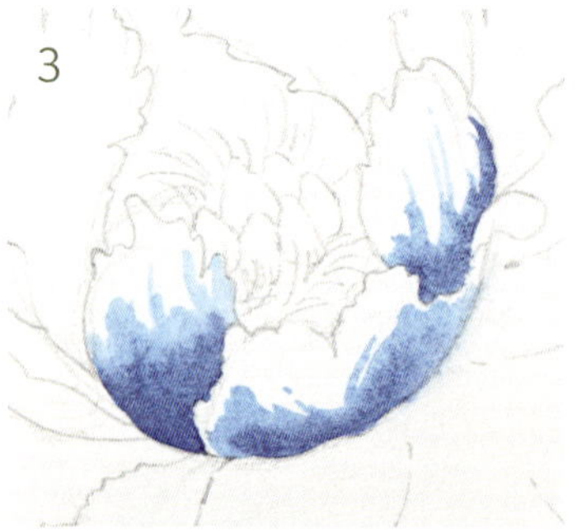

3

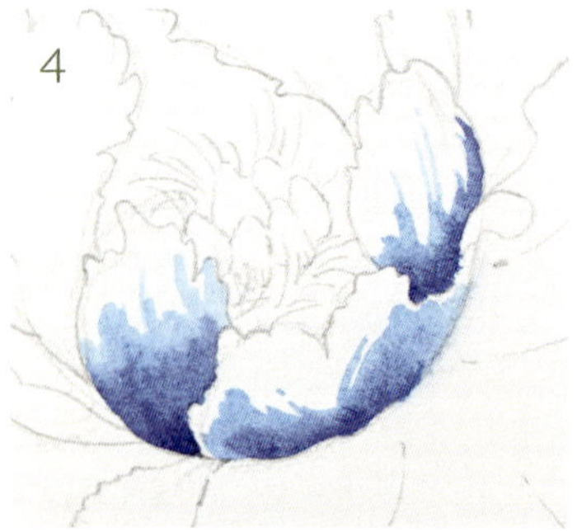

4

Start by coloring petals 1, 2, and 3, noting that these petals are facing away from us. Begin by applying color 600021 (Cerulean Blue Chromium) at the base of each petal, leaving a large blank area at the top. Keep your brushstrokes light and natural to allow the petal's vertical striping texture to appear at the edges of the color. Avoid outlining them as rigid arcs or straight lines. This approach will be applied to the coloring of the other petals as well.

While the petals are still wet, use color 600025 (Cobalt Blue) to dab to deepen the base of petals 1, 2, and 3.

While the petals are still wet, use color 600077 (Phthalo Blue) to further deepen the base of petals 1, 2, and 3. This will create a natural gradient effect, with the color transitioning from deep to light from the base to the top of the petals.

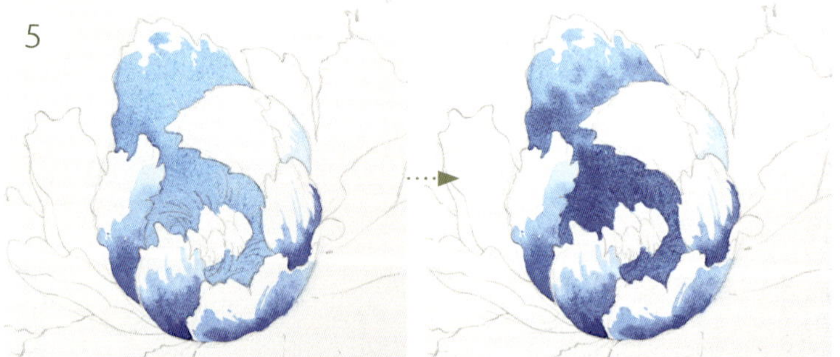

5

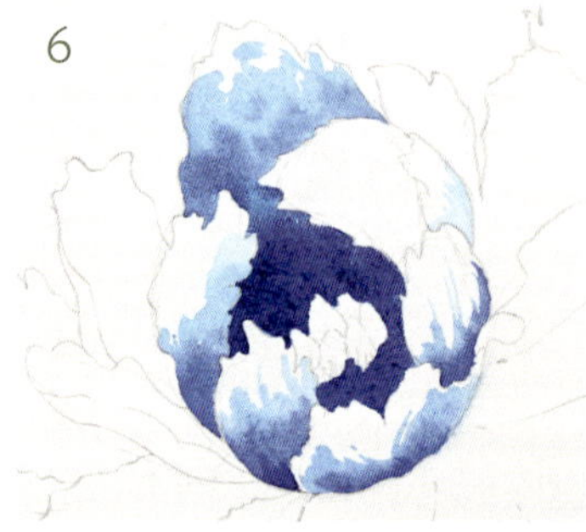

6

For petals 4 and 5, these two petals are also turned outward with their backs facing out, wrapping gently inward. Start by using color 600021 (Cerulean Blue Chromium) to apply color, and while the petals are still wet, use color 600025 (Cobalt Blue) to dab and deepen petal 4. For petal 5, you can choose whether to dab it, depending on your preference, to make the painting appear more natural and casual.

Next, paint petal 6, which is larger and faces toward us. The area close to the center of the flower will be the darkest. Start by using color 600021 (Cerulean Blue Chromium) for the base color, leaving a small area at the top blank. While the petal is still wet, deepen the color with 600025 (Cobalt Blue).

While the petal 6 is still wet, use color 600077 (Phthalo Blue) to dab and further deepen its inner part.

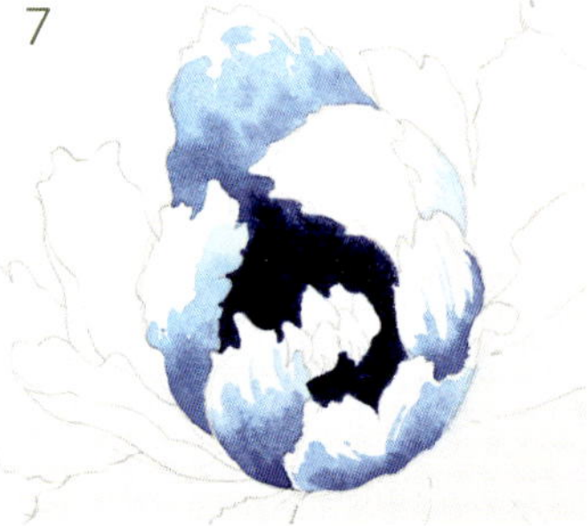

7

◀ While the petal 6 is still wet, use color 600082 (Prussian Blue) to deepen the darkest area.

▶ Start painting the petal 7. Due to the influence of the surrounding colors and to enrich the color layers of the painting, we can add a touch of green. Begin by using color 600021 (Cerulean Blue Chromium) to lay down the base color.

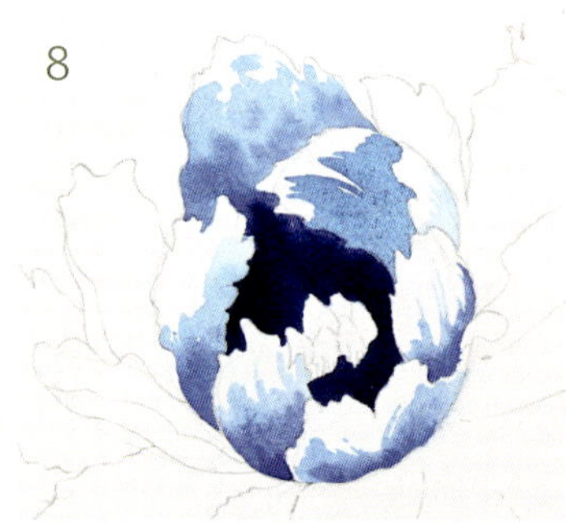

8

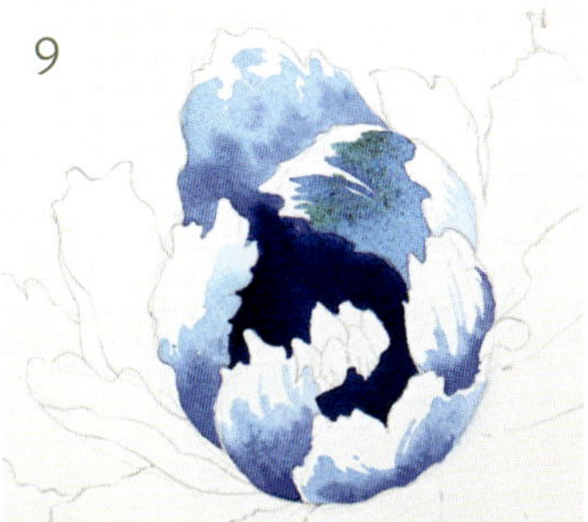

While the area is still wet, dab in some color 600142 (Cascade Green).

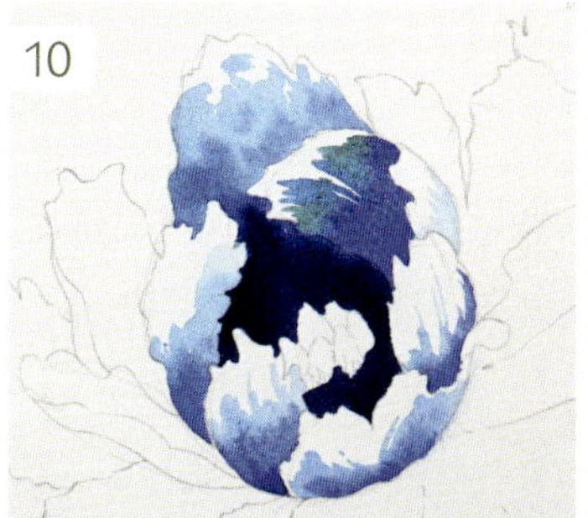

While the area is still wet, use color 600025 (Cobalt Blue) to deepen the base of the petal.

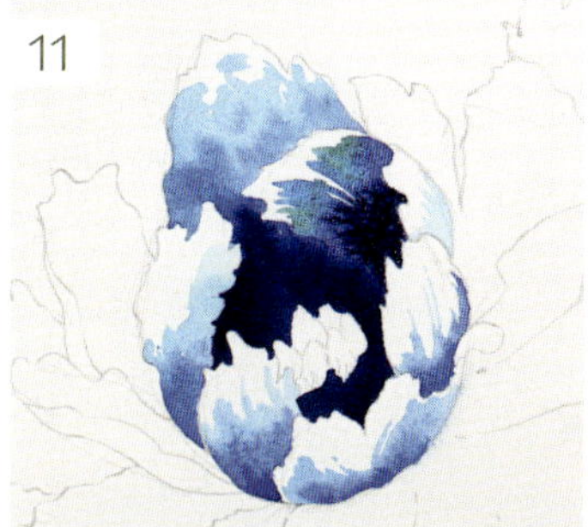

While the area is still wet, use color 600077 (Phthalo Blue) to further deepen the base of the petal.

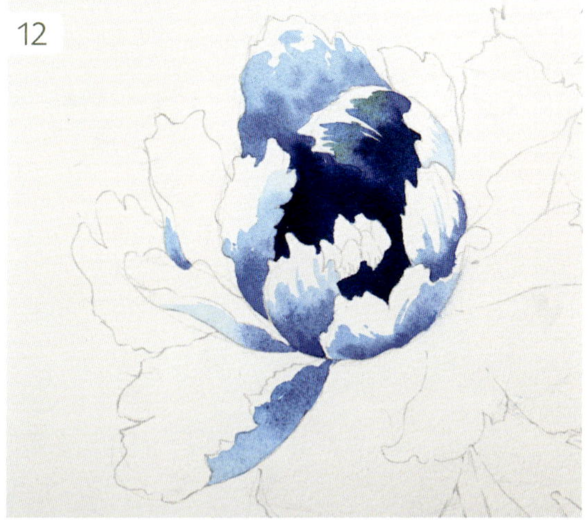

For petals 8, 9, and 10, which are the flipped sides of the petals, start by laying down a base layer with color 600021 (Cerulean Blue Chromium). While the area is still wet, use color 600025 (Cobalt Blue) to dab and deepen the shade. Be sure not to cover the entire petal with color. Leave some areas of the edge blank to emphasize the highlights on the petals, enhancing the three-dimensional effect.

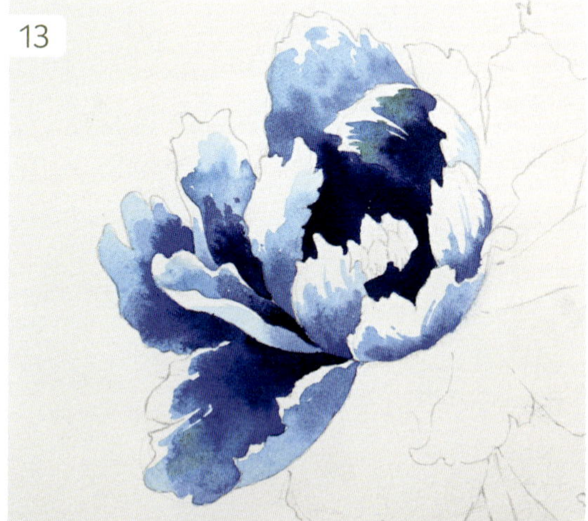

For petals 11 to 14, follow a similar method as the previous petals. Start by applying a base layer with color 600021 (Cerulean Blue Chromium), leaving the highlight areas unpainted. While the area is still wet, use color 600025 (Cobalt Blue) to deepen the petals from the base. Then, layer color 600077 (Phthalo Blue) and color 600082 (Prussian Blue) from the base, gradually deepening the color through layered dabbing. Finally, mix color 600082 (Prussian Blue) and color 600003 (Lamp Black) in a 5:1 ratio to create the darkest color, and apply a small amount to dab at the base of the petals. The colors are deepened layer by layer, with each successive layer covering a smaller area, completed in one go, gradually creating a smooth gradient effect from deep to light along the petals.

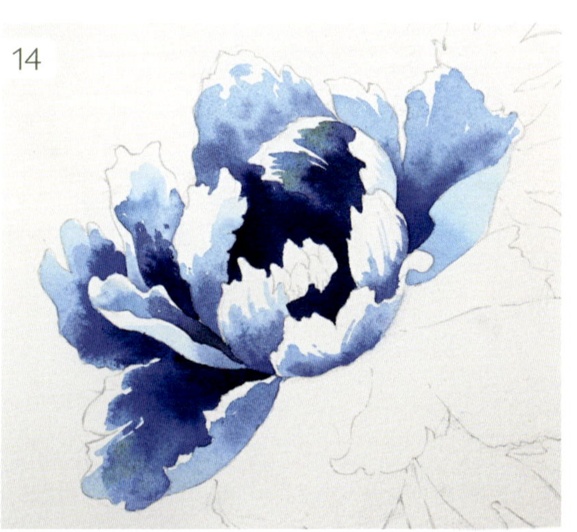

Petal 15 is on the inside, while petal 16 is the back-facing side, so the color of petal 16 should be slightly lighter than petal 15. Start by applying color 600021 (Cerulean Blue Chromium) as a base for both petals, leaving the top areas for highlights. Then, gradually deepen the color of petal 15 by layering color 600025 (Cobalt Blue) and color 600077 (Phthalo Blue) respectively from the base upward.

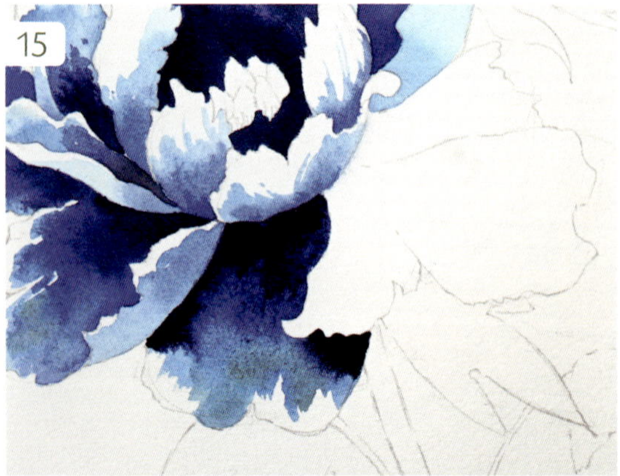

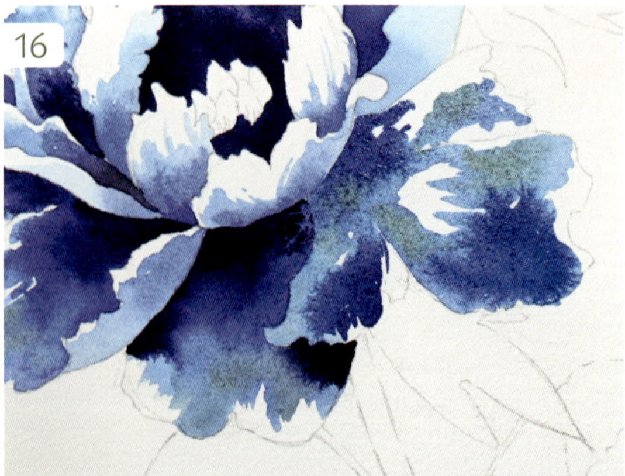

The coloring and method for petal 17 are the same as for petal 13. Here, we can add a touch of color 600142 (Cascade Green) to the top of the petal, as the top area is the highlight region. Due to the influence of the surrounding leaf color, it may have a slight green tint, which will make the overall composition more harmonious and natural.

For petal 18, start by applying color 600021 (Cerulean Blue Chromium) as the base color, making sure to leave the highlight areas white. While the paper is still wet, use color 600025 (Cobalt Blue) to add shading at the base of the petal. Then, use color 600077 (Phthalo Blue) and color 600142 (Cascade Green) to add dispersed touches of color throughout the petal.

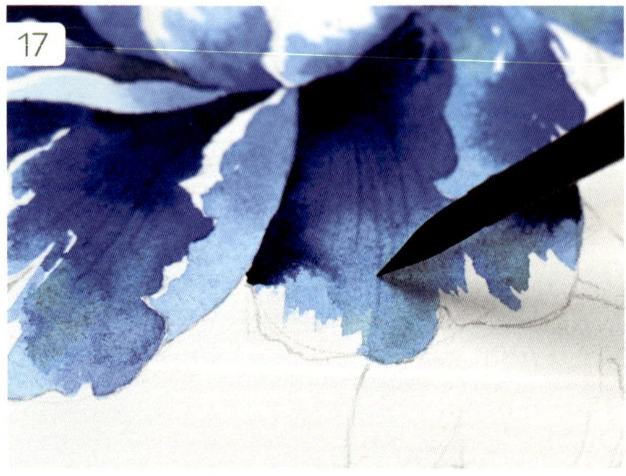

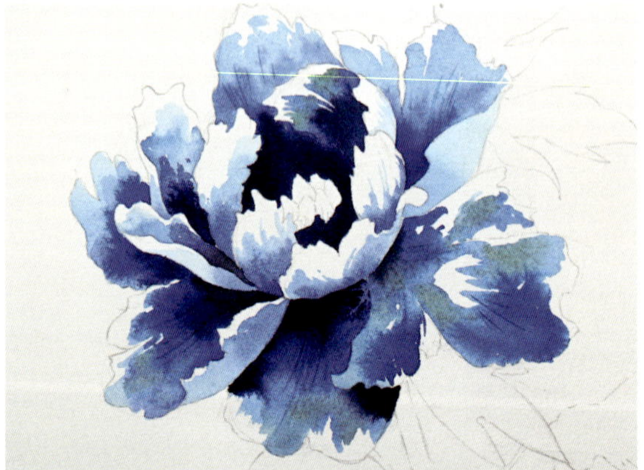

Use a light touch of color 600077 (Phthalo Blue) to outline some patterns on the petals. The image on the right shows the effect of all petals with their patterns completed.

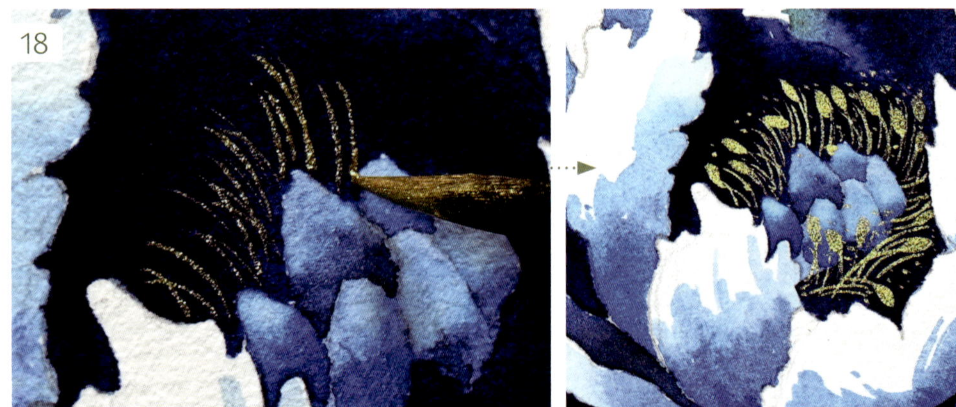

Refer to the above steps for the method of coloring the petals. Apply color 600021 (Cerulean Blue Chromium) and color 600077 (Phthalo Blue) to color the pistil of the peony. Then, with color 640017 (Iridescent Gold), outline the stamens, paying attention to their density and direction. Finally, use the same iridescent gold to paint the anthers on the stamens.

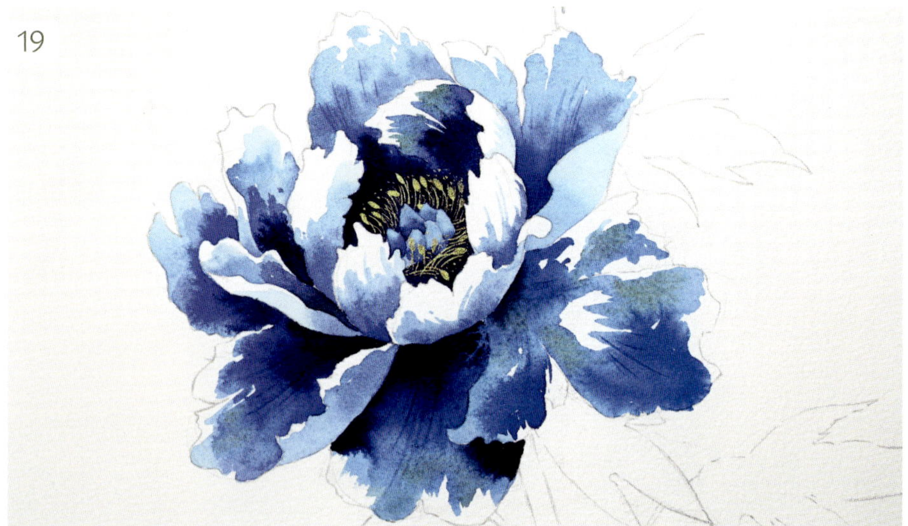

19

The image shows
the completed main
body of the peony
flower.

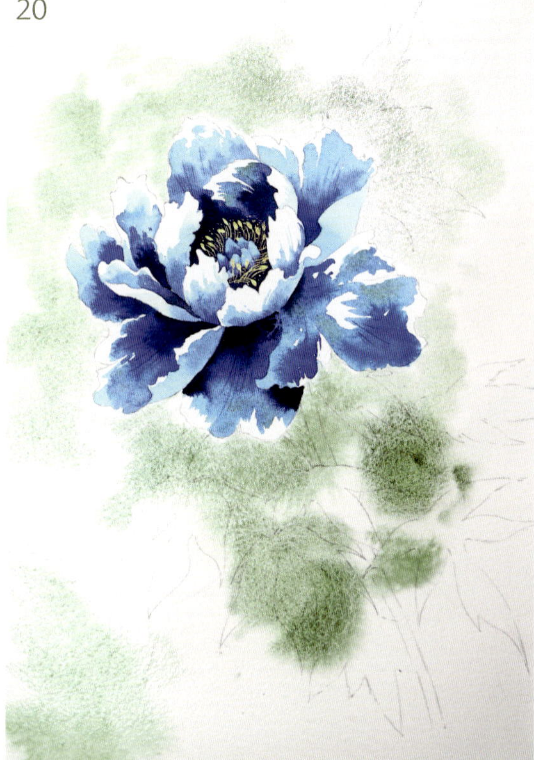

20

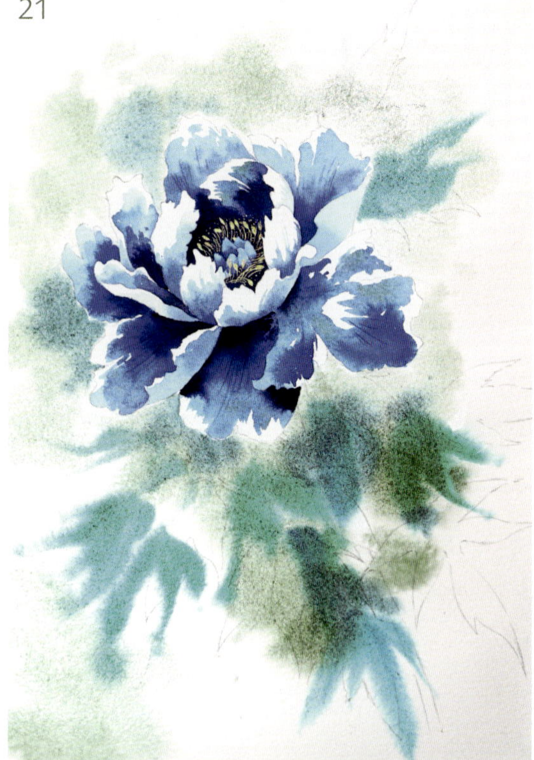

21

Paint the background. First, wet all areas outside the flower with clean water. Then use paint color 600024 (Chromium Green Oxide) to lay down a green background. Vary the sizes of the color patches and leave some white spaces in between. Let the paint flow naturally with the water. Once it spreads and settles, the background will have a light, airy feel.

While the paper is still wet, continue applying color 600029 (Cobalt Turquoise) to the darker areas of the background. Then, use color 600078 (Phthalo Green), as well as a cool green mixed in equal parts from color 600078 (Phthalo Green) and color 600025 (Cobalt Blue), to paint background leaves. The moisture on the paper will cause the paint to softly diffuse outward, creating a hazy, almost translucent effect. When painting these leaves, stay relaxed, and avoid fixating on precise shapes. Instead, aim to complete each stroke fluidly to evoke a natural atmosphere.

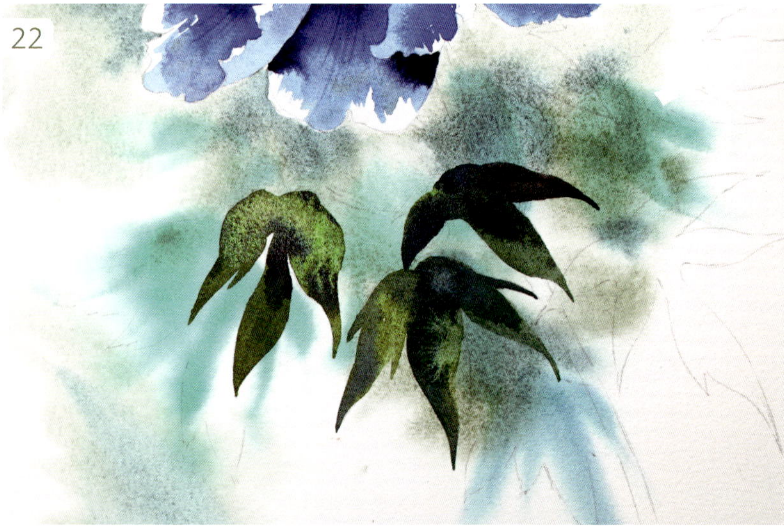

Use color 600197 (Green Apatite Genuine) to lay the base tone for the three leaves shown in the image. While the surface is still wet, deepen the darker parts of the leaves by dotting in a mix of color 600082 (Prussian Blue) and color 600003 (Lamp Black) in a 5:1 ratio. Finally, while the paint is still moist, randomly drop one or two small droplets of clean water onto leaves of your choice to create watermarks. Be mindful not to overdo it, just 1 to 2 drops per leaf are enough. In this stage, use the paint loosely, allowing it to blend naturally with the moisture to create a mottled appearance on the leaves.

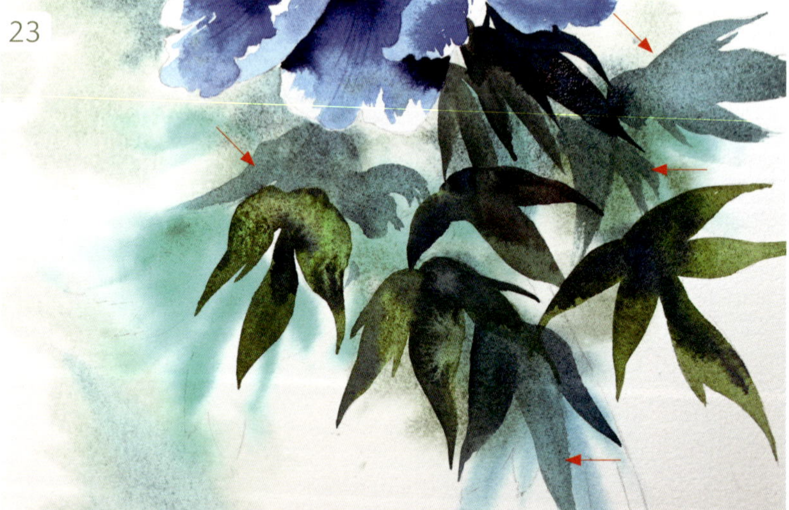

Use the same colors and techniques as before to paint the remaining leaves. Finally, use color 600029 (Cobalt Turquoise) directly to paint the few gray-green leaves indicated by the arrows in the image. By utilizing contrast in lightness and darkness, this helps to convey the layering between the foreground and background leaves.

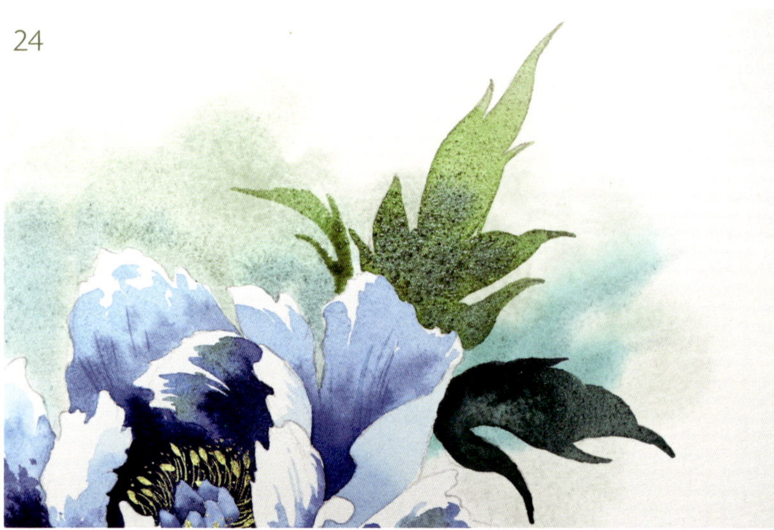

Use color 600197 (Green Apatite Genuine) to lay a base tone for the green leaf located above the flower. While the surface is still wet, use color 600078 (Phthalo Green) to dab in the darker areas.

For the leaf positioned lower down, apply a wash mixed in equal parts of color 600003 (Lamp Black) with a higher water content, and color 600077 (Phthalo Blue). While still wet, deepen the base of the leaf using a more concentrated (less diluted) application of color 600003 (Lamp Black). Finally, drop a single bead of clean water at the base to form a watermark, creating a mottled effect.

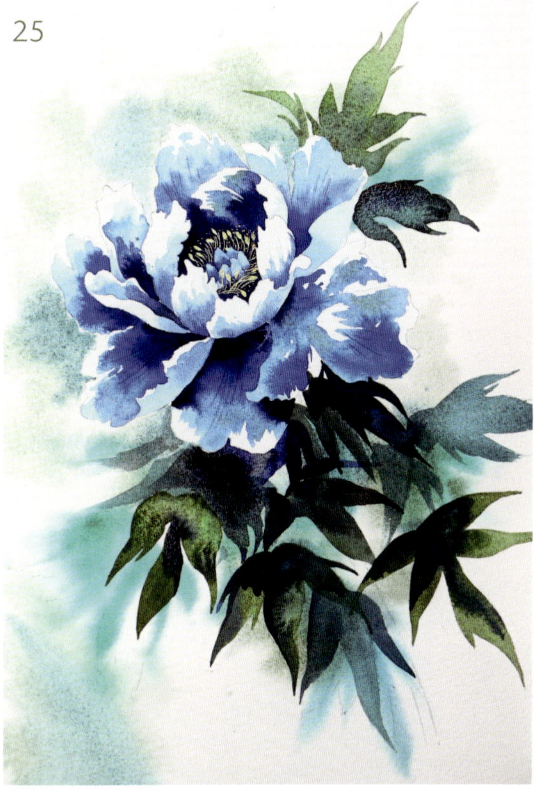

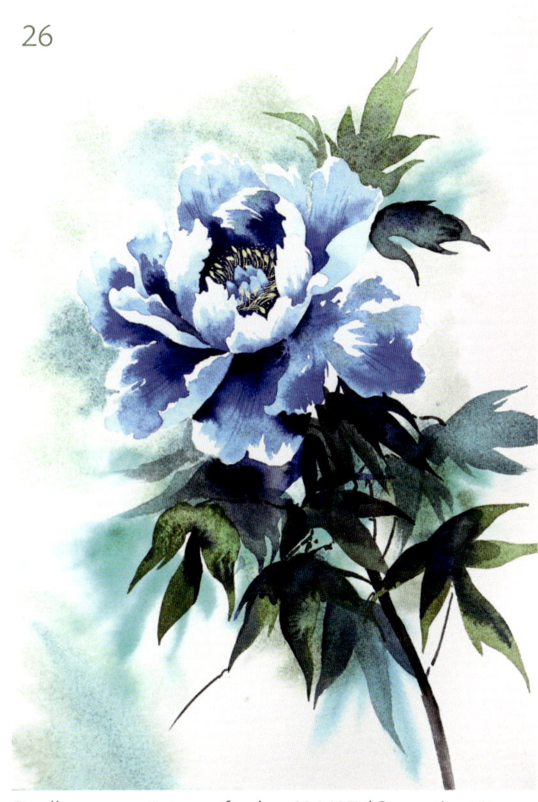

Apply color 600034 (French Ultramarine) to the surface of some leaves and between the leaves, deepening the shadows formed by overlapping leaves, and continue to enhance the sense of layering.

Finally, use a mixture of color 600197 (Green Apatite Genuine) and color 600003 (Lamp Black) in a 4:1 ratio to paint the flower stems and petioles interwoven among the leaves. With this final step, the peony painting is complete.

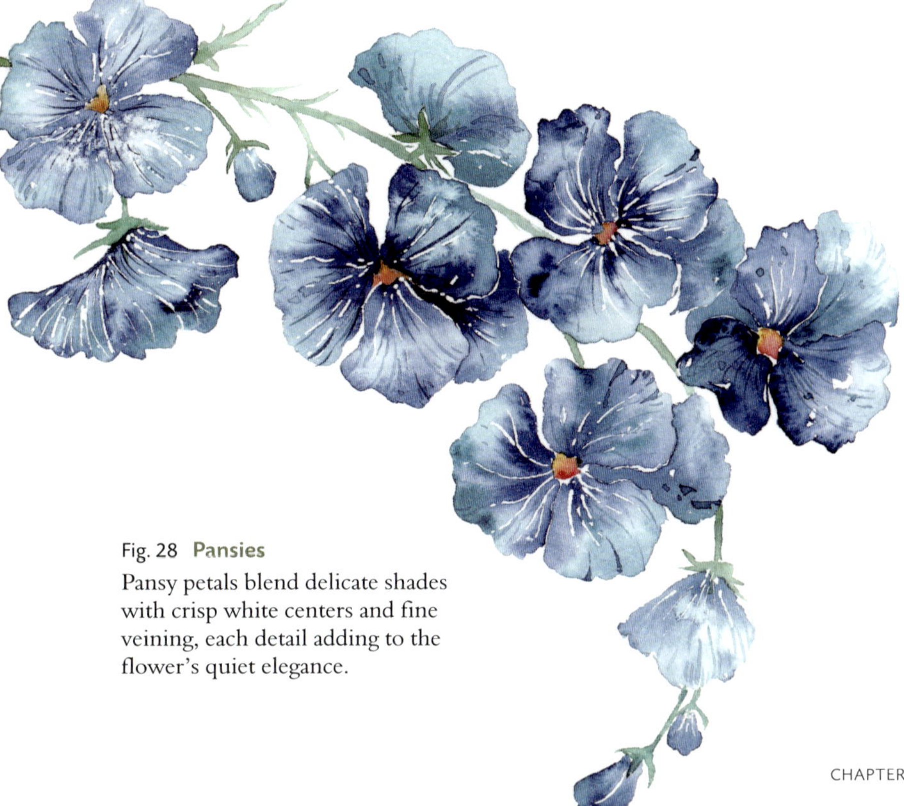

Fig. 28 Pansies

Pansy petals blend delicate shades with crisp white centers and fine veining, each detail adding to the flower's quiet elegance.

Cat

The cat crawls gracefully through the
garden, weaving skillfully between the
blooming flowers. She treads carefully
across a small pond, her paws gently
touching the water, creating tiny,
sparkling ripples. Her gaze is focused, as
if she has spotted something of interest.
At this moment, the entire garden
seems to hold its breath, waiting for the
excitement of this fleeting moment.

Paint Brand
DANIEL SMITH

Color Codes
- 600011: Burnt Umber
- 600244: Joseph Z's Neutral Grey
- 600198: Opera Pink
- 600082: Prussian Blue
- 600041: Hansa Yellow Light
- 600233: Raw Sienna Light
- 600010: Burnt Sienna
- 600003: Lamp Black
- 600064: Organic Vermilion
- 600021: Cerulean Blue Chromium

Auxiliary Material
Masking fluid

Recommended Watercolor Paper
ARCHES watercolor paper, cold pressed, 140 lb/300 g/m^2

Recommended Brush
Black Velvet 3000S brush for watercolor, size 8

Key Challenges
1. Shaping the form of the cat crawling forward.
2. Shaping the sense of volume of the cat.

Steps

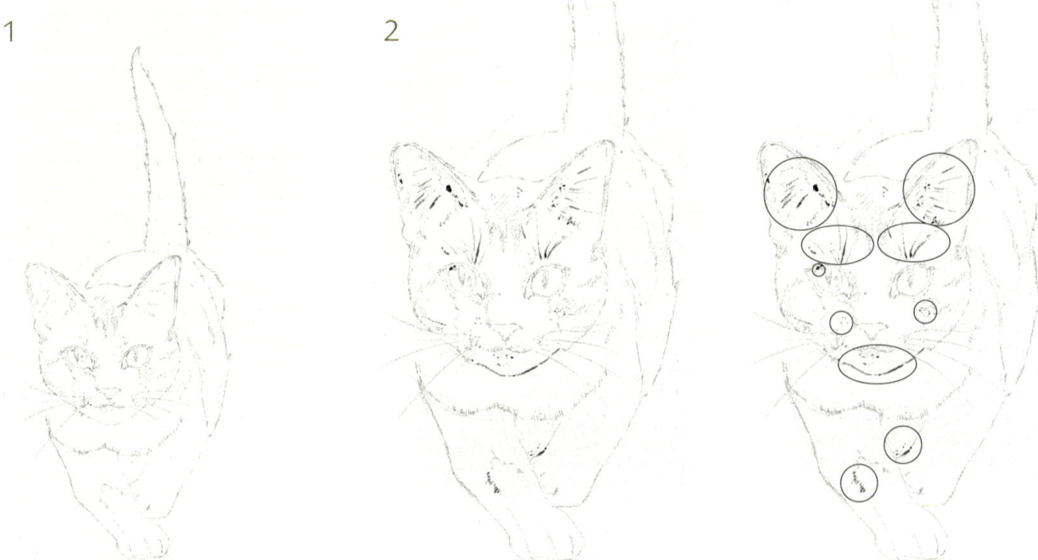

1.

Draw the cat's form using a pencil, paying attention to the crawling posture and the positioning of its legs as it moves.

2.

Apply masking fluid on the ears, cheeks, and front legs, especially on the fur of the ears, the eyebrows, the chin edge, around the mouth, and the front legs. The circled areas on the right picture are the key regions where highlights are needed.

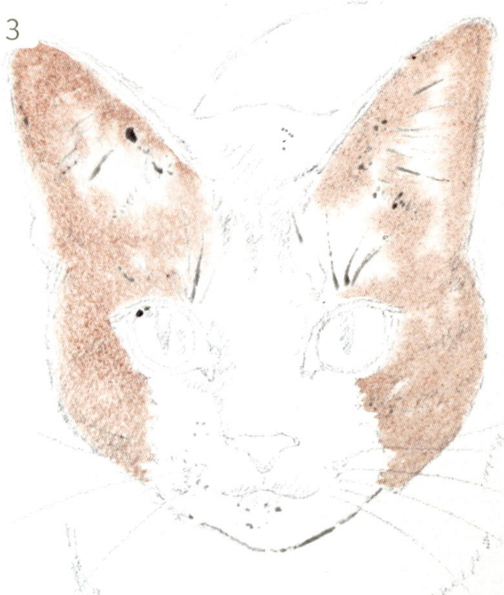

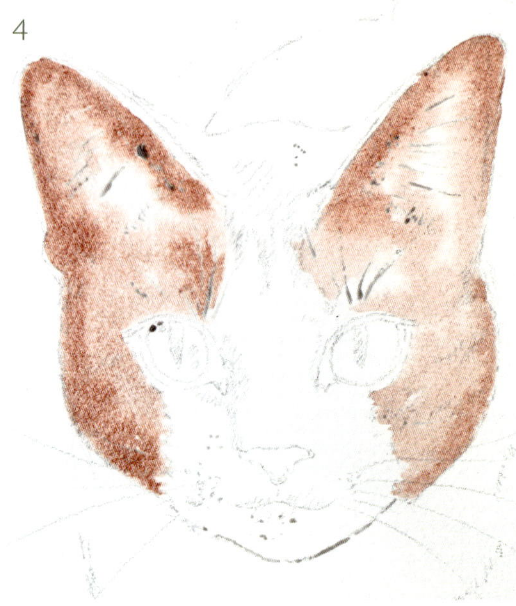

First, wet the cheeks and the ears on both sides with clean water. Once the water has soaked into the paper, use color 600011 (Burnt Umber) as the base layer. Be sure to leave the ear canal area unpainted and let the color diffuse naturally.

While the paper is still wet, use color 600010 (Burnt Sienna) to deepen along the outer contour of the cat's face and the brow ridge, enhancing the sense of volume.

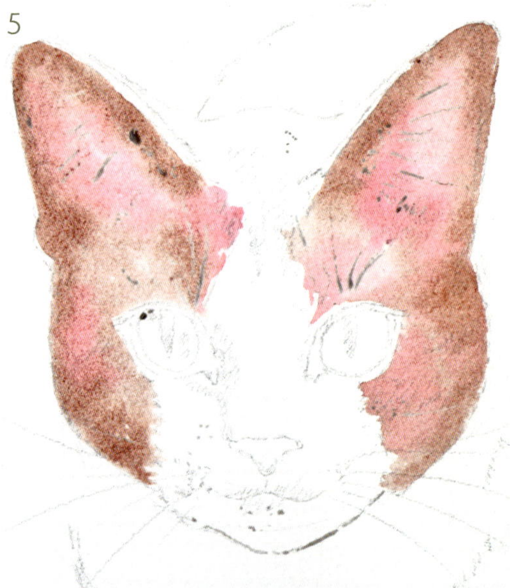

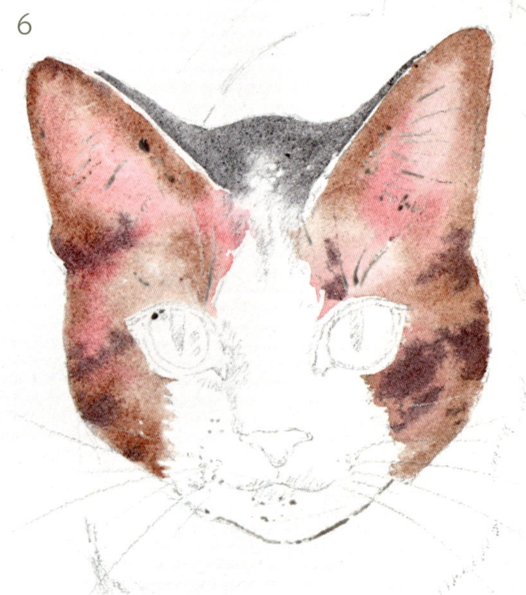

While the paper is still wet, mix color 600064 (Organic Vermilion) with 600198 (Opera Pink) in equal proportions to create a soft pink hue. Apply it lightly to the lighter areas of the cheeks and ears.

Apply a layer of clean water to the top of the head. While the paper is still wet, use color 600244 (Joseph Z's Neutral Grey) to lay down a base color, leaving the center area blank to allow the color to diffuse naturally. Pay attention to the junction with the ears, leaving a white line to prevent the gray from bleeding into the ear colors. Next, mix the soft pink hue prepared in step 5 with a bit of 600244 (Joseph Z's Neutral Grey) to create a deep gray shade, and use it to paint the dark patterns on both sides of the cheeks.

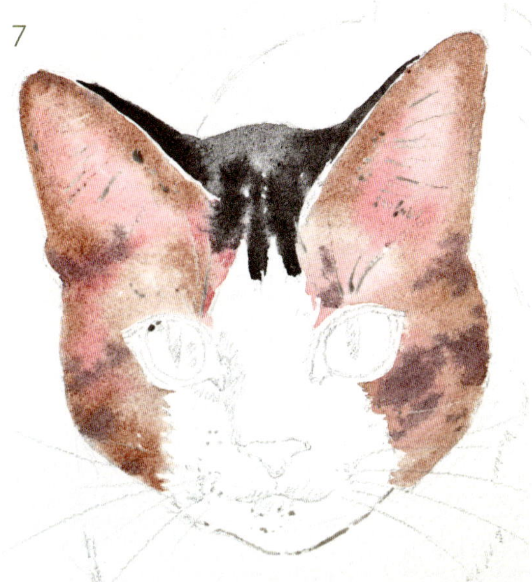

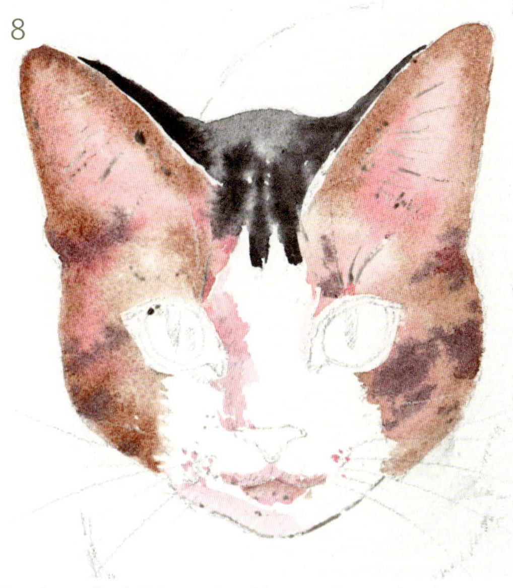

While the paper is still wet, use color 600003 (Lamp Black) to paint the black patterns on the top of the head.

Use the soft pink hue mixed in step 5 to paint the areas around the nose wings, lips, and chin. Note that the coloring in these areas primarily serves to depict facial shadows, thereby highlighting the volume of these three features.

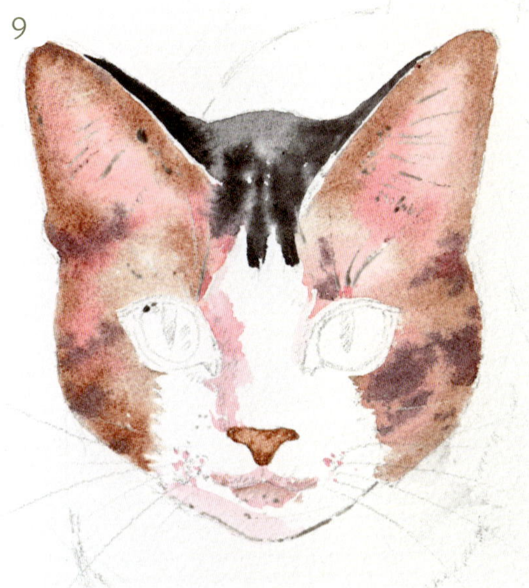

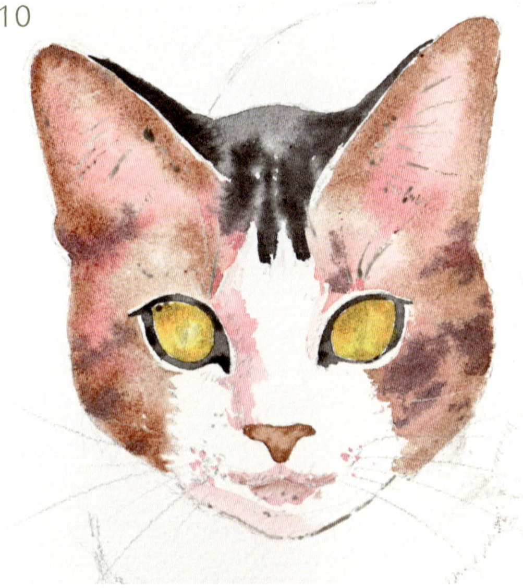

Use color 600010 (Burnt Sienna) to paint the nose tip. First, apply a layer of clean water, then lightly lay down a base color. Afterward, use a less diluted paint (with lower water content) to deepen the edges and create a sense of volume.

Use color 600003 (Lamp Black) to paint the lines around the eyes. First, apply a layer of clean water, then lightly add a base color. Next, use a less diluted paint (with lower water content) to deepen the eye socket area and certain parts of the upper eyeliner.

Next, paint the eye itself, keeping in mind that it should be treated as a sphere with distinct light and shadow areas. Start by applying a light yellow base using color 600041 (Hansa Yellow Light). While the paper is still wet, use color 600233 (Raw Sienna Light) to paint the shadowed areas on the outer edge of the eyeball, creating a sense of volume and dimensionality.

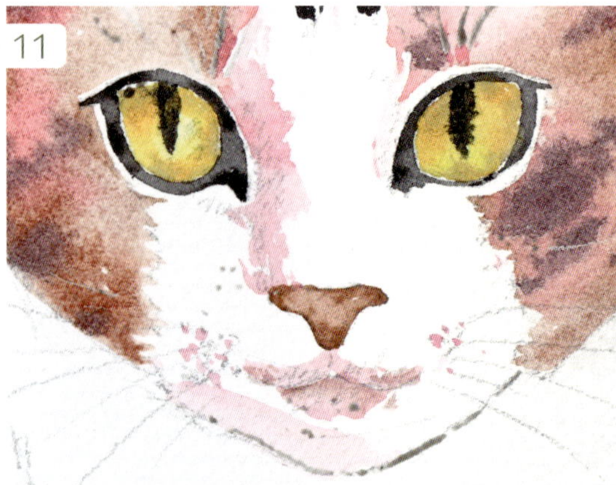

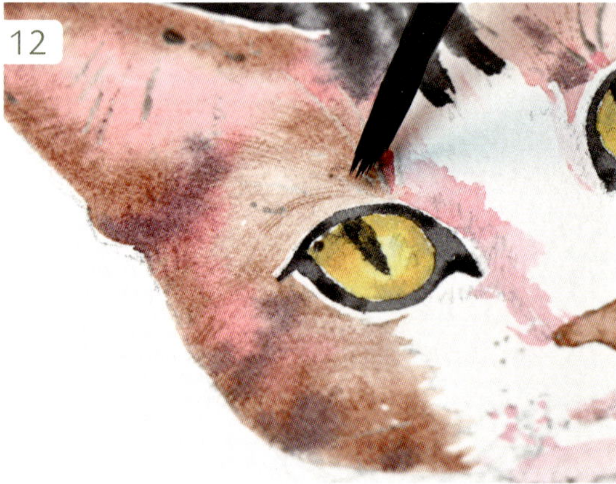

While the paper is still wet, use color 600003 (Lamp Black) to paint the pupil, allowing the color to spread naturally. This prevents the edges of the pupil from being too sharp, which would make it appear stiff and unnatural.

Dry the brush tip as much as possible using a paper towel, then gently rub the brush tip with your fingers to create a splayed shape. Dip the brush lightly into color 600011 (Burnt Umber) and carefully outline fine, fluffy fur textures along the edges of the ears, the brow ridge, and the cheeks.

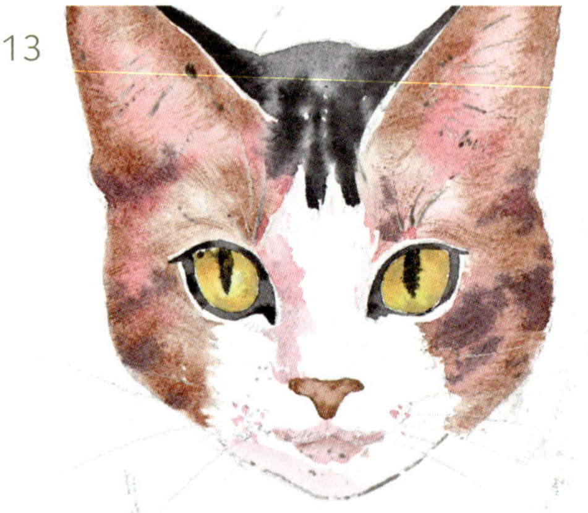

The shaping of the face is essentially complete.

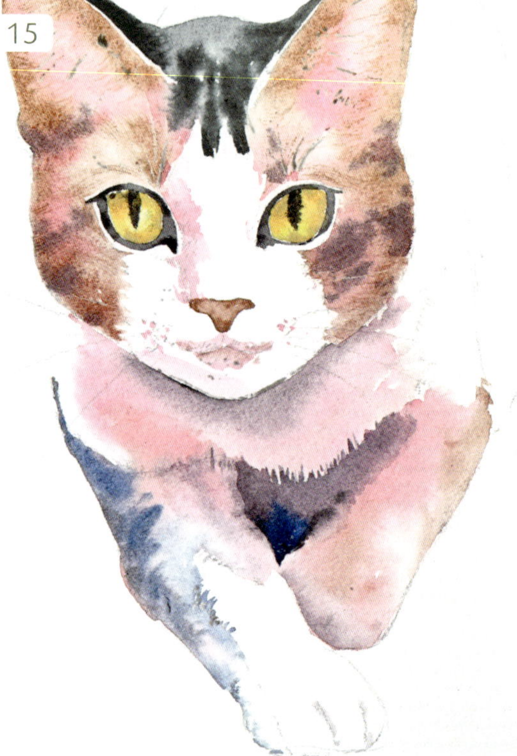

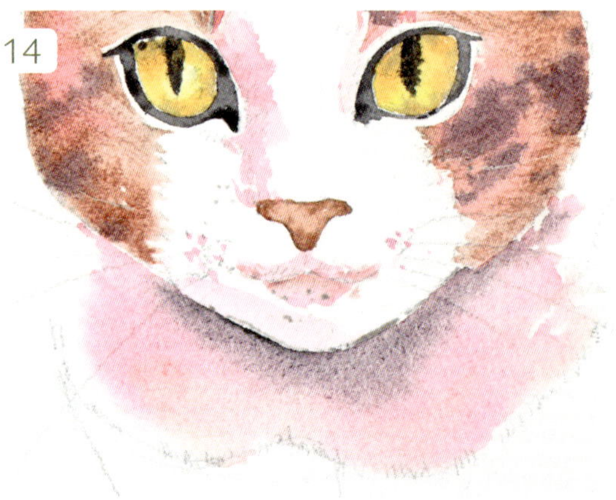

Wet the neck area with clean water and lightly apply a base layer using 600198 (Opera Pink) and 600011 (Burnt Umber). While the paper is still wet, blend in 600244 (Joseph Z's Neutral Grey) at the junction between the neck and the head to create the shadow effect.

Wet the front limb area with clean water and apply a light base layer using 600198 (Opera Pink) and 600011 (Burnt Umber). Blend in 600244 (Joseph Z's Neutral Grey) to depict shadows. Use 600021 (Cerulean Blue Chromium) to paint the outer part of the right front limb, highlighting shadows and creating volume. For the shadowed area of the chest between the two legs, mix all the colors from step 15 to create a deep gray. While the paper is still wet, add 600082 (Prussian Blue) to deepen the shadows at the bottom of the chest.

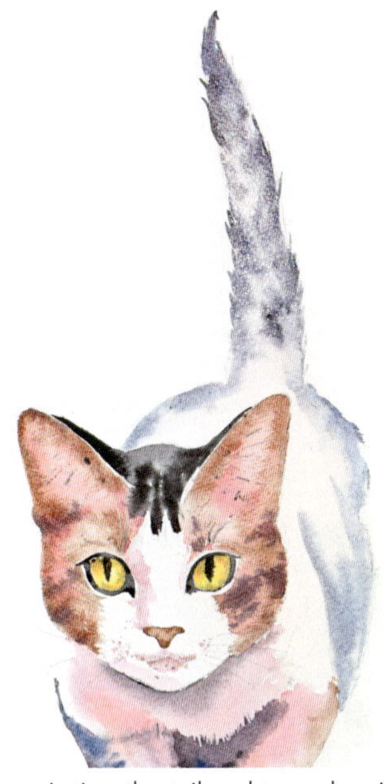

Begin painting the tail and torso by visualizing them as cylindrical shapes, with distinct light-facing and shadowed areas. Wet the edges of the tail and torso with clean water. Use 600021 (Cerulean Blue Chromium) to apply a base layer, representing the shadowed areas. Leave the center of the tail and the top of the torso, which are the light-facing areas, unpainted.

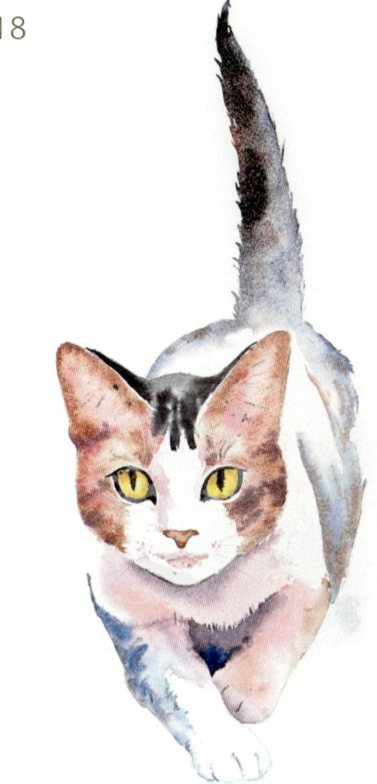

On the tail, while the paper is still wet, dab 600003 (Lamp Black) to depict the darker patterns.

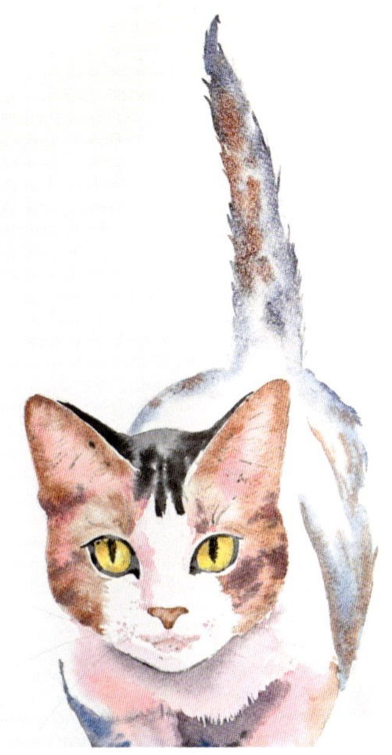

Next, while the paper is still wet, use 600011 (Burnt Umber) to dot the patterns, allowing the two colors to naturally blend and diffuse.

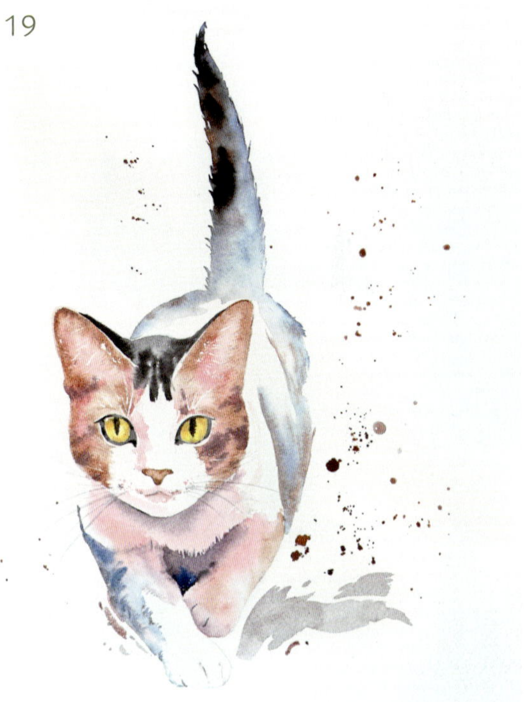

Rub off the masking fluid, and use 600244 (Joseph Z's Neutral Grey) to paint the whiskers. Add sufficient water to the existing colors on your palette, and gently dot in the splashing water with a light touch, varying the colors slightly to make the scene livelier.

And with that, the painting of a little cat strolling through a garden after the rain is complete.

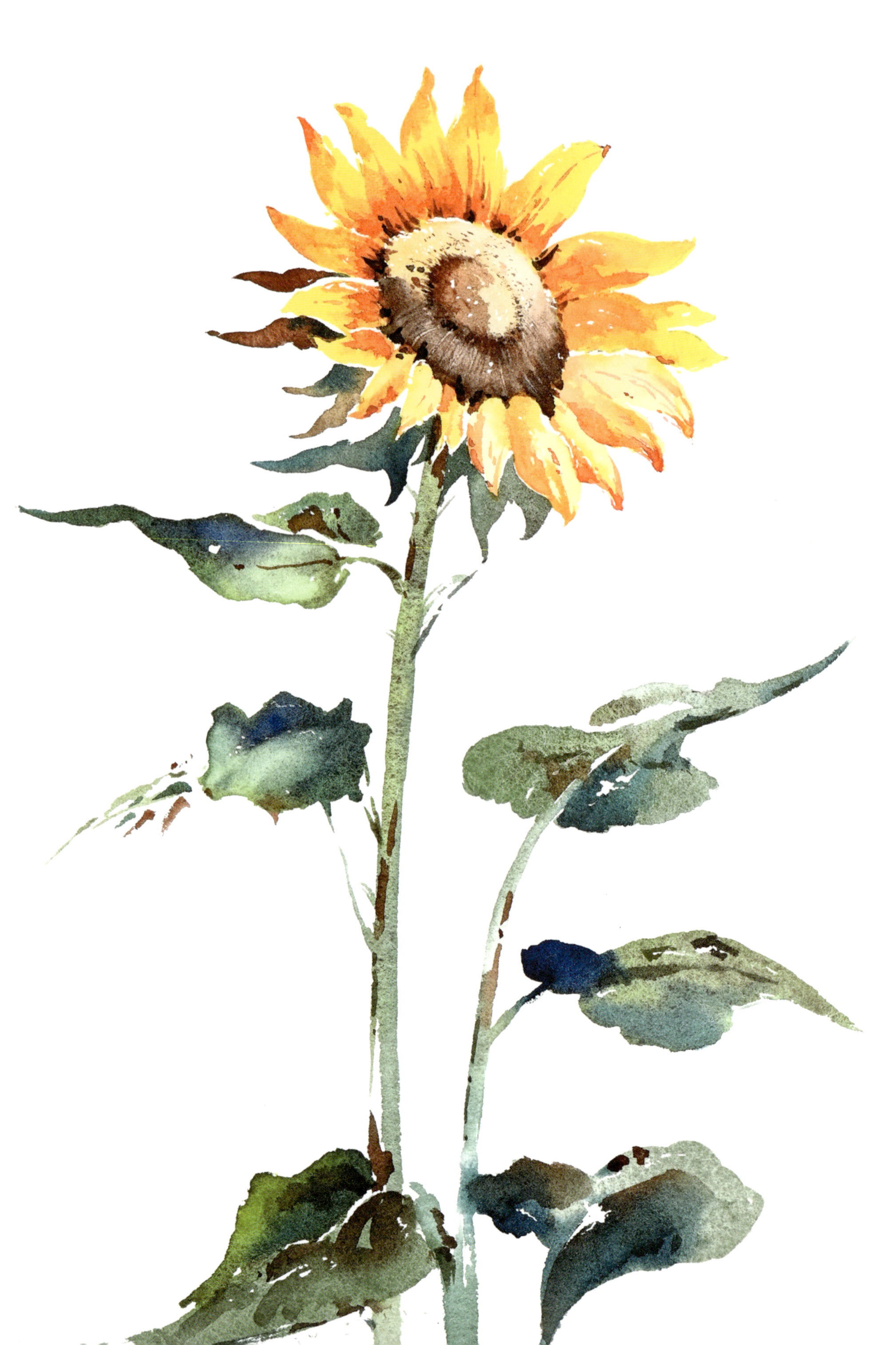

Sunflower

In my garden, a tall sunflower stands proudly in full bloom, with a bright, warm smile. It follows the sun, reaching toward the light, and competes with the sun, radiating vibrant energy. It constantly reminds me to stay positive, believe in a beautiful future, and encourages me to face life's challenges with courage, chasing the sunshine and hope within my heart.

Paint Brand
DANIEL SMITH

Color Codes
- 600041: Hansa Yellow Light
- 600234: Aussie Red Gold
- 600064: Organic Vermilion
- 600233: Raw Sienna Light
- 600034: French Ultramarine
- 600010: Burnt Sienna
- 600011: Burnt Umber
- 600197: Green Apatite Genuine
- 600080: Phthalo Turquoise
- 600003: Lamp Black
- 600024: Chromium Green Oxide

Auxiliary Material
Masking fluid

Recommended Watercolor Paper
ARCHES watercolor paper, cold pressed, 140 lb/300 g/m^2

Recommended Brush
Black Velvet 3000S brush for watercolor, size 8

Key Challenges
1. Shaping the form of the sunflower.
2. Handling the contrast between the light-facing and shadowed sides of the sunflower's leaves and central disc.
3. Detailing specific parts.

Steps

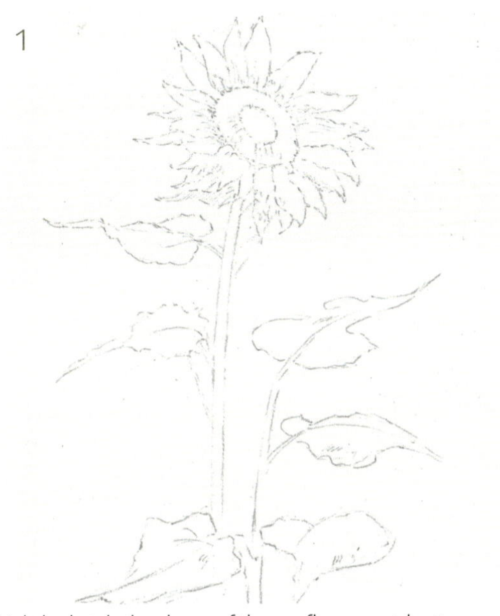

1

Lightly sketch the shape of the sunflower petals, stems, and leaves with a pencil. Ensure each petal and leaf is clearly defined, paying attention to the folding of the leaves. The flower's central disc is an almost flat round sphere, so be mindful of its shape when outlining. The entire flower faces the upper right, so keep the perspective in mind. When drawing the leaves, use light strokes, ensuring that the lines flow naturally and smoothly.

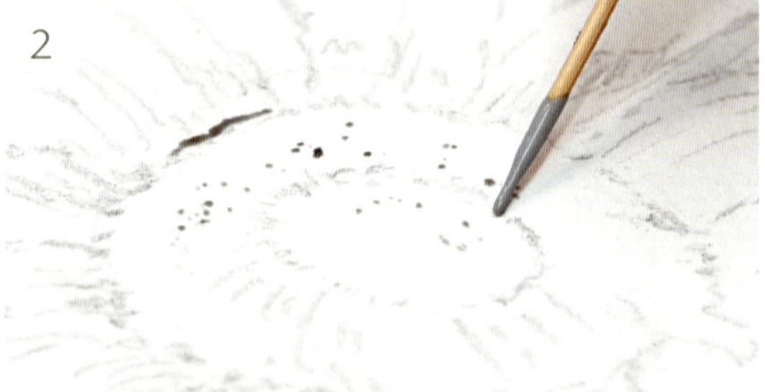

2

Use a toothpick to apply masking fluid and pinpoint the highlight areas.

3

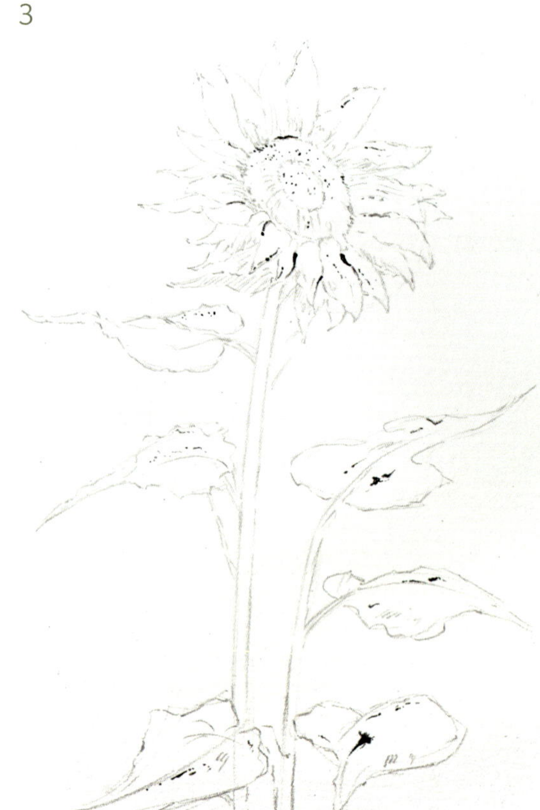

The black areas in the image indicate the areas where masking fluid has been applied.

4

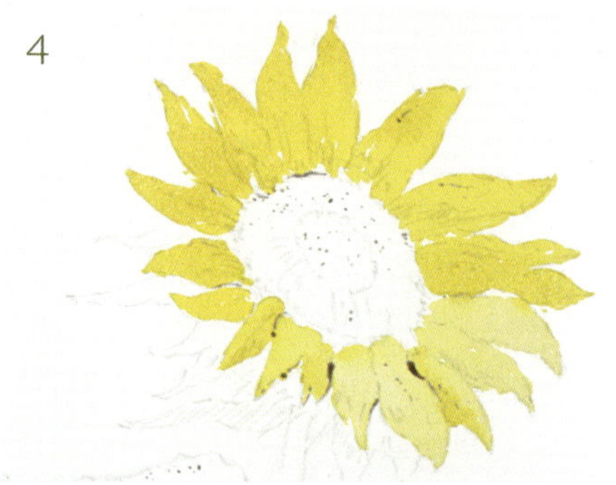

Use 600041 (Hansa Yellow Light) mixed with an ample amount of water, with a ratio of approximately 2:1 of water to pigment. After thoroughly diluting the paint, apply a generous flat wash to the petals.

5

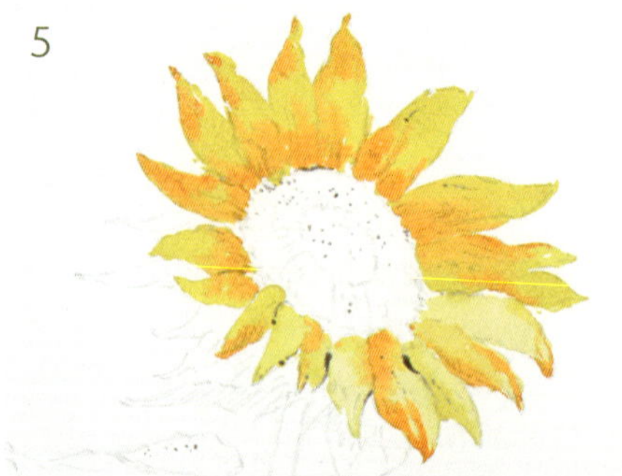

While the paper is still wet, use 600234 (Aussie Red Gold) to deepen the darker areas of the petals, as shown in the image.

6

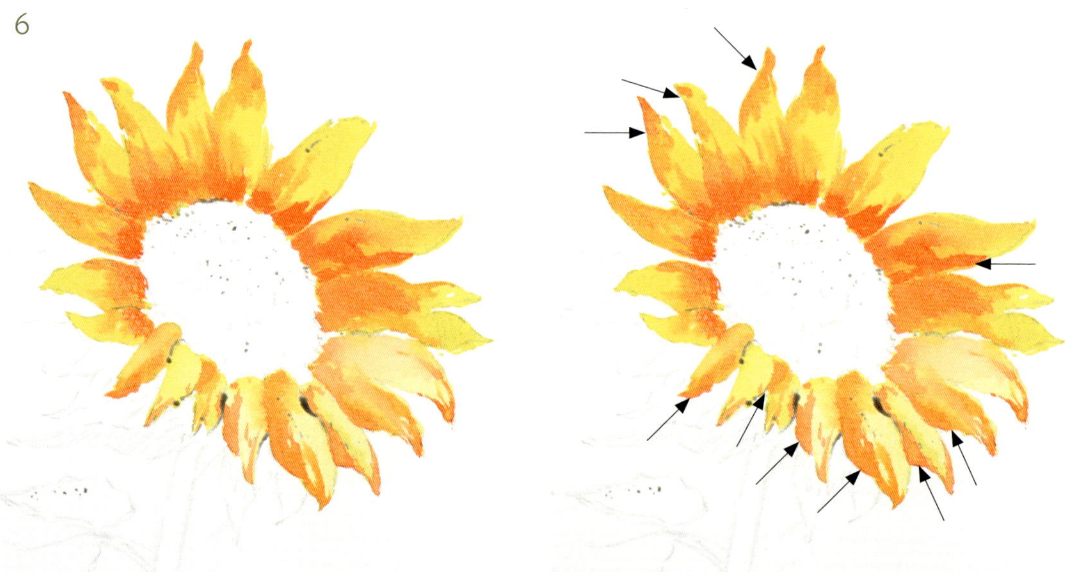

Mix 600064 (Organic Vermilion) and 600041 (Hansa Yellow Light) in a 1:1 ratio to create an orange-yellow color. Use this mixture to further deepen the darker areas of the petals and the parts of the petals that are folded (as indicated by the arrows in the right image). This will help shape the volume and depth of the petals.

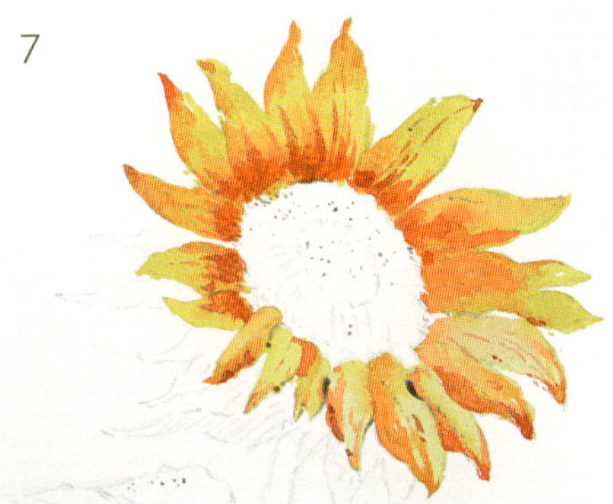

7

Use 600064 (Organic Vermilion) to continue deepening the petals, enhancing their layers. Be sure to apply the paint with a light touch and avoid overfilling the areas. Lightly sketch the texture of the petals.

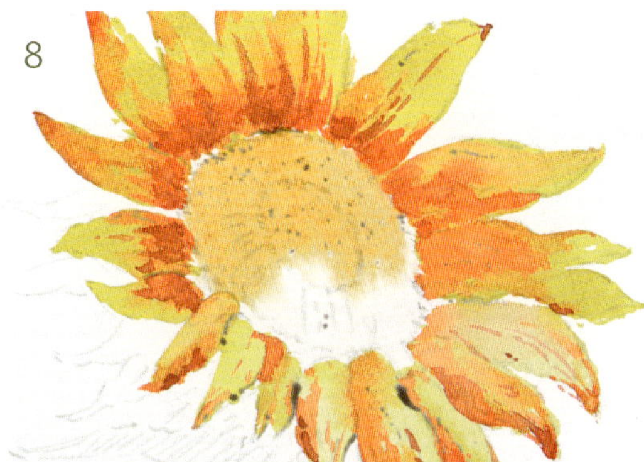

8

Paint the central flower disc. It resembles a flattened sphere, so it has a light-receiving side, a light-to-dark transition area, and a shadowed side. Start by moistening the entire disc area with clean water. While the paper is still wet, use 600233 (Raw Sienna Light) to gently paint the light-receiving region.

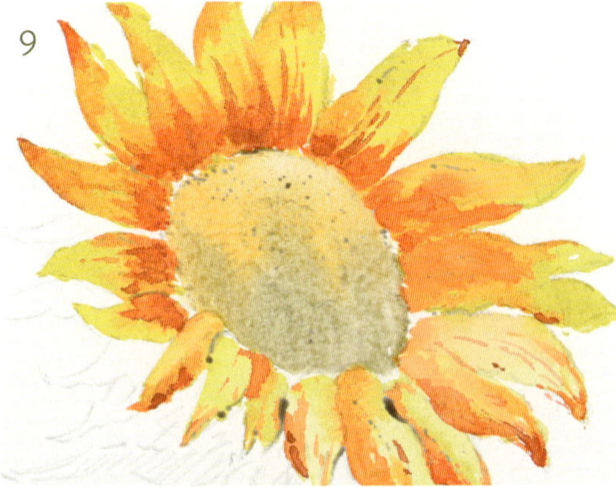

9

Mix 600233 (Raw Sienna Light) with a small amount of 600034 (French Ultramarine) to paint the light-to-dark transition area, as well as the shadowed area.

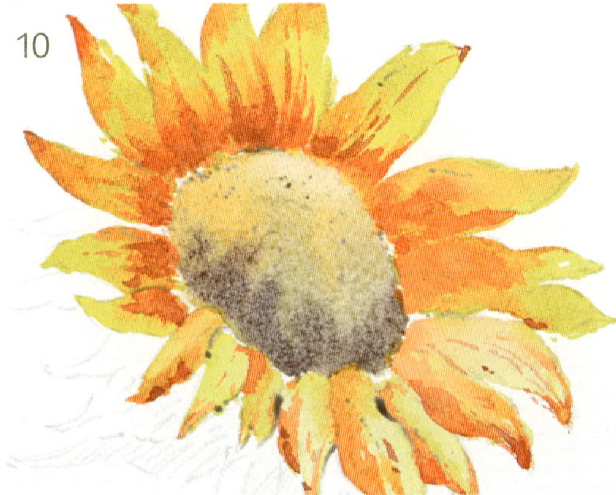

10

Mix 600010 (Burnt Sienna) with a small amount of 600034 (French Ultramarine) to deepen the shadowed area, enhancing the volume and dimension of the flower disc.

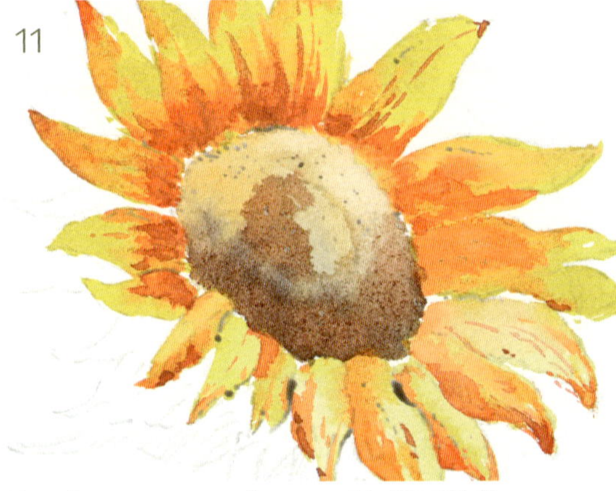

11

Mix a larger amount of water with 600011 (Burnt Umber) to paint the shadows in the middle and outer areas of the flower disc.

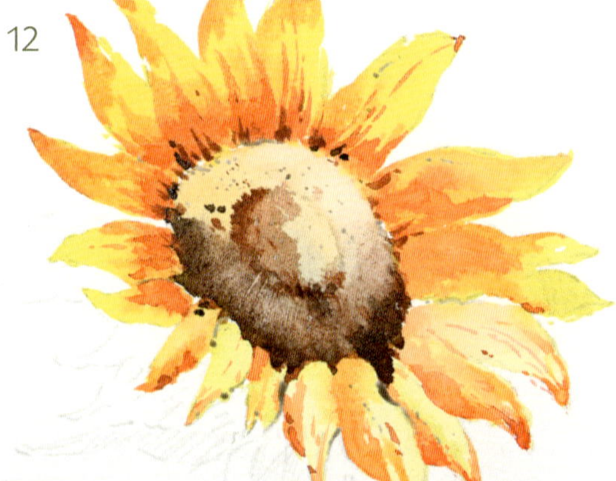

12

Using a more concentrated 600011 (Burnt Umber), deepen the shadowed areas of the flower disc, and where it meets the petals, to enhance the volume and dimension.

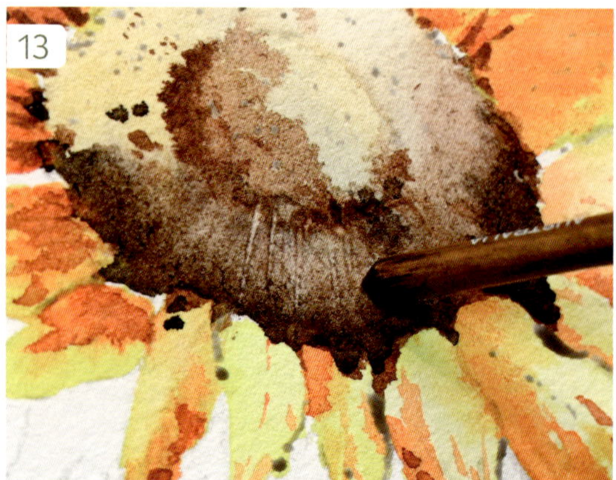

While the paint from step 12 is still wet, gently scrape out the texture of the flower disc using the end of your brush handle.

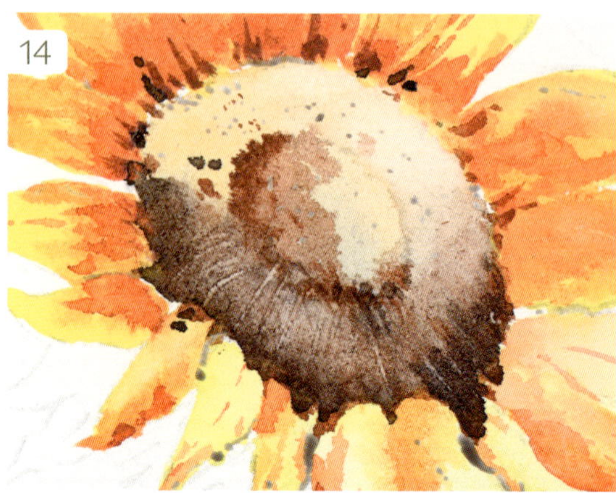

The texture of the flower disc only needs to be scraped in the dark shadowed area, as the light-receiving area is generally highlighted and does not require scraping to brighten.

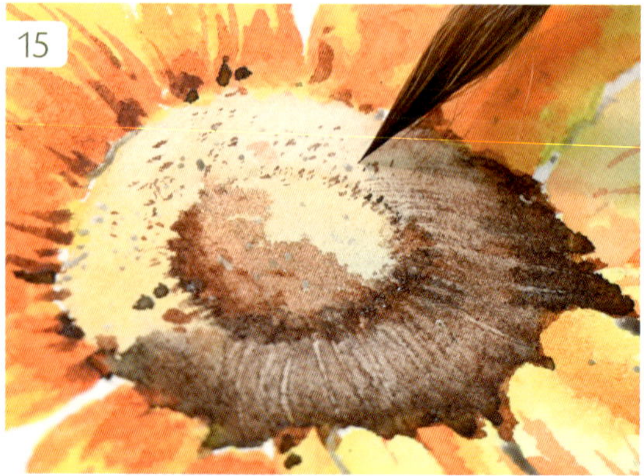

Mix 600011 (Burnt Umber) with a small amount of 600003 (Lamp Black) to create a very dark brown color. Use the tip of the brush to scatter and dot the seeds inside the flower disc.

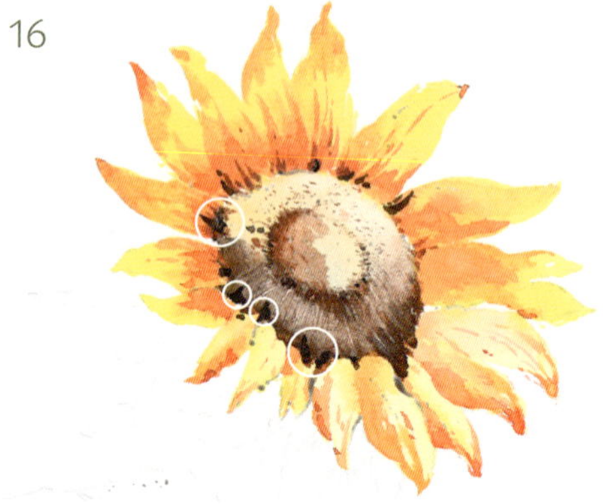

Similarly, use the deep brown color mixed in step 15 to lightly dot the junction between the flower disc and the petals (the areas circled in the image). This will add more depth to the flower's volume. With that, the creation of the sunflower is nearly complete.

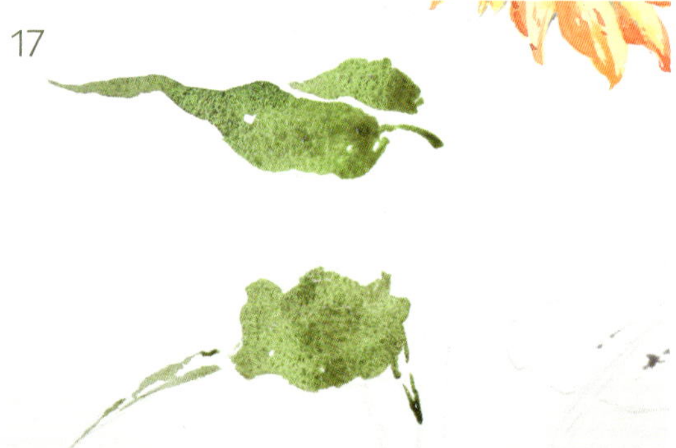

Use 600197 (Green Apatite Genuine) to paint the green leaves. Be mindful to use a light touch with the brush. Don't deliberately outline the shape of the leaves and apply a flat wash. Instead, follow the natural form of the leaf with single, confident stroke to depict its shape, leaving some areas of white space.

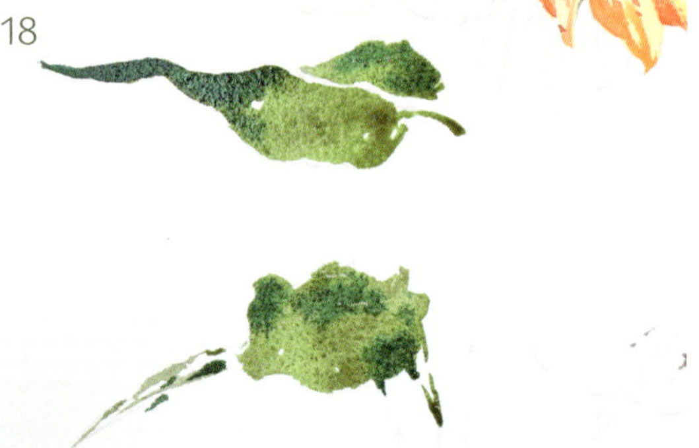

While the paint from step 17 is still wet, use 600080 (Phthalo Turquoise) to paint the darker areas of the leaves.

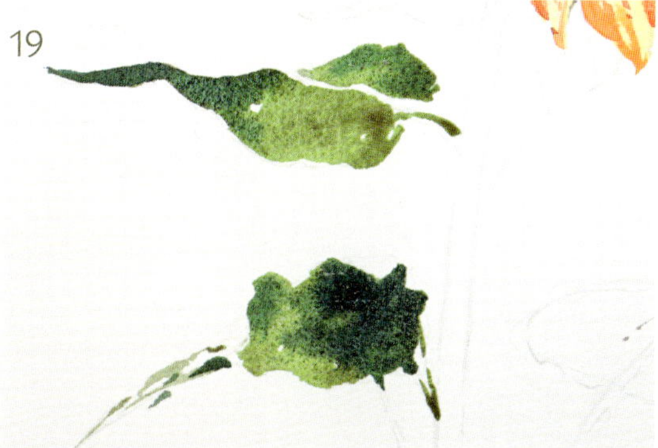

Mix 600080 (Phthalo Turquoise) and 600197 (Green Apatite Genuine) in a 2:1 ratio and use this mixture to further deepen the darker areas of the leaves.

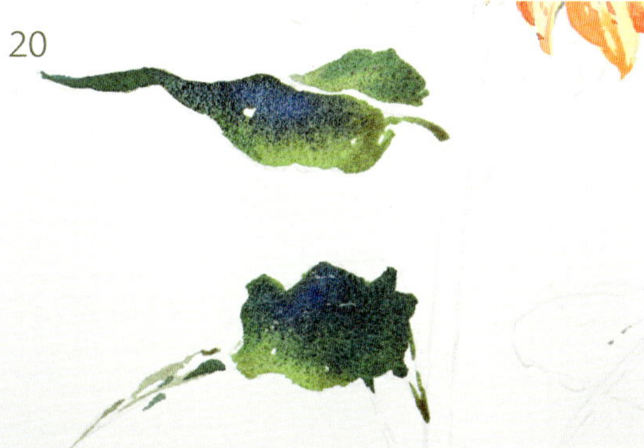

Directly mix 600034 (French Ultramarine) into the middle vein of the upper leaf and along the upper edge of the lower leaf. This will enrich the color of the leaves, creating a cooler deep green as the blue naturally blends into the green. This will enhance the depth and layers of the leaves.

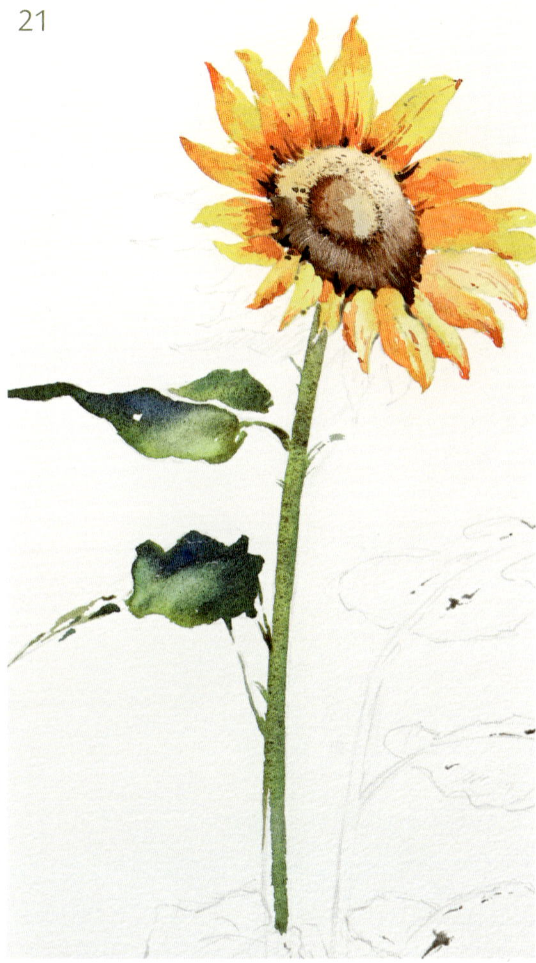

Use 600197 (Green Apatite Genuine) to paint the flower stem. During the painting process, as the water in the pigment evaporates, it will naturally create variations in the depth and intensity of the color.

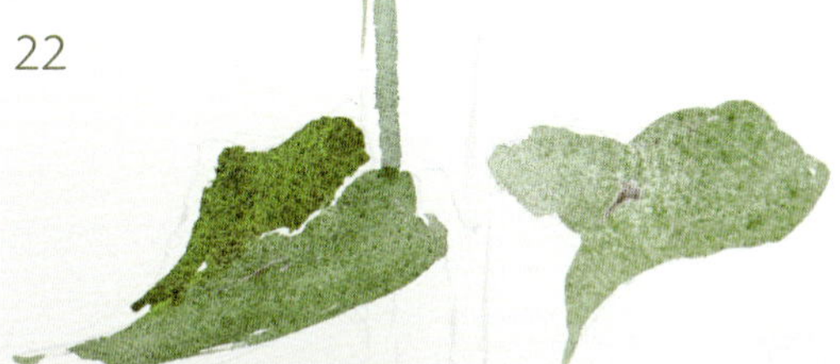

Use 600197 (Green Apatite Genuine) and 600024 (Chromium Green Oxide) to paint the two leaves at the bottom separately. Be sure to leave some areas blank. Don't worry about which specific green color should go on each leaf. Feel free to be spontaneous and free in your approach while painting.

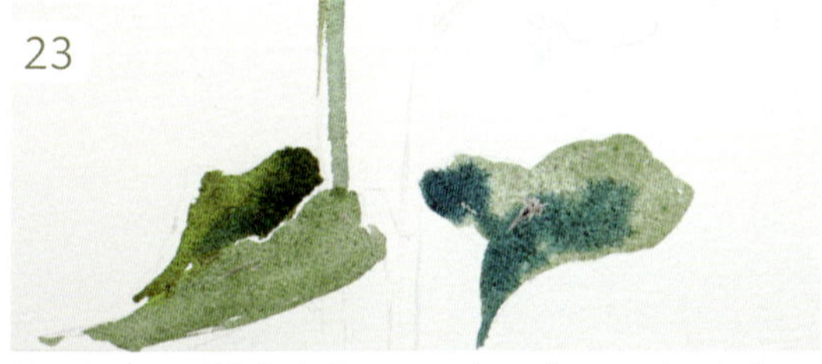

Use 600080 (Phthalo Turquoise) to deepen the dark areas of the leaves.

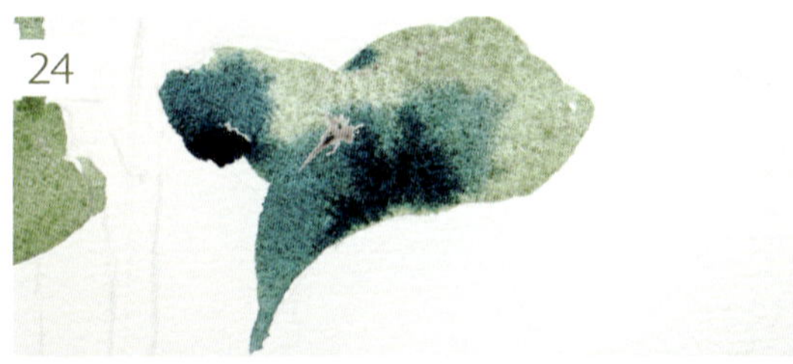

Continue by mixing 600080 (Phthalo Turquoise) and 600034 (French Ultramarine) in a 1:1 ratio to deepen the shadowed areas.

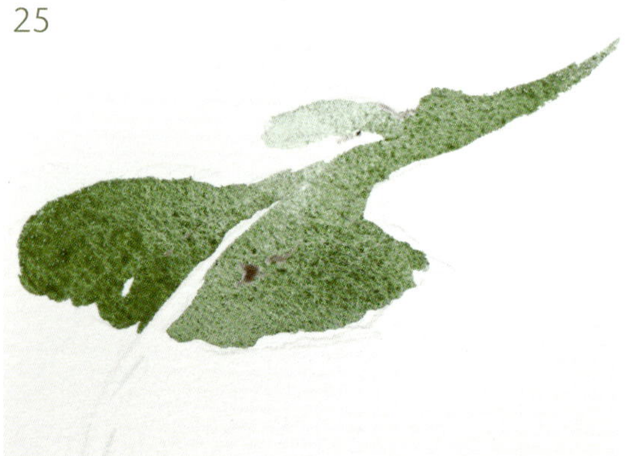

25

Paint the large leaf on the upper right. Mix 600197 (Green Apatite Genuine) and 600024 (Chromium Green Oxide) in a 1:1 ratio to paint the leaf, making sure to leave some areas white.

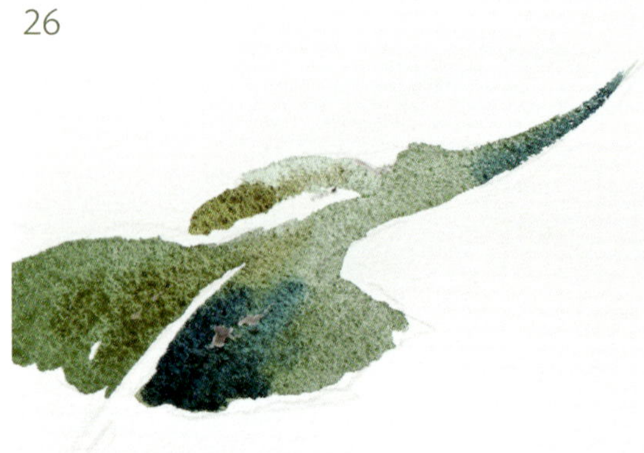

26

While the paint from step 25 is still wet, use 600080 (Phthalo Turquoise) to darken the shadowed areas.

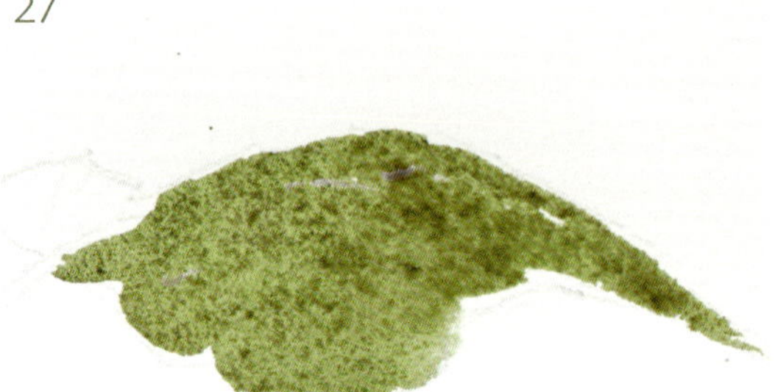

27

Use 600197 (Green Apatite Genuine) to paint the lower leaf, paying attention to its shape and form.

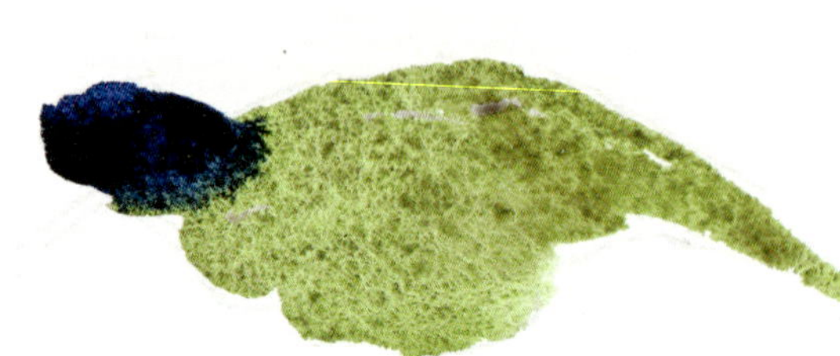

28

Use 600034 (French Ultramarine) to deepen the root of the leaf.

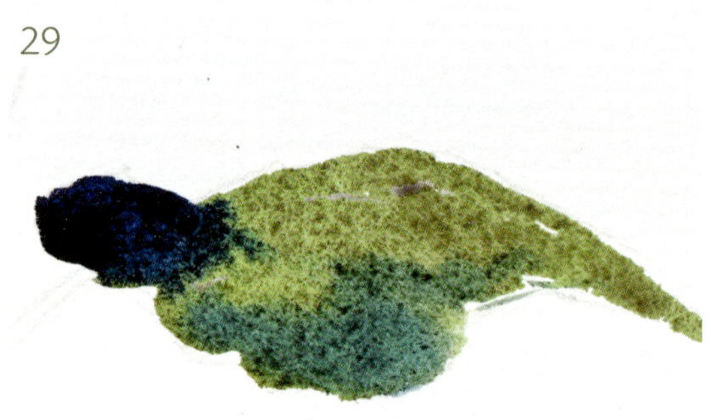

29

Use 600080 (Phthalo Turquoise) to deepen the shadowed area at the bottom of the leaf.

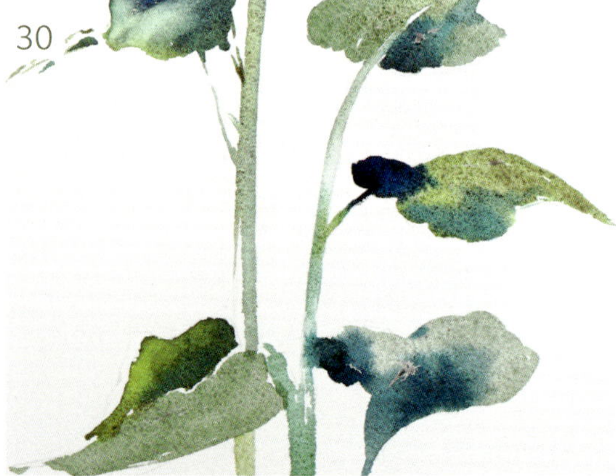

30

Mix 600197 (Green Apatite Genuine) and 600024 (Chromium Green Oxide) in a 1:1 ratio to paint the flower stem on the right side. For the highlight areas on the stem, use a clean brush to apply water and lift off some pigment to create the light spots.

31

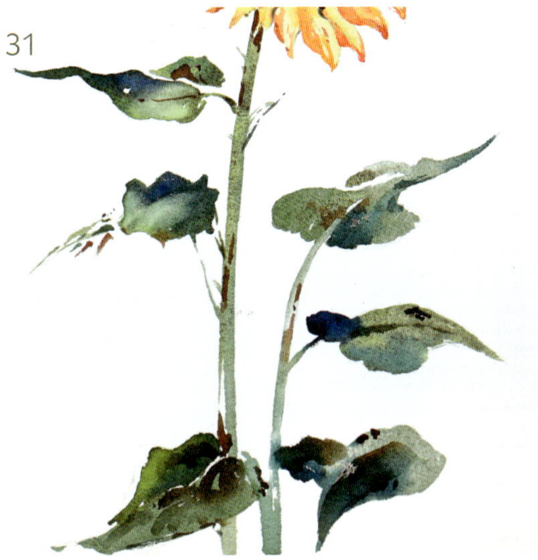

Use 600011 (Burnt Umber) to deepen the details of the flower stems and leaves.

32

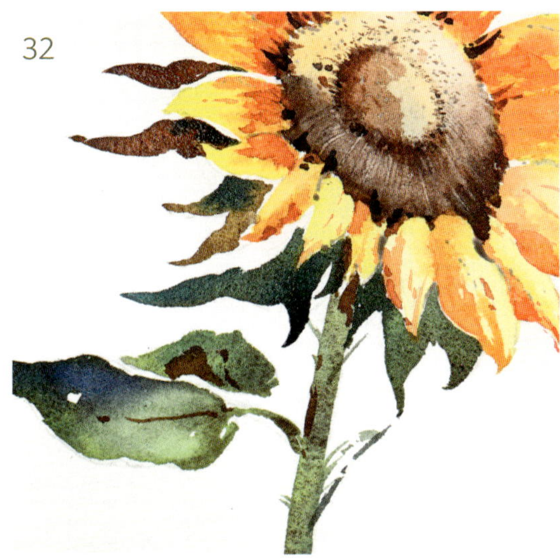

Mix 600197 (Green Apatite Genuine) and 600080 (Phthalo Turquoise) in a 1:1 ratio, then add a small amount of 600034 (French Ultramarine) to paint the leaves beneath the sunflower. Since these leaves are shaded by the sunflower, they appear as a cooler, darker color overall.

33

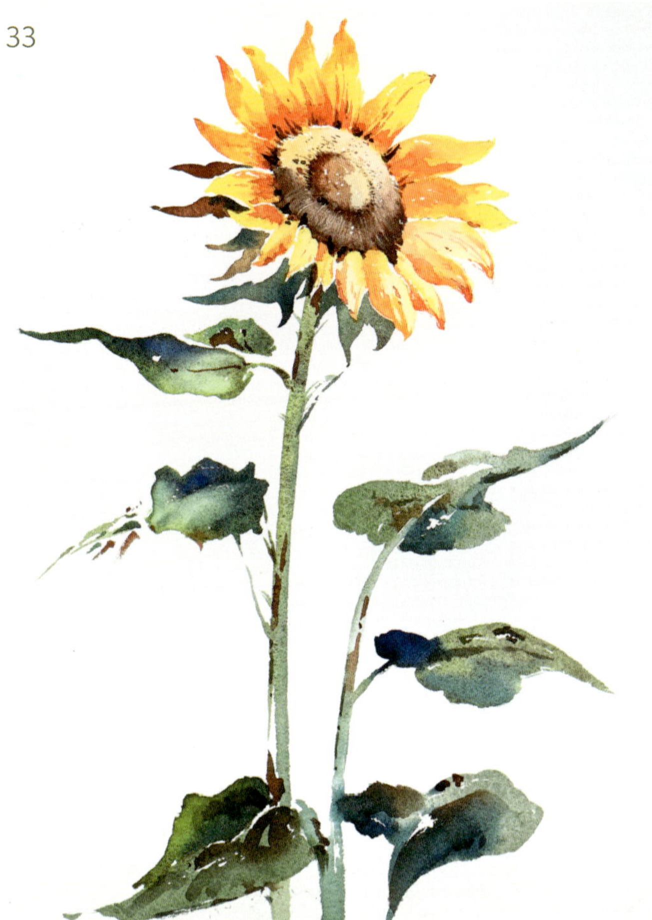

Use an eraser to remove the masking fluid, revealing the highlighted areas of the painting. This completes the sunflower in the garden.

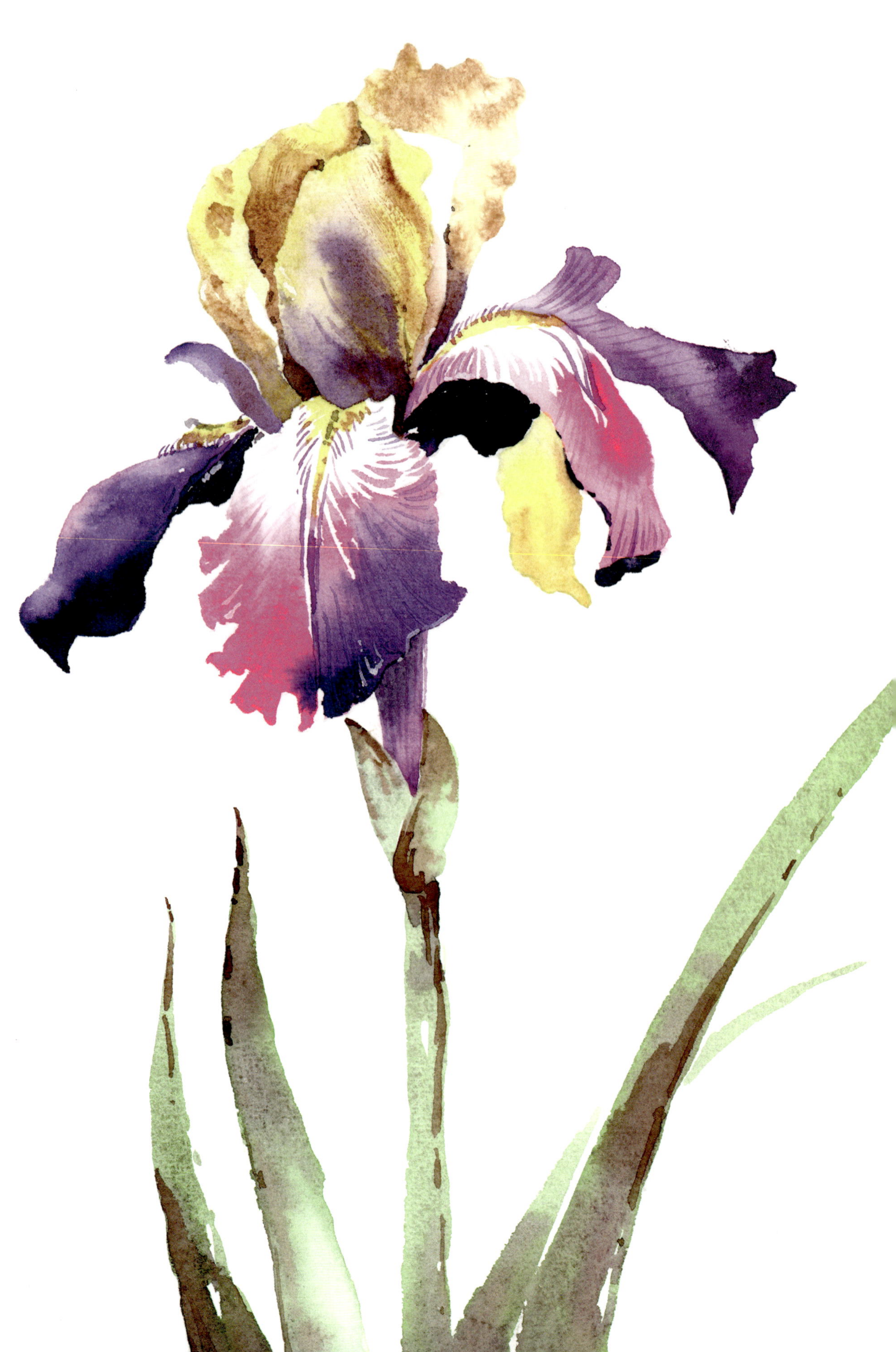

Iris

In the early morning garden, the blue violet irises bloom in quiet grace.
Their slender leaves resemble drawn swords, while the petals are light and
delicate, like butterflies in flight. Born by the water's edge and accompanied
by lake stones, they are grounded yet never forget to gaze at the stars. When
the wind rises, the irises gently sway, and their blue-violet forms evoke the
legend of transformation into butterflies, reminding us of the poetry found
in the simplicity of everyday life.

Paint Brand
DANIEL SMITH

Color Codes
600006: Aureolin (Cobalt Yellow)
600010: Burnt Sienna
600019: Carbazole Violet
600197: Green Apatite Genuine
600024: Chromium Green Oxide
600003: Lamp Black

600009: Buff Titanium
600198: Opera Pink

Auxiliary Material
NICKER opaque white gouache

Recommended Watercolor Paper
ARCHES watercolor paper, cold pressed,
140 lb/300 g/m^2

Recommended Brush
Black Velvet 3000S brush for watercolor,
size 8

Key Challenges
1. The shaping of the iris flower,
especially the folding relationship of the
petals.
2. The color layering changes between
the lit and shadowed sides of the petals.
3. When applying color, pay attention to
the airiness of the painting and learn to
leave areas of white space.

Steps

1

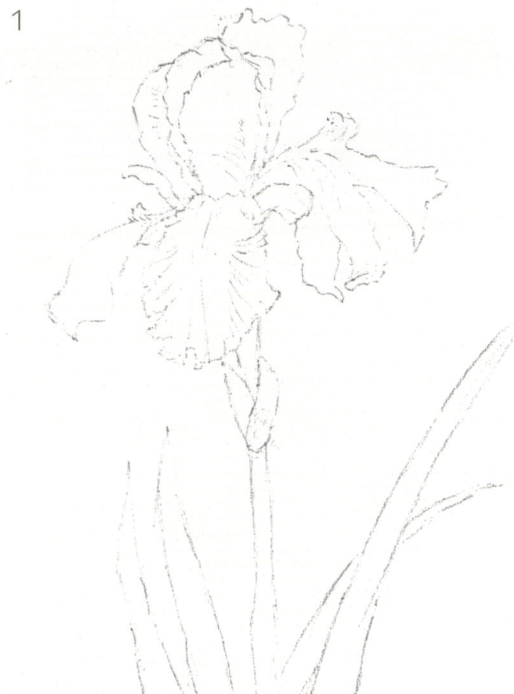

Draw the outline, paying attention to the proportion
between the image and the paper, and also the
overlapping relationships between the petals.

2

Start by painting the inner petals of the flower. Mix color 600006 (Aureolin) and color 600009 (Buff Titanium) in equal proportions, applying an even base layer of color to the inner petals. Make sure to leave white space between the petals to prevent the colors from blending into each other. This will help distinguish the relationship between the petals when you continue painting later.

3

While the previous layer is still wet, deepen the petals with color 600006 (Aureolin). Allow it to merge naturally with the previous color to create a seamless transition. Avoid covering the entire petal, which will make it difficult to show the relationship of light and dark on the petals.

4

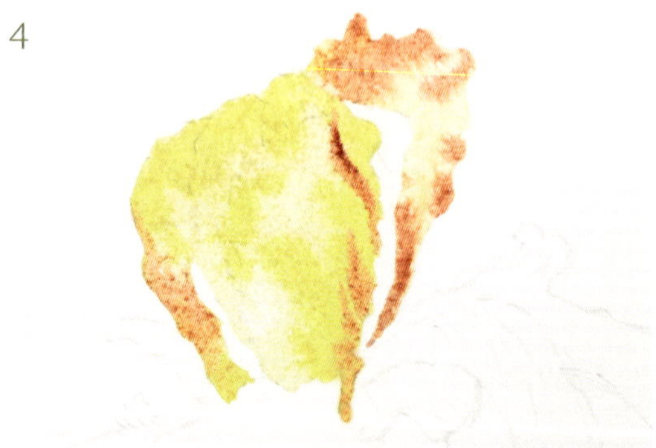

While the previous layer is still wet, use color 600010 (Burnt Sienna) to add the mottled spots on the petals and deepen the base of the petals. Control the moisture level carefully, avoid having it too wet or too dry. Keep the brushwork light and relaxed.

5

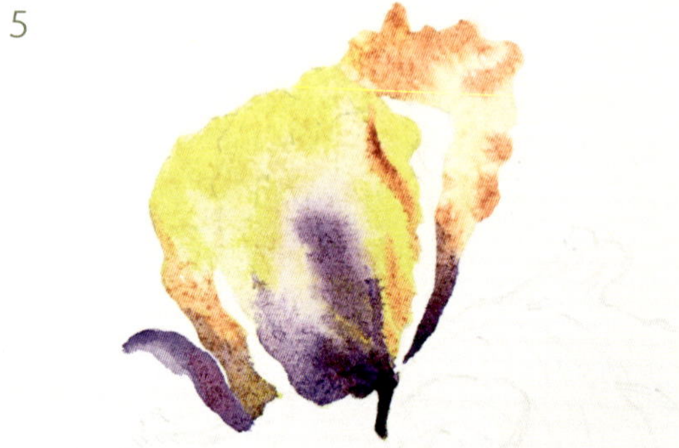

While still wet, use color 600019 (Carbazole Violet) to deepen the base of the petals. The contrast between this color and the yellow from the previous layer will enhance the layering of the flower.

6

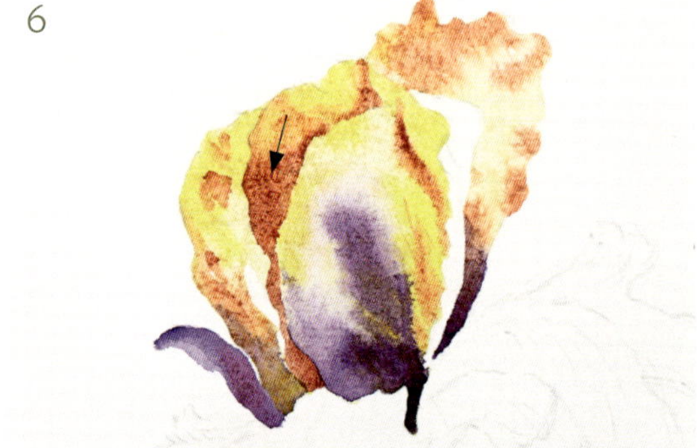

Continue using 600010 (Burnt Sienna) to color the inner part of the middle petals (as indicated by the arrow in the image). Since the inner part of the petals is darker, you can reduce the amount of water and apply the color more densely.

7

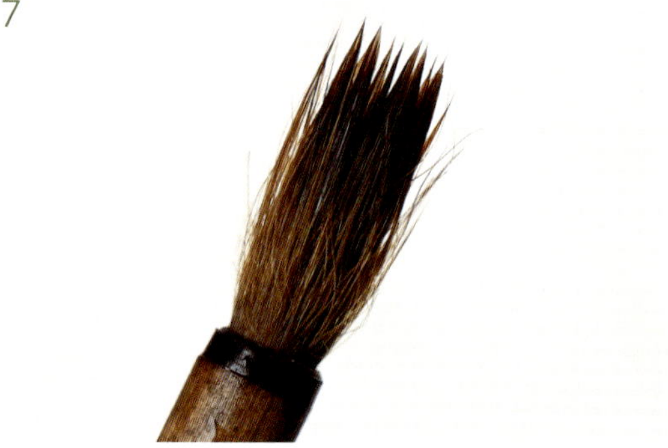

Begin painting the texture on the petals. You can gently blot the water from the brush with a tissue, and then lightly rub the tip of the brush with your fingers to make the bristles split apart.

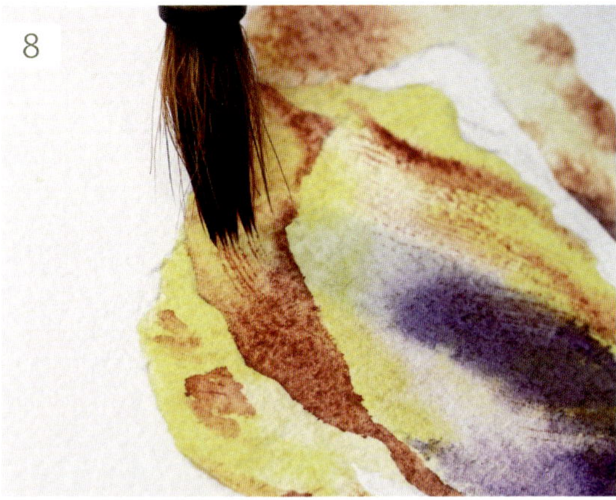

Load the brush with a small amount of color 600010 (Burnt Sienna), and lightly sweep a few strokes in the direction of the petals to create texture.

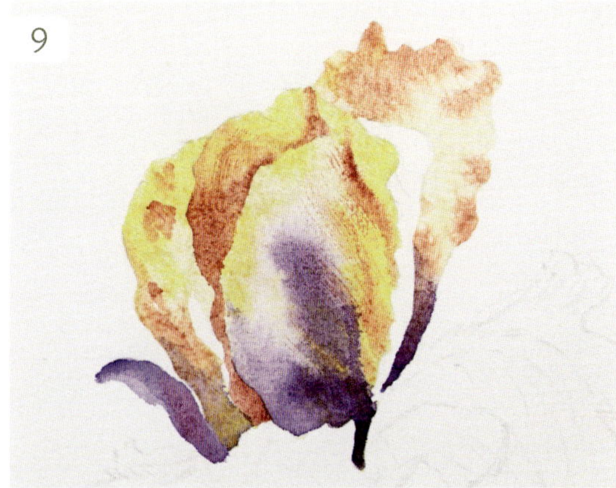

Avoid adding texture to every single petal, as this can make the painting look rigid and lifeless. This is an important principle to keep in mind when creating any artwork: learn to control and be purposeful.

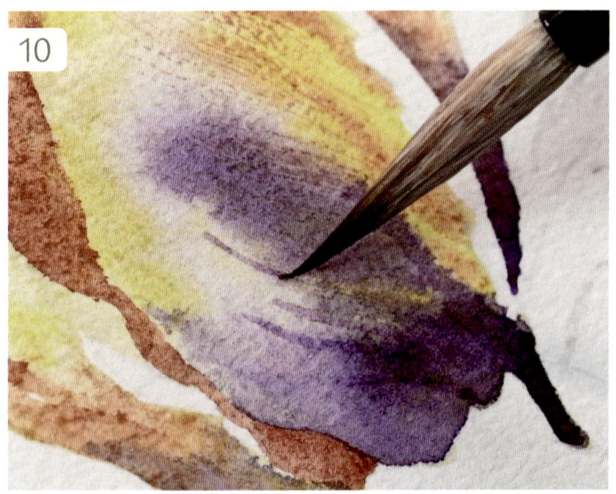

Use color 600019 (Carbazole Violet) to outline the texture of the petals.

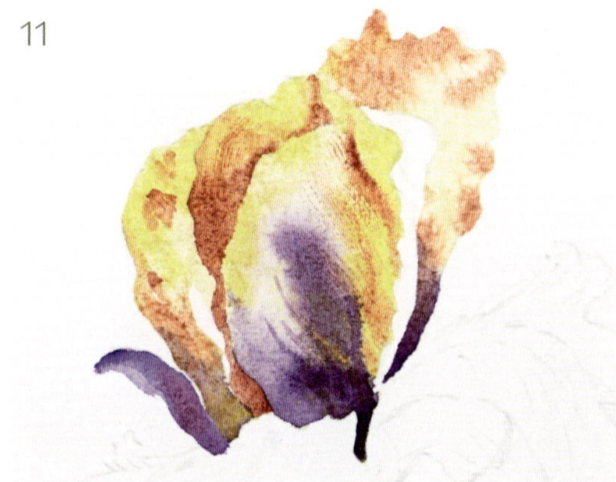

The shaping of the inner petals is now mostly complete.

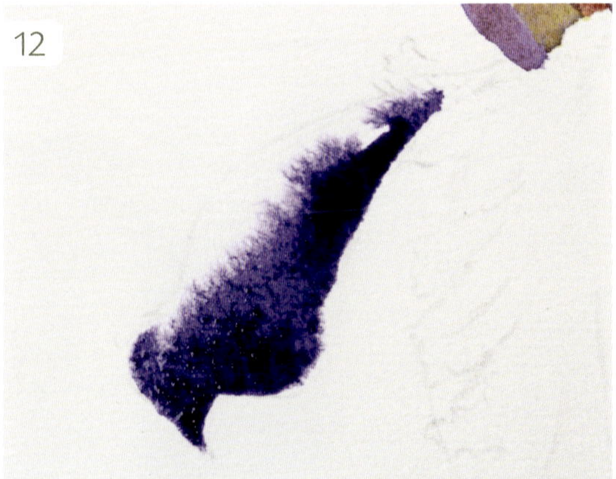

Next, start painting the outer petals. Begin by applying a layer of clean water to the leftmost petal. While still wet, use color 600019 (Carbazole Violet) to add color, allowing the color to naturally transition and leaving the highlight areas.

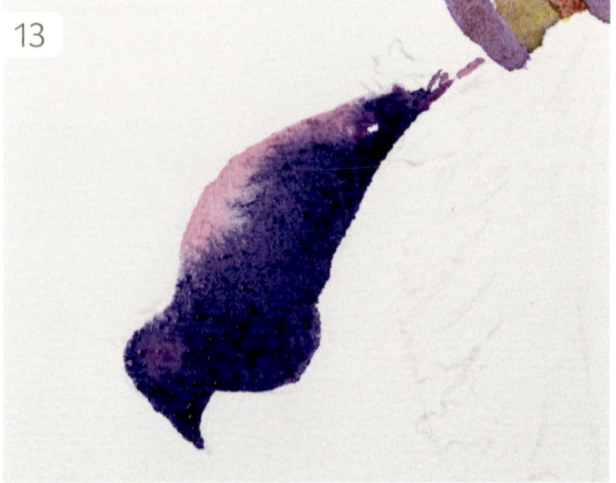

Then, use color 600198 (Opera Pink) to paint the highlighted areas, allowing it to blend naturally with 600019 (Carbazole Violet).

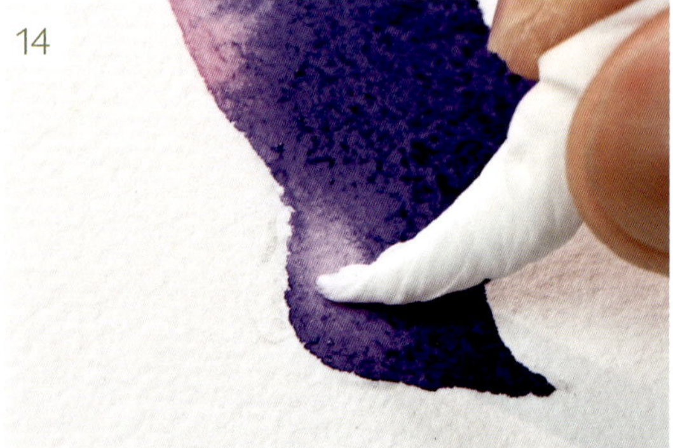

Use a tissue to gently blot out the highlighted areas, displaying the lighted regions of the petals.

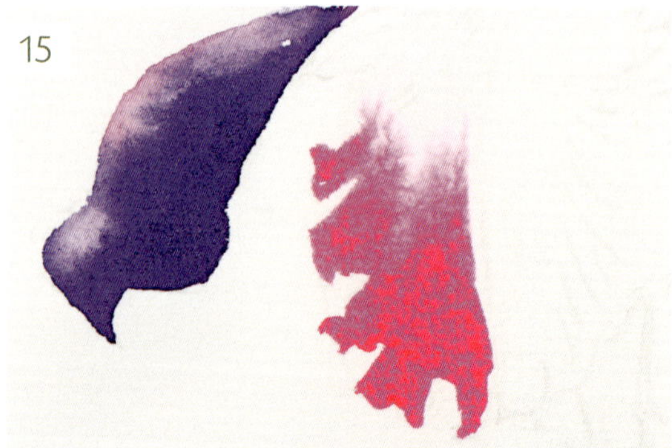

For the large petal at the bottom, we will divide it into two sections for painting. Start by applying clean water to the left half of the petal. While it's still wet, use color 600198 (Opera Pink) to begin painting from the top of the petal, allowing the color to naturally transition toward the root. At this point, you can tilt the painting surface to let the color flow naturally toward the lighter areas, or gently blow air toward the direction of the color flow to encourage a smooth gradient transition.

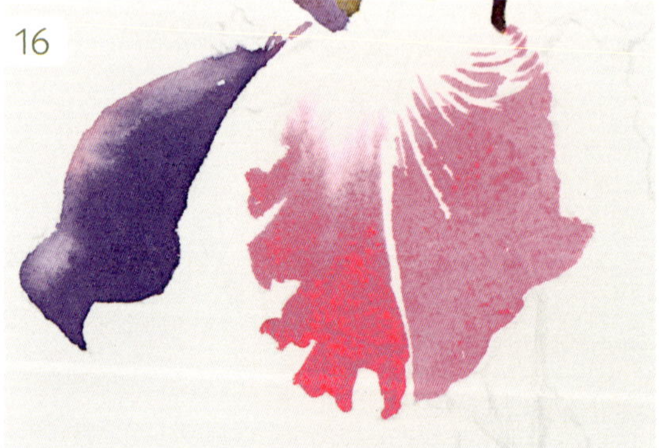

For the right half of the petal, apply color 600198 (Opera Pink) directly, but with more water added to the paint compared to the left half, so the color will be lighter. Be careful to paint the texture on the petal near the base. Also, make sure to leave a small gap in the middle between this petal and the left one.

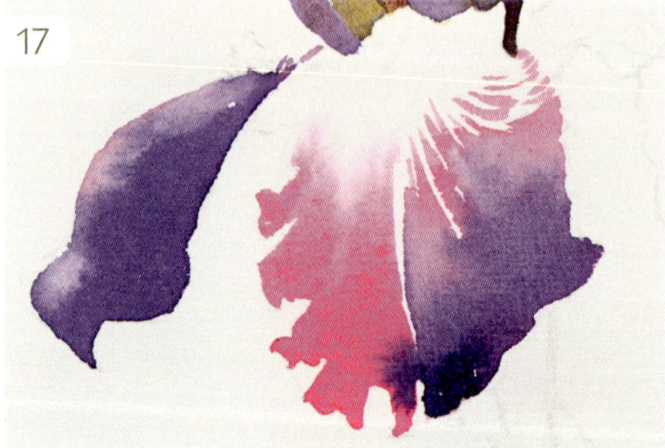

While the petal is still wet, use color 600019 (Carbazole Violet) to deepen the top part of the right half of the petal. Allow the two colors to naturally blend and merge together.

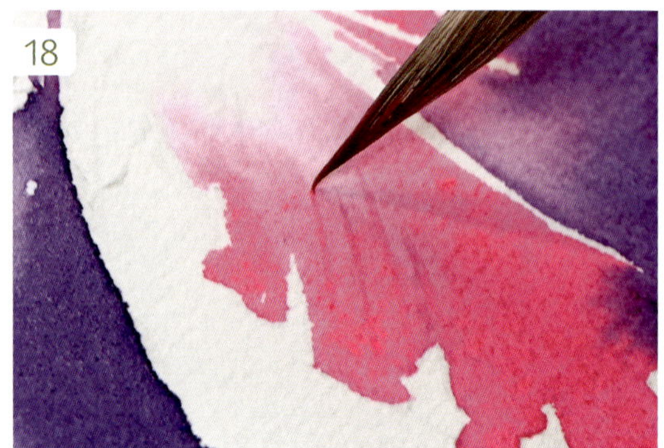

Gently outline the texture of the left half of the petal using color 600198 (Opera Pink), paying attention to the flow of the lines extending outward.

Gently outline the texture of the right half of the petal using color 600019 (Carbazole Violet), also paying attention to the outward flow of the lines.

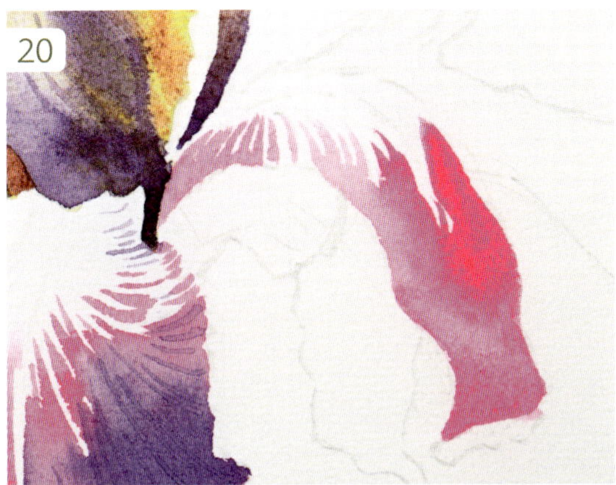

Use color 600198 (Opera Pink) to paint the pink petal on the right side, paying attention to the variation in the lightness and darkness of the color.

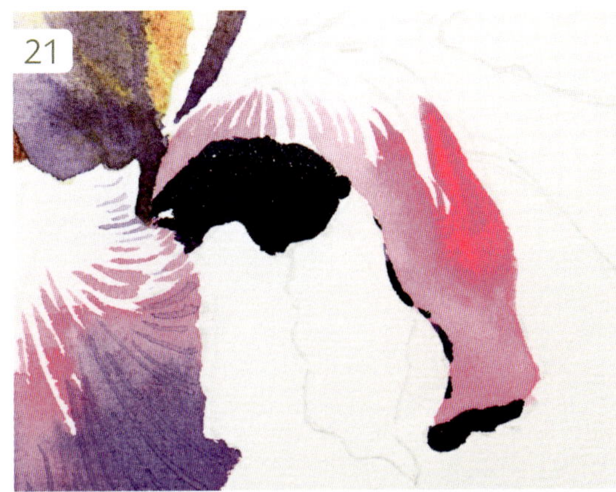

Mix color 600019 (Carbazole Violet) with a small amount of color 600003 (Lamp Black) to paint the back and folded parts of the petal, adding volume to the flower.

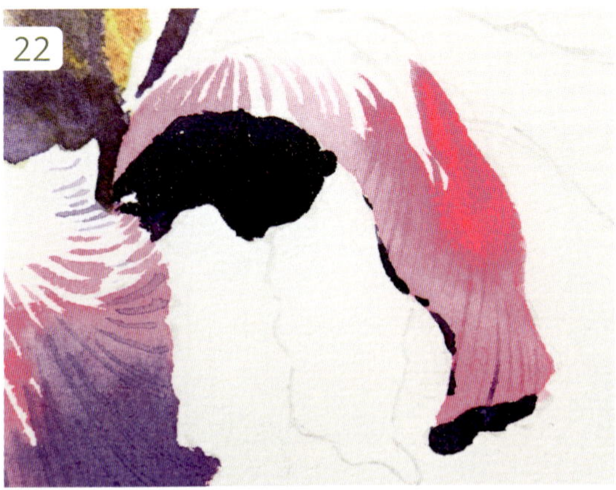

Use color 600198 (Opera Pink) to gently outline the texture of the petal.

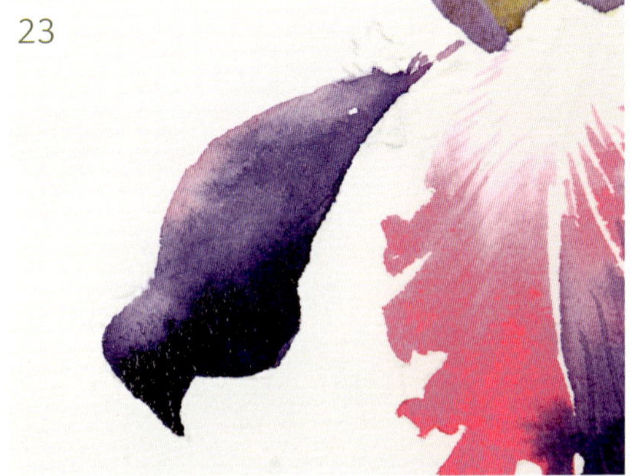

Continue using a 5:1 mixture of color 600019 (Carbazole Violet) and color 600003 (Lamp Black) to paint the dark areas of the leftmost outer petal, enhancing the petal's depth and layers.

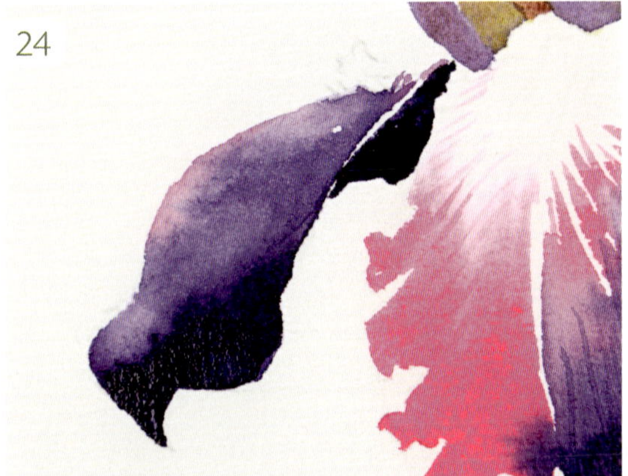

Similarly, use a 5:1 mixture of color 600019 (Carbazole Violet) and color 600003 (Lamp Black) to paint the backside of the petal.

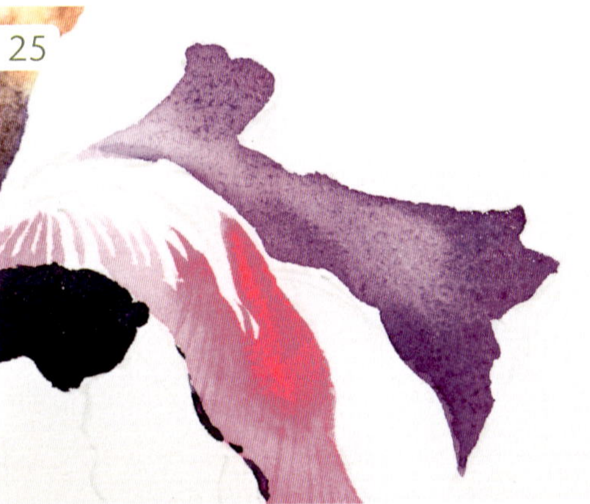

Use color 600019 (Carbazole Violet) to paint the rightmost outer petal. Then, wipe out the central highlighted area with tissue paper, bringing out the lightness in the petal's highlight region.

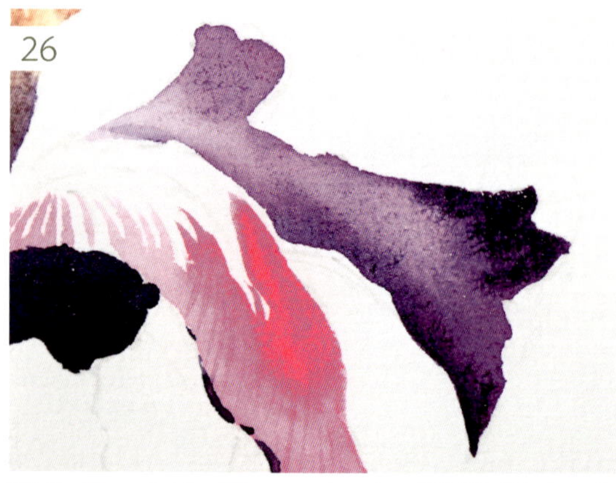

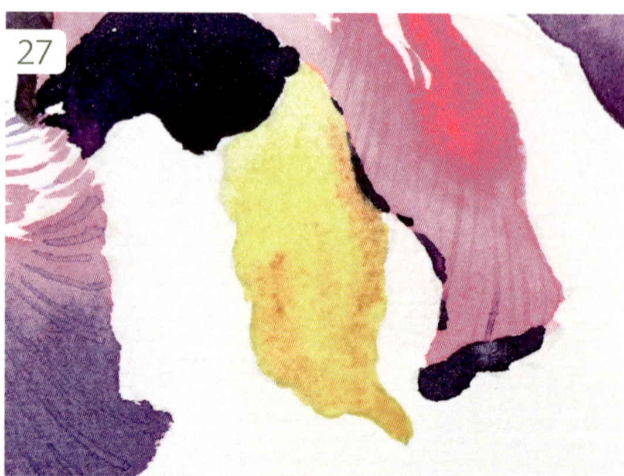

While the paint is still wet, mix color 600019 (Carbazole Violet) and color 600003 (Lamp Black) in a 5:1 ratio, and deepen the head (tip) of the petal. Allow the two colors to blend naturally.

Next, paint the yellow outer petal. Start by laying down a base coat with color 600006 (Aureolin), and while it's still wet, use color 600010 (Burnt Sienna) to deepen the color.

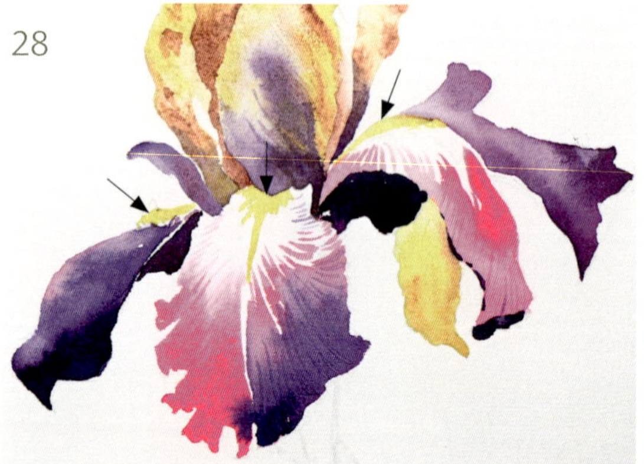

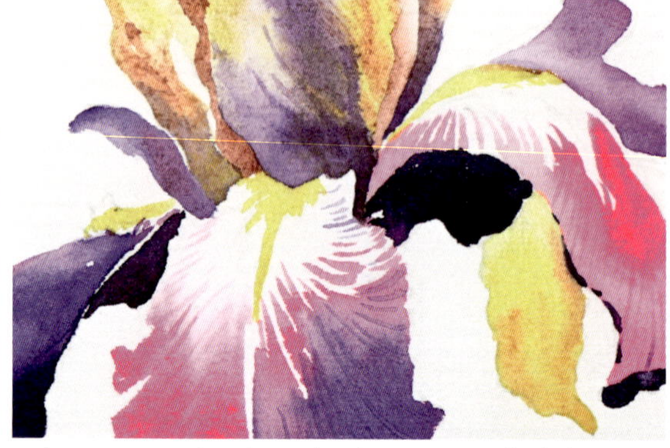

Using color 600006 (Aureolin), paint the hairlike structures on the outer petal as shown by the arrows in the left image.

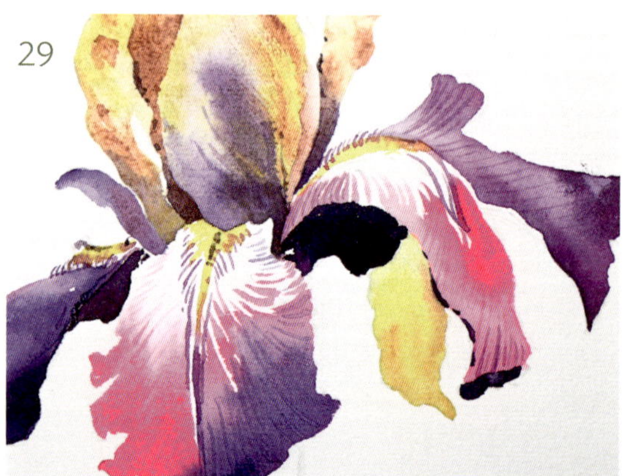

Using color 600198 (Opera Pink), outline the details on the hairlike structures and the veins on the far-right outer petal.

Use color 600198 (Opera Pink) to cover the base of the flower. While still wet, use color 600019 (Carbazole Violet) to paint the area near the sepals. Due to the petal's coverage, the area close to the base of the petals should be painted with a mixture of color 600019 (Carbazole Violet) and color 600003 (Lamp Black) in a 5:1 ratio, diluted with plenty of water to create a soft shadow effect. Finally, use color 600198 (Opera Pink) to paint the veins.

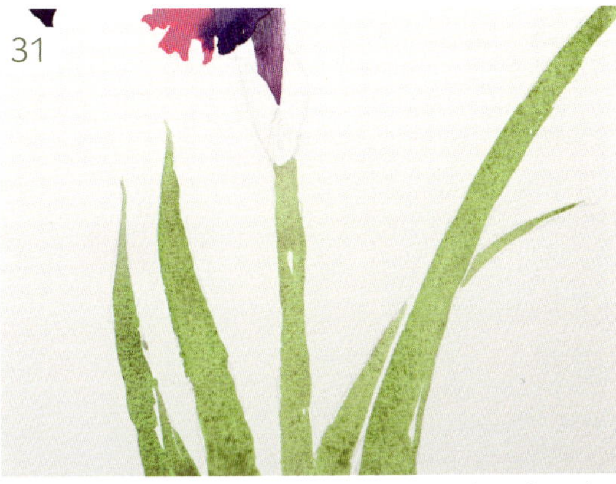

31

Use color 600197 (Green Apatite Genuine) to directly paint the shapes of the leaves and stem. Keep the brushwork relaxed, and leave appropriate white space, especially leaving a gap between intersecting leaves, to prevent colors from blending together when you add further layers of paint.

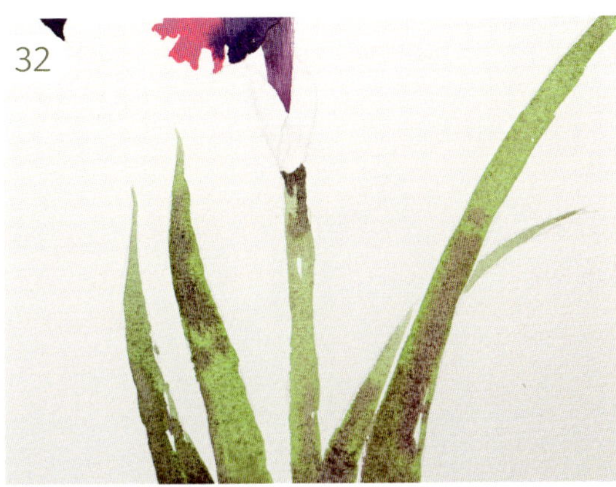

32

While the paint is still wet, mix color 600197 (Green Apatite Genuine) with a small amount of color 600019 (Carbazole Violet) to paint the darker areas of the leaves and create a mottled texture. Let the colors blend naturally with the moisture.

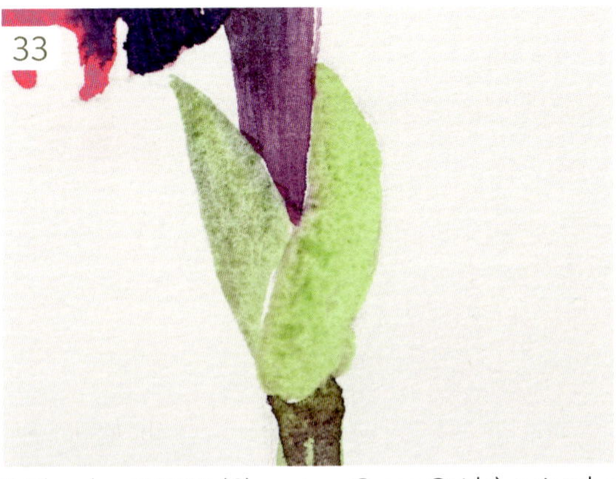

33

With color 600024 (Chromium Green Oxide), paint the left bract, and color 600197 (Green Apatite Genuine) for the right bract.

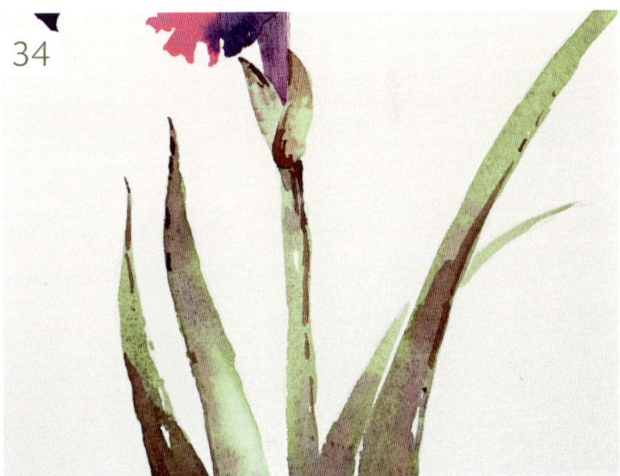

34

Mix color 600197 (Green Apatite Genuine) and color 600010 (Burnt Sienna) in equal proportions, then dilute the mixture with plenty of water. Use this blend to paint the details of the leaves, flower stem, and bracts. This will help enrich the layering and depth.

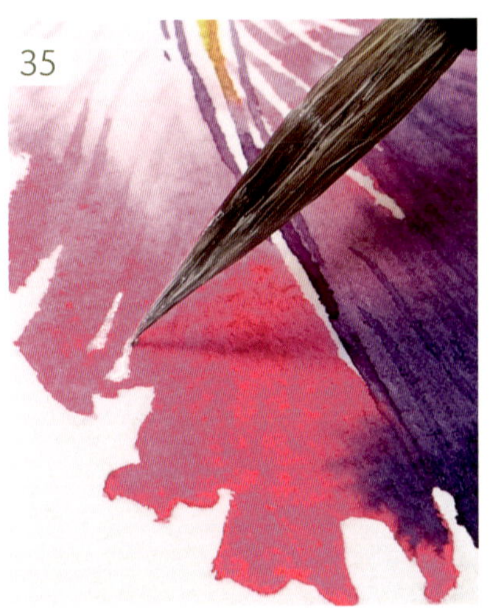

35

◄ To add more detail to the petals, we can dip into NICKER opaque white gouache and paint the highlighted areas on the petals. Just dab a few strokes casually here. Be careful not to overdo it.

▶ The iris flower is now complete.

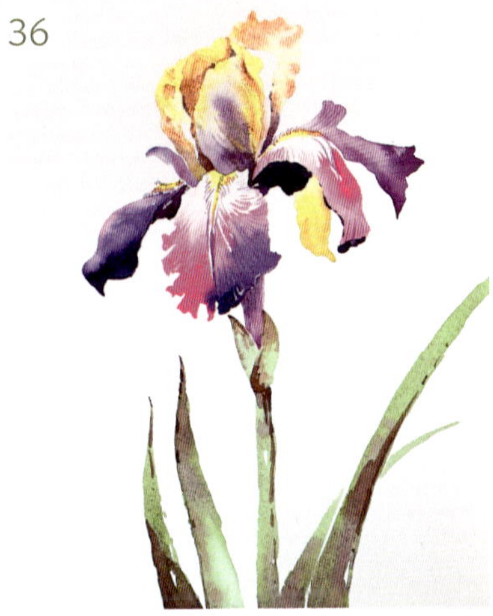

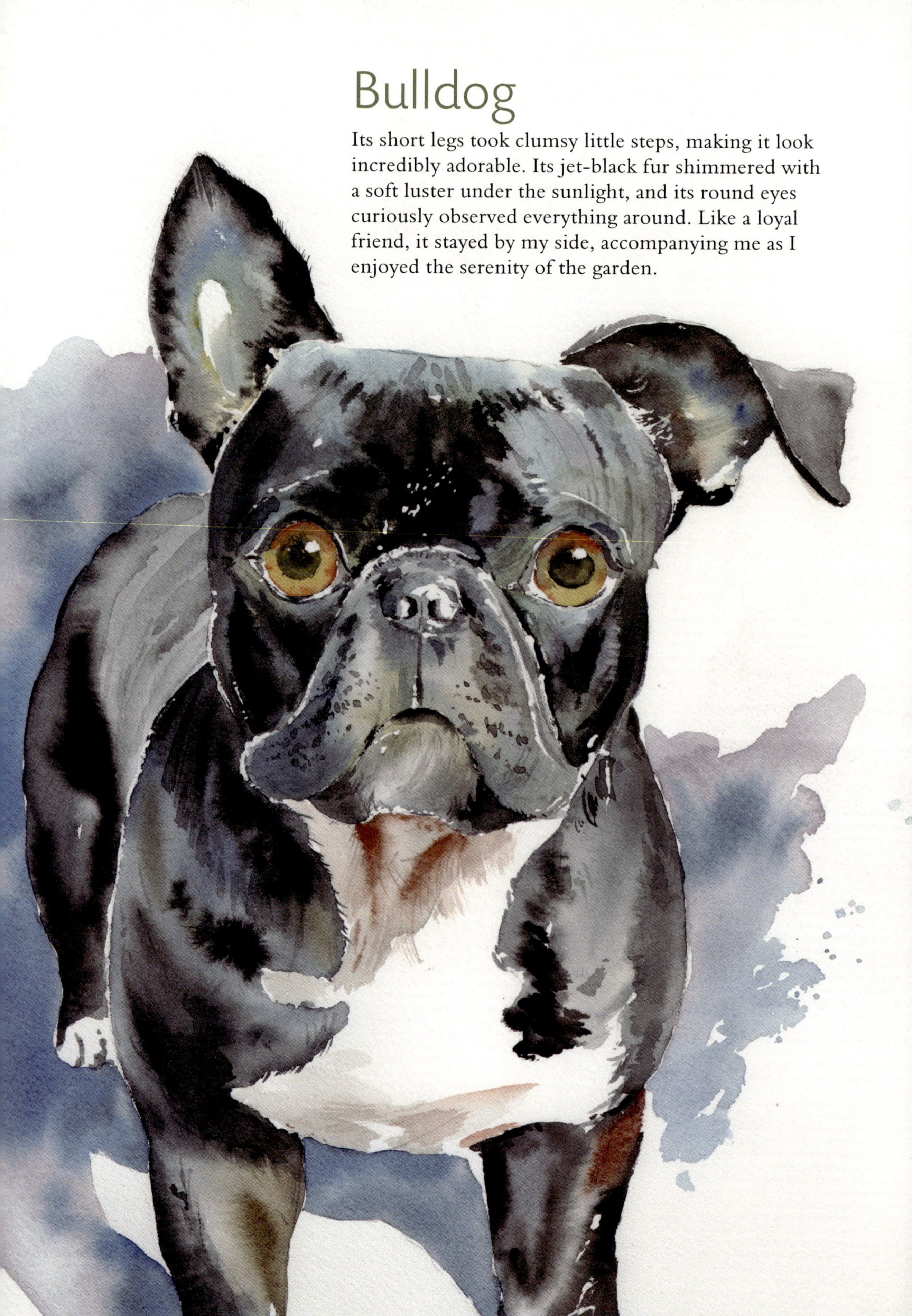

Bulldog

Its short legs took clumsy little steps, making it look incredibly adorable. Its jet-black fur shimmered with a soft luster under the sunlight, and its round eyes curiously observed everything around. Like a loyal friend, it stayed by my side, accompanying me as I enjoyed the serenity of the garden.

Paint Brand
DANIEL SMITH

Color Codes
- 600056: Monte Amiata Natural Sienna
- 600082: Prussian Blue
- 600003: Lamp Black
- 600029: Cobalt Turquoise
- 600242: Alvaro's Fresco Grey
- 600234: Aussie Red Gold
- 600033: Deep Scarlet
- 600010: Burnt Sienna
- 600057: Moonglow
- 600077: Phthalo Blue (Green Shade)

Auxiliary Material
Masking fluid

Recommended Watercolor Paper
ARCHES watercolor paper, cold pressed,
140 lb/300 g/m^2

Recommended Brushes
Black Velvet 3000S brush for watercolor,
size 8
Black Velvet 3000S brush for watercolor,
size 6
Hog bristle brush

Key Challenges
1. Capturing the dog's expression and
character.
2. Rendering the sense of volume in the
muscles and the texture of the fur.
3. Using color effectively to depict a
black dog without making the painting
look dull or heavy.

Steps

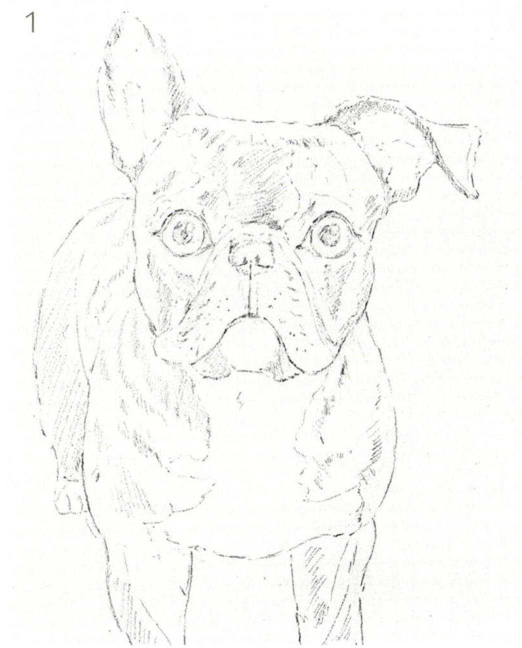

1

Sketch the basic outline of the dog in pencil. Indicate
the shadow areas on its body as well to guide the later
stages of coloring.

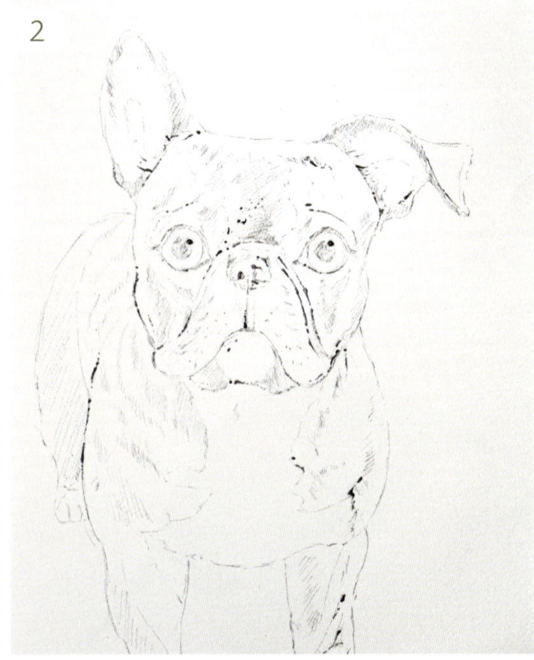

2

Apply masking fluid to certain edges. The black areas
in the image indicate the areas where masking fluid
has been applied. This allows you to better grasp the
structural relationships during the painting process, and
also to depict the highlights on the fur.

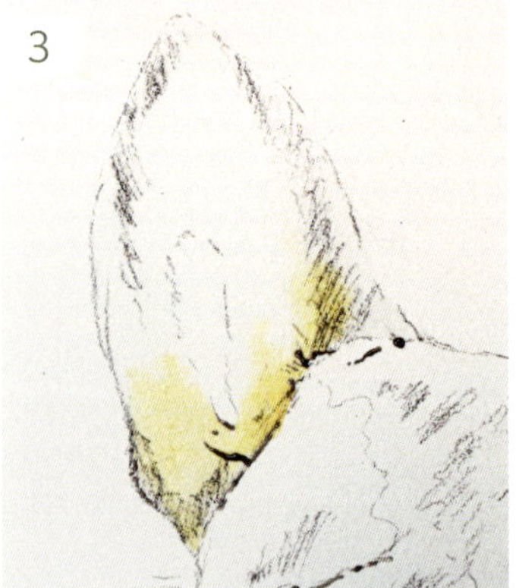

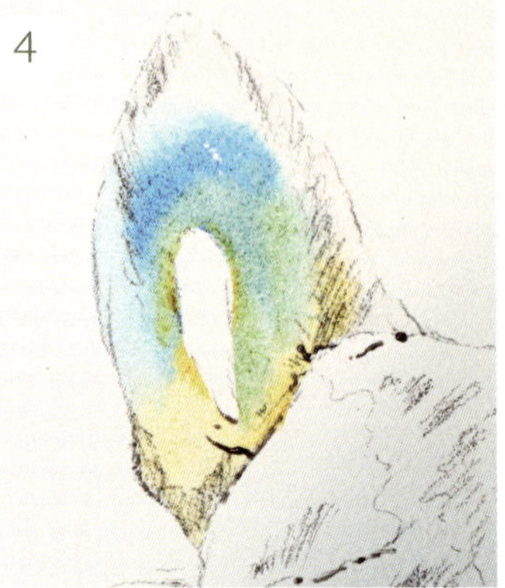

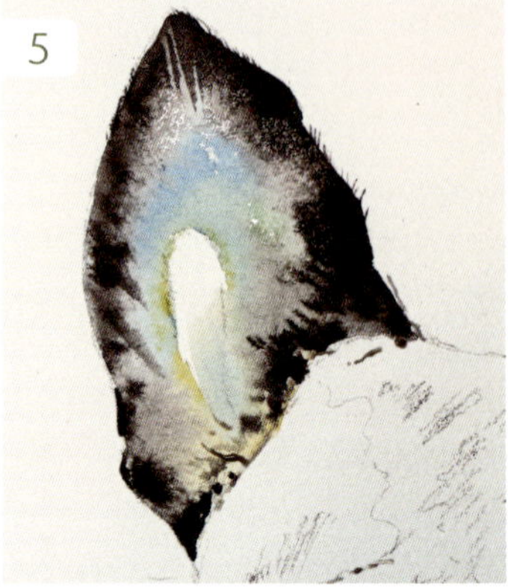

Start by painting the left ear. Begin with a wash of clean water, but be careful not to wet the center area where the ear canal is. If that part gets wet, the paint might spread across the entire ear, making it difficult to create a sense of three dimensionality. While the area is still wet, use color 600056 (Monte Amiata Natural Sienna) to dab in some color at the base of the ear.

While the area is still wet, use color 600082 (Prussian Blue) to paint the shadows around the ear canal. Let this color naturally blend with the previously applied color 600056 (Monte Amiata Natural Sienna) as the water spreads. The reason for choosing these two colors is that, even when painting a black dog, if we rely solely on black and gray, the result can easily look dull and lifeless. So, while staying true to the subject's appearance, we can also apply subjective colors flexibly to enhance the painting's sense of depth and transparency.

While the paper is still wet, continue by using color 600003 (Lamp Black) to further deepen the edges of the ear. Be sure to keep your brushstrokes light and relaxed. Use gentle dabbing motions to apply the color.

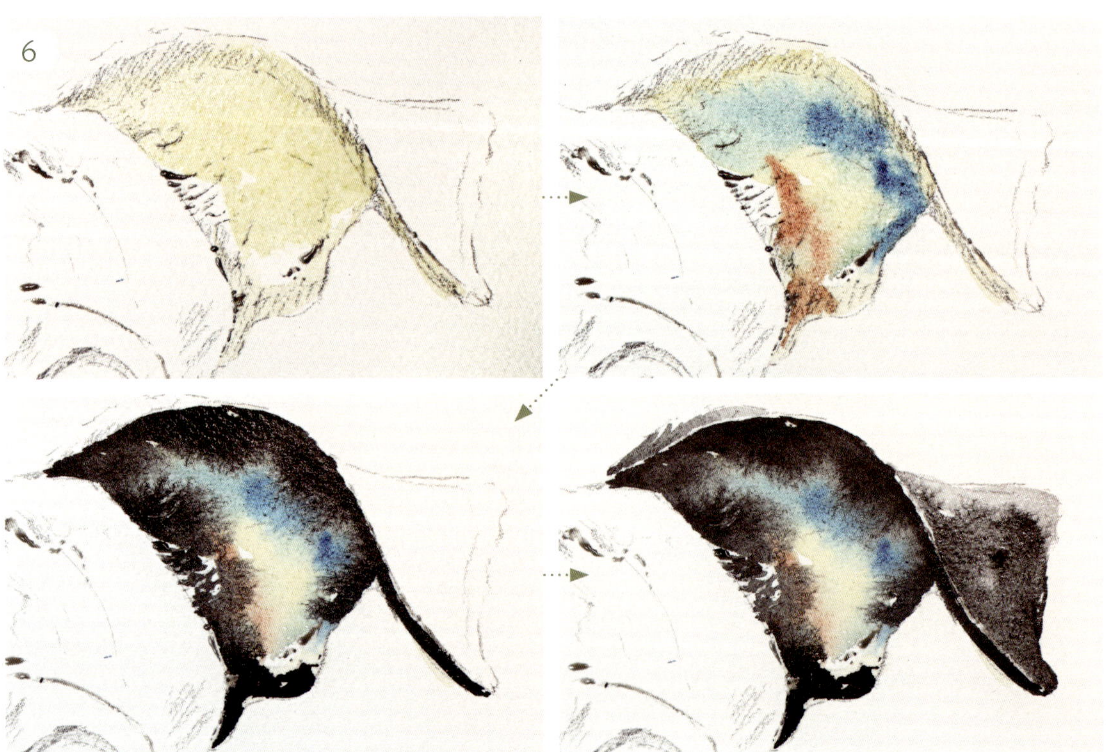

Refer to the colors and techniques used in steps 3 to 5 to paint the right ear. Use the same method as with the left ear to build up the ear's structural relationship.

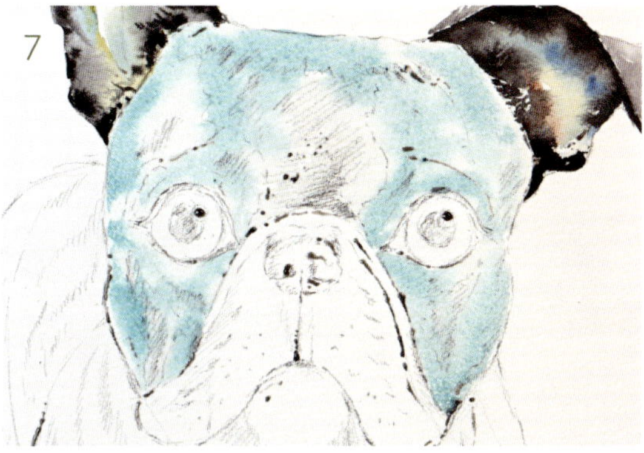

Next, paint the dog's face. Start by covering the entire face with clean water. While it's still wet, use color 600029 (Cobalt Turquoise) to add a light wash of shadow following the facial structure. Be sure to leave the highlight areas untouched.

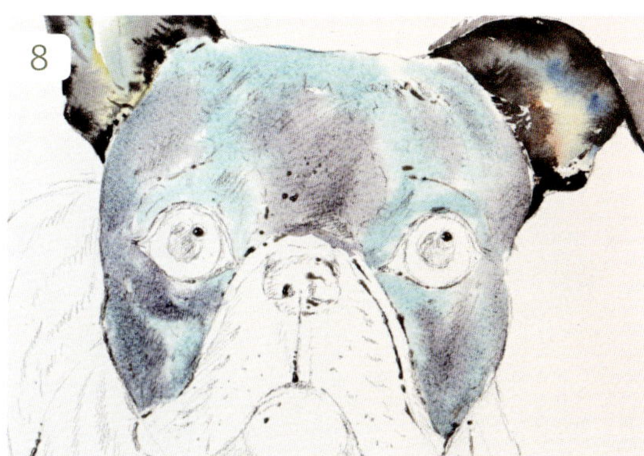

While the paper is still wet, use color 600242 (Alvaro's Fresco Grey) to further enhance the shadows. Continue to leave out the highlight areas to emphasize the sagging folds of the dog's face.

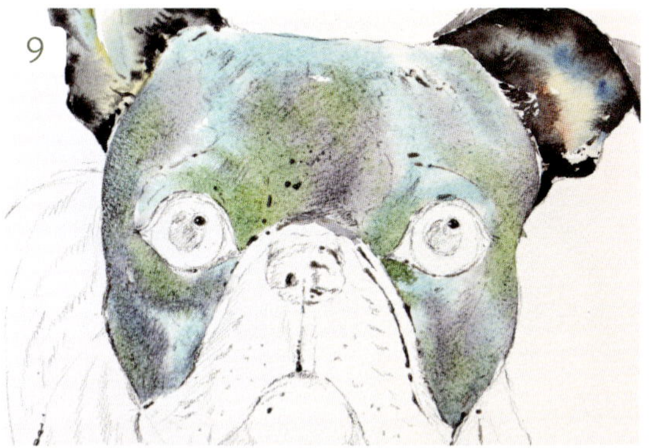

While still wet, use color 600056 (Monte Amiata Natural Sienna) to paint the raised areas of the facial muscles, especially around the forehead and eye sockets. Note: At this point, mixing color 600056 with the previously applied grey may result in a slightly greenish hue.

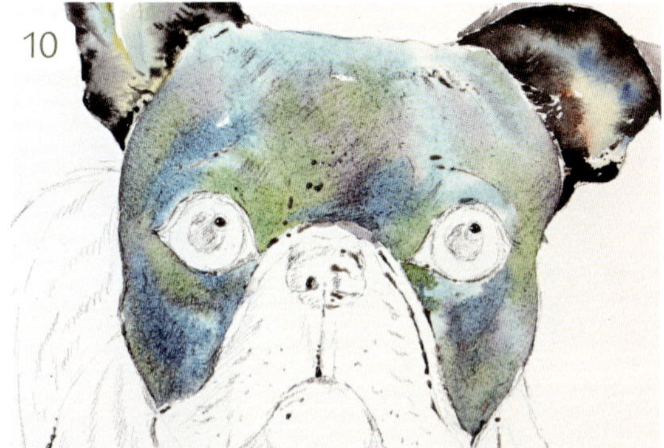

Mix color 600082 (Prussian Blue) and color 600003 (Lamp Black) in a 5:1 ratio, then dilute with plenty of clean water. Continue to deepen the shadows in the areas you painted in step 8.

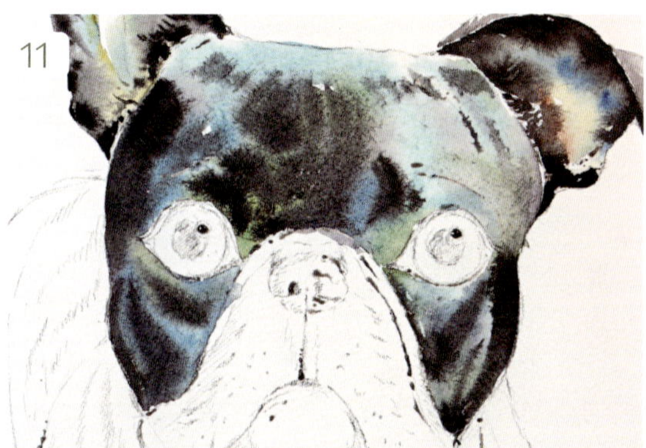

While the paper is still wet, paint the raised areas of the facial muscles with color 600003 (Lamp Black). Be sure to add more water to the color here so that it becomes lighter, helping to depict the folds and contours of the facial muscles.

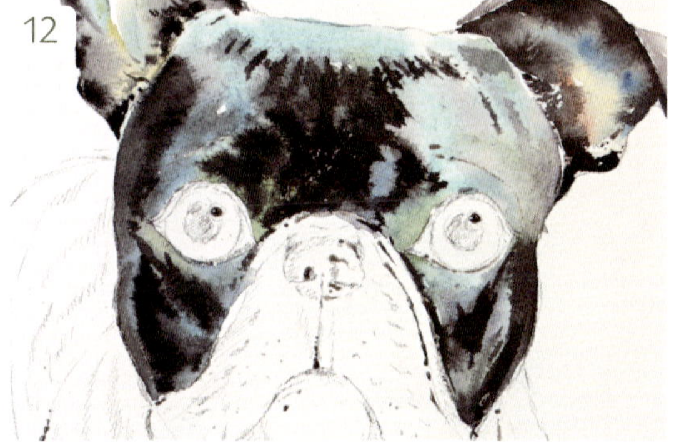

While the paper is still wet, mix a small amount of water with color 600003 (Lamp Black) to create a more concentrated color. Continue to deepen the folds of the facial muscles.

Note that the layers and sense of volume in the face are gradually built up with layers of color. It is important to keep the paper wet so that the colors can merge and blend, avoiding a dull or heavy appearance.

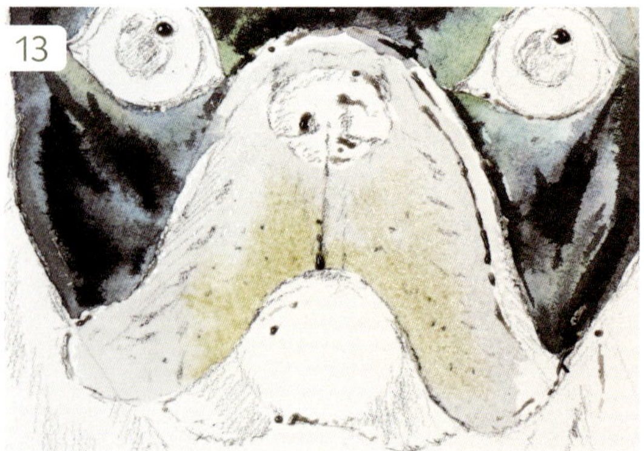

Apply a layer of clean water to the area, and while it's still wet, use color 600056 (Monte Amiata Natural Sienna) to paint the outline of the upper lip.

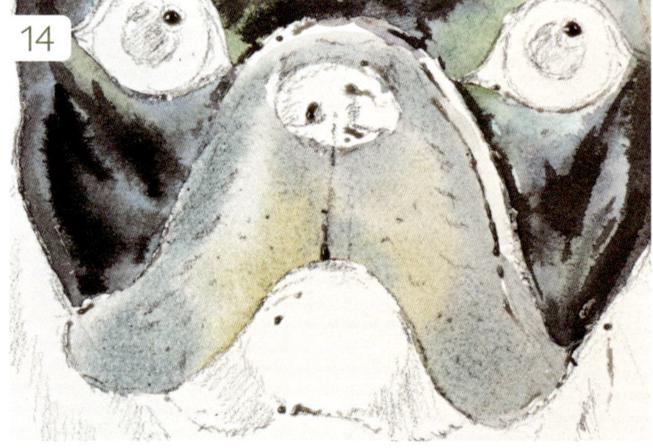

While the area is still wet, use color 600242 (Alvaro's Fresco Grey) to further enhance the shadows around the upper lip.

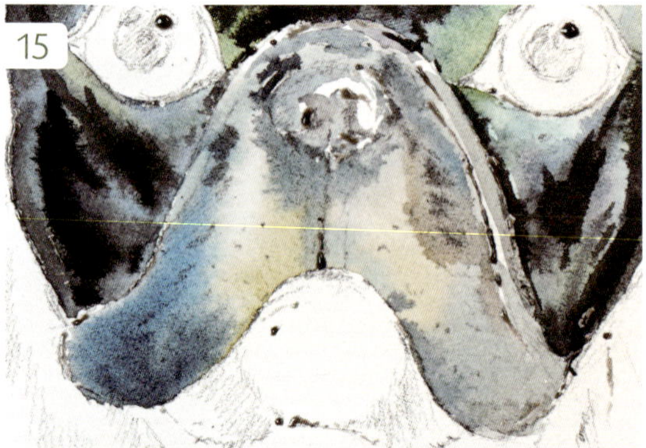

While the area is still wet, mix color 600082 (Prussian Blue) with a small amount of color 600003 (Lamp Black) roughly in a 5:1 ratio, and use this mixture to deepen the shadows around the lower part of the upper lip, as well as the nose and its surrounding areas. This will help shape the volume of the upper lip and nose.

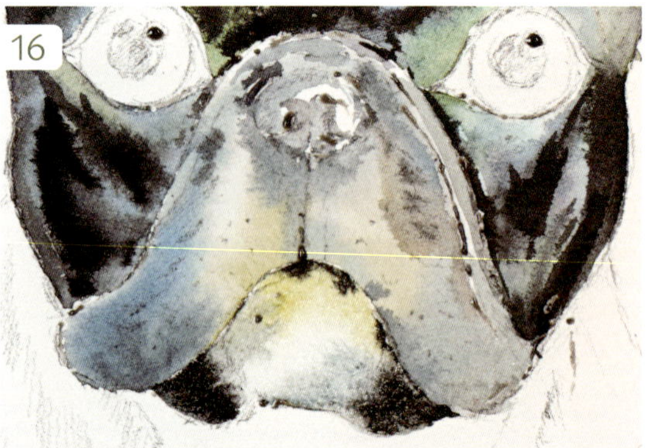

Paint the lower jaw. Start by applying clean water to the jaw area as a base. While the area is still wet, use color 600056 (Monte Amiata Natural Sienna) to paint the upper edge of the lower jaw. Then, with color 600242 (Alvaro's Fresco Grey), add shadows to the lower part of the jaw. Finally, use color 600003 (Lamp Black) to lightly paint the sides of the jaw and the junction between the jaw and upper lip, creating the volume and shape of the mouth area.

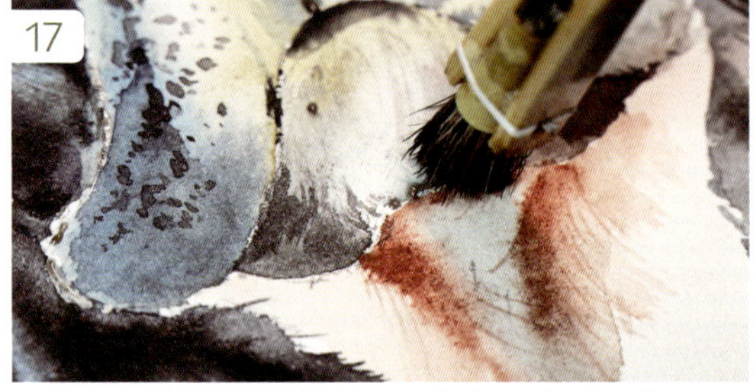

Using a dry hog bristle brush, gently draw the fine fur on the bulldog's face. The firm texture of the hog bristle brush, when dry, causes the bristles to separate, allowing you to easily create the texture of fur. Note that you do not need to depict fur in every area, just lightly sketch a few strokes on the jaw, upper lip, around the face and eyes, and on the chest. You can alternate between color 600010 (Burnt Sienna) and color 600242 (Alvaro's Fresco Grey) for the fur, or mix these two colors in any proportion.

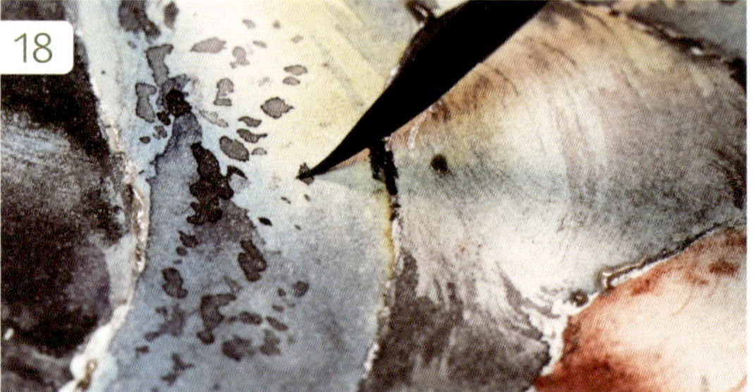

Mix color 600003 (Lamp Black) with a large amount of water to dilute the paint, making it lighter. Use this diluted mixture to paint the pores of the mustache on the upper lip.

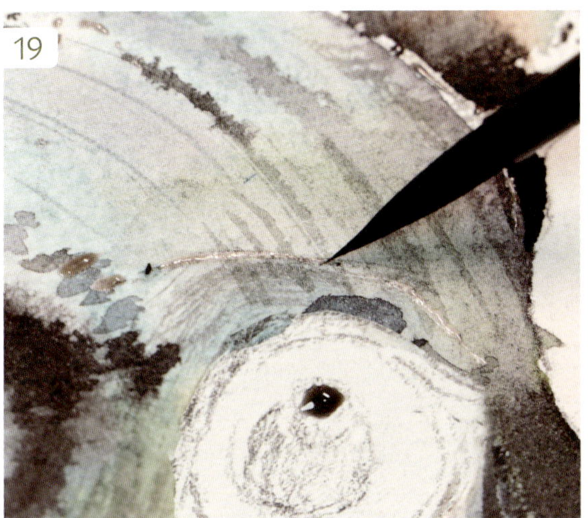
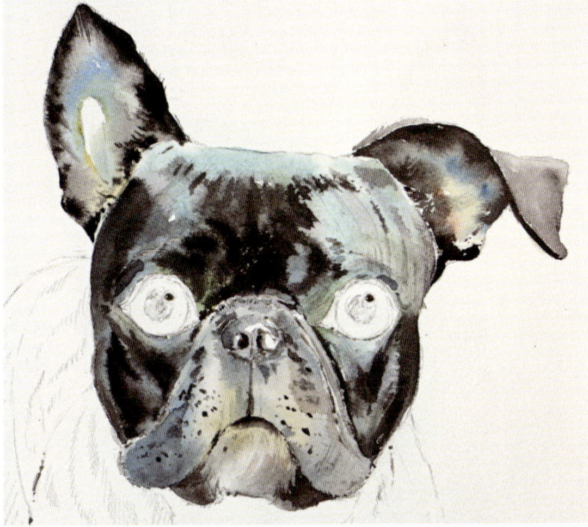

Mix color 600242 (Alvaro's Fresco Grey) with a sufficient amount of water to lighten the color. Use this diluted mixture to outline some of the facial wrinkle lines and add detail. At this point, the depiction of the bulldog's face is essentially complete, as shown in the right image.

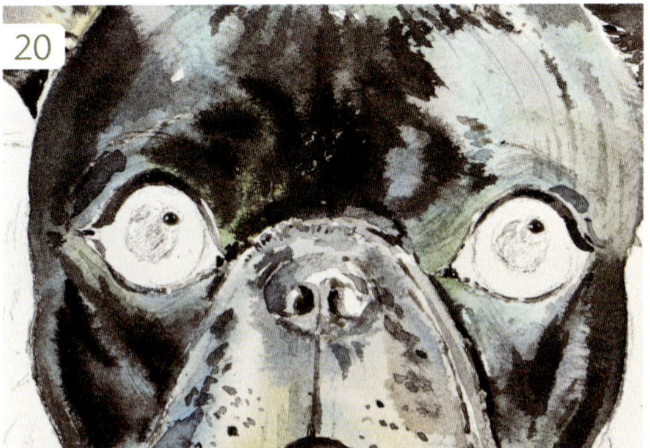

Next, shape the dog's eyes by first using color 600003 (Lamp Black) to outline the upper eyelid. Pay attention to the variations in light and dark on the eyelid.

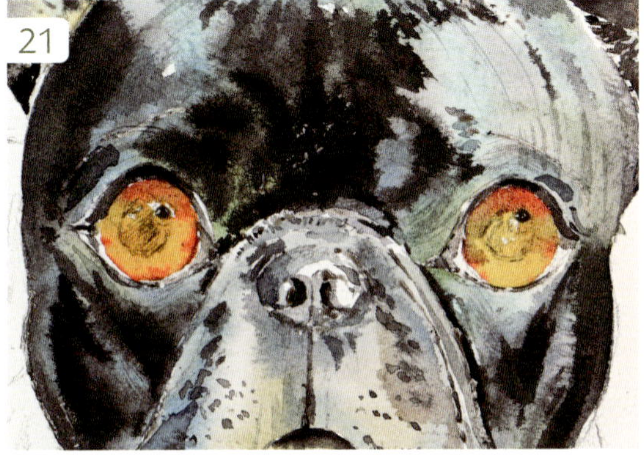

Wet the eyeball area with clean water, making sure to keep the edges sharp. Use a light wash of color 600234 (Aussie Red Gold) to create the base color of the eyeballs. Then, apply color 600033 (Deep Scarlet) to depict the darker areas, especially the shadow below the upper eyelid, which represents the eyelid's projection onto the eyeball.

At the same time, the white of the eye also receives some shadow from the upper eyelid. Use a light gray color with a simple stroke to suggest it. Just a simple touch will do.

Use a light wash of color 600003 (Lamp Black) to paint the dark pupils. Be mindful not to focus solely on creating a deep color or fully filling in the pupil. Due to light, the pupil will show variations in darkness. Adjust the color intensity and brushstroke pressure to capture the layered effect and light reflections on the pupil.

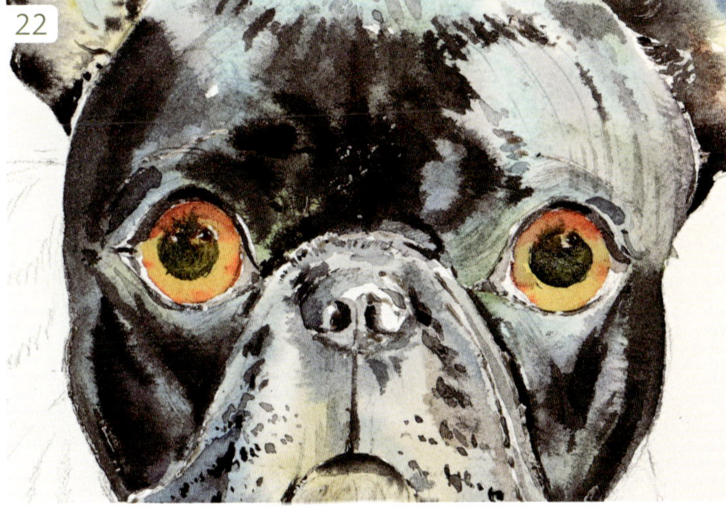

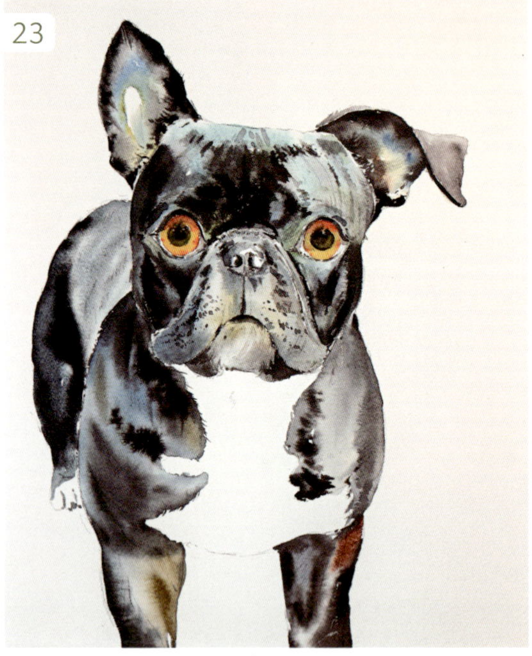

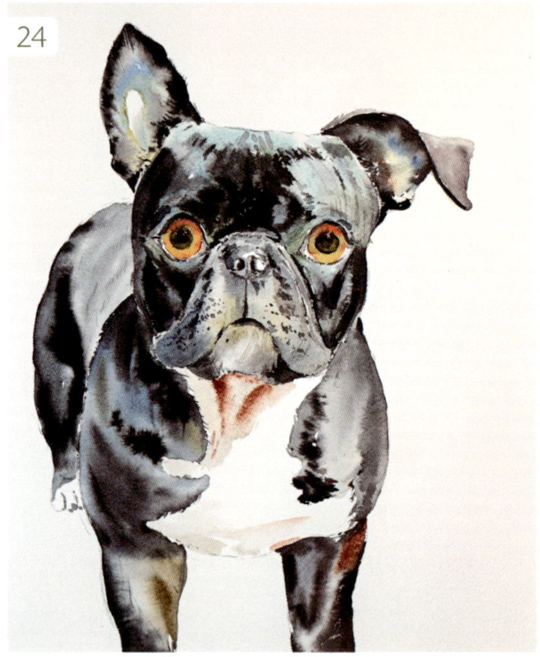

Start by applying a wash of clear water to the dog's entire body (except for the chest area). While it's still wet, apply color 600029 (Cobalt Turquoise) to create a base layer of color. Then, while the paper is still wet, use color 600242 (Alvaro's Fresco Grey) to add shading to the sides of the body, the sides of the limbs, and along the back, to define the body structure. Next, add color 600082 (Prussian Blue) around the junctions between the limbs and body, and between the front chest and head, to enhance the shadow areas.

While the paper is still wet, apply color 600010 (Burnt Sienna) to the shadowed areas of the front limbs.

Finally, while the paper is still wet, apply color 600003 (Lamp Black) along the edges of the hind limb, on both sides of the front limbs, and in certain areas of the body to enhance its structure.

Use a light wash of color 600010 (Burnt Sienna) to gently depict the shadowed areas of the white fur on the chest. Be sure to keep the application light and relaxed.

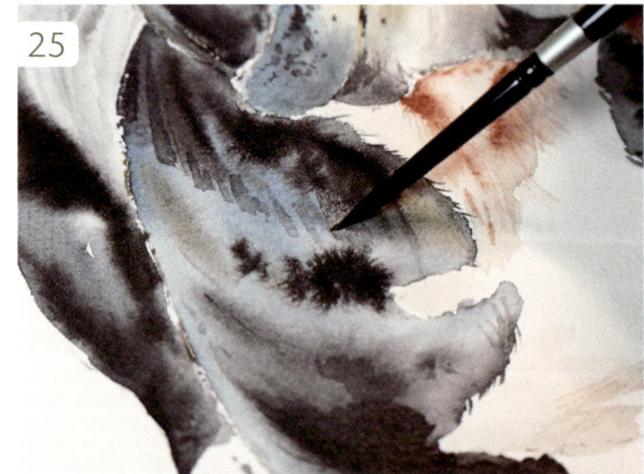

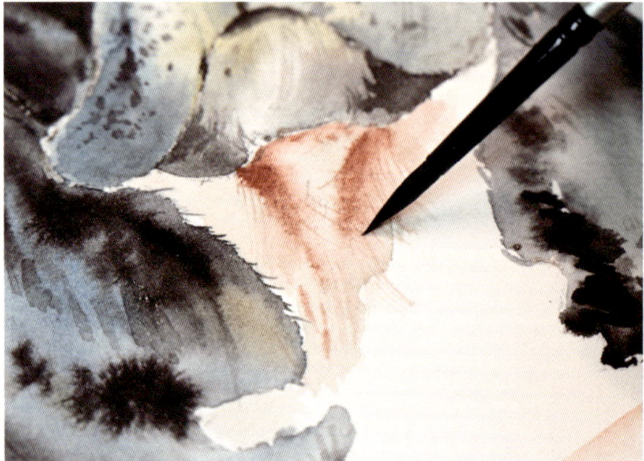

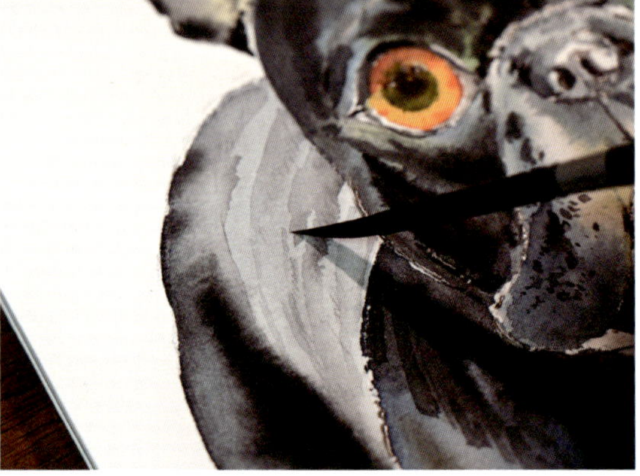

Using a fine-tipped brush, dip into color 600242 (Alvaro's Fresco Grey) to depict the details of the body muscles and fur texture. Be mindful not to make the colors too dark while depicting these details.

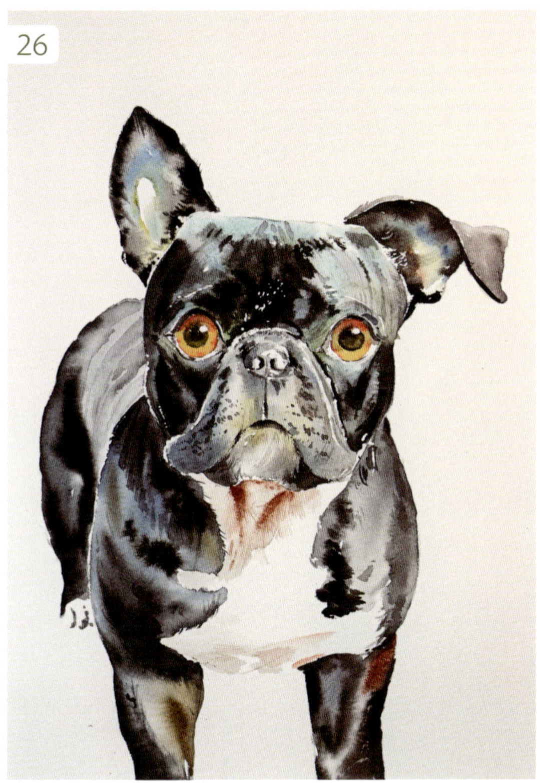

Remove the masking fluid.

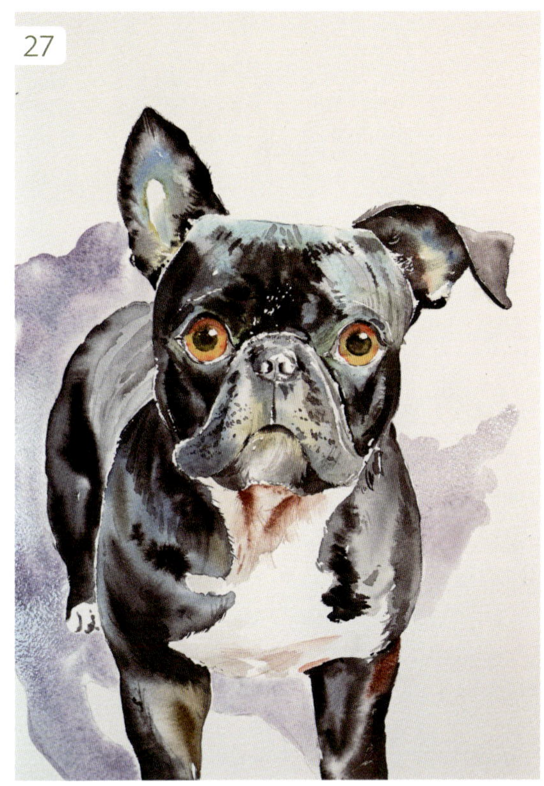

Use clean water to roughly outline the shadow of the dog's body. While it's still wet, gently apply a light layer of color 600057 (Moonglow) to establish a base color.

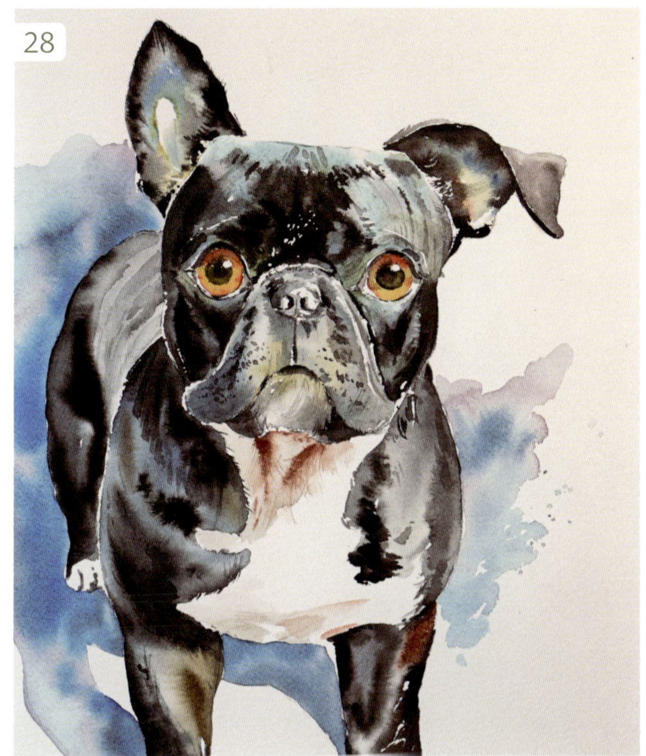

While the paper is still wet, mix in color 600077 (Phthalo Blue) to strengthen the shadows. When painting shadows, avoid fully saturating the entire area with one color. The color will naturally flow and blend with the water, allowing the variations in shadow depth to form naturally. This will give the dog in the garden its final look.

Line Art

W e've prepared 16 high-definition line drawings of the works for you. You can either trace them, tear them along the cutting lines for use and framing, or even use other media, like colored pencils, to create your own versions of these pieces. In short, you can either rework the originals or let your creativity flow freely. Now, go ahead and unleash your artistic inspiration.

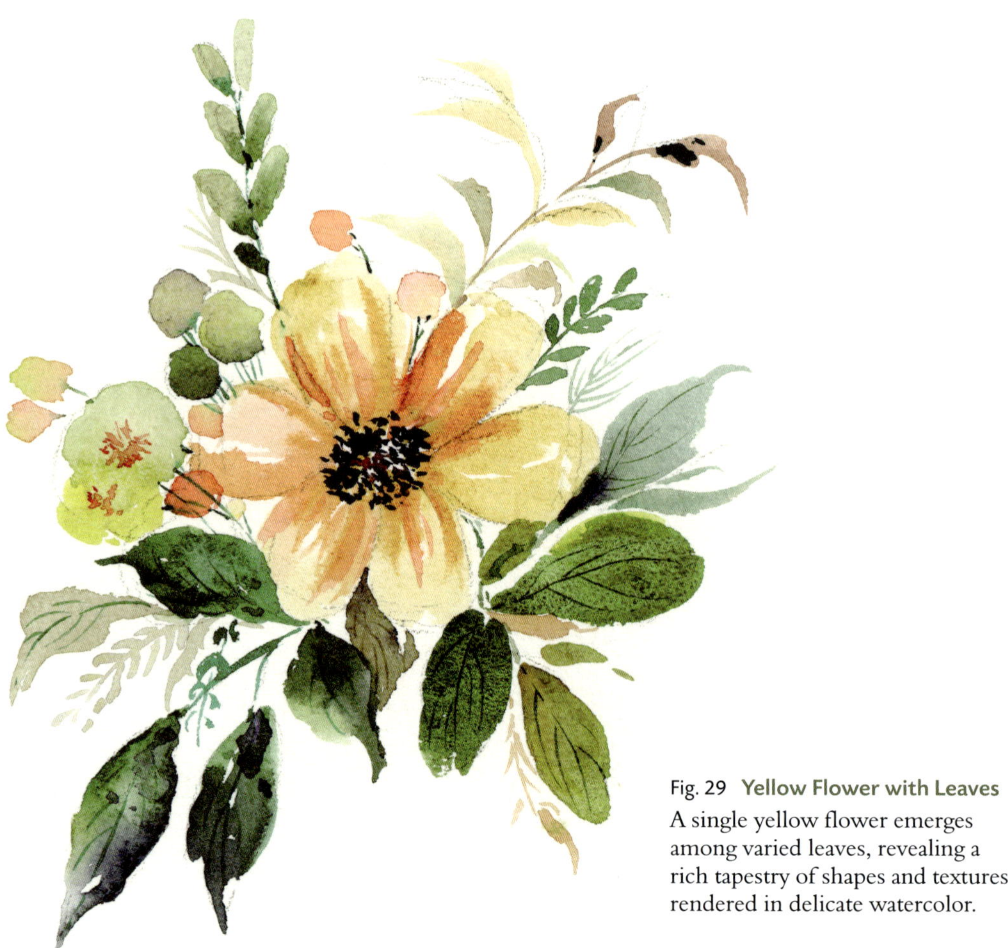

Fig. 29 Yellow Flower with Leaves
A single yellow flower emerges among varied leaves, revealing a rich tapestry of shapes and textures rendered in delicate watercolor.

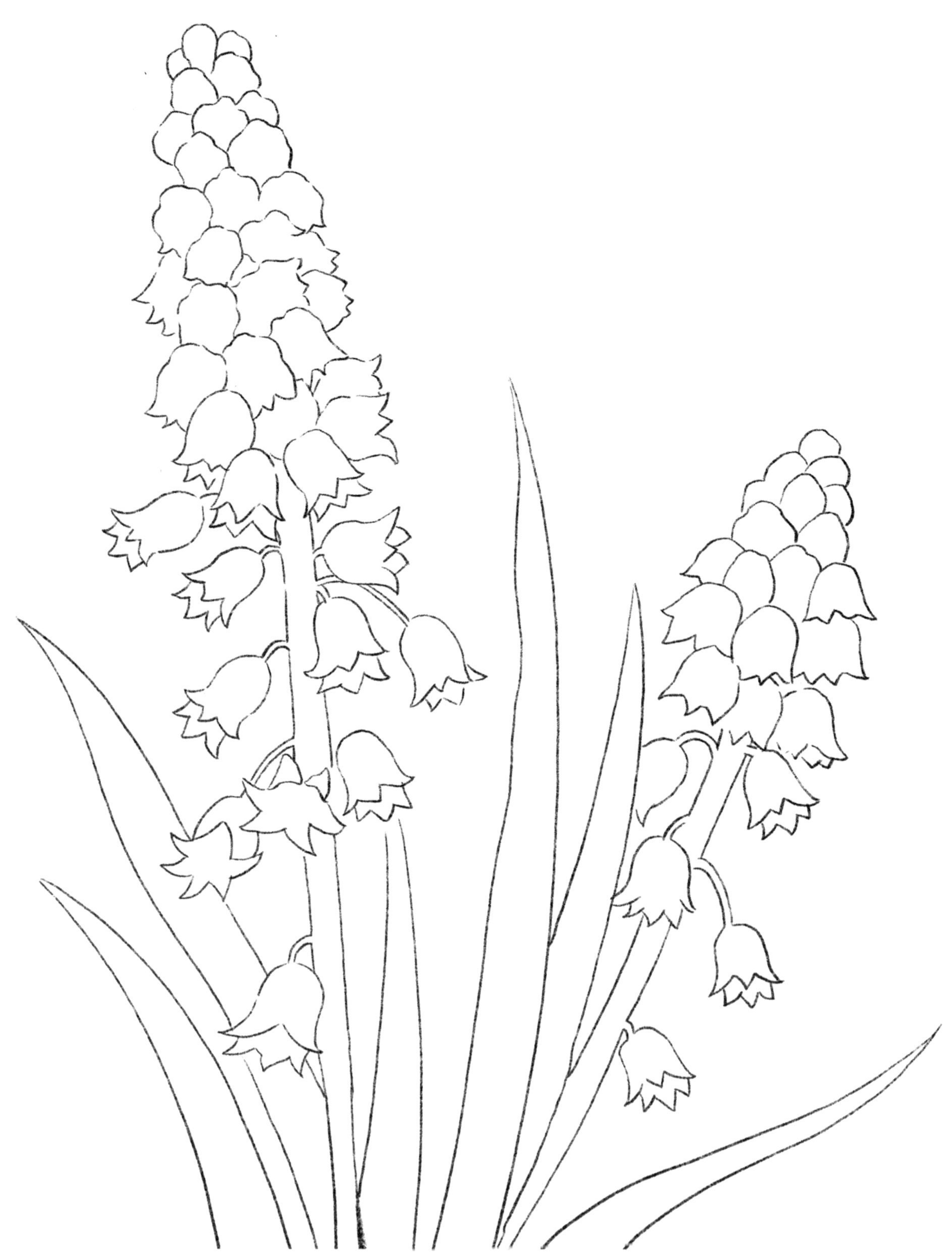

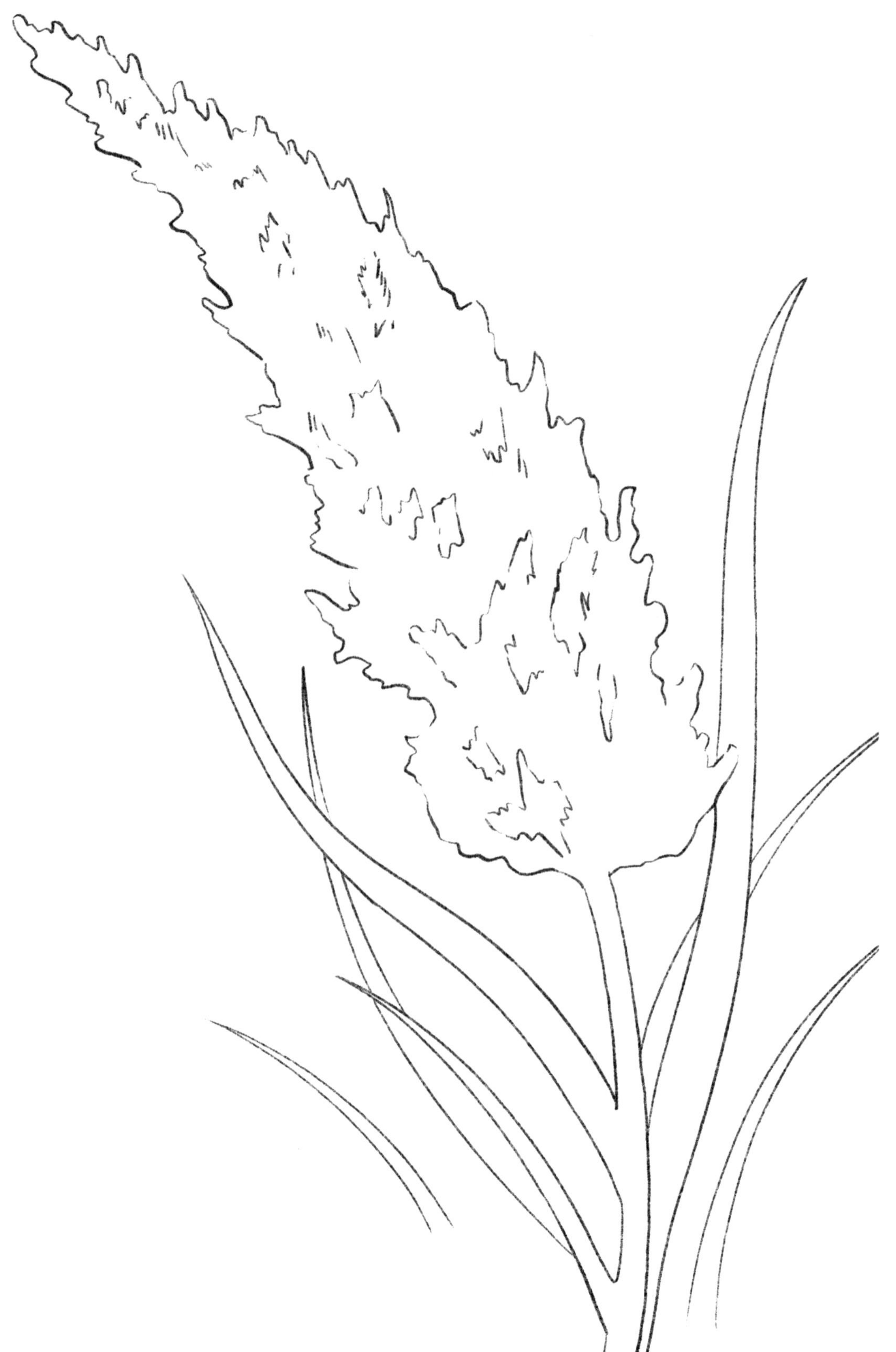

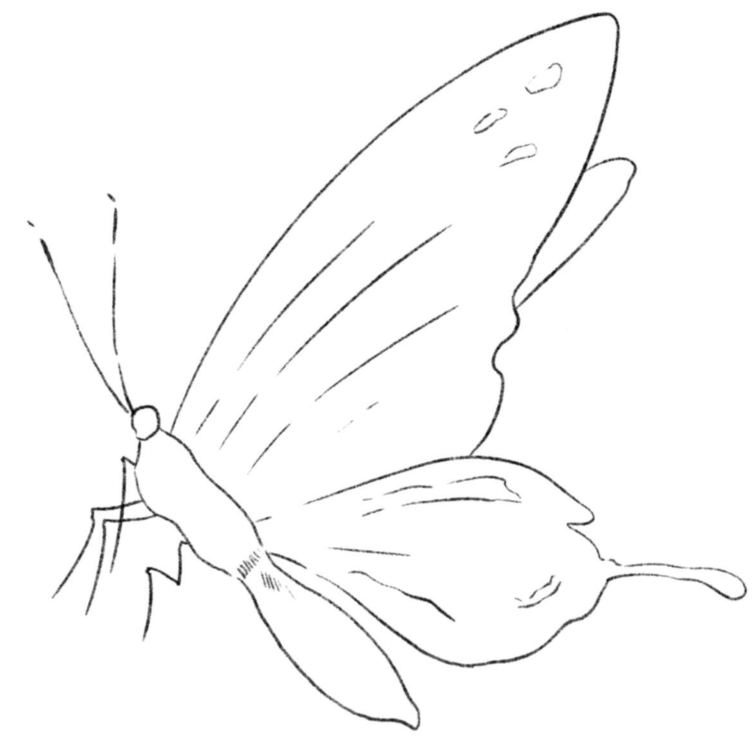

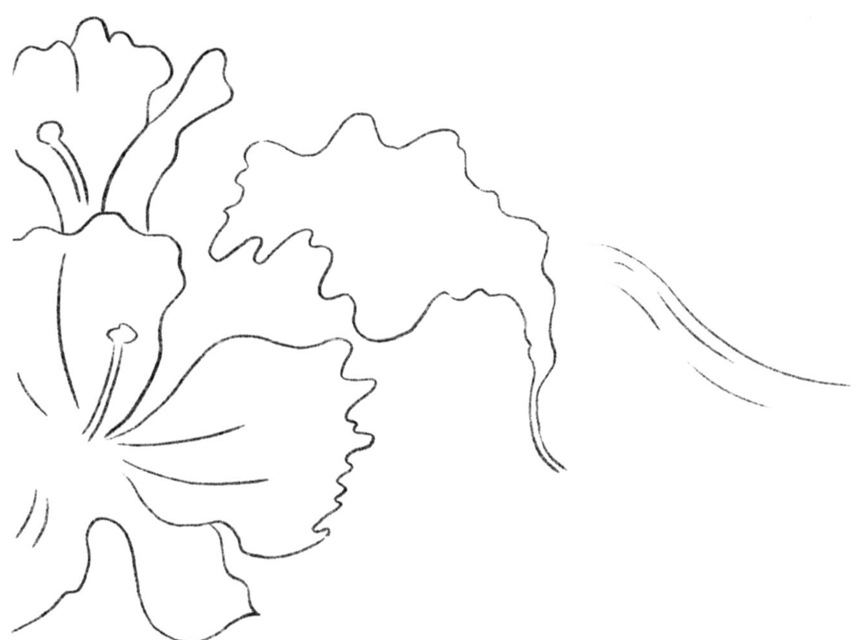

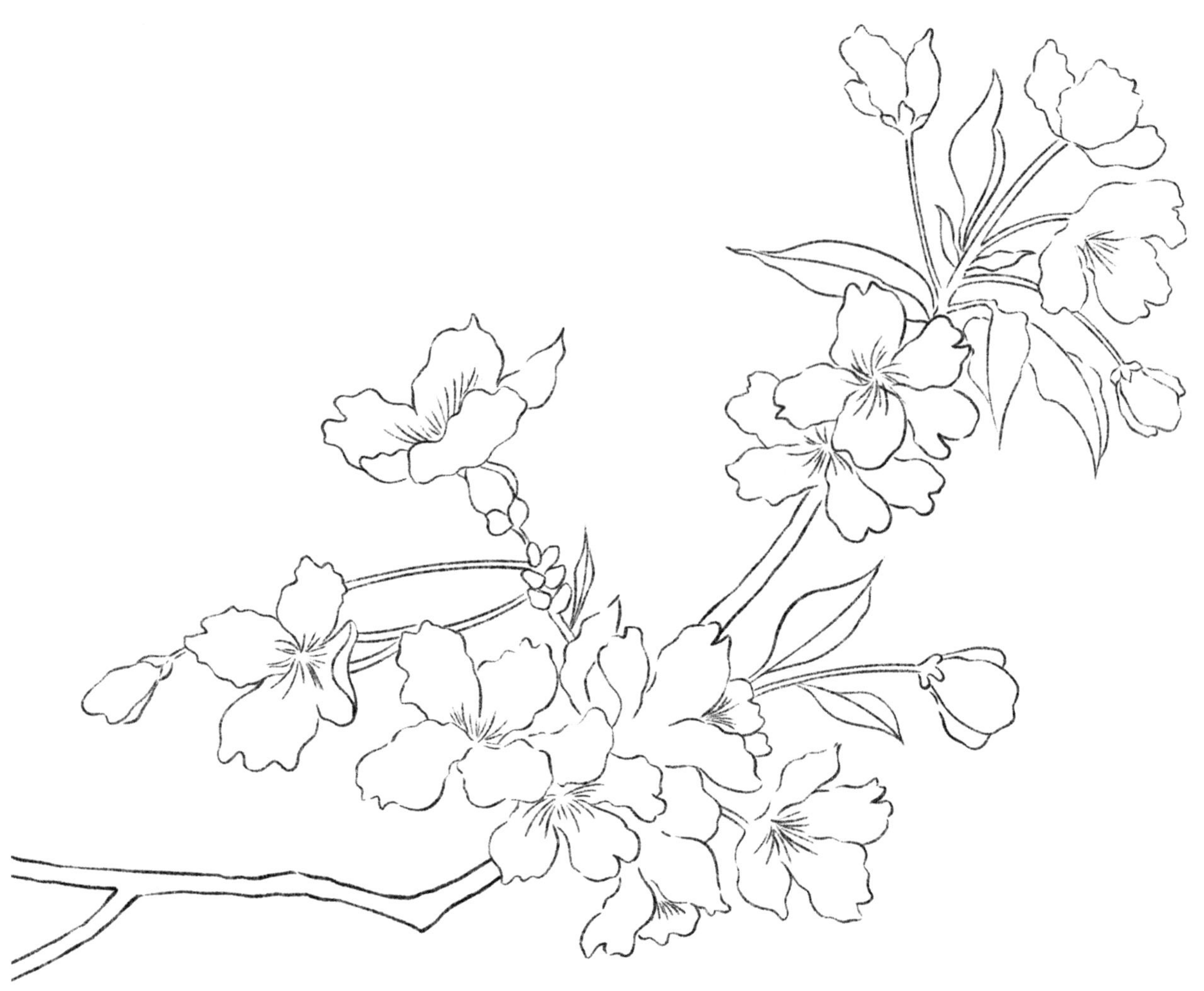

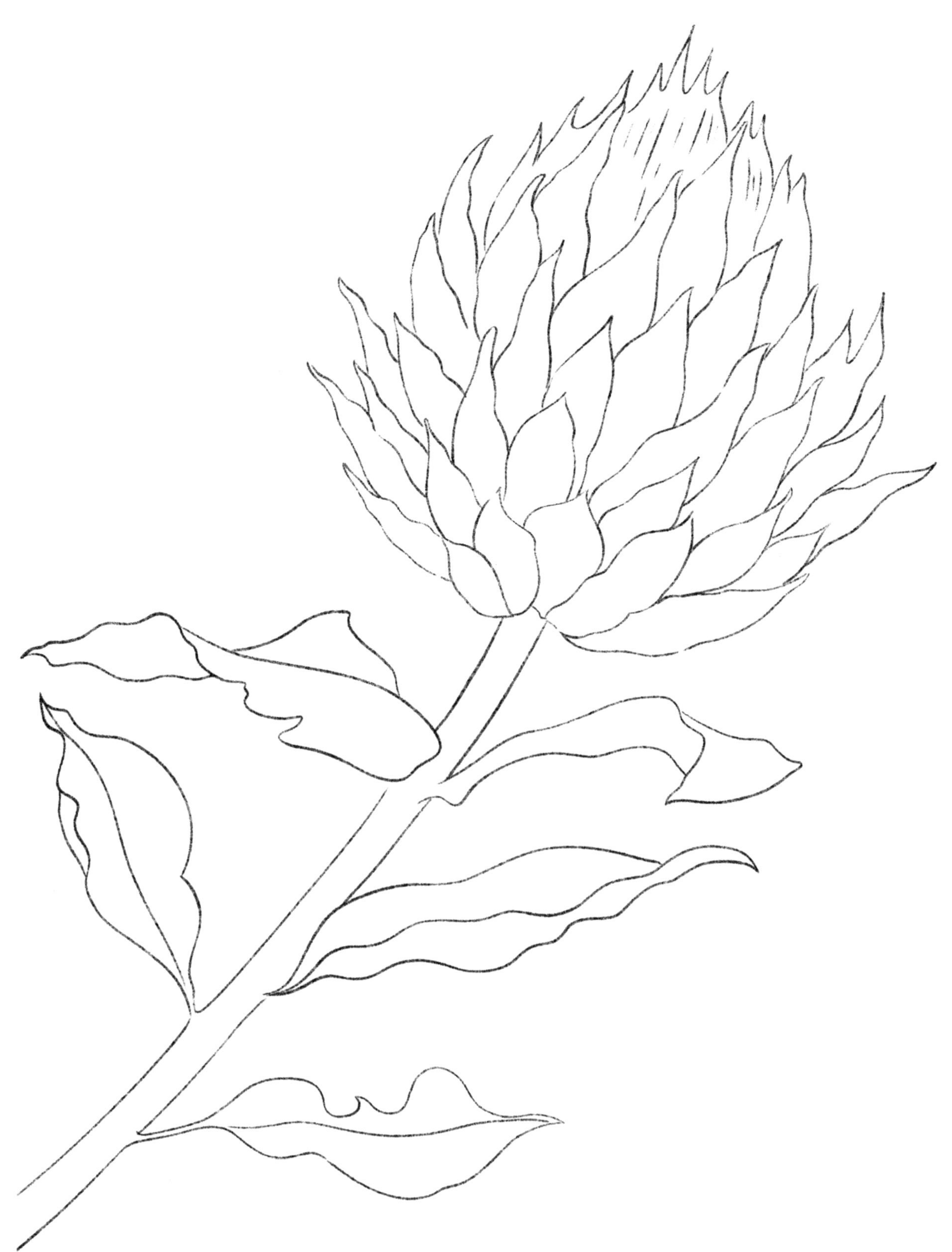

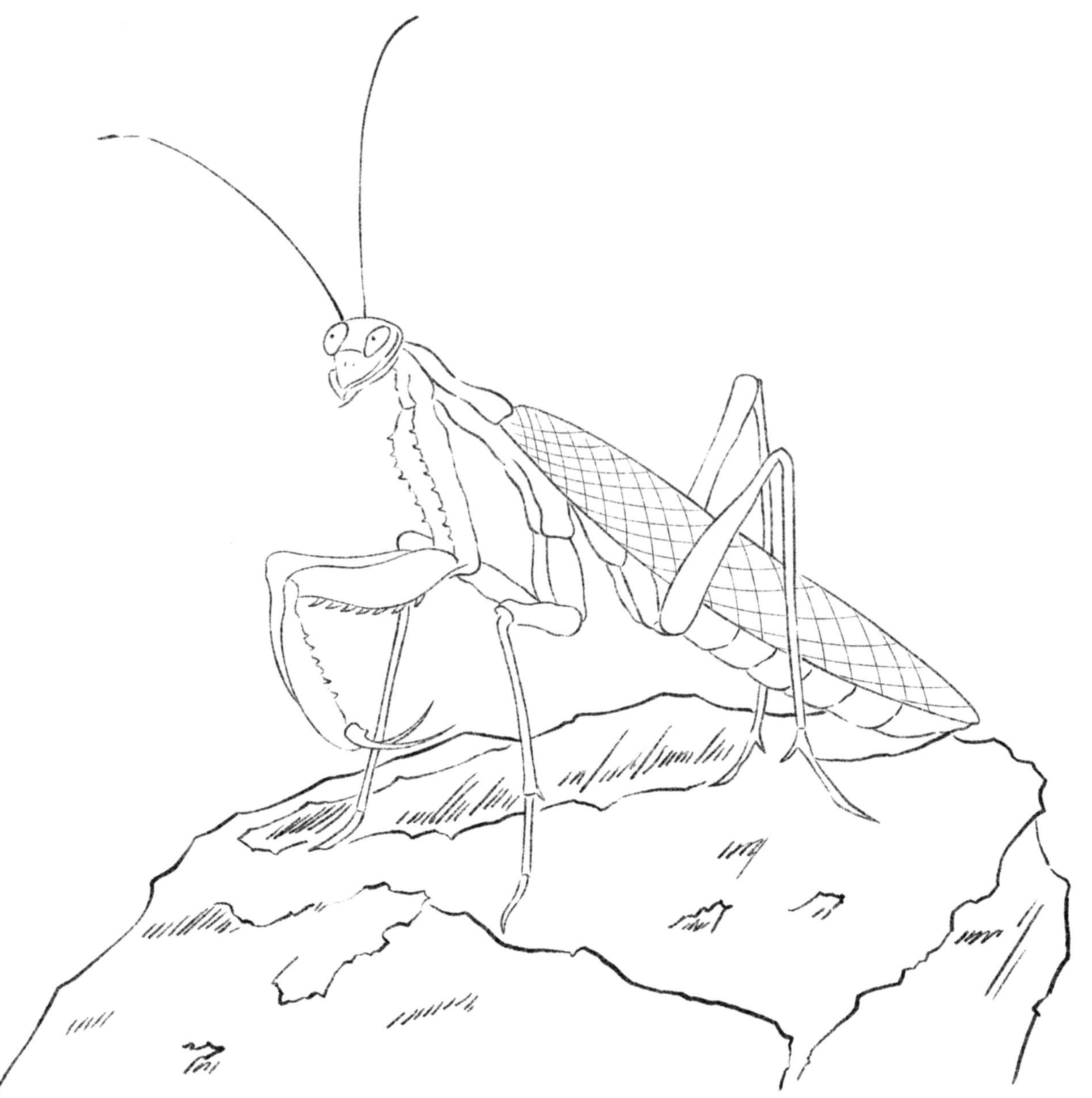

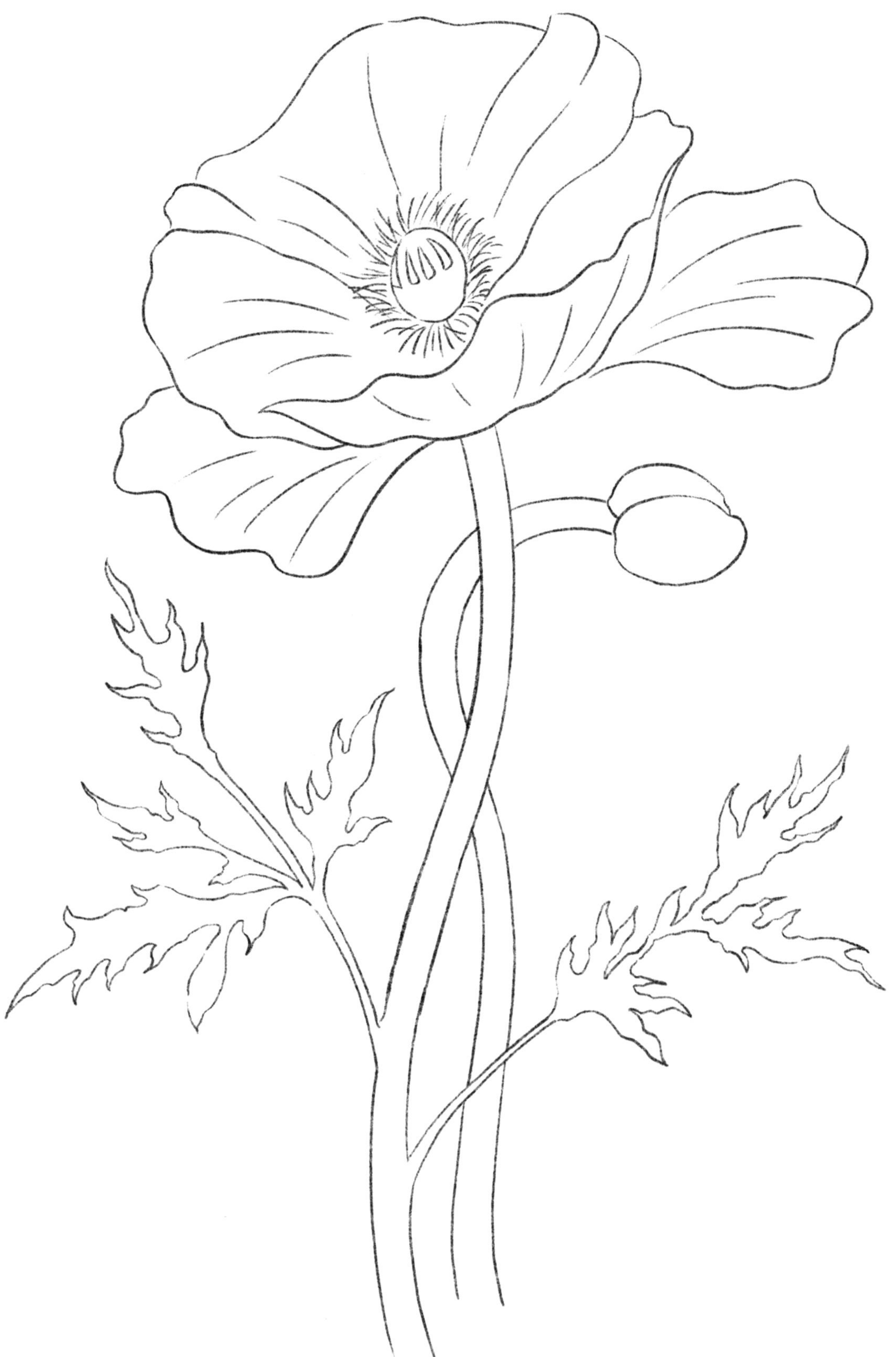

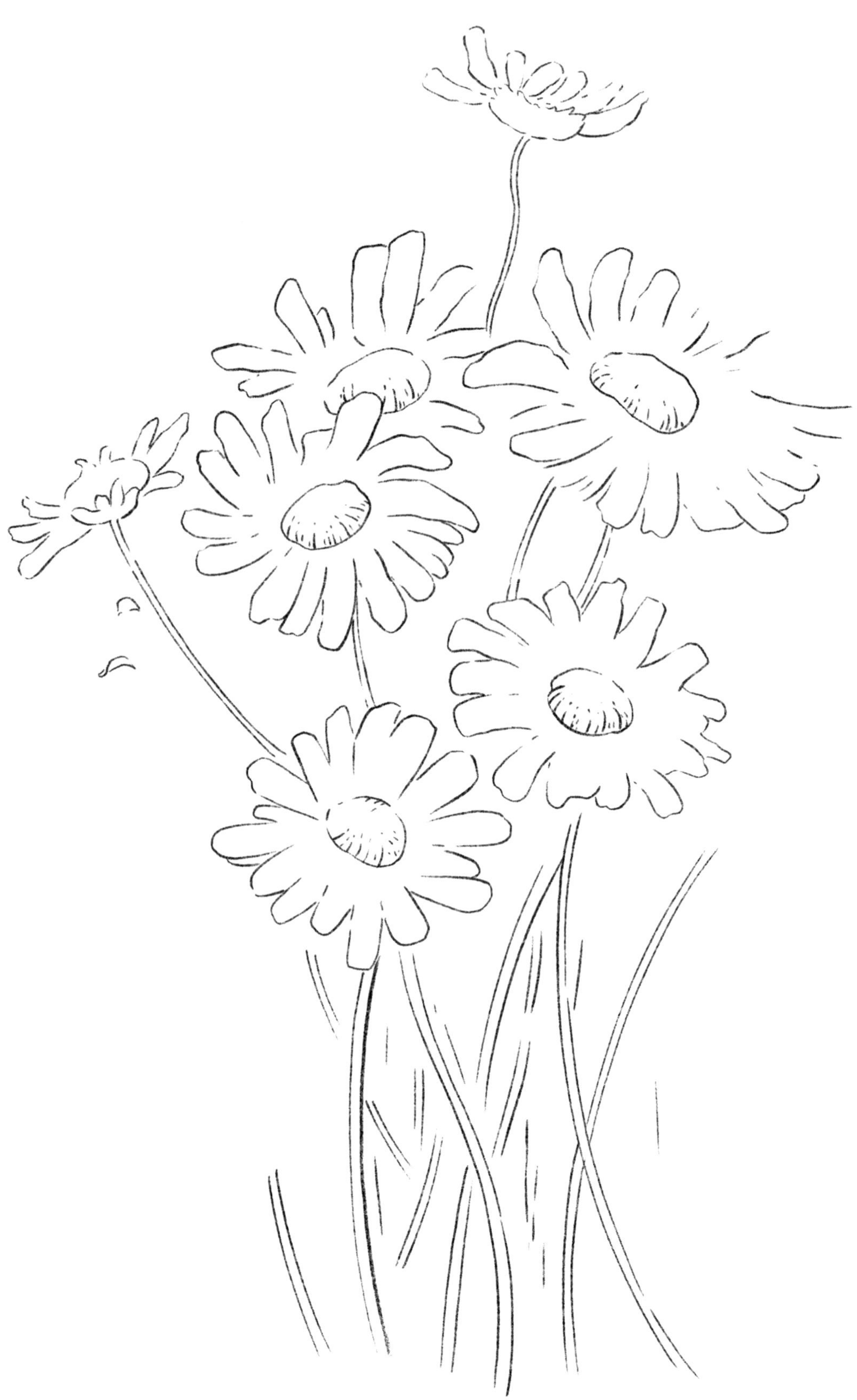

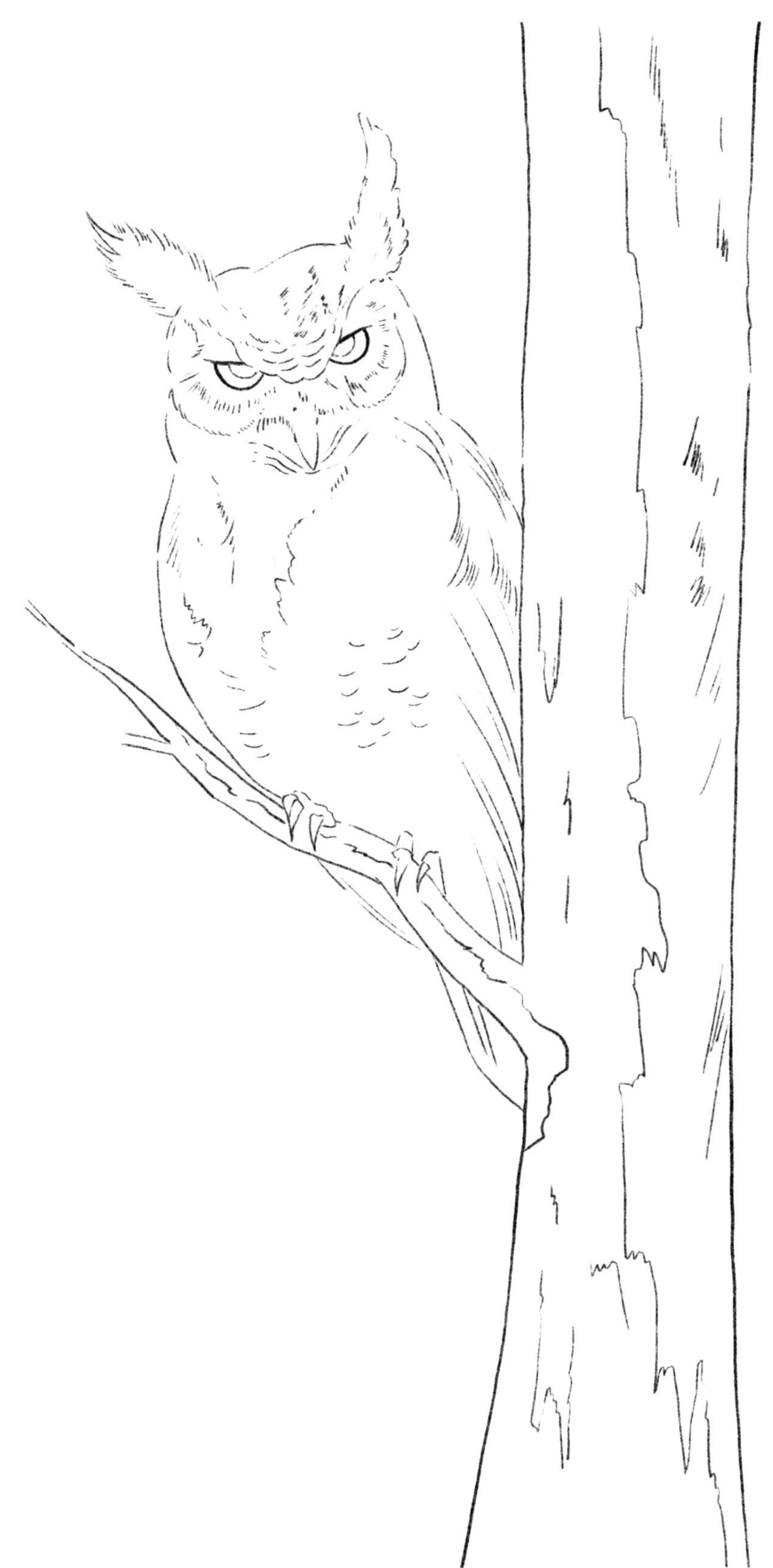

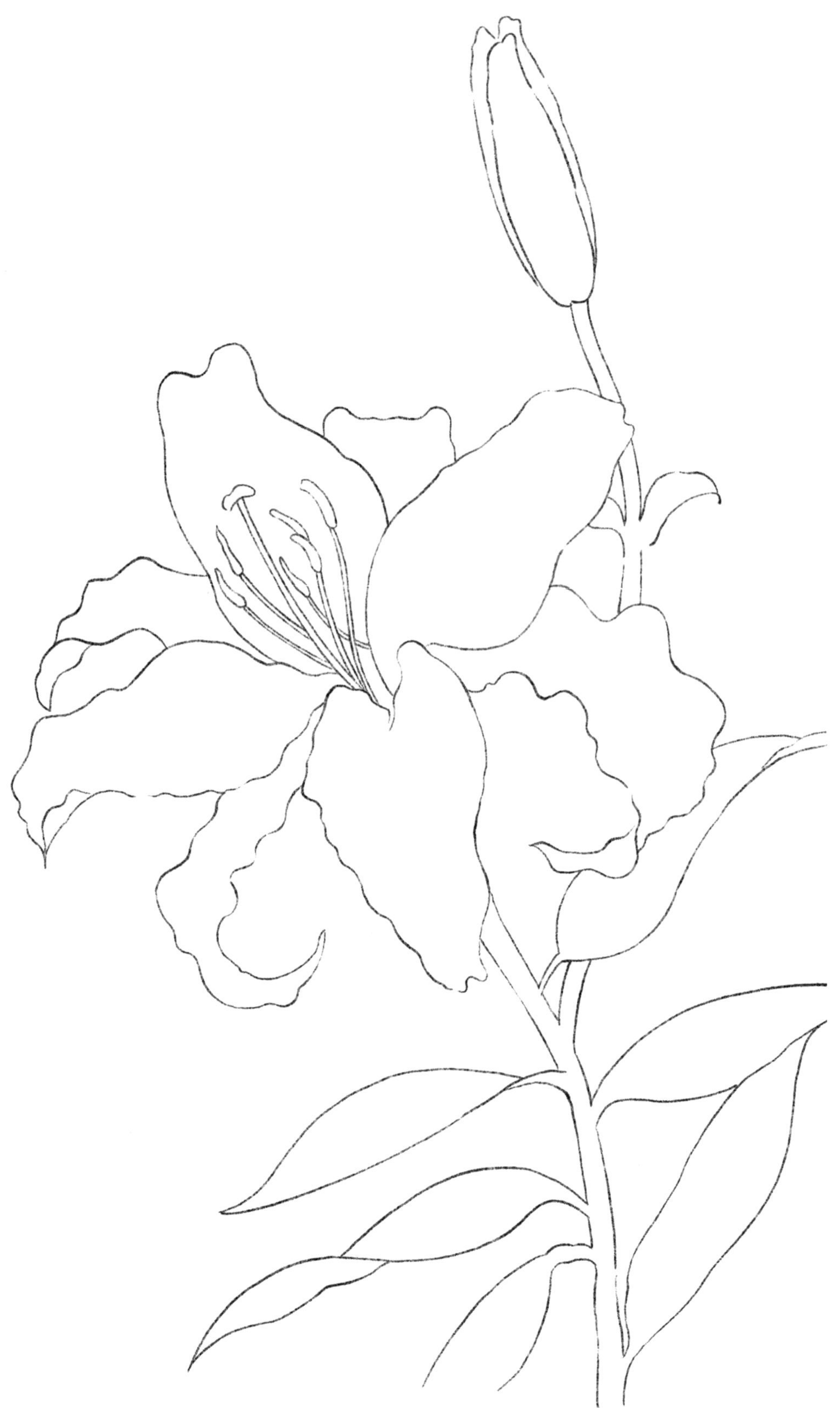

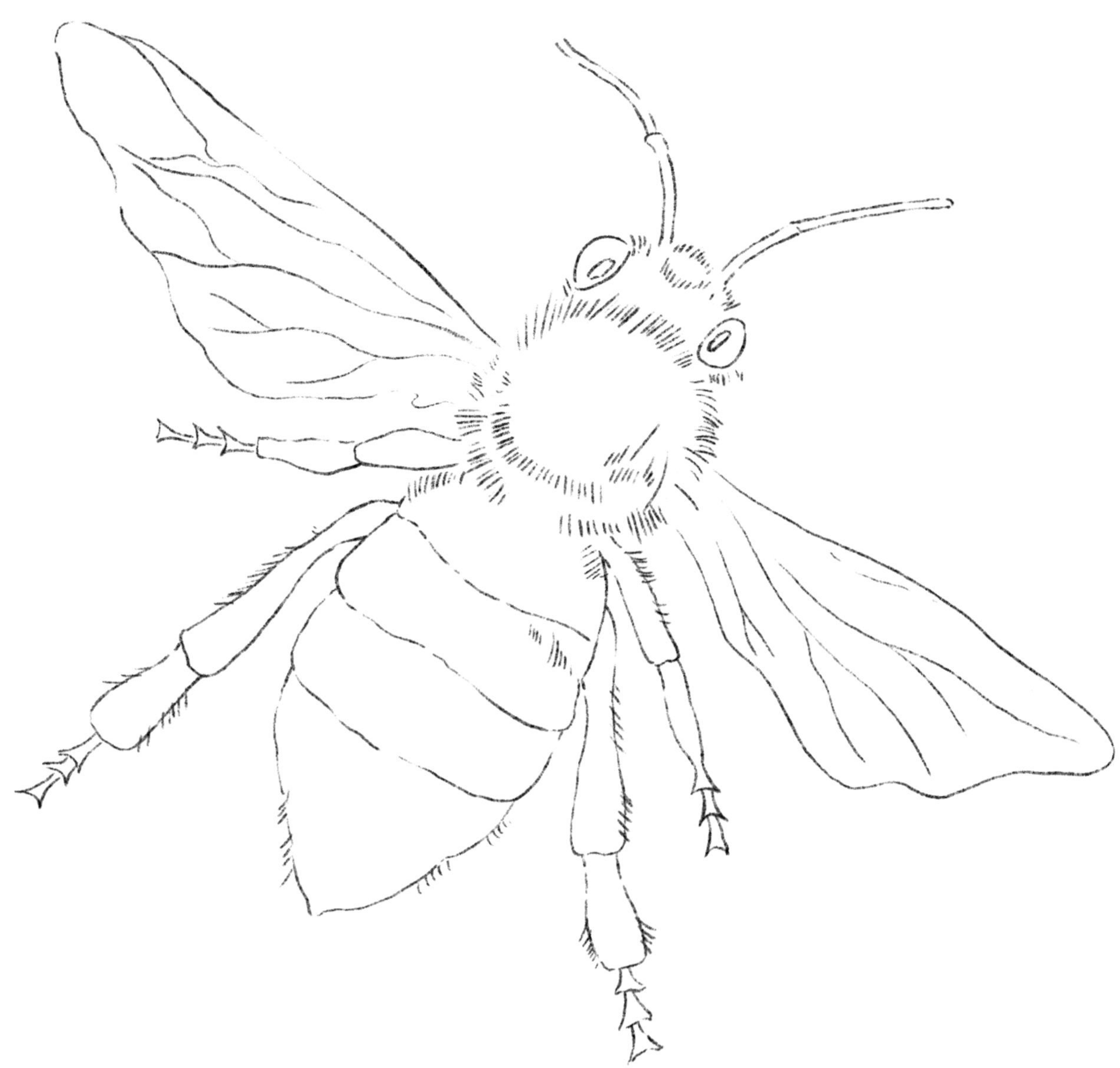

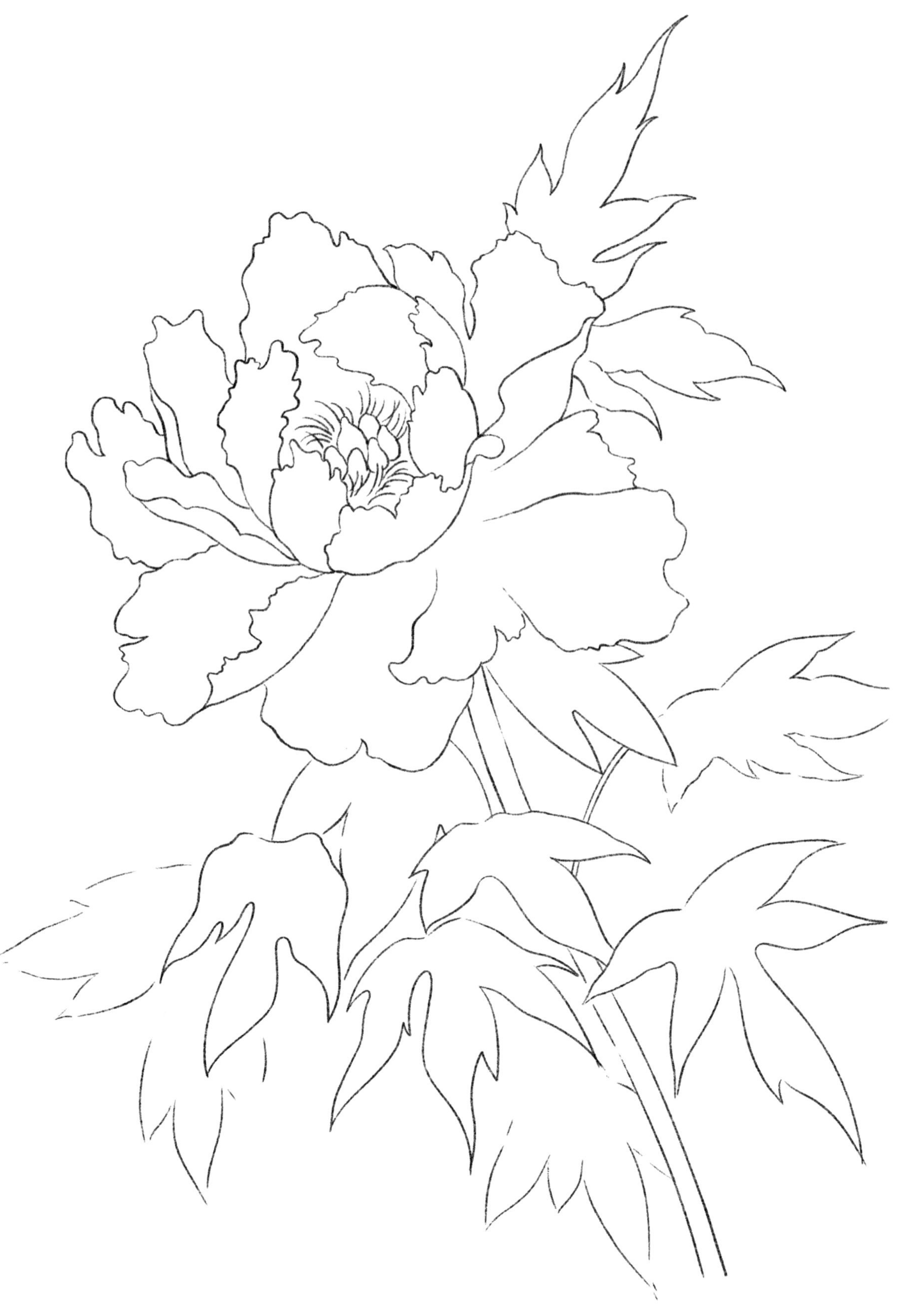

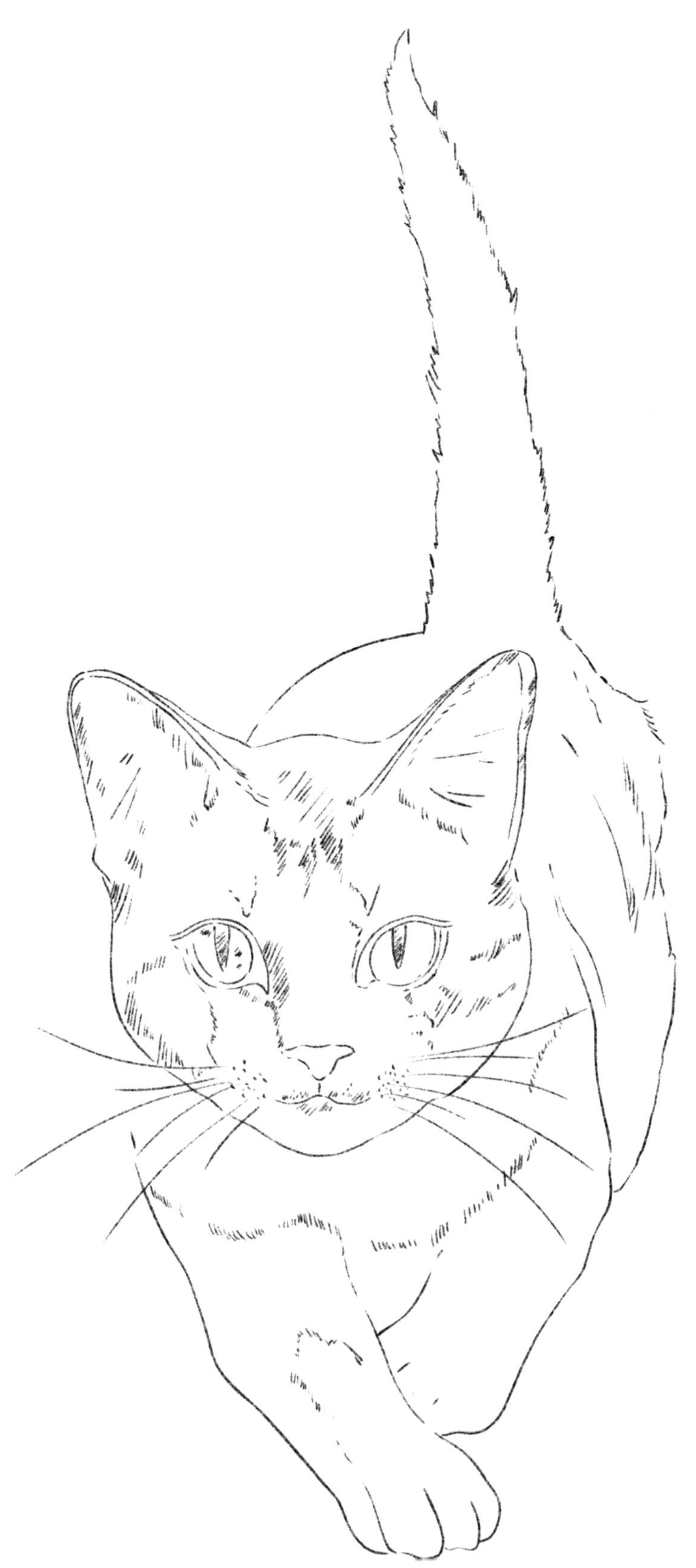

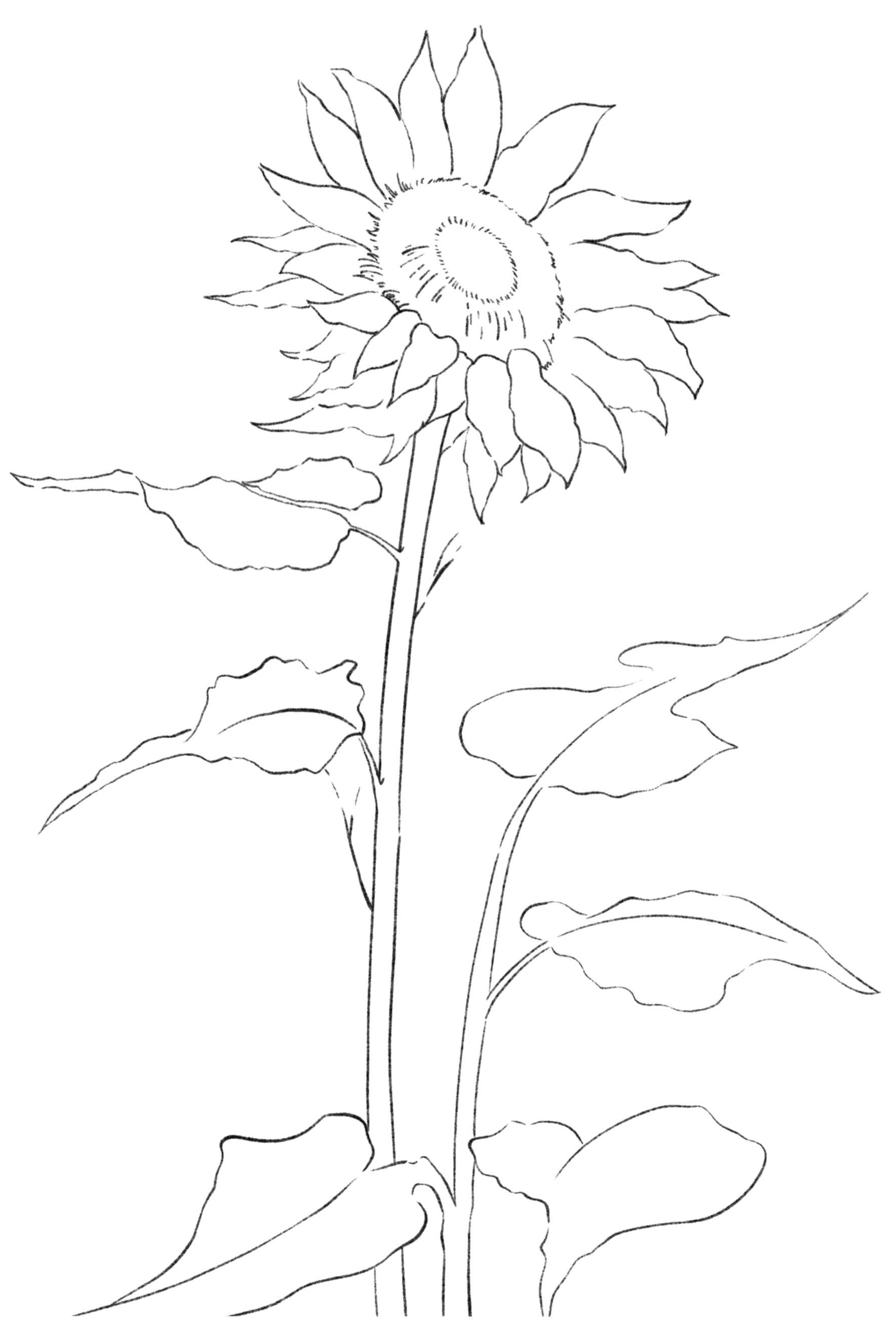

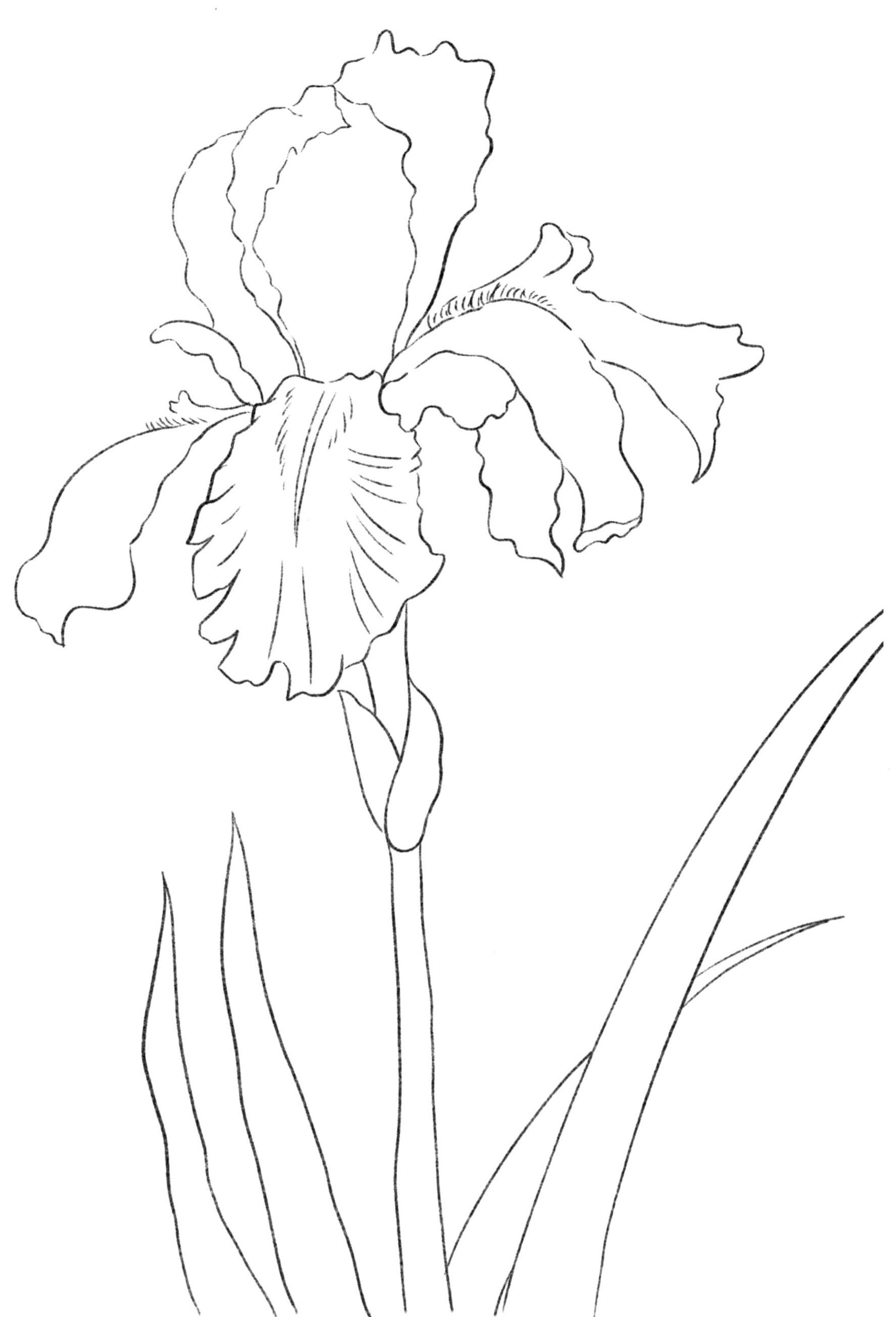

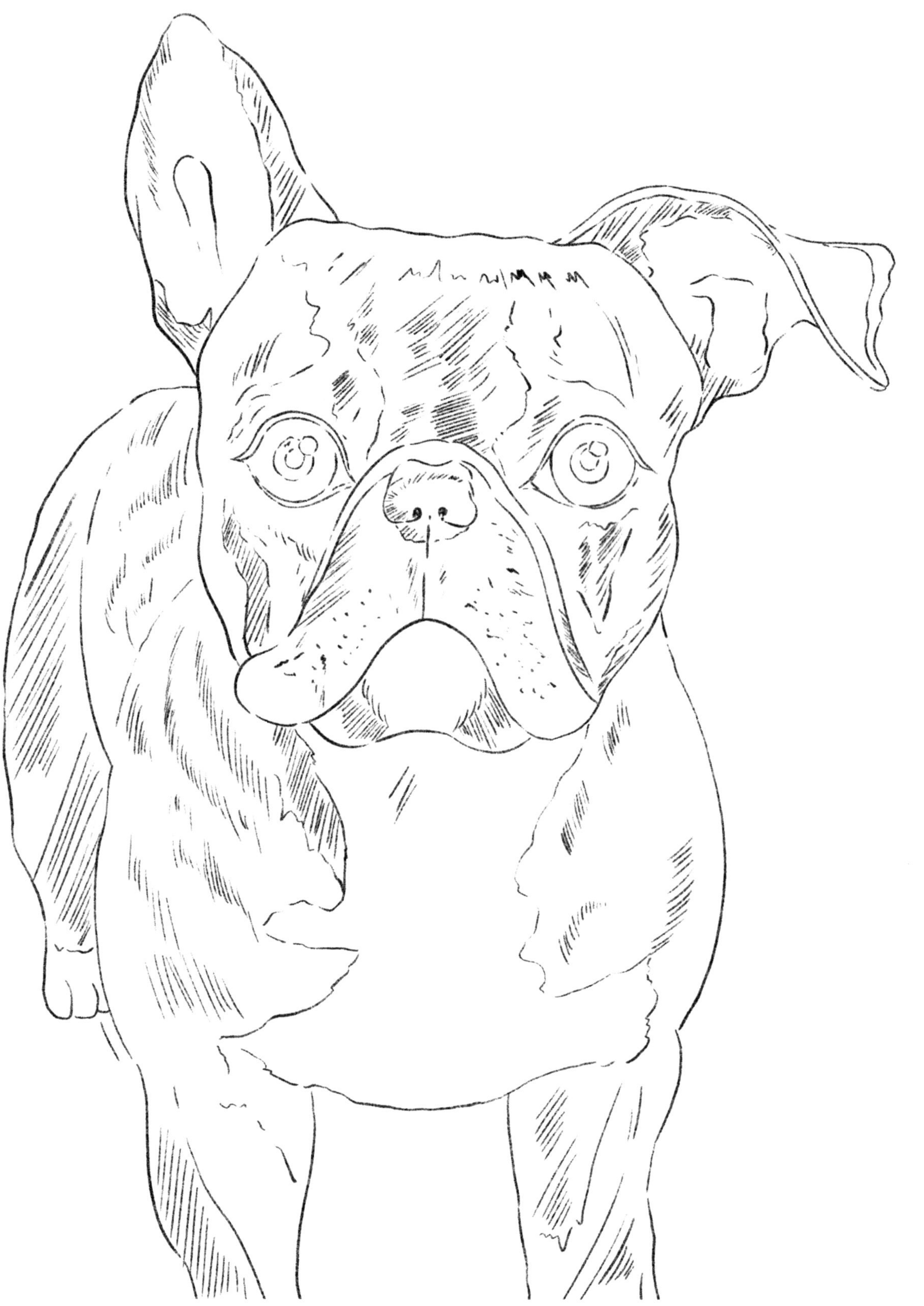